ARTHURIAN STUDIES VII

THE LEGEND OF ARTHUR IN THE MIDDLE AGES

ARTHURIAN STUDIES

I

ASPECTS OF MALORY

Edited by Toshiyuki Takamiya and Derek Brewer

II

THE ALLITERATIVE MORTE ARTHURE

A Reassessment of the Poem

Edited by Karl Heinz Goller

III

THE ARTHURIAN BIBLIOGRAPHY

I Author Listing

Edited by Cedric E. Pickford and Rex Last

IV

THE CHARACTER OF KING ARTHUR
IN MEDIEVAL LITERATURE

Rosemary Morris

V

PERCEVAL

The Story of the Grail
Chrétien de Troyes

Translated by Nigel Bryant

VI

THE ARTHURIAN BIBLIOGRAPHY

II Index

Edited by Cedric E. Pickford and Rex Last

ISSN 0261 – 9814

THE LEGEND OF ARTHUR
IN THE MIDDLE AGES

Studies presented to
A. H. DIVERRES
by colleagues, pupils and friends

Edited by P. B. Grout, R. A. Lodge,
C. E. Pickford and E. K. C. Varty

D. S. BREWER

Published by D. S. Brewer
240 Hills Road Cambridge
an imprint of Boydell & Brewer Ltd
PO Box 9 Woodbridge Suffolk IP12 3DF
and by Biblio Distribution Services
81 Adams Drive, Torowa,
PO Box 327, New Jersey 07512, U.S.A

First published 1983

British Library Cataloguing in Publication Data

The Legend of Arthur in the middle ages. –
(Arthurian studies ISSN 0261-9814)
1. Arthur, King – Addresses, essays, etc.
2. Diverres, A. M. – Addresses, essays, etc.
I. Grout, P. B.   II. Diverres, A. M.
III. Series
398'.352   PN57.A6

ISBN 0-85991-132-2

Phototypeset in Great Britain by
Rowland Phototypesetting Ltd, Bury St Edmunds, Suffolk
Printed by St Edmundsbury Press, Bury St Edmunds, Suffolk

Contents

Contents

Preface

THE following volume of studies presented to Professor A. H. Diverres grew out of a Colloquium held in his honour at Gregynog Hall, Newtown, Powys, from 13 to 15 March 1981. Six papers were delivered at the Colloquium and these are printed here, together with eleven others contributed by scholars in the Arthurian field. In selecting material for this volume, an attempt has been made not only to represent different languages in which Arthurian texts appeared in the Middle Ages, but also to reflect some of the important phases of Professor Diverres's career: the connection with the International Arthurian Society and with the University of Manchester, to name but two.

Particular thanks are due to Professor C. E. Pickford and the Eugène Vinaver Fund for their invaluable assistance with the printing and financing of this volume.

The editors also wish to thank those who organized the Colloquium: Dr C. J. Gossip, and the Warden of Gregynog, Dr G. T. Hughes. In addition they express their sincere gratitude to those who, although not members of the editorial board, gave generous assistance with the preparation of the text for publication: Mrs F. M. Alexander, Dr W. R. J. Barron, Dr R. Bromwich, Dr C. J. Gossip, Professor B. F. Roberts.

Armel Hugh Diverres

A. H. DIVERRES has spent the greater part of his career in three centres of learning: Manchester, Aberdeen and Swansea. After studying at Swansea Grammar School where Dylan Thomas was one of his contemporaries, he entered the University College of Swansea where he graduated with First Class Honours in French in 1936. Two years later he obtained the Licence-ès-Lettres at the University of Rennes and the MA of the University of Wales for a thesis on the Breton writer Paul Féval. After two years of service in the artillery, he transferred to the Intelligence Corps where he remained until demobilisation in 1946. Appointed Assistant Lecturer in French at Manchester, then Lecturer, he remained there until 1954, when he moved to a Senior Lectureship at Aberdeen. He succeeded Professor F. C. Roe in the Carnegie Chair of French in 1958 and held it until 1974, at which date he was appointed to the Chair of French at Swansea.

During the sixteen years he spent as Head of Department in Aberdeen Armel Diverres threw himself with characteristic zest into all aspects of University life. He was a member of the Library Committee from 1962 to 1968 and during the last two years he was Chairman, with the title of Curator of the Library. From 1971 to 1974 he was a member of the University Court. His Deanship of the Faculty from 1967 to 1970 coincided with a period of very rapid University expansion with all its attendant problems: the introduction of new subjects, the recruitment of suitably qualified staff, the provision of adequate teaching accommodation. In his own department, which doubled in size in the space of a few years, he brought about through his initiative some important developments. He introduced, in 1961, a Single Honours in French as an alternative to the traditional Scottish system of Joint Honours in two languages. In 1965 he introduced a postgraduate Diploma, later to become an M.Litt., in Medieval Studies, a co-operative venture of all departments which

9

had medieval interests of any kind, and he chaired the relevant committee throughout his time in Aberdeen. In addition to his activity in furthering medieval studies, his was one of the main influences responsible for the creation of the Departments of History of Art and of Linguistics, and the starting of the TV Service. He was also largely responsible for the institution of the new language laboratory, opened in 1973 in a purpose-designed building with the latest equipment, and which is now one of the biggest Language Centres in the country.

He was also keen on forging close links with France and set up two exchange scholarships with Rennes and Geneva and three exchange lecteurships with Rennes, Pau and Clermont-Ferrand. His achievements in the field of expanding French studies in Scotland were recognized by the award by the French Government of the Palmes Académiques in 1971.

Armel Diverres's interests are wide-ranging. His early love of Romantic literature to which his MA thesis on Féval bore witness came to the surface again many years later in his edition of 1967 of Vigny's *Chatterton*. But his main contribution to scholarship has been in the field of medieval language and literature. His edition of Froissart's *Voyage en Béarn* was published in 1953, followed by an edition of *La Chronique métrique attribuée à Geoffroy de Paris*, based on his doctoral thesis of 1950. Numerous articles have followed throughout the years on Froissart and on Chrétien de Troyes. A founder member of the International Arthurian Society, he served as Vice-President of the British Branch from 1963 to 1978, as President from 1978 to 1980. This was crowned by his two-year appointment as International President of the Society, the last manifestation of which, before he retired, was the highly successful congress held in Glasgow in August 1981.

The last seven years of his career were spent in Swansea where he renewed a family link, since his father had been a member of staff in the department of French from 1923 until his retirement in 1946. Faced with new challenges, Diverres tackled them with his usual brio. He restructured the teaching programmes and developed academic links with the universities of Brest, Mannheim and Angers. As in Scotland, so in Wales. He gave his time unstintingly in the service not only of the University but also of several extra-mural bodies. He served on the University of Wales Press Board and as a Governor of the National Museum of Wales, and on the wider national plane, he served on the CNAA Modern Languages Board, Humanities Board and Research Committee, and as a Governor of the Centre for Information on Language Teaching and Research. From 1976 to 1978 he was President of the Society for French Studies.

On the personal level, when one thinks of Armel Diverres, the first word that comes to mind is warmth. The friendliness and generosity of the man are remembered by all those who came into contact with him in the University world and beyond. In Aberdeen at Christmas time, he would visit all colleagues in the French Department with small children and distribute toys to them, a practice he continued in Swansea. All this in the greatest simplicity and with a total lack of condescension. His memory for faces and names is legendary. Anyone setting out for Lerwick or Stornoway would be immediately asked to remember him to Mr Mc so and so. His likes and dislikes are expressed with equal warmth. Althought he is essentially kind-hearted, his innate charity does not impair the lucidity of his judgment. His students held him in a mixture of awe and affection. His tremendous enthusiasm for his subject, his gift of communicating this, and in particular his readiness to discuss his own field with non-specialists account for the awe, and the affection is attributable to his approachability, his complete lack of pompousness and his genuine interest in the student as an individual. Son of a Breton father and a Welsh mother, he epitomizes the pure Celt. Indeed, he is very proud of his Welsh background: an engineer from Cardiff who had come to install some equipment in the language laboratory in Aberdeen was somewhat taken aback to find that Armel refused to talk English to him.

Armel Diverres's friends and colleagues offer him this volume of essays to mark their appreciation of forty years of scholarly activity and to wish him many years of active and happy retirement.

F. E. SUTCLIFFE

Bibliography

The Publications of A. H. Diverres

I EDITIONS

Froissart, *Voyage en Béarn*, Manchester University Press, 1953, xxx–159 pp.

La Chronique métrique attribuée à Geoffroy de Paris (Publications de la Faculté des Lettres de l'Université de Strasbourg, Fascicule 129), Paris, Les Belles Lettres, 1956, 359 pp.

Alfred de Vigny, *Chatterton*, University of London Press, 1967, 176 pp.

II ARTICLES AND LECTURES

'*Le Miroir de Mort* by Charles Chastellain', *The National Library of Wales Journal*, I (1940), pp. 218–19.

'Le Patois gallot dans les oeuvres de Paul Féval', *Nouvelle Revue de Bretagne*, II (1948), pp. 280–4.

'Chateaubriand et la complainte du Major André', *Revue de littérature comparée*, XXIII (1949), pp. 412–16.

'Le Folklore breton dans les oeuvres de Paul Féval', *Nouvelle Revue de Bretagne*, III (1949), pp. 339–46.

'Paul Féval et le roman historique', *Nouvelle Revue de Bretagne*, IV (1950), pp. 401–6.

'L'Histoire de Bretagne dans les romans de Paul Féval', *Nouvelle Revue de Bretagne*, VI (1952), pp. 245–53.

Sixty-one short articles on medieval French authors in *Cassell's Encyclopaedia of Literature*, 1953, recently revised.

'Jean Froissart', *Encyclopaedia Britannica*, 1964 edition, vol. IX, pp. 953–4, recently revised.

Bibliography

Bibliography

'Jean Froissart's Journey to Scotland', *Forum for Modern Language Studies*, I (1965), pp. 54–63.

'The Geography of Britain in Froissart's *Meliador*', *Medieval Miscellany presented to Eugène Vinaver* (edited by F. Whitehead, A. H. Diverres and F. E. Sutcliffe), Manchester University Press, 1965, pp. 97–112.

'An Anglo-Norman Life of Saint Melor', *The National Library of Wales Journal*, XV (1967), pp. 167–75.

'Froissart's *Meliador* and Edward III's policy towards Scotland', *Mélanges offerts à Mme Rita Lejeune*, Gembloux, 1969, vol. II, pp. 1399–1409.

'The Irish Adventures in Froissart's *Meliador*', *Mélanges offerts à Jean Frappier*, Paris, 1970, vol. I, pp. 235–52.

'Some Thoughts on the *sens* of *Le Chevalier de la Charrette*', *Forum for Modern Language Studies*, VI (1970), pp. 24–36.

'Laurent Joubert's system of orthography in 1578–1580', *History and Structure of French. Essays in Honour of Professor T. B. W. Reid*, Oxford, 1972, pp. 89–98.

'Chrétien de Troyes and his sources' (review article), *Forum for Modern Language Studies*, IX (1973), pp. 298–300.

'Chivalry and *fin'amor* in *Le Chevalier au Lion*', *Studies in memory of F. Whitehead*, Manchester, 1974, pp. 91–116.

French at the Universities, University College of Swansea, 1977, 19 pp.

'The Pyramus and Thisbe story and its contribution to the Romeo and Juliet legend', *The Classical Tradition in French Literature*: *Essays presented to R. C. Knight by colleagues, pupils and friends* (edited by H. T. Barnwell, A. H. Diverres, G. F. Evans, F. W. A. George and Vivienne Mylne), London, 1977, pp. 9–22.

'St. Melor: what is the truth behind the legend?', *Amesbury Millenium Lectures*, Amesbury Society, 1979, pp. 9–19.

'Paul Féval and the Novel', *Mélanges offerts à Garnet Rees*, Paris, 1980, pp. 131–44.

'Les Aventures galloises dans *Meliador* de Froissart', *Mélanges offerts à Charles Foulon*, Liège, 1981, vol. II, pp. 73–9.

'Yvain's Quest for Chivalric Perfection', *An Arthurian Tapestry. Essays in Memory of Lewis Thorpe*, ed. Kenneth Varty, University of Glasgow, 1981, pp. 214–28.

'*Iarlles y Ffynnawn* and *Le Chevalier au Lion*: Common Source or Adaptation?', to appear in *Studia Celtica*.

In addition there are numerous reviews in learned journals.

13

'The Treson of Launcelote du Lake': Irony in the Stanzaic Morte Arthur.

FLORA M. ALEXANDER

THE story of the death of Arthur and the ruin of the Round Table is inevitably an ironic one. An excellent society is destroyed from within, as a result of the collective actions of Agrawayne, Mordred, Launcelot, Gawayne, and Arthur himself. Most significantly, the two best characters, Launcelot and Gawayne, make major contributions to the disaster. Agrawayne and Mordred are characterized as evil and treasonable, but their malice would have nothing to work on if it were not for the opportunities presented to them, first by the adulterous relationship between Launcelot and Gaynor the Queen, and, in consequence of that, by the feud that arises between Launcelot and Gawayne after the deaths of Gawayne's brothers. Irony enables the poet who told the story in Le Morte Arthur to express a view on the behaviour of Launcelot and Gawayne. Further ironies are employed to show how other characters bring suffering upon themselves and others, and also how misfortune interacts with the weakness of men to make destruction inevitable.

Structural irony allows a writer to imply judgements without actually stating them, by manipulating a character so as to reflect on another character, or a situation so as to reflect on another situation.[1] In Le Morte Arthur the figures of Gawayne and Launcelot are balanced against each other, because they are outstanding in different ways, and the strength of each provides a perspective which exposes the weakness of the other. Launcelot is conspicuously courteous, and faithful to his lover, but his commitment to Gaynor involves of necessity the deception of King Arthur: he is defective in that quality of loyalty which is prominent in Gawayne. Gawayne is supremely loyal to the memory of his dead brothers, but this quality, on the face of it admirable, becomes obsessive. He is driven by an unreasonable desire to be revenged on Launcelot, who is not in fact responsible for their deaths, and he is shown to be incapable of dealing flexibly and sensitively with other people, as Launcelot does.

15

Through the interaction of the two, the poet is able to show two contrasting types of human fallibility.

The courtesy of Launcelot is established most effectively when Arthur, by this time his adversary at the siege of Joyous Gard, reflects:

> How corteise was in hym more
> Then euyr was in any man.[2]

This thought is provoked by Launcelot's action in placing the King on his own mount after he has been unhorsed. His courtesy is consistently displayed throughout both sieges. At Benwick he twice refrains from killing Gawayne in spite of intense provocation,[3] and the virtue displayed is the more impressive because he allows himself, in a remark addressed to King Arthur, to betray the extent of his exasperation with Gawayne's intransigence.[4] The joy that is felt by the court at his presence, and the corresponding distress caused by his absence, confirm his outstanding qualities.[5]

It is only in the deception of Arthur that he is open to criticism. An explicit judgement on the love between him and Gaynor is made by means of her parting statement:

> throw thys ylke man and me,
> For we togedyr han loved vs dere,
> All thys sorowfull werre hathe be.
> My lord is slayne, that had no pere,
> And many a doughty knyght and free.
>
> (3639–43)

Love that has been so dearly bought can only be regarded as tarnished. The poet leads up to this position with indirect indications, earlier in the poem, that he sees and regrets the disloyalty involved in Launcelot's love for the Queen. The deception of Arthur is emphasized by the repeated references to Launcelot's visits taking place immediately the King has gone out.[6] Even allowing for the fact that secrecy was necessary and conventional, and for the frequently antithetic style of the poem, the accumulation of sequences like:

> The kynge satte vppon his stede
> And forthe is went vppon his way . . .
> Launcelott forth wendys he,
> Unto the chambyr to the quene;
>
> (57–8; 65–6)

seems, in the context of the contrast between Launcelot and Gawayne, to hint at more than is said. The awareness of dishonesty is heightened by the brazen nature of Launcelot's communications to Arthur after the discovery. At the siege of Joyous Gard he sends a message, by a maiden, to the effect that:

> lyes were sayde hym vppon;
> Trewe they were by day and nyght.
> (2066–7)

The claim is repeated after it has been agreed that Launcelot should return the Queen. He hands her back with the unsuitable comment that she is given:

> As lady that is feyre and shene
> And trewe is bothe day and nyght;
> (2384–5)

and repeats the offer, made on the previous occasion, to fight in proof of her purity. He even goes on to say that Arthur is misled because of listening to liars. The best that can be said for Launcelot here is that he tells his lies with confidence.

There is a further indication, in the use of the word 'treson', that the poet means to draw attention to dishonesty in the hero. The word is used insistently in the part of the poem which deals with the discovery of the lovers. Agrawayne, planning the disclosure, uses 'treson' and 'trator', referring to Launcelot's behaviour towards the King.[7] Then, in the actual scene in which the lovers are trapped, 'treson' occurs in three successive stanzas. After telling us that Launcelot went unarmed to see Gaynor, the poet adds

> Off tresson dred he hym ryght noght;
> (1797)

and virtually the same comment is made in the following stanza. But in the next stanza after that, Agrawayne and Mordred and the twelve other knights come and:

> Launcelot of tresson they begredde,
> Callyd hym fals and kyngys treytoure.
> (1812–3)

Very shortly thereafter the word is applied by Bors to the actions of Agrawayne and his companions.[8] It can be assumed that the repetition is deliberate. The language of the poem is repetitive in its nature, but it is not poverty-stricken or careless. Here the poet is, by design, depicting the treacherous Agrawayne charging the hero with treason. We may wish to discount his accusation as unreliable and malicious. But because of the facts that have been put before us we are not free to do this. We know that Launcelot *is* in this respect disloyal to Arthur. And so we are compelled to take note of the incongruous truth that there is something in common between the hero of the story and one of its villains. It is the one flaw in his otherwise fine character, and it is highlighted by being placed in the perspective afforded by Gawayne.

Equally, Gawayne's intransigence is seen to be a failing because it is seen in relation to relevant aspects of Launcelot's courtesy: his care for the dignity of his opponents, his remembrance of old ties of friendship,[9] and his concern for the suffering that the prolonged conflict causes to his people –

> Thys land is of folke full thynne,
> Bataylles has it made full bare,
> Wete ye welle it were grete synne
> Crysten folke to sle thus more.
> (2598–601)

Launcelot responds sympathetically and appropriately to situations as they arise, whereas Gawayne, who was initially full of warmth and goodwill, is hardened by bereavement into a condition of fanatical hatred. The poet's practice of composing in pairs of incidents, which in some sense balance each other, enables him to use an earlier episode to reflect ironically on a later one, thus exposing Gawayne's dogged hostility. On each of the occasions when Launcelot is besieged by Arthur and Gawayne, he sends out a damsel to try to make peace. This is modelled on what takes place in *La Mort le Roi Artu* at the siege of Joyous Gard, although in the French text the negotiation at the siege of Benwick takes a different form, in that Gauvain and Lancelot talk directly at Gauvain's request.[10] By using the same form, with a maiden dressed in green riding out with a message on both occasions, the poet directs his listener or reader to compare the two episodes. In the first case, at Joyous Gard, Launcelot is sending an untruthful and defiant message, much more abrasively worded than the message he sends in *Mort Artu*[11], denying the adultery and offering to fight. Arthur and Gawayne both react aggressively to his words. The point of the comparison with the second peace mission is that on the second occasion the situation is substantially different. Launcelot has returned the Queen to Arthur, and has subsequently been pursued by Arthur and Gawayne to his own land, and besieged there. Furthermore, Launcelot's attitude is now entirely different. He is asking for a twelve-month truce, and offering to go into exile and live the rest of his life in the Holy Land.[12] Arthur is disposed to accept Launcelot's offer, and it is only because Gawayne's attitude is quite unchanged that the fighting continues.[13] The only development in Gawayne's position is between:

> His dedis shall be bought full sore,
> Bot yife no stele nyll in hym go;
>   (2076–7)

and:

> To Yngland will I not torne agayne
> Tylle he be hangid on a boughe.
>   (2680–1)

Constancy so extreme that it is unchanged in a thoroughly changed situation cannot be seen as an unqualified virtue, and the difference between Gawayne and Launcelot confirms the impression that the poet intends Gawayne's shortcomings to emerge here.

The same strategy of using contrasting figures and attitudes to provide ironic comment is evident in the presentation of love in the poem. Gaynor and the Maid of Ascalot are alike in that they both love Launcelot passionately. The Maid's self-destructive feelings for Launcelot are presented without explicit criticism from the narrator, although it is clearly unreasonable for her to accuse Launcelot of lack of courtesy in his behaviour to her. Her last letter presents an account of her 'trewe lovynge' in such a way as to provoke sympathy. But a different perspective is put on the letter by the final statement in which Gaynor renounces her love for Launcelot. This resembles the letter formally: the letter is addressed to King Arthur and the knights of the Round Table, and occupies six stanzas, and Gaynor's speech, addressed initially to the Abbess in the presence of Launcelot, occupies five. There is also a thematic connection between the two utterances. It would be misleading to imply that the positions of the two women are fully comparable, since Gaynor has to reproach herself with vast and disastrous public repercussions of her love, whereas the Maid is destroying only herself. Yet it is significant that the Maid is shown dying egoistic and unrepentant[14] (with no disposition at all to leave earthly thoughts, as Malory's Elaine is exhorted to do in the same circumstances), whereas Gaynor has developed new values and now sees as her highest priority the salvation of her soul:

> My sowle hele I wyll abyde,
> Telle god send me som grace,
> Throw mercy of hys woundys wyde.
>   (3655–7)

By implication this is bound to make the Maid's limited view appear inadequate.

Another variety of irony prominent in this story is the dramatic irony that

19

arises when characters are unaware of some important matter, while poet, audience, and possibly other characters know the true situation. One of the most obvious examples of this lies in Arthur's unawareness, during most of the first half of the poem, that Launcelot and Gaynor are lovers – a fact which, as the poet makes clear at an early stage, is well known to the world at large:

> For men told in many a thede
> That Launcelot by the quene lay.
>
> (61–2)

There is no suggestion that Arthur suspects the truth until Agrawayne tells him,[15] so that throughout the episodes of the Winchester tournament and the poisoned apple we assume that he is happily ignorant of the real situation. The sudden awakening to unhappy knowledge lacks the psychological interest of the treatment in *Mort Artu*, in which Agravain mentions the idea to Arthur early in the story. Thus, although the King does not at first believe it, the effects can be seen working gradually in his mind, and preparing him for the revelation through the pictures he sees in Morgain's castle.[16] The early disclosure also makes possible the ironic situation in which Arthur assumes that Lancelot's presence at the tournament, when he might have stayed at Camelot to be with the Queen, is proof that they are not lovers.[17] The different effect chosen by the English writer lacks the subtlety of the French. On the other hand, the sudden revelation is appropriate to his consistent interest in the harsh contrast between 'wele' and 'wo' (as is seen, for instance, in the way that widespread delight at Launcelot's return to the court is rapidly succeeded by general distress as a result of his quarrel with Gaynor and hasty departure).[18]

A similar type of dramatic irony, which occurs more extensively in the poem, is that in which a character believes that he or she knows something which is in fact not the case. Indeed a number of the most crucial points in the story turn on a character acting on a false perception. The Maid of Ascalot leads Gawayne to believe that she and Launcelot are lovers, and Gawayne passes on this misconception in good faith to Gaynor. (It seems clear to me that when Gawayne later regrets that he 'gabbyd on' Launcelot the meaning must be that he passed on false information unwittingly, not that he told a malicious lie. Otherwise it is very difficult to explain his very evident anxiety to put things right immediately he discovers the truth of the situation.)[19] As a result of this misinformation Gaynor quarrels with Launcelot and he leaves the court. Therefore in the crisis of the poisoned apple she is initially left without his support, and she has difficulty in finding another knight to help her, because they are all angry that her quarrel with Launcelot has deprived them of his company. When Gaynor realises that the report about the Maid was wrong she reproaches herself forcefully for having believed it:

Herte, allas, why were thou wode
To trowe that Launcelot du lake
Were so falsse and fykelle of mode
Another lemman than the to take?
(1176–9)

She is a victim of misunderstanding, but there is also an indication that she is over-hasty and has been lacking in trust. So she helps to bring about her own difficulties, although the extreme nature of her plight is out of all proportion to the extent of her fault. The actual accusation that she was responsible for the killing of the Scottish knight is also due to people believing they know something which is actually untrue. The knights believe, because they saw the Queen handing the fruit to the victim, that she must have been guilty of poisoning it. The narrative makes abundantly clear to the listener or reader that the culprit is the squire who wished to slay Gawayne, and calculated wrongly that Gaynor would offer him the best fruit.[20] So here we are made to look on while characters say, individually and collectively, that they 'say the sothe' which we know is no truth at all.[21] This whole segment of the story displays, through its ironies, how fragile peace and goodwill are, and how easily simple misunderstandings can shatter them. The confidence with which people are prepared to act on a mistaken belief anticipates the ultimately more disastrous confidence with which Gawayne acts on the wrong assumption that Launcelot has killed his brothers.

Accidents interact with misapprehensions so as to tilt the scales towards an unfortunate outcome. The poet tells us very pointedly in two successive stanzas that Gawayne sets off to visit Launcelot at Ascalot, but by that time Launcelot has taken his leave and gone.[22] If the two had in fact met, Gawayne would not have acquired his mistaken belief about Launcelot's relations with the Maid, and much distress would have been avoided. More terrifyingly, accident provides the occasion for a fatal misunderstanding in the account of the last battle. It is clearly understood, through the advice given to Arthur in his dream by the dead Gawayne,[23] that it is vital that he should not fight now but should wait for a month for Launcelot to come to his assistance. Because of his lack of confidence in his truce with Mordred, Arthur orders his men to attack if they see a weapon drawn.[24] In the circumstances it is the cruellest misfortune that an adder should glide forth and cause a knight to draw his sword, while the two armies are facing each other, so that Arthur's men attack unnecessarily, and all is lost.

The irony of lack of self-awareness appears in the crucial episode in which Agrawayne catches the lovers together. Bors warns Launcelot not to visit the Queen because Agrawayne is watching for him. But Launcelot feels that it is safe to disregard the warning, because, as he says, he intends only to pay a short visit, to talk with Gaynor, and to return directly. Therefore he goes dressed

21

only in his robe, and without armour. But he has underestimated the power of
their love, and in the event they disregard the danger, which turns out to be
only too real:

> For sothe, they neuyr wolde wene
> That any treson was ther dyght.
> So mykylle loue was hem bytwene
> That they noght departe myght;
> To bede he gothe with the quene
> And there he thoughte to dwelle alle nyght.
>
> (1802–7)

This treatment of the lovers' meeting is unlike the French, in which Lancelot
sets out with the intention of passing the night with the Queen.[25] The effect of
Launcelot's mistaken belief that he can restrict himself to a brief visit is to show
the fallibility of his human nature, and also to demonstrate, more powerfully
than any direct method could, the extreme force of the passion that unites him
and Gaynor.

Irony of events is that in which the turn of events frustrates a character's
expectations or designs.[26] There is a risk of finding irony in every unexpected
misfortune, and applying the term so widely that it loses significance. But we
can usefully say that it is ironic when people contribute to their own problems,
and we may suppose that if they could foresee the consequences that actually
ensue, they would behave differently. The case of Launcelot, who has to deal
with the unwanted devotion of the Maid of Ascalot, is ironic in that he does his
best to treat her with sympathy and consideration, and yet he is reproached in
her dying letter for being discourteous:

> So vnhend of thewis is ther none,
> His gentillnesse was all away,
> All churlysshe maners he had in wone.
>
> (1081–3)

In an attempt to comfort her he wears her sleeve at the Winchester tournament,
and afterwards leaves his shield with her. These things are done purely out of
compassion, and without any sense of commitment to her as a lover. But the
shield, when Gaynor hears of it, appears to be evidence of unfaithfulness, and
so the lovers' quarrel ensues. And in spite of all the repercussions, the Maid's
sorrow is not assuaged by Launcelot's attentions, so nothing is gained.
Launcelot, acting with the highest motives and out of concern for both women,
becomes as a result of his efforts the target of the reproaches of both. Through
this comically painful situation, the poet shows that there are some difficulties
to which there is no solution. The English handling of this part of the story

emphasizes the extent to which the hero brings trouble upon himself, since he offers freely to wear the sleeve and leave her his shield,[27] whereas in *Mort Artu* the *damoisele* manipulates Lancelot into the position of accepting the sleeve,[28] and it is by accident that Gauvain sees his armour while it is temporarily in her keeping.[29]

Several aspects of the central disaster show events contradicting expectations, so that people bring about results which they never intended. Agrawayne's motives for betraying the lovers are not analysed in any detail, but it seems safe to assume that his concern over the deception of the King would not drive him to expose them if he were able to foresee that he would lose his own life in the consequent fighting. Arthur orders Gaheriet and Gaheries to be present at the burning of Gaynor, against their will,[30] and it is as a result of this unnecessary presence that they are killed, and all hope of restoring the fellowship of the Round Table is lost. Again in this part of the story the English version lays more stress on the idea that people contribute to their own troubles. In *Mort Artu*, while it is similarly Arthur who is responsible for the brothers being there, this is because he is following a suggestion made by Agravain (who in this version has not yet himself been killed).[31] In *Le Morte Arthur* there is nothing to explain why Arthur should order them to be present against their wills, so a stronger impression is created that he wilfully does something which is to have very grave consequences. There is a similar irony involved in the placing of Mordred in charge of the kingdom when Arthur goes overseas in pursuit of Launcelot. In *Mort Artu*, Mordret puts himself forward as guardian of the Queen, and Arthur accepts the offer and goes on to give Mordret the keys of his treasure and to command his people to obey him.[32] Thus again there is the evil knight manipulating, and Arthur acceding to suggestions. In the poem, Mordred is chosen by the knights of the Round Table, because:

> Full mykelle they dred hem all bydene
> That alyens the land wold take;

and they:

> said, for sothe, that so them thought
> That Syr Mordred the sekereste was,
> Thoughe men the reme throwoute sought,
> To saue the reme in trews and pees.
> (2514–5; 2517–20)

Just as Arthur did in overruling the wishes of Gaheries and Gaheriet, the knights of the Round Table collectively take an initiative which will lead to dire consequences. In addition to the faulty judgement that Mordred is the most

23

trustworthy, there is the further reason given for his being chosen that he is the King's nephew, and also his son,[33] and in his treatment of what follows the poet points out most insistently that it is his father that Mordred is attempting to keep out of the kingdom, and his father's wife that he is attempting to marry.[34] In this way the magnitude of the error of judgement in trusting him is brought to our attention.

The irony of events is intensified by the ability of the audience to foresee the outcome of which the characters are ignorant. It appears that the poet is writing for an audience already aware of the basic outline of the action, since the tale is told with very little concern to establish background or to explain characters and relationships. Even a listener who did not know the key points of the plot would at least learn from the first stanza that this is the story of:

> there endinge,
> That mykell wiste of wo and wele;

whereas the actors in the story are of course unaware that it is their ending that they are playing out. Anyone who knew that the disaster is due to Launcelot's love would perceive ironically the many references to joy felt at his achievements, or his presence, or at news of his safety.[35] Arthur's comment when he reads the Maid's accusation that Launcelot has been 'vnhend' and 'churlysshe' in his treatment of her, is to say to Gawayne that in refusing her Launcelot:

> had hym wonne a reproovyng
> For euyr and a wikkyd fame.
> (1100–1)

Not only is the judgement inaccurate, in that Launcelot has incurred no reproach in his dealings with the Maid, but there is the further ironic point that in the near future Launcelot will, from Arthur's point of view, win ill repute not for refusing a lady but for adhering to one.

The idea of the coming destruction is adumbrated through comments made by the characters, at first ironically, because the speakers cannot appreciate the full implications of what they are saying, and progressively with greater accuracy, and so less irony, as they realise the magnitude of the crisis they face. When Launcelot leaves the court as a result of the quarrel with Gaynor, Bors, Lionel and Ector comment, with infinitely greater significance than they are yet able to recognise:

> 'Allas' they sayd, 'Launcelot du lake
> That euyr shuldistow se the quene.'
> (796–7)

24

There follows a series of reactions which are apposite, but insufficient in that they do not comprehend the full magnitude of what is happening. Gawayne says, when it becomes clear that Agrawayne is going to tell the king about the adultery:

> Here now is made a comsemente
> That bethe not fynysshyd many a yere.
> (1726–7)

When, remarkably quickly thereafter, the lovers are caught and Agrawayne killed, Launcelot says to Bors, who had given him warning:

> For it is sothe that thou me tolde,
> We haue begonne thys ilke nyght
> That shall brynge many a man full colde.
> (1885–7)

Bors in reply declares himself prepared 'aftyr the wele to take the wo', but at this stage only the first part of the calamity has been revealed. No one can yet anticipate the horror of the feud that will ensue after the deaths of Gawayne's two other brothers. It is immediately Launcelot hears of these deaths that he grasps the full significance of what has come about, and utters the words that put everything else into a new and truer perspective:

> A sorye man is Syr Gawayne;
> Acordement thar me nevyr wene,
> Tille eyther of vs haue other slayne.
> (2027–9)

The narrator of the poem uses from time to time the understated verbal irony that is familiar in English literature from the Old English period onwards. When Launcelot and Ector fight at Winchester he says:

> Bytwene them was no childis play.
> (304)

In an infinitely more serious situation, when news is brought of Mordred's insurrection, the tone is much the same:

> There was no man that thought it goode.
> (2947)

The effect is to direct the audience to create for themselves the feeling of

25

admiration, or fear, or whatever is appropriate. R. A. Wertime has suggested that we have in this poem a narrator deliberately handled by the poet so as to produce 'a basic and meaningful discrepancy . . . between the narrator's point of view and the poet's pattern of events.'[36] He proposes this as explanation of the fact that the narrator's responses are consistently compassionate and do not seem to take full account of the characters' faults – in particular the responsibility of Gawayne for the final disaster. Wertime is right when he points to the description of Gawayne as 'hende and fre', at precisely the point where he rides out and challenges Launcelot with peculiar aggressiveness, as challenging our expectations. However it should not be assumed that the narrator is naïve in the manner of many of Chaucer's narrators – unable to see what is plain to poet and audience. Rather the point is being established, and appreciated by the narrator, that human nature is complex. Gawayne is both excellent and destructive, and the praise is present in this context to remind us of the inadequacy of simple judgements.

Structural and dramatic irony, irony of events and verbal irony all contribute something to this poem. In the early stages of the story some of the ironies are comic, e.g. Launcelot's confidence that he is unknown at the tournament, when he has in fact been recognized, because of his excellence, by Arthur and Evwayne, and his threat to be revenged on the unrecognized opponent who is in fact Ector.[37] Even in the portrayal of Launcelot being blamed by both ladies for his treatment of them, when he has done his best to avoid hurting either, there is an element of comedy which clashes with the undoubted pain. But the ironies become increasingly sombre, and their principal function is to highlight the weakness and misfortune which in combination with the evil of Agrawayne and Mordred will destroy.

In *Mort Artu* the thought that men are victims of Fortune is more powerfully present than it is in *Le Morte Arthur*. In particular, the words of Sagremor li Desreez:

> Sire, ce sont li geu de Fortune; or poez veoir qu'ele vos vent chierement les granz biens et les granz honors que voz avez eü pieça;

(§190, 5–7)

are not reflected in any way in the English poem. Although the Wheel of Fortune is retained, the treatment of it is curtailed and does not contain Fortune's explanation that no one is seated so high that he can avoid falling from earthly power.[38] Nor does the poet include the incident in which Arthur is confronted with the rock on Salisbury Plain inscribed with a prophecy of the 'bataille mortel'.[39] Because of these differences the inexorable nature of Fate is less strongly felt. Wertime chooses to regard the poem as a 'tragedy of consequence' rather than a tragedy of Fate or Fortune, and argues that 'the forces of destiny are imbedded in the structure of chivalric society and in the natures of its individual members, whose actions . . . govern, almost entirely, the course of events'.[40] In fact misfortune and fault are necessary, to make the story turn out as it does. But this poet has a distinctively well-developed interest in the way that not only the unmistakable evil of malicious knights, but also the weaknesses and misjudgements of basically good characters, combine with misfortune in a deadly process.

The inclination to question or to modify earlier concepts of the heroic is a marked feature of English literature in the fourteenth century.[41] M. W. Bloomfield, examining the problem of the hero in the later Middle Ages, finds 'a strong suspicion of earthly achievement along with a fascination with it'.[42] In *Le Morte Arthur* the awareness of the fallibility of good men, and of the instability of secular institutions, leads naturally to the new perspective provided towards the end by the emphasis on religious values. In the context of penitence and salvation, the desires that had moved the characters come to be seen as relatively unimportant. The Archbishop, receiving the intimation of Launcelot's death and entry into Heaven, laughs, echoing the laughter of Troilus from the eighth sphere. The ironies which throughout the work have created a degree of detachment prepare the audience to accept this laughter, and to see a fitting end in the burial of Gaynor beside her husband, in the care of the monks of Glastonbury.

The Ambivalence of Adventure: Verbal Ambiguity in 'Sir Gawain and the Green Knight', Fitt I

W. R. J. BARRON

IN the scruffy little manuscript containing the supposed work of the *Gawain*-poet, now BL MS Cotton Nero A.x, Art. 3, none of the four texts is titled.[1] What would a contemporary reader, glancing at the opening of the fourth, have judged its literary category to be?

> Siþen þe sege and þe assaut watz sesed at Troye,
> þe borӡ brittened and brent to brondez and askez,
> þe tulk þat þe trammes of tresoun þer wroӡt
> Watz tried for his tricherie, þe trewest on erthe:
> Hit watz Ennias þe athel, and his highe kynde . . .
>
> (1–5).[2]

Initially he might assume it to be an epic on the Matter of Antiquity, then, as the first laisse moves on to the founding of Rome, various Italian provinces and the realm of Britain, change his mind in favour of a chronicle of world history. Even when Arthur enters the poem at line 26 he might merely narrow his conception to a British chronicle. And when, in the following lines, the poet himself turns from the matter of his work to speak of the literary tradition to which it belongs, what he says does nothing to resolve the uncertainty as to its category. Lines 31–6 may refer to the antiquity and authenticity of the text or, equally, to the antiquity of the alliterative style as a traditional English medium – some critics see the ambiguity as deliberate.[3] The category to which he specifically assigns it in line 30 – *laye* – hardly resolves the ambiguity: though the overtones of the word, self-consciously literary and antique, may seem appropriate to the opening of the *Gawain* text, its lyric origins and associations with brief tales on Celtic matter of love and magic are at variance both with the

28

alliterative tradition and with the epic scale and classical and historical subjects so far suggested.[4]

On grounds of scale alone we might have expected the poet to prefer 'romance' to 'lay'; certainly that is the category evoked from line 37 onwards by a description of Arthur's court full of the conventions and verbal formulas of *roman courtois*. He actually uses the word only at the very end of the poem, when the issue of the category to which it belongs is raised again. In saying that the story he has just told 'is breued in þe best boke of romaunce' (2521), he seems to be using the term in its basic sense: 'The vernacular language of France as opposed to Latin' (*OED* I), referring to his source, real or figmental, as warrant for the truth of the poem's contents – as at line 690 when he says 'þe bok as I herde say.' It is also guaranteed by 'þe Brutus bokez' (2523) or British chronicles, history rather than *roman courtois*. The vagueness of its use here may remind us that the term originally referred not to a literary category but to a linguistic medium,[5] and that, long after the *roman courtois* had evolved, it continued to be applied to a wide variety of vernacular literature intended for secular audiences.[6]

Romance has presented enormous difficulties of definition for modern critics. It cannot be defined by subject, since the classic medieval division into the *matières* 'De France, et de Bretaigne, et de Rome la grant'[7] makes no distinction between their treatment in Chronicle, Epic or Romance; nor by audience, since the primary audience of all three forms was the French aristocracy who first patronized secular literature in the vernacular. Though the linear procedures of literary history have taught us to associate the Matter of France with Epic, the Matter of Antiquity with romanticized Epic, and the Matter of Britain with the romance proper, it is doubtful if these distinctions would have been apparent to contemporaries who labelled examples of all of them *romanz*. Faced with the impossibility of defining the genre by such criteria, scholars have recently fallen back on characterizing it by its essential concerns and conventions of expression.[8] Though in retrospect the conventions have become more positively identified with the romance form than they were at its inception, the mode was from the beginning an essentially mixed one not rigidly separable from other literary expressions of the interests and values of the secular aristocracy.[9]

The problem is not merely one of the initial evolution of the genre. Despite England's inheritance of the French tradition in its maturity, the term 'romance' is applied to as wide a range of literary texts in the one language as in the other.[10] The modern bibliographies and literary histories identify and classify the Middle English romances with confidence, though not without occasional embarrassments.[11] Yet even within the comparatively late, alliterative corpus to which *Sir Gawain* belongs the width of subject matter and diversity of interpretative approach is evident. Some of the texts might best be described as chronicles with epic overtones – *Alexander A*, *The Destruction of*

Troy, Morte Arthure, The Siege of Jerusalem, The Wars of Alexander (to which the earlier *Brut* of Laȝamon might be added); others are predominantly moral and didactic in interpretation – *Alexander B*, *The Awntyrs off Arthure, Joseph of Arimathie*; only *Golagrus and Gawain* and *Sir Gawain* itself superficially conform to conventional conceptions of the romance.[12] In an age when many so-called romances were specifically historical, and versions of the Troy legend in particular represented themselves as authentic histories,[13] rigid distinctions of narrative kind, clearly separating fact from fiction, had apparently not yet developed. This is reflected in the absence in Middle English of any neutral terminology for the various narrative genres:

> As a result, Middle English writers classify their narratives with a number of different terms, reflecting such criteria as relationship to actual events (*storie, fable*), mode of narration (*spelle, tale*), language (*romaunce*), literary tradition (*romaunce, legend, lyf*), proportion of represented action to argument (*geste, treatise*), and movement of the fortunes of the protagonist (*tragedie, comedie*). These criteria were not mutually exclusive, and several terms could be applied to a single work.[14]

In the light of these terms, which predominantly reflect content rather than form, it is perhaps significant that the *Gawain*-poet, even before using the unhelpful term *laye*, emphatically announces the type of matter with which his poem is to be concerned:

> . . . an aunter in erde I attle to schawe,
> þat a selly in siȝt summe men hit holden,
> And an outtrage awenture of Arthurez wonderez.
>
> (27–9)

But the key word here is a complex one:

> *MED aventure* n., 1(a) Fate, fortune, chance; one's lot or destiny. 2(a) Something that happens, an event or occurrence; an experience; an accident. 3(a) Danger, jeopardy, risk. 4(a) A venture, an enterprise; a knightly quest; (b) An adventure, an exploit, a daring deed. 5 A marvellous thing (action, occurrence), a wonder, a miracle. 6 A tale of adventures, an account of marvellous things.[15]

Though the literary context might suggest sense 6 as the most appropriate here, *schawe* ('reveal, declare') and the indication that the poet is concerned with something already known and judged by others rather suggest 2(a) or 4(a), an event not a narrative.

Adventure, Northrop Frye tells us, is the essential element of plot in Romance; but it is equally essential in other narrative forms, such as the saints' legends which rely no less heavily on miraculous violations of natural law for their interest as stories.[16] The *Gawain*-poet acknowledges the supernatural associations of adventure by coupling it initially with *selly* and *wonderez*; but at the same time he insists on the actuality, the reality of his subject-matter as an 'aunter in erde,' a 'selly in si3t.' The two prepositional phrases could be dismissed as conventional tags employed for alliterative convenience and largely devoid of meaning.[17] Editors who interpret them as having full semantic value (*in erde*: Waldron – 'real-life'; Barron – 'actual'; *in si3t*: Waldron – 'manifest'; Barron – 'veritable')[18] strengthen the impression that the ambiguity of category implied by the opening lines also extends to the content of the poem. What sort of narrative are we to expect – fantasy or reality? What credence does the poet himself give to it?

Once the narrowing focus of the narrative fixes our attention upon Camelot, both the atmosphere established – 'With rych reuel ory3t and rechles merþes' (40) – and the courtly festivities described are redolent of Romance. True, the Christmas sports with their jousting, kissing games, and the seasonal 'custom' of the king closely reflect contemporary reality. And there are critics who sense ambivalence in the atmosphere, reading *rechles* as 'carefree, careless, reckless'; in reactions to the kissing game – 'Ladies la3ed ful loude, þo3 þay lost haden, / And he þat wan watz not wrothe' (69–70); and in the personality attributed to Arthur, 'so joly of his joyfnes, and sumquat childgered' (86) (*MED child* n., 13(d) Boyish, light-hearted), motivated by 'nobelay' but also by 'his 3onge blod and his brayn wylde' (89). Others reject any idea of ambivalent social behaviour and personal motivation, the half tones of real life, as inappropriate to the ideal world of Romance. Though on a second reading, to which the circular form of *Sir Gawain* invites, anticipation of later events may cast an ironic light on this opening scene, it is difficult at first sight to be certain where the ambiguities lie.

But, even approached in the open-hearted spirit appropriate to Romance, there seems to be something ambivalent in Arthur's 'custom':

> . . . he þur3 nobelay had nomen, he wolde neuer ete
> Vpon such a dere day er hym deuised were
> Of sum auenturus þyng an vncouþe tale,
> Of sum mayn meruayle, þat he my3t trawe,
> Of alderes, of armes, of oþer auenturus,
> Oþer sum segg hym biso3t of sum siker kny3t
> To joyne wyth hym in iustyng, in jopardé to lay,
> Lede, lif for lyf, leue vchon oþer,
> As fortune wolde fulsun hom, þe fayrer to haue.
>
> (91–9)

What does its fulfilment require – narrative, as lines 92–5 suggest, or event, as implied by lines 96–9? If the former, what sort of narrative? An *vncouþe* (*OED uncouth* n., 1 Unknown. 3 Of an unknown or unfamiliar character; unusual, strange; marvellous. 4 Of a strange and unpleasant or distasteful character) tale of some *auenturus* matter (the adjective shares the wide ranging meaning of *aventure*). But which sense is appropriate here: event, daring exploit, marvellous occurrence, accident, dangerous event, miraculous occurrence? The coupling with *mayn meruayle* suggests the darker, supernatural end of the range, but *meruayle* too refers to a wide range of events, from the surprising to the miraculous or monstrous, and the narratives in which they are recorded.[19] The examples of subject-matter given in the next line are vague and literary, though not specifically romantic, and *auenturus* remains undefined. The type of event which would satisfy the royal 'custom', a challenge to jousting, is reminiscent both of the tale *of armes* desired by Arthur and one of the Christmas sports in which the court participates at Camelot. But the remainder of the sentence reminds us that jousting, even in sport, puts life in jeopardy, subject to fortune, inherently fickle in medieval conception. We may foresee a range of events from the harmless, formal joust of Romance, through fatal jousts in Romance and in contemporary life, to the trial by combat of medieval legal usage. Both the key terms used take us back to *aventure*, one of whose senses (3(a)) is 'jeopardy', while the goddess Fortuna, Dame Fortune is sometimes called Dame Aventure. And both remind us of the element of chance beyond human control in adventure as in games – *MED juparti* (e) (< OF *jeu parti*) n., 3(a) Uncertainty, doubt, suspense. 4(a) A problem in chess; also a trial or stratagem in chess; (b) a trial. Arthur's 'custom' appears ambiguous both in formulation and in implication. If the literary category to which *Sir Gawain* belongs is to be determined by its subject-matter, the ambivalence of adventure seems likely to affect judgement on both content and form.

Arthur's 'custom' is almost immediately fulfilled (130–231) in a form which proves equally ambivalent. As if his seasonal challenge were a challenge to the unknown, the unknown arrives in a nameless form – 'an aghlich mayster' (136) – combining aspects of the conventional Knight Challenger of Romance and the *wodwos* ('satyr, troll, Wild Man of the Woods'), part of the folklore inheritance of the romance at the opposite pole, socially and morally, from the knight. Confrontation with such a creature, irrational but made credible, almost tangible, by the poet's vivid description, is the kind of episode which distinguishes Romance from Epic:

> . . . what is lacking in the typical epic is 'aventure', the opening out to the unexpected, the encounter with the unknown.[20]

Familiar as they are with the *auenturus* both in literature and life and eagerly expectant of the one or the other (90–9), Arthur's court is startled, puzzled, alarmed by the form in which it presents itself:

For wonder of his hwe men hade

(147)

For vch mon had meruayle quat hit mene my3t

(233)

The poet veils their humiliation in ambivalence, passing delicately from the reactions of the servants to those of the company in general, to those of the nobles in a way which blurs social distinction in favour of their common humanity:

> Al studied þat þer stod, and stalked hym nerre
> Wyth al þe wonder of þe worlde what he worch schulde.
> For fele sellyez had þay sen, bot such neuer are;
> Forþi for fantoum and fayry3e þe folk þere hit demed.
> þerfore to answare watz ar3e mony aþel freke,
>
> (237–41)

Their stunned silence is attributed to an ambivalent motivation – 'I deme hit not al for doute, / Bot sum for cortaysye' (246–7) – which, for the moment, redeems Camelot's reputation for courage and courtesy. But the terms now associated with the already familiar concomitants of adventure – *wonder*, *meruayle*, *selly* – emphasize the darker, supernatural end of its semantic range (sense 5): *MED fantom* n., 2(b) An illusory experience or object; an apparition, a specter; *fairie* n., 2(a) Supernatural contrivance; enchantment, magic, illusion, also, something supernatural or illusory; a phantom. But other senses of these cognates echo the overtones of uncertainty, dubiety, illusion, fiction – *fantom* n., 1 That which has only a seeming reality, permanence, or value. 5 *Med.* morbid experience of hallucination or bad dream; delirium; *fairie* n., 2(b) Something incredible or fictitious, a figment – associated with the idea of adventure: *MED aventurous* adj. 1(a) Occurring by chance, accidental; (b) governed by chance, insecure, doubtful. The court's identification of the visitant, though it has ominous implications, still leaves much uncertain.

The responsibility for deciding how to respond to him falls upon Arthur:

> þenn Arþour bifore þe hi3 dece þat auenture byholdez,
> And rekenly hym reuerenced, for rad was he neuer,
>
> (250–51)

The occurrence here of the key term suggests that Arthur recognizes the response to his desire for adventure, but *hym* in the following line shows that it must refer to the Green Knight, a person rather than the expected narrative or event. Such a use is unusual, presumably to be understood as an extenstion of sense 5 'A marvellous person' – but Arthur's understanding of the nature of the

33

visitant remains undeclared. This point represents the hinge of the first fitt, since upon Arthur's response to the Green Knight and his challenge depends the Round Table's involvement in the quest, which constitutes the narrative thread of the romance and the moral testing ground of the hero. It is marked by the term whose ambivalence queries the nature of romance and its relation to reality.

Arthur responds to the *auenture* before him with regal calm and courtesy which turns to puzzlement, then to anger as he struggles to comprehend the nature of the Green Knight's challenge to his court (250–342). Referring to the Round Table's chivalric reputation on the battle-field and off – 'Preue for to play wyth in oþer pure laykez' (262) – and to the holly branch he carries as a sign of peace (ignoring the monstrous axe in his other hand), he requests of Arthur: 'grant me godly þe gomen þat I ask / bi ryȝt' (273–4). Despite the stranger's insistence that had he come in force, in martial fashion, he would have armed himself for combat, Arthur responds as if to the conventional Knight Challenger of Romance, apparently taking *gomen* in the sense 'a tournament or jousting; a battle' (*MED gomen* n., 3(a)): 'If þou craue batayl bare, / Here faylez þou not to fyȝt' (277–8). The ambiguity of *bare* may reflect Arthur's uncertainty as to what sort of challenge is implied by the Green Knight's ambivalent appearance, to single combat or to combat without armour.[22] He arrogantly rejects any military contest with the 'berdlez chylder' of the Round Table and reiterates his request for a 'Crystemas gomen', a game of pluck buffet, of blow for blow undefended – but with the giant axe he carries! Despite the deadly implications of such a one-sided contest, it is evidently proposed as a festival pastime fit for children, evoking innocent senses of *gomen*. But the word is to be a key term in complex verbal patterns which extend, interlinking with each other, throughout the poem.[23] And it has overtones which are to seem ominously appropriate to various aspects of the narrative as it evolves: when the first blow ends in the survival of the headless Green Knight, we may guess the game to be 'a scheme, trick, plot' (5(c)) only to find it ultimately dismissed as 'a joke, jest, a ridiculous circumstance' (4(a)) resulting in the hero's humiliation; during the inter-linked hunting and wooing scenes of the third fitt we may suspect a thematic relationship from the associated senses 'amorous play, love-making, especially sexual intercourse' (2(d)) and 'game killed or caught, the kill, the catch' (6(a)). Even here we may note that the contest is spoken of in terms which mingle the vocabulary of game – *gomen, gyft, barlay* – with that of law and justice: *court, quit-clayme, diȝt, dom, barlay, respite*. When the terms of the compact are formally exchanged between the Challenger and Gawain (377–416), the playful vocabulary of sport – *buffet, dint, tape, cnokez* – is still mingled with that of legal contracts: *refourme, forwardes, couenaunt, siker, trawþe, wages, swere, soþe*. But when they are repeated for the third time by the Green Knight's severed head (448–56), the legal words survive – *lelly, hette, herande, charge, disserued, ȝolden, recreaunt* –

while only the ambiguous *dunt*, half ominous, half playful (*MED dunt* n., 1(a) The blow of a weapon; 2(b) a buffet of the fist or hand), remains from the vocabulary of play.

Once the technical nature of the challenge has been made clear, the whole court responds with stunned silence until Arthur, stung by the mocking laughter of the Challenger and his accusations of cowardice, reacts with intemperance: 'He wex as wroth as wynde' (319), leaping forward to take the axe from the Green Knight's hand. If we suspect that the challenge, directed to anyone 'so bolde in his blod, brayn in hys hede' (286) – echoing the terms in which the youthful Arthur was initially characterised (cf. line 89) – was designed to provoke such a response, we may be concerned that the king nonetheless judges it *nys* (323) and *foly* (324). Gawain's intervention to draw the challenge upon himself, 'syþen þis note is so nys þat no3t hit yow falles' (358), underscoring the way in which the king's actions are at variance with his judgement, may make us query his own motivation – social tact to save Arthur from an embarrassing involvement in an inappropriate sport, or courageous self-sacrifice to save the head of state from certain death? – and therefore his judgement of the nature of the challenge. And when the court concurs 'To ryd þe kyng wyth croun, / And gif Gawan þe game' (364–5), we may wonder whether the other members are conscious of danger to the sovereign and what they judge the nature and implications of 'þe game' to be.[24]

Judgements on the game must depend on the nature of the *aventure*, person and event, with which the court is faced. But when, still headless, he rides away from Camelot, his identity, like his destination, remains as mysterious as at his arrival, even though he has given Gawain equally mysterious instructions for finding him:

> To quat kyth he becom knwe non þere,
> Neuer more þen þay wyste from queþen he watz wonnen.
>
> (460–1)

The direct intervention of the poet asking 'What þenne?' (462) breaks the mood of stunned suspense which has persisted since his entrance, challenging our judgement of what has passed in the interim. Gawain, whose urbane self-control has previously been contrasted with Arthur's intemperance, is associated with him in his ambivalent response: 'þe kyng and Gawen þare / At þat grene þay la3e and grenne' (463–4). If the king's laughter is unfeigned, it may confirm earlier impressions of the facile element in his personality; *grenne*, which has no humorous senses in Middle English, suggests fear, anger, mockery, suppressed for social appearances. Gawain is not to speak again in this fitt and not until the final fitt (2193–4) does he clearly express his opinion of the nature of the adventure to which he is now committed. His fellow courtiers, however, now declare their judgement openly: 'breued watz hit ful bare / A

35

meruayl among þo menne' (465–6). Any remaining ambiguity in their use of *meruayl* is resolved, on the ominous supernatural side, by their private acknowledgement that the adventure will end in Gawain being 'britned to noȝt, / Hadet wyth an aluisch mon' (680–81) – *MED elvish* adj., (a) possessing supernatural skill or powers; (b) mysterious, strange; (c) elf-like, other-worldly.

Arthur too has secret thoughts behind his too-ready laughter: 'þe hende kyng at hert hade wonder' (467), but the imprecise term used does not indicate the precise degree or cause of his feeling. What is really in his heart is concealed behind the elaborate public response by which he tries to defuse the ominous implications of the event by likening it to Christmas entertainments, 'Laykyng of enterludez' and other courtly diversion (470–73). In reassuring the queen and ignoring the amazement of the court, Arthur is displaying the courtesy, tact and social judgement expected of a great king. But remembering the intemperance of his personal response to the Green Knight we may wonder whether, in his heart, he really equates that strange apparition with a theatrical event, or whether his description of it as *craft* consciously or unconsciously includes the pejorative overtones of the word – *MED craft* n¹., 2(b) Skill in deceiving, trickery; 8(b) A trick, wile. His final declaration 'I haf sen a selly' does not resolve the ambiguity since he interprets the *selly* as fulfilling the ambivalent terms of his festive 'custom' (474–5, cf. 90–99) and the word itself is too general in sense (*OED selly* n., Marvel, wonder; something wonderful) to define the nature of his expectation or the manner in which it has been fulfilled. His attitude to the tangible evidence of the event, the Green Knight's axe left in Gawain's hands, underscores the issue: does he intend his comment 'heng vp þyn ax' (477) merely in the literal sense or, ironically in view of the return blow to which Gawain must eventually submit, the figurative one – 'have done with this business'?[25] The axe is hung upon the wall:

> þer alle men for meruayl myȝt on hit loke,
> And bi trwe tytel þerof to telle þe wonder.
>
> (479–80)

Are we to see it as a memento of a *wonder* past and done with – as it is implied others will do – or as a *memento mori* for the future? Much must depend on what opinion we have formed of the nature of 'þe wonder' and the threat which it implies to Camelot and to Gawain in particular. If the ambiguities surrounding it have escaped us, the poet jolts us into reconsidering the whole *auenture* so far by ending the fitt with a direct personal address to Gawain, silent amidst a renewal of the 'rechles merþes' (40) with which the Camelot episode began, suggesting what may be passing through the hero's mind:

> Now þenk wel, Sir Gawan,
> For woþe þat þou ne wonde

þis auenture for to frayn
þat þou hatz tan on honde.
(487–90)

Though the most appropriate sense for *auenture* in this context might be 'venture, enterprise, knightly quest' (4(a)), the suggestion that a renowned chivalric hero might shrink from pursuing it implies an exceptional, if undefined, degree of danger. The reader's own judgement of the degree and nature of the danger involved is immediately challenged in the opening lines of the next fitt (491–9) with their ambiguous comments on the significance of the previous action and sibylline hints as to its future outcome. As repeatedly throughout the first fitt, much depends on our understanding of *auenture*. The second fitt opens:

This hanselle hatz Arthur of auenturus on fyrst
In ӡonge ӡer, for he ӡerned ӡelpyng to here.
(491–2)

The implication seems to be that Arthur, who wished for a tale of 'sum auenturus þyng' (93), has experienced an actual *auenture*; that it may prove a token of good or ill luck in the new year (*MED hanselle* n., (a) A token or indication of luck, good or bad; (b) something given (especially in the New Year) as a token of good luck) as ambivalent as the forfeits in the kissing game amongst his courtiers (66–70); that the challenge (*ӡelpyng*) he longed for may actually have been invoked by his court's pride in its chivalric reputation (*OED yelping* n., 1 Boasting, proud or pompous talk); that what began happily as a game may end sadly in earnest:

Gawan watz glad to begynne þose gomnez in halle,
Bot þaӡ þe ende be heuy haf ӡe no wonder;
(495–6)

Throughout the remainder of the action we shall continue to be puzzled by the nature of the game in which Gawain is inescapably involved, anxious as to the seriousness of its outcome. Though we may have seen no connection between it and the innocent, if ambivalent, kissing game which preceded it in the Christmas festivities at Camelot, we will find it difficult to ignore the parallelism between the compact for an exchange of blows which it involves and the compact for an exchange of winnings which forms part of the Christmas festivities at Hautdesert. When the triple pattern of that game, with its seemingly innocent forfeits of kisses, is interlinked with three violent hunts for whose quarry they are exchanged, we may begin to query the innocence of the courtly love-play in which they were obtained, and the significance of the

37

luf-lace gained in the process and illicitly retained in breach of the exchange compact. And when the outcome of the compact made at Camelot, which threatens the hero's destruction, proves to depend upon that breach in the compact made at Hautdesert, resulting in no more than a trifling wound, the token punishment of a game of forfeits, we may begin to doubt our ability to distinguish between sport and earnest, social game and moral test. The nature of Gawain's failure – social peccadillo or mortal sin? – still divides critics and their disparate reactions suggest that the reader's moral perception (and his sense of humour) is as much under test as the hero's.

By presenting the adventures of his romance as a complex of inter-related games, by using the key term *auenture* in a variety of ambiguous contexts and linking it with others which compound rather than resolve the ambiguity, the *Gawain*-poet would seem to be stimulating the reader's scrutiny of the events he narrates: conventional quest confirming the values of chivalry, or conflict with supernatural powers bent on undermining them? The technique has an obvious functional value in restoring narrative tension to a traditional form in which the hero's survival is normally assured. But it also has a thematic function, querying the relationship between appearance and reality (the hero's bodily survival and his spiritual peril) within the narrative and, by using *auenture* to refer to narrative as well as event, the relationship between romance and reality. The issue, implicit in all romance, is generalized by the contrast between the conventional procedures of *Sir Gawain* and the vivid realism of the narration and moral earnestness of the hero. It is explicitly posed when the moral theme and the reality of the *auenture* are related to the whole record of human experience in the poem's historical frame which sets this incident in the stream of time:

> þus in Arthurus day þis aunter bitidde,
> þe Brutus bokez þerof beres wyttenesse;
> Syþen Brutus, þe bolde burne, boȝed hider fyrst,
> After þe segge and þe asaute watz sesed at Troye,
> (2522–5)

> þe borȝ brittened and brent to brondez and askez,
> þe tulk þat þe trammes of tresoun þer wroȝt
> Watz tried for his tricherie, þe trewest on erthe:
> (2–4)

The ambivalent reputation of Aeneas, the *tulk* who, tested like Gawain under a double obligation, redeemed his betrayal of Troy to the Greeks by his admirable deception in concealing Polyxena from them, is associated with that of his great-grandson Felix Brutus, ironically so called since his mother died giving birth to him and he later killed his father by accident, yet upon exile from Italy founded Britain:[26]

Where werre and wrake and wonder
Bi syþez hatz wont þerinne,
And oft boþe blysse and blunder
Ful skete hatz skyfted synne.

(16–19)

The Trojan heroes and their descendants, legendary founders of European nations and models for western chivalry, would appear to have imparted their own ambivalence to Arthur's Britain. Of the terms in which its history is summarized, *werre* invokes the perennial ambivalence of warfare, not least in an age which deplored the internecine conflicts of Christian princes as a distraction from the just war against the power of Islam; *wrake* ranges in meaning from suffering in the abstract, through malicious injury, to the retributive vengeance which contemporary law often incorporated and justified (*OED wrake* n., 1 Retributive punishment, vengeance, revenge. 2 Hostility, mischief. 3 Pain, suffering, misery); and *wonder*, rooted in the idea of astonished reaction to a fact or event either good or bad, can express both 'marvel' and 'atrocity'.[27] The oppositions inherent in these words are made explicit in the tying together of *blysse* and *blunder* expressing the glories and disasters of British history. But both have moral overtones applicable to the element of self-discovery in the hero's quest: *MED blis(se)* n., 2(c) A source of joy, a cause of happiness; sexual gratification. 3 *Theol.* (a) Spiritual exultation or ecstasy; (b) heavenly bliss; the state of those in bliss, beatitude; *blonder* n., Disturbance, strife; trouble, distress, *cf. blonderen* v., (a) To walk without seeing, go blindly; (b) to proceed ignorantly, act blindly or irrationally.

Gawain's adventures have been said to take place in a world in which the rituals of chivalry follow Nature which in turn takes its course from the mysteries of God, but which is also dangerously cleft between appearance and reality:

Whereas his *blysse* would have been a state in which the heroic rituals of men accord with Nature and with the mysteries of God, his *blunder* is a state of deception which results from man's abuse of ritual and, hence, his separation from Nature and God.[28]

In allowing the reality of human fallibility and sin to obtrude upon the ritual of courtly games, the poet has juxtaposed the romantic and mimetic modes in a way which challenges the reader's judgement of the category to which the work belongs.[29] Romance, Northrop Frye tells us, is essentially a mixed form, satisfying man's perennial desire to see his aspirations and ideals achieved by superior members of an ideal society in whom, nonetheless, he can recognise himself and the world in which he lives.[30] By playing upon the ambivalence of its basic component, adventure, the *Gawain*-poet creates in his reader that

39

willing suspension of disbelief combined with moral awareness which is essential if Romance is to speak to him meaningfully of human experience past and present.[31] And in the epilogue he indicates the perpetual remedy for all human error:

> Mony aunterez here-biforne
> Haf fallen suche er þis.
> Now þat bere þe croun of þorne,
> He bryng vus to his blysse! AMEN
> (2527–30)

Celtic Elements in Arthurian Romance: A General Survey[*]

RACHEL BROMWICH

THE nature of the indebtedness of continental Arthurian romance to antece-dent Celtic sources, together with that of the likely channels by which Celtic material reached the continent, has been a matter of hot debate for the best part of a century. In the light of the advances which have been made in Celtic scholarship during the same period, however, I hope that it may now be possible to establish certain basic principles concerning this transmission which will prove acceptable to Romance scholars and to Celticists alike – that is, acceptable both to those whose main concern is with the early indigenous literature of the Celts in Wales, Cornwall, and Brittany, and to those who look back from the high noon of Arthurian romance as this is reflected in the later prose and verse masterpieces in French, English, and German, but who nevertheless retain some interest in the question of 'origins'.

I begin by setting forth four basic propositions which I shall elaborate in the course of this paper. These are:

i) that the personal nomenclature of French Arthurian romance, in so far as it is of Celtic derivation, is derived from the names of characters who played a part in antecedent Welsh, Cornish, and Breton tradition, and who are fre-quently identifiable in Welsh sources which are too early to have been subjected to continental influences;

ii) that the development of Arthur as the centre of a cycle, drawing into his orbit the names of a number of independent figures belonging to this native tradition, is an indigenous development which took place in Celtic countries at too early a date to have been influenced from without;

iii) that the Brittonic names which entered French romance in this way did

[*] Based on a lecture delivered to the British Branch of the International Arthurian Society at the 'Arthurian weekend' held at Swansea in July 1978.

41

not necessarily do so in combination with any narrative elements previously attached to those who bore them in the native records, but that Celtic names and Celtic story-themes for the most part penetrated continental romance independently of each other;

iv) that the question of Arthur's rise to fame in western literature is essentially a Welsh literary problem, and that the scanty references to Arthur in early sources can only be interpreted in the light of a full understanding of the character and development of the literature to which they belong.

Firstly, then, the question of Arthurian names. The name 'Arturus' appears first in the Latin of the Welshman who redacted the *Historia Brittonum* some time in the early ninth century, and as 'Arthur' in several Welsh poems which are believed to go back approximately to the same date – one of them indeed, the famous reference to Arthur in the *Gododdin*,[1] may even be considerably earlier. Arthur's two most frequent companions in a number of early sources are Cai and Bedwyr[2] (*Keu* and *Bedoier*, Kay and Bedivere), and these appear as his companions already in one of the poems to which I refer, *Pa gur*[3] (=*Pa wr*) 'What man is the gatekeeper?', of which I offer a tentative translation below. The names of both Arthur[4] and Cai (*Caius*) are generally believed to be of Latin derivation, but this, if it be accepted, need prove no obstacle, for names derived from Latin are by no means rare among the names in the early Welsh genealogies, for men who were born approximately between the dates AD 300 and 450: they become less common after that date.[5] (The name of St Patrick, from *Patricius*, is an example). Arthur's queen Gwenhwyfar (*Guenievre*) 'fair enchantress',[6] though not attested quite so early as these latter names, does seem to belong to the early native tradition, if we are to believe the Triads, and Geoffrey of Monmouth latinizes her name as *Guanhumara*, a form which he must have derived from a written source in Old Welsh. The names of a number of independent heroes who at varying dates became absorbed into the Arthurian complex or 'brought to Arthur's court' may also be here referred to – examples are Gwalchmai, Peredur, Drystan. Loose approximations were made in French in the cases of the first two when they became *Gauvain* and *Perceval*,[7] while the last was borrowed in the written form in which it is early attested in Old Welsh as *Tristan*. This name is attested, quite independently of the romance hero, as the name of a witness to a charter in the *Book of Llan Dâv* (early 12th century, but based on older sources), and this appears to be a unique instance in which this name is recorded in Welsh for a character other than the Tristan of the romances.[8] 'Gauvain' and 'Perceval' are loose approximations to the antecedent Welsh forms, but they are no looser than is 'Merlin' (Geoffrey's *Merlinus*) derived from the name of the Welsh prophetic poet Myrddin.[9] 'Perceval' is an instance in which a French name has taken the place of a Brittonic name which sounded somewhat similar; a parallel instance is 'Isolt' from Welsh and Cornish Esyllt, Eselt.[10] The very looseness of such borrowings as these is an indication that they derive from oral rather than from written sources – it would be only too easy for the French narrator of a tale transposed from Welsh or Cornish or Breton to reproduce such names incorrectly, or to conflate them with existing names of a kind more familiar to him. On the other hand it is certain that some names, such as that of Tristan, were borrowed through *written* sources, because they were pronounced quite differently in the two languages. *Yvain* from Welsh Owein, Ywein or Ewein (from Latin *Eugenius*) is another instance, like that of 'Tristan', in which the obscure vowel represented by *i* or *y*, *o*, or *e* in Welsh was given an entirely different sound in French.[11] The transposition of 'Owein fab Urien' into *Yvain li fiz Uriens* is also particularly interesting from another point of view: it is one of only three examples in which a personal name, together with its patronymic, are seen to have been borrowed together from Welsh into French. The other two instances of this are for quite minor characters – *Ider* or *Yder fiz Nut* from 'Ede(y)rn fab Nut (Nudd)' who is listed in *Culhwch and Olwen*,[12] and *Giflet fiz Do* from 'Gilfaethwy fab Don' in *Mabinogi Math*.[13] Another quite exceptional occurrence is for a name to be transferred together with its Welsh epithet: 'Uthyr Pendragon' (U. 'head of Dragons', i.e. 'leader of warriors')[14] of the poem *Pa gur*, preserved in almost identical form in the chronicles and in the poems of Chrétien, is one such example. The transposition of 'Caradawc Freichfras[15] (Old Welsh *Brecbras*) into *Caradues Brie(f)bras* is a fascinating instance, in which the original epithet meaning 'strong arm' was misinterpreted in French as 'short arm', giving rise to a new story, found in the First Continuation of the *Conte del Graal*, to account for the manner in which Caradawc lost his arm. According to Piette[16] this name must have entered French through a written borrowing from a source in Middle Breton rather than in Welsh, since the Breton endings *-oc* and *-uc* (corresponding to Middle Welsh *-awc*) were rendered in French as *-ue(s)*. The case of *Tristan* is somewhat similar, for here a misinterpretation of the name as containing the French adjective *triste* gave rise to the story of the hero's 'sad' birth.

The names borrowed from antecedent stories which have not survived in Welsh included even the names of animals. The most famous of these is Kein Caled,[17] or the 'hard-backed', the horse of Gwalchmai who is listed in the Triads of Horses, and who gave in French the name of Gauvain's horse *le Guingalet*, the English *Gryngolet* in *Sir Gawain and the Green Knight*. Another is the Cath Palug,[18] the cat-monster of Anglesey, who became in French *le Chapalu*, a new story being evolved which described Arthur's fight in a bog with a monstrous cat – the same kind of ingenious misinterpretation of a Brittonic name (Fch. *palus* 'marsh, fen') as though it were French that we get in the cases of *Caradues Briebras* and *Tristan*; in all of these instances new stories were evolved in order to give intelligible explanations of these names for French audiences. Another horse, Lluagor,[19] the 'host-splitter', the steed of Caradawc Freichfras according to the Triads of Horses, supplied the name of the foal *Lorzagor*, the congenital animal companion born at one birth with

Caradues Briebras, according to the *Livre de Carados*. Similarly the ferocious boar known from *Culhwch and Olwen* as the Twrch Trwyth, appears as the boar *Tortain*[20] in the same source. It is therefore an established fact that a number of personal names of Brittonic derivation – whether Welsh, Cornish, or Breton – have passed into twelfth-century French romance. The animal-names even retain their animal identity after the transference. Such name-borrowings are particularly rich in the poems of Chrétien, although the large number of obscure names found in his works and in those of his contemporaries and continuators leaves room for a considerable margin of doubt concerning some of the particular derivations which have been proposed, since many of these names have come down in so corrupt a form as to be unrecognisable in any language, and some of the Celtic derivations which have been advocated are far from satisfactory, indeed quite unacceptable. I would certainly not go so far, for instance, as to claim any Celtic antecedent for the name and character of Lancelot[21] – still less for that of his son Galahad.[22] These are French creations, and they originated entirely in the post-Celtic development of the romances. Although a proportion of the names in Chrétien correspond with names in the existing Welsh poems and triads and native tales, the large number of names in the French romances which cannot be explained, and which have obviously been borrowed in forms which are corrupt, favours the belief that oral transmission was by far the more frequent and widespread means for the transference of Celtic names and stories into French; though we must allow always for several significant instances of written borrowings. This is indeed what one would expect to find, in view of the essentially oral nature of the Celtic tradition right down through the Middle Ages and beyond – so that what actually became preserved in writing in early Welsh sources is, so to speak, the mere tip of an iceberg. This, coupled with the fact that the medieval oral literature of Cornwall and Brittany is almost entirely lost, is the reason that the *disjecta membra* of Brittonic names and stories which have come down in the French romances are so interesting and present so challenging a problem to the Celticist, even though the attempts to interpret them have so often led merely to a wild surmise. It follows also that strict philological rules do not apply to such borrowings, but that a number of very loose approximations were made: classic examples are *Merlin* (*Merlinus*) from Welsh Myrddin, *Perceval* from Welsh Peredur, and *Gauvain* from Welsh Gwalchmai. And further, as Piette has emphasized,[23] very little headway can be made on purely linguistic criteria in distinguishing borrowings from Welsh as distinct from Cornish or Breton, since these languages were so close until as late as the twelfth century. As it is, Welsh literature is almost exclusively our source for detecting such borrowings.

The next point that I wish to emphasize is that early Welsh literature provides abundant evidence in poetry, triads and tales, for the fact that Arthur was already becoming the centre of a cycle of stories at a date too early for there to be any question of back-influence from continental sources. The earliest evidence for this cyclic development of Arthurian material in Wales is the dialogue poem *Pa gur* in the Black Book of Carmarthen,[24] to which I have already referred, and which may be dated to before 1100 – perhaps more than a century earlier. This poem begins with a verbal interchange between Arthur and a certain Glewlwyd Gafaelfawr[25] ('G. Mighty Grasp'), who is the gate-keeper of a hostile fortress to which Arthur is seeking to gain admittance for himself and his men. He lists a number of the names of these, and refers to their wonderful feats in slaying monsters and witches. The conclusion of the poem is absent, owing to the loss of a leaf from the manuscript, but in spite of this, and in spite of some obscurities which I cannot here discuss in detail, it is on the whole straightforward, if in places disjointed, and the following translation[26] will serve to give its substance. (I have used italics for the lines and half-lines presumably spoken by Glewlwyd; it will be seen that the poem rapidly develops into a monologue spoken by Arthur).

What man is the gate-keeper? *Glewlwyd Might Grasp.*
What man asks it? Arthur and fair Cai.
What (company) goes with you? The best men in the world.
Into my house thou shalt not come unless thou disclose(?) them.
I will disclose(?)[27] them, and thou wilt see them.
Wyth(n)eint, Eléi, and Ssiwyon[28](?) all three,
Mabon son of Mydron,[29] the servant of Uthyr Pendragon,[30]
and Gwyn Godyfrion.[31] My servants were harsh in defending (or 'fighting
   for') their rights:
Manawydan son of Llŷr,[32] profound was his counsel.
Indeed Manawyd brought shattered shields from Tryfrwyd;[33]
and Mabon son of Mellt, he spotted the grass with blood;
and Anwas the Winged, and Llwch of the Striking Hand,[34]
they were defending Eidyn[35] on the border.
A lord would satisfy them where(?) he would recompense[36] (them).
Cai entreated them as he hewed them down by threes.
When Celli[37] was lost men endured savagery.[38]
Cai mocked them as he cut them down,
Arthur, though he laughed, the blood was flowing,
in the hall of Afarnach,[39] fighting with a hag.
He smote the 'Cudgel-head' in the settlements of Dissethach,
on the mountain of Eidyn he fought with the 'Dog-heads'.[40]
They fell by the hundred, by the hundred they fell
before Bedwyr Perfect of Sinew;[41]
on the banks of Tryfrwyd[41a] fighting with a 'Rough Grey',[42]
furious was his nature, with shield and sword,
A host was futile compared with Cai in battle;

45

he was a sword in battle, to his hand was given a pledge.[43]
They were steadfast leaders of an army for the benefit of their country,
Bedwyr and Brydlaw. Nine hundred to listen,
six hundred to scatter, his onslaught would be worth.
I used to have servants – it was better when they were alive.
Before the lords of Emrys[44] I saw Cai in haste.
He carried away booty, the 'long man'[45] was hostile(?);
heavy was his vengeance, fierce was his anger.
When he drank from a buffalo-horn he drank for four,
when he came into battle he slew for a hundred.
Unless it were God who caused it, Cai's death were impossible.
Fair Cai and Llachau,[46] they made slaughter before the pang (ie. 'death')
   from blue spears;
on the uplands of Ystafngwn[46a] Cai killed nine witches.
Fair Cai went to Môn to destroy lions(?);[47]
his shield was a fragment against Palug's Cat.[48]
When people ask 'Who killed Palug's Cat?'
nine score warriors would fall as her food,
nine score champions . . .

The narrative background of the poem is obviously similar to that of a part of *Culhwch and Olwen*. Obvious parallels exist in the episode in which Cai seeks to gain admittance to the fortress of the giant Wrnach Gawr, and that in which Glewlwyd Gafaelfawr acts as Arthur's own gatekeeper and demands Culhwch's credentials before admitting him to Arthur's court. Another suggested parallel is to be found in the scene depicted on the Modena archivolt,[49] in which Arthur and Cai discourse with a porter who guards the fortress where Winlogee (Guinevere?) is imprisoned. There is also an early and significant mythological parallel in Irish,[50] in the *Battle of Moytura* in which the god Lugh (Lleu) enumerates his qualifications before gaining admittance to the fortress of Tara. The priority which the poem gives to the feats of Cai (and in a lesser degree to those of his companion Bedwyr) is significant in view of the deterioration of Cai's character in later sources. Others of the characters named in the poem are commemorated in the Triads or in the tale of *Culhwch* (*circa* 1080), where the wonderful and incredible list of heroes assembled at Arthur's court includes many who had no original connection with Arthur at all – even *Gwilenhin brenin Ffrainc* ('William king of France', i.e. William the Conqueror) and the protagonists of the Irish Ulster Cycle. In the Triads the 'Arthur's Court' framework is similarly used on occasion as an umbrella formula for bringing together a number of independent and unrelated heroes such as Llywarch Hen, a dramatic figure in the Powys englyn cycle.[51] All these things provide clear evidence for the cyclic development of the Arthurian legend at an early date in Wales.

After this rapid survey of the extent of the name-borrowings made into Arthurian romance from Brittonic sources, I pass on now to consider the nature of the traditions which were introduced into Europe from the Celtic world. How much of this material was historical or semi-historical, how much mythology, how much deliberate fiction? It is certain that these borrowings were not all from Celtic mythology, as has sometimes been too readily assumed. Early heroic narrative concerning prominent Brittonic heroes also formed a very important ingredient. Probably the most outstanding example of this is the case of Owain fab Urien who became in French *Yvain li fiz Uriens*,[52] the famous son of an early historical ruler in southern Scotland, known as Urien of Rheged.[53] Both father and son are the subject of eulogies and an elegy by the poet Taliesin, and these poems are authoritatively believed to have been originally composed as early as the end of the sixth century. We do not know at what stage Owain first became associated with Arthur, since there is no evidence for this earlier than the romance of *Owain* (Chrétien's *Yvain*). Geoffrey of Monmouth presents Urien as Arthur's contemporary, but makes it clear that he regarded his son Owain as belonging to a later generation.[54] A similar case could be made for Gwalchmai and Peredur, who are both independent legendary – and possibly historical – heroes who belonged to the 'Old North', the early British kingdoms which were situated in southern Scotland and northern England. There is also Chrétien's Erec (*Guerec*), whose name originates in that of the legendary founder of the Breton kingdom of Vannes (*Guerocus*)[55]. But I would feel much less certainty in advocating the historicity of Arthur's two early companions Cai and Bedwyr, of whom the earliest mention is found in the poem *Pa gur*, where they appear in company with such obviously mythological figures as Mabon, who is the Celtic god *Maponos* (though described in the poem as 'servant of Uthyr Pendragon') and Manawydan,[56] originally also a deity known to both the Irish and the Welsh. Mythical elements undoubtedly formed a large part in the Arthurian tradition from an early date – witness the 'Marvels' attached to Arthur's name in the *Historia Brittonum* – and it is indeed often difficult, if not impossible to draw a clear distinction between the elements of heroic legend, myth, and fiction. The widespread notion that all early Celtic literature is 'Celtic myth' has, however, often formed the basis for a belief that Arthur himself was no more than a 'myth.' But to recognize the degree to which the *dramatis personae* of Arthurian romance are indebted, not only to mythology, but also to 'saga' concerning legendary Brittonic heroes of whom some, such as Urien and Owain, certainly had a historical existence, is in itself a strong plea for Arthur's own historicity. This plea gains additional support from the very early allusion to Arthur in the *Gododdin* poem.

A related question, about which there is room for speculation and debate, is the extent to which the body of narrative attached to the heroic, legendary, and mythical figures I have mentioned formed part of a common inheritance of traditional lore and belief which was shared by *all* the Brittonic-speaking Celts, from the 'Old North' down through the whole length of Wales to Devon and Cornwall, and across the sea to the colony in Brittany. For instance, there is evidence to believe that the cult of Arthur as a returning hero or promised deliverer was more firmly entrenched in the south-west and in Brittany than it was in Wales. But as Piette emphasized, this cult must have been imported *from* Britain as the result of the common cultural tradition shared between Wales, Cornwall, and Brittany down to at least the ninth century; it is most unlikely to have originated as far back as the age of the sixth-century Breton migrations, which were too close to Arthur's own time; and a certain time-lapse must be allowed for between the date of a hero's death and the evolution of a legend concerning him. As evidence for the community of culture shared between Bretons and Welsh during the second half of the ninth century we have a significant statement found in the Book of Llan Dâv [57] concerning a certain Welsh nobleman called Guidnerth who was sent to do penance for the crime of fratricide in the cathedral church of Dol in Brittany, and the text explains that he and the Britons of that diocese were *unius linguae et unius nationis*: they spoke the same language and belonged to the same nation, although divided by the sea, so that to go to Brittany was not for Guidnerth like undertaking to do penance in a distant and alien country. Although at the end of the ninth century the Scandinavian invasions threatened the communications between Britain and Brittany, it is significant that Giraldus Cambrensis,[58] writing in the late twelfth century, states that the Cornish and the Bretons speak a language similar to Welsh and for the most part easily understood by Welsh people, though it is interesting that he offers the opinion that the speech of the former 'approaches more nearly to the ancient British idiom.'

It has been rightly emphasized (most recently by J. R. F. Piette) that the absence of any appreciable amount of early literature from either Cornwall or Brittany is no argument that such did not once exist. The Celtic cultural tradition was essentially an oral one, as has been previously emphasized, and it is of the nature of an oral tradition that an immeasurable amount is liable to be lost through failure to be recorded. There is a small but significant amount of evidence that the Breton poets once practised techniques similar to those practised in Wales. Fifteenth-century verse in the Breton language[59] preserves traces of a rudimentary from of *cynghanedd lusg* (i.e. rhyme of the penultimate syllable in a line with a preceding syllable), and also of something like the device known as *cyrch gymeriad*, in which the rhyme is carried on from the final of one stanza into the beginning of the next: a fact which offers eloquent testimony for the survival of a learned order of professional poets for a considerable period after the migration. As in Wales also, it was no doubt these professional poets who were the primary custodians of the Breton dynastic genealogies which have come down in the cartularies and in the saints' Lives, sometimes in forms which correspond closely with those from Wales,[60] and which show interestingly archaic linguistic features. Evidently the Bretons regarded themselves in the ninth century, and to an appreciable, though gradually decreasing extent for some centuries afterwards, as being of the same nation as the insular Britons. They shared with them the memory of a great hero called Arthur, and this belief implied far more than the mere fact itself, for it meant that they were partners in a body of tradition about their national past which linked the two peoples closely together, including also the western Britons of Devon and Cornwall.[61] The Bretons had their own origin legends about the foundation of the kingdoms which formed their emigrant colony,[62] and these follow a pattern which is pan-Celtic, being recognisable in both medieval Welsh and Irish literature. Traces of this have come down in such of the so-called 'Breton lays' (in French) as relate to the traditional founders of these kingdoms, as well as in Chrétien's poem about *Erec* or *Gueroc*, the traditional founder of the Breton kingdom of Vannes, for whom the Welsh version substitutes the Devon hero Gereint. The substitution in Wales of Gereint for *Erec* is indeed a symptomatic indication of a significant fact: for although it would seem that the Bretons clung tenaciously to the national traditions which they inherited from insular Britain, the same did not happen in reverse, since the legends of the founders of the Breton kingdoms made no impact upon the general corpus of native Welsh traditions, which tell us nothing of such heroes as *Gradlon Mor* (the founder of Breton Cornouailles) or *Guingamor*[63] (a name borne by successive Counts of Léon) any more than they do of *Gueroc* the founder of Vannes. The only minor exception to this that I have noted is the appearance in Welsh sources of that indeterminate figure 'Emyr Llydaw,' whose name means merely 'an emperor (ruler) of Brittany' and his son Howel,[64] a figure borrowed from Geoffrey of Monmouth. The Bretons preserved their own version of the story of the settlement of their country by Maximus's soldiers, a story which existed already in Brittany in the tenth century,[65] in a version evidently used by Geoffrey of Monmouth, and one which is independent from the narration of the same events in the Welsh tale of the 'Dream of Maxen.' And the Bretons appear to have contributed is no small measure to the story of the romance-hero Tristan, in the final form in which his story reached the French, contributing to it both a birth-tale, and the final episode of Tristan's marriage and death, in the theme of the second Isolt. Although it is apparent from the analogy of the Gaelic world[66] that community of culture can, and does, over-ride political divisions, and can even survive a dividing sea, it is nevertheless a striking fact that traditions of the legendary Breton heroes were not apparently re-absorbed into Wales by a process similar to that which saw the re-localization in medieval Wales of the stories of the prominent heroes of the 'Old North',[67] such as Owain ab Urien, Gwalchmai, Peredur, and others – some but not all of whom became subjected to the further transference from Wales into continental Arthurian romance.

Irish personal names in Arthurian romance are virtually non-existent. A striking and wholly exceptional instance in that of *le Morholt* in the *Tristan* romances. It is impossible to reject some ultimate connection between this name and that of the Irish mythical monsters known as the *Fomóire*, who levied a human tribute from Ireland and from the western islands of Scotland, just as did *le Morholt* from Cornwall. Their exaction of a human tribute from the Hebridean islands is recounted in the story of the Pictish hero Drust mac Seirb, who is the ultimate original of Tristan.[68] R. S. Loomis advocated an original in the Irish common noun *bachlach* ('churl, rustic') for the 'Green Knight' in *Sir Gawain and the Green Knight*,[69] but any Celtic derivation for this name is no longer convincing in view of the most recent opinion that the manuscript reading of the name (which only occurs once) is *Bertilak* and not *Bercilak*.[70] But when we turn from personal names to the story-themes of Arthurian romance, the evidence is entirely different. Owing to the fact that a considerable number of parallels undoubtedly do exist between these themes and themes which occur in early Irish tales, there has been a widespread view held among Arthurianists that the majority of such themes are of Irish origin, and that they passed over from Ireland into Britain, to be transferred again by the Welsh and Cornish to the Normans and French. But this is extremely improbable, as Kenneth Jackson and others have frequently reiterated.[71] While it is evident from a study of the *Mabinogi* that Irish story-themes certainly *did* enter Wales in the early Middle Ages – and we actually have in *Culhwch and Olwen* the names of a group of Irish heroes who are presented as members of the court of Arthur – the views which have frequently been expressed on this matter have been not a little distorted by the fact that so much more early Irish literature has been preserved than has come down in Welsh: perhaps, as Proinsias Mac Cana has recently suggested,[72] because the learned and literary classes in Ireland concerned themselves with committing their oral literature to writing at a much earlier date than did the corresponding classes in Britain. But here again we must remind ourselves of the essentially oral character of the Celtic tradition wherever it existed, and of the numerous pointers which are to be found, in the Triads and elsewhere, to the richness and 'density' of the oral tradition in Wales. The explanation is simply that Welsh stories failed to be committed to writing in anything like the abundance enjoyed by the early Irish tales. This is an accepted fact among Celticists: the debate is now no longer whether or not it was so, but concerns rather the speculation as to why it was that Irish stories received so much fuller a documentation than did Welsh. Whatever the reason may have been, there can be no doubt of the great value for comparative purposes of early Irish literature, no less than that of Welsh, for the Arthurianist.

Coming now to my third proposition, I have always regarded it as a general maxim that we should look primarily to Welsh sources for the personal nomenclature of Arthurian romance, but to Irish for parallels to the narrative themes.[73] Just as names may be freely transferred right out of their original narrative context, so it can be shown that story-motives moved about freely *within* the field of Celtic literature, passing from one character to another, in the same way as they did subsequently after their transference into continental Arthurian romance. An example of such a 'movable' theme within the Celtic field is that of the 'Boyhood Deeds' of a hero, leading to his arrival as an awkward initiate at the court of the supreme ruler, whether this be King Conchobar mac Nessa or King Arthur: this theme is associated with the Irish heroes Cú Chulainn and Finn, and in Wales with Peredur, the prototype of Chrétien's Perceval; and there are indications also of its association with Tristan, though it can hardly be proved that these belonged to the Celtic vernacular tradition of Brittany. Another theme which required the publicity of a royal court for its proper presentation is that of the 'Beheading Game', associated with Cú Chulainn at the court of Ulster in *Bricriu's Feast*, but with Gawain and Arthur's court in *Sir Gawain and the Green Knight*, (following various intermediary versions). Yet another 'movable' theme is the dynastic myth of the 'Sovereignty', which is found attached to the names of the founders of dynasties in Ireland, Wales, and Brittany, in one or both of two forms – the 'Chase of the White Hart' and that of the 'Transformed Hag.'[74] There are, of course, a few outstanding exceptions in which particular story-themes attached to particular characters have survived the transference from a Celtic source into Arthurian romance. Examples of this are the variant forms of the rape or elopements of Guinevere; and another very striking instance is the theme of the Fisher King with his disabling wound through the thighs, which appears to go back to the prestigious figure of Brân Fendigaid in the *Mabinogi* who, in the words of the story, was 'wounded in the foot with a poisoned spear.' The Perseus-Andromeda-like theme of the Dragon Fight, first attested in western Europe in the story of the Pictish *Drust*, the likely prototype of Tristan, has clung tenaciously to his successor in the romances,[75] being repeated no less than three times in the different versions based upon the poem of Thomas. These are, however, the exceptional examples which traditionally go to prove the rule. It is now becoming generally and increasingly recognized that we should think far more in the terms of a common fund of narrative themes which were once shared among *all* the Celtic peoples and moved about freely among them, to be appropriated to different heroes as local and national interests dictated – to King Conchobar mac Nessa, Cú Chulainn, and Finn mac Cumhaill and the heroes who surrounded them in Ireland, but to Arthur and to his attendant warriors in Britain.

There are certain themes later transferred into Arthurian romance which make their earliest appearance in association with figures in the Welsh *Mabinogi*: the 'Waste Land', which is very clearly delineated in the enchantment which descended upon the land of Dyfed, leaving it completely barren and waste, in the tale of *Manawydan*, and the often repeated introduction to

Arthurian adventures, by which the Arthurian court is holding high feast at Pentecost or some other festival, and the king refuses to eat until some marvel appears before him. This theme is anticipated in the First Branch of the *Mabinogi* when the hero Pwyll goes up to the mound of Arberth – a centre for magical happenings – between the first and second courses of his meal, in the hopes of seeing some marvel, and this marvel presently occurs when his magical wife Rhiannon appears. These two themes are what I would call 'Arthurian commonplaces.' But the latter, the court scene, is a simple narrative device which served again and again as the send-off for an Arthurian quest, while the former, the 'Waste Land' theme, is obviously loaded with mythological import, however difficult it is for us to recover its full significance today. There are a number of other 'Arthurian commonplaces' which are significantly paralleled in antecedent sources in Welsh or Irish. It is somewhat perilous to embark upon even a preliminary list, since no doubt analogies for each one of them can be cited from elsewhere, but here are some: magic fountains and magic mists, frequent transformations of humans into birds or animals, quests – often involving Otherworld visits – for a magic animal or a magic talisman (e.g. the Grail), cauldrons of plenty or re-birth, sword-bridges and revolving castles, dismembered heads on stakes. These may be called 'commonplaces' in the sense that they are continually repeated in the romances, so that any original mythological meaning they may once have held has long since become obliterated and forgotten.[76] Nevertheless, it is in relation to such themes as these that the term 'Celtic myth' may with some appropriateness be employed, because what we have in them is the débris of an imperfectly understood mythology. This mythology, based upon pagan Celtic religious belief, formed the substratum upon which much of the elaborate Arthurian superstructure became erected, and it was a possession which belonged in common to the whole of the Celtic world – to ancient Gaul, as far as our evidence goes – no less than to Britain and Ireland. We can deduce from the evidence available that pagan Celtic religion recognized a multiplicity of gods and goddesses who were tribal and local rather than representative of specific functions;[77] and it is indeed the consequent strongly localized character of early Celtic religion which lies at the basis of the great importance attached to place-name lore (the Irish *dindshenchas*) in all medieval Celtic literature. These concepts, inherited from primitive mythology and handed down almost exclusively by oral tradition, gave to the storytellers in Celtic countries the immense repository of imaginative, colourful, and even fantastic story-themes on which their high reputation was based, and which proved to have such a rare attraction for foreign audiences.[78] The great difference between Ireland and Wales lay in the different legendary and geographical backgrounds to which the traditional concepts became related, each country realizing similar ideas in terms of its own native heroes. As the Arthurian tradition crystallized in Wales, there is no doubt that the remembered heroes of the lost kingdoms in the 'Old North' formed a significant part: I have already instanced the cases of Urien Rheged, and his son Owain, together with Gwalchmai and Peredur. There were of course heroes from Wales as well, such as Caradawg Friechfras, who seems from the earliest sources to have once held a greater prominence than came to be his lot in the extant romances, and Gereint son of Erbin, a hero who belonged to Devon and Cornwall but who was also known to tradition in south-eastern Wales. It was the names of these and other Brittonic heroes, some of them belonging to quite independent stories, which became grouped around the central figure of Arthur in Welsh sources, and which eventually came, with Arthur himself, to form the names of the leading heroes of continental romance. No doubt some of these names and stories may have been transferred to the French through oral sources in Brittany, since the Bretons continued for long to remember the heroes who were celebrated in Britain itself, even though their own heroes failed to win any comparable recognition, and made hardly any impact upon the traditions of Britain as a whole. In the twelfth century it can be accepted that there was in circulation among all the Brittonic peoples a body of stories, derived from heroic saga, Celtic and international folk-tale motives and pan-Celtic mythology, representing a corpus of tradition which was their common property, and to which all had made a contribution of one kind or another.

My fourth and final proposition concerns Arthur himself. The cyclic development of the Arthurian material may be presumed to have taken place in Britain and Brittany by successive stages between the ninth and eleventh centuries, unaffected by any external influences from the continent of Europe. We find that as early as the ninth century, in the Arthurian *Mirabilia* attached to the *Historia Brittonum*, Arthur appears as a folk-hero whose deeds are associated with the mountain-top of Corn Gafallt (*recte Carn Cafall*) in Radnorshire,[79] where his dog's footprint was to be seen, and to a grave-mound at Gamber Head in Herefordshire, said to be that of his son *Amr* or *Anir* (unknown from any other source). Similarly stories of a folk-tale type, dispersed widely over Wales and the south-west, are to be found in Welsh saints' Lives redacted in the eleventh and twelfth centuries. It is however from Cornwall, in the early twelfth century, that we first hear of Arthur as a messianic hero who will return and lead his people to victory.[80] A similar concept, though under a slightly different form, reappears in different places all over Britain (but particularly in the Celtic areas and places adjacent to them) where the legend is localized that Arthur is sleeping in a cave, surrounded by his warriors, awaiting the final trumpet-call to action in the hour of his country's greatest need.[81] This portrayal of Arthur as the hoped-for deliverer, a *defender* of his people against all kinds of enemies including giants, witches, and monsters, seems to characterize the indigenous popular traditions concerning him and to have survived both in Welsh folk-tradition and in the early sources we have been considering – a plausible memory, perhaps, of a great leader who in the remote past had once led a British force against an enemy of foreign invaders.

There are a number of indications that Geoffrey of Monmouth came into contact with an Arthurian tradition localized in the south-west of Britain, since he seems to have known a curiously circumstantial story about Arthur's birth which involved a Cornish duke Gorlois and his fortresses at Tintagel and Damelioc (identified with Domellick, near St Denis) and a tradition which localized his last battle on the river Camel in Cornwall. There is also the significant fact that both the Triads and the tale of *Culhwch and Olwen* claim that Arthur's chief court was at 'Celli Wig in Cornwall':[82] a place whose identification is not certain, but which with a certain amount of probability has been identified with Killibury or Kelly Rounds, in the parish of Egloshayle near the north coast. It is impossible to know how old may be the name of Celli Wig for Arthur's court in Cornwall, but we have seen above that there is a possible allusion to it in the line relating to *Celli* in the poem *Pa gur*. If this were the only evidence concerning the sphere of activity of an early hero named Arthur, it would constitute a substantial case for the belief that the birth-place of the Arthurian tradition lay in the south-west of Britain.

But to conclude thus would not be a fair presentation of the evidence for the sphere of Arthur's original activities. We have yet to consider the evidence which associates Arthur with the 'Old North' – the Brittonic kingdoms north of the Border which extended southwards into Cumbria, Yorkshire and Lancashire. What may well be the oldest of all the references to Arthur is the one which is found in the early Welsh poem known as the *Gododdin*, a series of elegies on the British warriors who had come down from their tribal territory situated around Edinburgh to present a fruitless opposition to the invading Angles at a great battle at Catterick in Yorkshire, about the year 600.[83] Of one of these warriors it is said that he performed great deeds of valour *ceni bei ef Arthur* 'though he was not Arthur.' This reference comes from the earlier of the two texts of the poem: it may go back to the ninth century, it may even be older and date from the original redaction of the poem, whether in oral or written form, in the seventh century. No evidence exists on which this can be decisively proved, either positively or negatively. Whatever the date, the importance of the allusion consists in two facts – its north-British provenance, and the evidence it provides for Arthur's historicity. Some years ago Professor Thomas Jones[84] pointed out that in the context of a heroic poem such as the *Gododdin* no name would be cited for eulogistic comparison in this way unless it belonged to a hero who was believed to have really existed – no fictional or mythological figure would have served for such a purpose. The fleeting unexpanded allusion strongly suggests that the poet who made it placed full reliance on his hearers' cognizance of all the circumstances of Arthur's career, and recognized his name as a famous name to be conjured with in the society to which his listeners belonged – the name of a hero who, like the Gododdin warriors, had fought against the English invaders in an earlier generation.

There are two other important sources of information about Arthur which may be credibly supposed to antedate the ninth-century documents in which they first appear. One is the account of Arthur's twelve victorious battles in the *Historia Brittonum*; the other comprises the two allusions in the *Annales Cambriae* to Arthur's victory at Mt Badon, and to the battle of Camlann at which he and Medraut both fell. There is much to be said concerning the significance of both sets of passages: the battle-list is now generally believed to derive from a battle-listing poem of a kind for which there are several analogies in early Welsh. It is unlikely that all the named battles could have been fought by Arthur himself, or that they were indeed all fought against the English, rather than against the Picts, Scots, or rival British factions. It has been suggested with some plausibility that the battle of Mt Badon or *Mons Badonicus* may have been quite wrongly associated with Arthur and was not necessarily fought by him at all.[85] My present concern, however, is with the likely source of these entries, rather than with their historical import.

We are indebted to Kenneth Jackson for stressing the high significance of the British kingdom of Strathclyde,[86] which preserved its independence for several hundred years after the neighbouring kingdoms of the Gododdin and of Rheged had in the course of the seventh century fallen to the invaders. The capital of Strathclyde was at Dumbarton – the 'Fortress of the Britons' – and its ecclesiastical centre was at Glasgow. There is some evidence which suggests that it was here, at Glasgow itself, that the vernacular records of the 'Men of the North' were conserved and developed and at least partially committed to writing between the seventh and the ninth centuries. It was from this latter date onwards that many of them became transferred to Wales: we have evidence for the general movement of much of the poetic remains, chronicle material, genealogies and oral traditions of the northern Britons, including those relating to such figures as Myrddin, Urien Rheged and Owain, Rhydderch Hael, Llywarch Hen, probably also Tristan, Peredur and Gwalchmai – some but not all of whom were to reappear later in continental Arthurian romance in the role of the most prominent of Arthur's 'knights.' All, however, were important figures in early Welsh literature before this transference took place. The movement southwards and fresh localization in Wales of much heroic tradition which stemmed originally from the 'Old North' is therefore a fact of seminal importance for any discussion of the genesis of the legend of Arthur.[87] Historical and archaeological speculation concerning Arthur's possible identity, together with the proper interpretation of the early documentary references to him, must therefore take full account of this movement as one of the basic facts of Welsh literature. It cannot be too strongly stressed that the problem of Arthur is first and foremost a Welsh literary problem.

L'Autre Monde celtique et l'élément chrétien dans les lais anonymes.

JACQUES DE CALUWÉ

AU moyen âge, comme à toutes les époques, les guerres, les conquêtes, les croisades, ont mis en présence des peuples et des cultures, mais les contacts ainsi établis se sont souvent soldés par des résultats contradictoires. La religion des autres, notamment, apparaît tantôt comme un facteur fondamental de conflits, tantôt comme un réservoir commode où puiser de nouveaux ingrédients pour l'imaginaire. Aux dieux 'diaboliques' des musulmans épiques et à l'effort soutenu de conversion chrétienne à leur profit s'opposent, dans la littérature romanesque, et surtout dans les lais, l'attrait et la magie de l'Autre Monde celtique, accueillant aux héros chrétiens qui paraissent pouvoir y entrer sans pécher.

On pourrait tenter de résoudre ce paradoxe apparent en partant du principe – mais n'est-ce pas une illusion ou, au moins, un anachronisme? – que le poète serait libre et que, la fiction prenant le pas sur les réalités, nos lais pourraient bien s'abstraire d'un climat religieux qu'ils laisseraient à l'épopée. Mais penser ainsi serait oublier la présence, ne fût-ce que littérale, de l'élément chrétien dans ces mêmes lais.

En examinant dans cette perspective les textes de Marie de France, je crois avoir pu montrer l'importance du rôle joué par la problématique religieuse.[1] Dieu s'y sépare de l'Eglise chaque fois que l'épanouissement de l'amour humain se heurte aux lois morales traditionnelles, et c'est précisément l'apparition de l'Autre Monde celtique qui permet d'abolir les tabous religieux.[2]

Mais Marie ne constitue-t-elle pas un cas unique? 'Psychologist of courtly love',[3] elle privilégie 'une élaboration chevaleresque et courtoise, chrétienne à l'occasion',[4] avec des raffinements peu communs. Trouvera-t-on dans les lais anonymes, 'plus près des vieilles légendes celtiques, plus simples, sans but psychologique ou moral',[5] un profondeur comparable?

C'est la question que je voudrais poser ici en partant de cette dernière remarque de Prudence Tobin. 'Plus près des vieilles légendes celtiques', les lais anonymes pourraient, en effet, avoir conservé plus vif l'élément religieux qui sous-tend ces légendes, comme ils pourraient avoir évité de mettre en présence l'univers chrétien et l'Autre Monde celtique. Ils pourraient l'avoir fait, mais l'ont-ils fait? Il suffit, pour le vérifier, de soumettre les textes à la lecture attentive et naïve que l'on qualifie aujourd'hui d'"anecdotique', en laissant à d'autres, plus subtils, le soin d'en débusquer le symbolisme latent . . .

L'index des noms propres établi par P. Tobin[6] présente trop d'erreurs ou d'omissions, *sub verbo* 'Dieu' notamment, pour que nous puissions en tirer de premières conclusions légitimes. Vérification faite, il apparaît que, parmi les onze lais édités, deux ne présentent aucun élément chrétien littéral: il s'agit de *Nabaret* et du *Trot*.[7] Et nous pouvons y ajouter, sans grand risque de fausser les statistiques, le *Lechëor*, car il serait seulement cocasse de retenir pour notre propos le fait que les paroles cyniques des dames anti-courtoises sont prononcées à l'occasion de la saint-Pantaléon (v. 1). Notons toutefois qu'il ne s'agit peut-être pas d'un pur hasard chez un auteur aussi léger: à l'époque où l'on situe la composition du lai, le culte du saint martyr, décapité au IVe siècle, connaissait un regain d'intérêt; une église lui fut dédiée à Troyes en 1216 et Pantaléon était le nom du pape Urbain IV, lui-même né à Troyes[8] . . .

Restent huit lais, dans ce *corpus*, où le nom du Dieu chrétien apparaît au moins une fois. Mais, faut-il le dire, ses apparitions n'ont pas toutes la même importance.

Dans *Doon*, la seule allusion intervient au moment où le héros quitte son épouse en la recommandant à Dieu:

Sa fame a a Dieu commandee.
(v. 165)

Dans *Tydorel*,[9] où se déploie sans souci moral un adultère qui rend chacun heureux, même le mari trompé, les quatre appels à Dieu sont assez curieusement concentrés dans la deuxième partie du lai, alors que l'élément chrétien est totalement absent au début. La mère du jeune orfèvre nantais que Tydorel a fait appeler recommande son fils à Dieu:

Diex te doinst vers lui bon eür;
(v. 294)

et le jeune homme lui-même, avant de troubler Tydorel par la singulière révélation qu'il tient de sa mère, évoque Dieu dans une autre formule stéréotypée:

57

Sire, fet il, onc ne contai,
si m'aït Dex, ne ne chantai.
(v. 307–308)

Lorsqu'il apprend qu'il n'est pas fils d'un homme, Tydorel se rend chez sa propre mère qui le reçoit avec quelque étonnement:

Filz, fet ele, por Deu merci,
qu'est-ce? que querez vos ici?
(v. 345–346)

Tydorel perd alors son sang-froid:

Par Deu! fet il, toute i morrez,
ja de mes mains n'eschaperez,
si vos ne me dites le voir
qui filz je sui, je veil savoir.
(v. 347–350)

Il s'agit sans doute là de 'clichés' plutôt que de formulations sémantiquement pleines. Elles apparaissent pourtant au moment précis où le héros va s'interroger sur ses origines avant de renoncer à la nature humaine pour choisir, lui qui fut baptisé (v. 178), l'Autre Monde celtique de son père.

Nous trouvons un autre exemple d'allusions concentrées dans *Mélion*. Le héros y salue la princesse d'Irlande, qui va devenir sa femme:

del Glorious le roi Iesu;
(v. 102)

formule moins fréquente, plus 'liturgique' pourrait-on dire, et, trois ans plus tard, mais seulement quelques vers plus loin, Mélion sertit entre deux évocations de Dieu sa métamorphose volontaire en loup-garou:

Dame, dist il, por Deu merci
(v. 153)
[. . .]
Por Deu vos pri, ci m'atendés.
(v. 167)

Clichés encore, ou subtile récupération chrétienne d'un motif païen destinée à disculper le héros? Il ne faut pas oublier, en effet, qu'ici comme dans le *Bisclauret*,[10] c'est le personnage 'enchanté' qui reste vertueux et c'est la femme trompeuse que la morale condamne:

> Melïons dist 'Ja ne faldra
> que de tot sa feme kerra,
> qu'en la fin ne soit malbaillis;
> ne doit pas croire tos ses dis.'
>
> (v. 587–590)

Les lais de *Guingamor* et de *Graelent* se situent, on le sait, dans le prolongement du *Lanval* de Marie de France, mais, comme l'a fort bien montré François Suard[11] dans un récent article, chaque oeuvre possède son originalité. Le rôle de l'élément chrétien pourrait bien en apporter une preuve supplémentaire.

Dans *Guingamor*, le roi et les chevaliers appellent la protection de Dieu sur le chevalier avant son départ pour la chasse au blanc porc:

> a Dieu du ciel l'ont conmandé.
>
> (v. 312)

La formule n'a pas plus d'importance que les interventions de Gauvain et d'Yvain dans *Lanval*.[12] Mais ici, c'est la fée qui bientôt prendra Dieu à témoin de la mauvaise action accomplie par Guingamor lorsqu'il s'est emparé des vêtements de la jeune femme:

> Ja Deu ne place ne ne voille
> qu'entre chevaliers soit retret
> que vos faciez si grant mesfet
> d'embler les dras d'une meschine
> en l'espoisse de la gaudine.
>
> (v. 448–452)

Evoqué par la fée-maîtresse, Dieu s'empare d'un rôle qu'il ne jouait pas dans *Lanval*, mais qu'il jouera aussi dans *Graelent*. Là, c'est au nom de Dieu que, pendant le procès, un valet annonce l'arrivée des pucelles de l'Autre Monde:

> en la cort vienent dex puceles,
> el roiame n'avoit plus beles;
> al cevalier molt aideront,
> se Diu plaist, sel delivreront;
>
> (v. 559–562)

c'est au nom de Dieu que ces mêmes pucelles demandent deux fois à la fée-maîtresse de pardonner à l'amant indiscret:

> Damoisele, por Dieu merci,
> aiés pitié de vostre ami.
> $\qquad$ (v. 683–684)
> [. . .]
> Dame, voiiés, l'onde l'en mainne,
> por Diu, car le getés de painne.
> $\qquad$ (vv. 689–690)

Graelent, enfin, s'adresse lui-même à Dieu lorsqu'il veut revoir son amie:

> a s'amie crie merci,
> por Diu qu'il puist parler a li.
> $\qquad$ (v. 509–510)

On a pu croire qu'une cinquième évocation de Dieu se trouvait au vers 90 de *Graelent*, lorsque le héros disserte, devant le reine, sur l'amitié selon Cicéron et qu'il affirme:

> boins amors n'est si de dex non.

Assez curieusement, P. Tobin renvoie à ce vers *sub verbo* 'Dieu' dans l'index des noms propres tout en expliquant ailleurs qu'il ne peut s'agir que du mot 'deux'.[13] C'est ainsi que comprennent, dans leurs belles traductions, Danielle Regnier-Bohler:[14]

> L'amour n'a cure de compagnon: l'amour véritable
> n'engage que deux êtres, deux corps, deux coeurs;

et Herman Braet:[15]

> L'amour sans partenaire ne signifie rien:
> L'amour véritable n'existe qu'entre deux êtres;
> Deux corps, deux coeurs, l'un pour l'autre.

Dans *Tyolet*, l'auteur nous dit qu'il n'existait nulle créature de *Dieu* (v. 47) susceptible de résister au sifflement du héros. Plein d'admiration pour le cerf devenu chevalier, Tyolet évoque Dieu dans les questions frénétiques qu'il lui adresse:

> Sire, fet il, vostre merci,
> Car pleüst Dieu qui ne menti,
> que j'eüsse tiex garnemenz
> con vos avez, e tel chapel.

> Or me dites, chevalier béste,
> por Deu e por la seue feste,
> se il est auques de tiex bestes
> ne de si beles con vos estes;
> (v. 183–192)

et il demande aussi à la divinité la grâce de devenir un chevalier-bête comme ceux qui servent le roi Arthur:

> Car pleüst or Dieu a sa feste
> que je fusse chevalier beste!
> (v. 217–218)

La fée, enfin, se présente au roi en glosant une formule traditionnelle qui, seule, pourrait paraître gratuite:

> Rois Arthur, sire, Dex te saut,
> le tot puissant qui maint en haut.
> (v. 334–335)

Le lai de l'*Espine* et le lai de *Désiré* se déroulent dans une ambiance générale qui fait apparaître, dès une première lecture, l'importance plus grande de l'élément chrétien.

Dès les premiers vers (v. 8), l'auteur de l'*Espine* nous dit que le souvenir de l'histoire qu'il raconte fut conservé dans un monastère de Bretagne; plus tard, il fixera l'épisode central de son récit la nuit de la saint-Jean.

Séparé de celle qu'il aime, le fils du roi se lamente en implorant Dieu et en regrettant son péché:

> Diex, quel eurë et quel peciés.
> (v. 121)

Inquiet pour son fils qui se rend au gué de l'Epine, le roi le recommande deux fois à Dieu:

> Or tost, fait il, a Dieu congié,
> e si soies preus e seürs,
> e Diex te doinse bon eürs.
> (v. 216–218)

Quant à la jeune fille, elle se meurt d'inquiétude et prononce une très douce prière, la seule que nous rencontrions dans nos textes:

61

Seule s'en entre en un vergier,
por son ami vuolt a proier
que sainc e saus Diex le ramaint.
Giete un soupir e dont se plaint,
puis s'est assise sor une ente,
a soi meïsme se demente,
e donques dist: 'Pere celestre
se onques fu, ne ja puet estre,
c'onques avenist orement
e chou c'on prie a nule gent,
par coi nus hom fust deshaitiés,
biaux Sire, prenge t'en pitiés
que li miens amis od moi fust
e jou od lui, s'estre peüst.
E Diex, conseroie garie.
(v. 233–247)

Elle s'endort bientôt d'un mystérieux sommeil au cours duquel elle est non moins mystérieusement transportée au gué de l'Epine. Elle y retrouve son ami qui la rassure:

S'en Dieu as part, soies seüre
(v. 281);

et, elle n'en doute plus, sa prière a été exaucée:

He! Diex! ce dist, con sui garie;
Sire, j'ai esté vostre amie.
Diex a oïe ma priere.
(v. 293–295)

Dans son index des noms propres, déjà évoqué, P. Tobin ne renvoie pas, *sub verbo* 'Dieu',[16] au lai de *Désiré*. En fait, on devrait trouver six références. Et cette abondance relative n'est guère étonnante dans un lai où il est beaucoup question de pèlerinage, d'hermite, de chapelle, de péché, de messe et de confession.[17]

Les premières allusions tournent autour des prières et du pèlerinage que font à saint Gilles de Provence les futurs parents de Désiré. Ils souhaitent ardemment que Dieu leur donne un enfant:

e a Deu priënt mut sovent,
par sa pité les confortast
ke fiz ou file lur donast.
(v. 22–24)

[. . .]
de Deu en ad ottrei e grace
nomeement d'aver enfant.
(v. 34–35)

Deux autres fois, Désiré invoquera Dieu dans des formules peu significatives:

pur les seinz Deu ne me ociez!
(v. 492)
[. . .]
M'amie, Deus! fet Dessirez,
dunc sui jo mut ben assemez;
(v. 597–598)

et il en va de même pour une réflexion du roi:

Deu! dit li reis a Desiré,
nus sumes tut enfantesmé.
(v. 435–436)

La dernière référence est plus intéressante, parce que prononcée par la fée-maîtresse:

Quant vus irrez desk'a muster
la messe oïr e Deu preier,
delé vus me verrez ester
e la pain beneït user;
(v. 387–390)

mais nous allons y revenir . . .

De tous les textes que nous venons d'envisager, le lai de *Désiré* est le seul à poser le problème religieux en termes très explicites. Comme la mère d'Yonec dans le lai de Marie, Désiré doute de l'orthodoxie de ses amours avec l'être mystérieux venu de l'autre monde, et il va, dans son désarroi, jusqu'à s'en ouvrir à un ermite au cours d'une confession. La fée lui reprochera ce doute, mais, comme le chevalier-oiseau d'*Yonec*, elle 'prouvera' à Désiré qu'elle peut accomplir, quoique venue de l'Autre Monde celtique, les gestes du culte chrétien.[18] N'avait-elle pas, au demeurant, déjà prouvé sa connaissance du dogme en adressant ses reproches au héros après la confession:

Ke valt li pecchez a geïr
deci ke hom le voille guerpir?
(v. 381–382)

'Il n'en est pas moins vrai', écrit Omer Jodogne, 'que, dans les deux cas où les héros protestent de leur inféodation au Christianisme, leur déclaration va d'emblée jusqu'au défi, jusqu'à l'épreuve non sollicitée: elle devient ostentatoire'.[19] Il n'en est pas moins vrai non plus, me semble-t-il, que, comme chez Marie de France, c'est au moment précis où des personnages s'abandonnent à des actes que la loi religieuse condamne que se fait le plus fortement sentir la présence d'un Dieu prompt à comprendre et à pardonner. Car nous avons affaire ici, ne l'oublions pas, à l'histoire d'une fée et d'un héros chrétien qui furent heureux, eurent beaucoup d'enfants et se marièrent ensuite, devant Dieu et devant les hommes. La notion de péché est présente, exprimée en termes univoques, et c'est elle qui crée, au plan de la morale religieuse, un conflit dynamique entre l'élément celtique et l'élément chrétien.

Pourtant 'aucun auteur', écrit encore Omer Jodogne, 'n'a osé introduire un prêtre ni même la croix dans les châteaux de l'Autre Monde',[20] et il semble bien, en effet, qu'il y ait là une limite que l'on ne peut ni atteindre ni dépasser. En revanche, que d'êtres, que d'objets, que de contraintes, que de 'geis' équivoques dans cet 'Autre Monde' où l'on fait difficilement le départ entre les sources incontestablement celtiques et les exotismes strictement imaginaires.

Pierre Jonin conclut un récent article sur Marie de France devant la matière celtique[21] en insistant sur le passage marqué du monde rural des légendes celtiques, rude et souvent belliqueux, à un univers aristocratique plus sensible aux blandices de la courtoisie et de l'acte gratuit. Le rôle du merveilleux, introduit par l'élément celtique, est, dans cet esprit, réduit au plaisir du dépaysement: 'Un souffle d'air frais vient balayer des vies un peu monotones', écrit Philippe Ménard. 'Tout change, tout commence. On passe du clos à l'ouvert, on quitte la fixité et l'uniformité du quotidien pour entrer dans le mouvement et le renouvellement.'[22]

Mais cet apport incontestable à la dynamique narrative n'épuise pas l'intérêt du merveilleux, pas plus chez Marie de France que dans les lais anonymes. En de nombreuses circonstances, les poètes n'hésitent pas à poser le problème éthique des relations entre des êtres qui appartiennent à des religions différentes. Toutefois il semble bien, selon nos textes, que la rencontre et l'entente ne puissent s'accomplir qu'au travers de certaines concessions: le héros chrétien qui succombe au péché trouve dans sa propre vie les justifications de son acte, justifications qui, à défaut de pouvoir être prises en considération par la loi religieuse, peuvent être comprises par Dieu (mal-mariée dans *Yonec*, 'fatalité' dans *Eliduc*, générosité dans *Fresne*,[23] séparation arbitraire des jeunes amants dans l'*Espine*). De leur côté, l'amant magique ou la fée maîtresse[24] se trouvent chargés d'un pouvoir ensorcelant bénéfique et ils ne manifestent aucune hostilité à l'égard de la religion chrétienne. Au contraire, ils n'hésitent pas, le cas échéant, à sacrifier à ses rites. Sans prêtre ni croix, l'Autre Monde celtique ne substitue au Dieu chrétien aucune divinité ni aucune loi morale à la loi religieuse. Mais ne juxtapose-t-il pas parfois la grâce laïque à la grâce codifiée?

L'Autre Monde celtique coïncide souvent avec une imagination poétique que l'on voudrait concilier avec les réalités humaines, c'est la projection d'un rêve de fuite ou d'immersion dans un monde enchanté, un paradis qui conserverait les plaisirs terrestres. C'est peut-être surtout la concrétisation d'un éternel désir: celui de déculpabiliser l'amour parce qu'il est naturel, sans pouvoir pour autant nier les tabous du dogme. Désir de s'abandonner et de trouver chez l'autre le plaisir sans péché et la transcendance sans ennui, désir d'entendre chez le même être, enfin en harmonie, les soupirs de la sainte et les cris de la fée.

	TEXTE	TRADUCTION
7396	Tant vont que au pié del degré	Ils marchent jusqu'au moment où, au pied de l'es…
	qui estoit devant le palais,	qui était devant le palais,
	truevent sor un trossel de glais	ils rencontrent, assis sur une botte de joncs,
	un eschacier tot seul seant	un homme unijambiste, tout seul,
7400	qui avoit eschace d'argent	qui avait une jambe artificielle en argent
	et desus estoit bien doree	et elle était, par-dessus, recouverte d'or,
	et fu de leus an leus bandee	et, de place en place on l'avait cerclée
	d'or et de pierres precïeuses.	d'or et de pierres précieuses.
7404	N'avoit mie ses mains oiseuses	Le mutilé ne gardait pas ses mains inactives,
	li eschaciers, car il tenoit	car il tenait
	un quanivet, et si doloit	un petit couteau et il polissait ainsi
	un petit bastonet de fresne.	une petite canne de frêne.
7408	Li eschaciers de rien n'aresne	Le mutilé à la jambe artificielle n'adresse
	ces qui par devant lui s'an vont	aucune parole à ceux qui passent devant lui
	ne cil un mot dit ne li ont.	et ceux-ci ne lui ont pas dit un mot.
	Et il notoniers a lui tire	Mais le nautonier prend à part
7412	mon seignor Gauvain et dit: 'Sire,	monseigneur Gauvain et dit: 'Seigneur,
	de cest eschacier que vos sanble?	que semble de ce mutilé?'
	– S'eschace n'est mie de tranble,	– Sa jambe artificielle n'est pas faite de tremble,
	fet mes sire Gauvains, par foi,	par ma foi, répond monseigneur Gauvain,
7416	que mout m'est bel ce que ge voi.	en sorte que j'apprécie fort ce que je vois.
	– Enon Deu, fet li notoniers,	– Par Dieu, réplique le nautonier,
	il est riches, li eschaciers,	il est riche, le mutilé,
	de mout granz rantes et de beles!	et il a beaucoup de belles et bonnes rentes.
7420	Vos oïssiez ja tex noveles	Mais vous auriez pu entendre des nouvelles
	qui vos enuiassent mout fort,	qui vous auraient fait très grande peine,
	se ne fust ce que ge vos port	s'il n'y avait eu ce détail, que je vous tiens
	conpaignie et si vos condui.'	compagnie, et que je suis votre conducteur.'

Un Personnage mystérieux du Roman de Perceval le Gallois: L'eschacier *dans la Seconde Partie du* Perceval

C. FOULON

DANS son roman, qu'il intitule *Perceval* ou le *Conte du Graal*, Chrétien de Troyes a raconté les aventures non seulement d'un, mais de deux héros. Fascinés par la beauté et le mystère du Château du Graal, nous ne voyons souvent, particulièrement dans nos Universités, que le jeune chevalier 'nice', qui, de 'sauvageon', devient 'initié', Perceval. Mais si la première partie nous parle essentiellement des épreuves de ce jeune homme, et s'arrête au vers 4785, la seconde, qui va du vers 4786 au vers 8960,[1] narre les exploits ou les mésaventures de Gauvain. Certes, cette deuxième partie est elle-même interrompue par la rencontre du Vendredi-saint (300 vers environ); mais Gauvain est le vrai protagoniste dans les épisodes de la fin. Il est vrai que l'oeuvre est inachevée, et nous ne savons pas si l'intention de Chrétien était de réunir les deux héros avant le dénouement.

L'habitude des critiques est de privilégier Perceval aux dépens de Gauvain; et il a fallu un livre original, celui de Madame Le Rider, *Le Chevalier dans le Conte du Graal*,[2] pour remettre Gauvain à sa vraie place. En effet, jusqu'alors, on voyait surtout les défaites et les humiliations de Gauvain: assiégé et presque vaincu par la Commune, insulté et raillé par la Mauvaise Pucelle, privé de son cheval Gringalet par l'impudent Greorreas; manquant de se noyer au Gué Périlleux, enfin devenant prisonnier du Château des Pucelles, il paraît à beaucoup de lecteurs comme une sorte de repoussoir de Perceval: car celui-ci monte, de victoire en victoire, jusqu'à conquérir presque, dans la rencontre avec l'ermite, une sorte d'auréole de sainteté. Faut-il penser que Gauvain est l'éternel vaincu, et que son histoire pourrait être le roman de l'échec? Nous ne le croyons pas.

En effet s'il reste le chevalier galant, tendre avec la fillette que l'on nomme 'La Pucelle as Manches Petites',[3] entreprenant avec la Demoiselle d'Escavalon, qui d'ailleurs ne lui refuse pas ses faveurs;[4] s'il est en somme, avant la lettre,

67

le Don Juan des Romans de la Table Ronde, il sait punir ceux qui ne se conduisent pas courtoisement vis-à-vis des Dames et des Demoiselles.[5] Il défend la justice, et il le proclame hautement. Il triomphe, malgré son mauvais roncin, du neveu de Greorreas.[6] Mais de plus, il ne recule pas devant le danger, au contraire: ayant appris qu'au-delà de la 'bone de Galvoie'[7] est la limite d'un territoire d'où 'nus n'est eschapez',[8] il continue sa route, s'écriant avec audace:

> Je irai çà tant que je voie
> Por coi retorner an n'an puet.[9]

Or ses aventures entraînent Gauvain (comme précédemment Perceval) vers un monde étrange, qui est, tout autant que le Château du Graal, une figure de l'Autre Monde. C'est le Château aux cinq cents fenêtres; car, bien défendu par cinq cents arbalètes, il cache dans ses murs certaines dames qui ont quitté depuis longtemps la vie des mortelles: Ygerne par exemple, mère du roi Arthur; elle parle de ce roi comme d'un enfant; mais c'est un enfant centenaire:

> Il est anfes, li rois Artus.
> S'il a C.anz, il n'a pas plus,
> ne plus ne puet il pas avoir.[10]

Et Gauvain, plus heureux que Perceval, y trouve aussi sa mère, disparue depuis vingt ans.

Il y a toutefois des particularités intéressantes dans ce château: nul n'y peut entrer, nul n'y peut rester, s'il n'est pas doté de certaines vertus:

> chevaliers n'i puet ester
> une liuee vis ne sains
> qui de coardie soit plains
> ne qui ait an lui nul mal vice
> de losange ne d'avarice.
> Coarz ne traïtres n'i dure,
> ne foimantie ne parjure:
> cil i muerent si a delivre
> qu'il n'i pueent durer ne vivre.[11]

Ainsi que le dit le nautonier qui a conduit jusqu'au château Gauvain, tous les habitants du lieu attendent la venue d'un chevalier parfait:

> qu'il le covandroit a devise
> saige et large, sanz coveitise,
> bel et franc, hardi et leal,
> sanz vilenie et sanz nul mal.[12]

Ce chevalier existe, et naturellement c'est Gauvain. Constatation importante: les habitants de ce monde étonnant le reconnaissent: et il fera chevaliers les valets, et il est prêt à marier les damoiselles (mais le roman s'interrompt avant cette conclusion aussi courtoise que plaisante).

Gauvain est également devenu, dans cette partie du roman, une sorte de sage; il enseigne le savoir-vivre à la Mauvaise Pucelle:

> Et il li respont: 'Belle amie,
> vos diroiz ce que boen vos iert.
> mes a dameisele n'afiert
> que ele soit si mesdisanz
> puis que ele a passé X. anz,
> einz doit estre bien anseigniee
> et cortoise et bien afeitiee.[13]

De là vient la réplique irritée de la Pucelle:

> Chevaliers, par male avanture,
> de vostre anseignement n'ai cure.[14]

Or, si la pucelle change de caractère, si elle se repent, si elle va jusqu'à demander à Gauvain, qu'elle a tant malmené, de 'prendre justise' d'elle[15], le bon chevalier lui pardonne et répond:

> a moi que monte
> que ge de vos justise face?
> Ja le fil Damedeu ne place
> que vos por moi nul mal aiez;
> mes montez, si ne delaiez,
> s'irons jusqu'a ce chastel fort.
> Veez le notonier au port
> qui nos atant por passer outre.[16]

Gauvain, non content d'avoir franchi toutes les épreuves, peut entrer au Château de l'Autre Monde, mais il peut aussi en sortir, et il devient ici le conducteur des damoiselles repentantes, se transformant en une sorte de Psychopompe, de merveilleux introducteur à l'Au-delà. Ne peut-on dire que, même s'il est devenu l'habitant d'un Autre Monde, il soutient la comparaison avec Perceval, à la fois par sa prouesse et par sa sagesse?

Ces divers détails n'étaient pas inutiles au moment d'aborder celui qui est le sujet de mon propos, à savoir un mystérieux personnage, qui n'apparaît qu'une fois, que nous ne revoyons plus par la suite, et qui a intéressé bien des commentateurs: il s'agit de l''eschacier', c'est-à-dire l''unijambiste', car ici l' 'eschace' est une jambe artificielle, et non pas, comme naguère une *échasse*, une sorte de long bâton muni d'un étrier pour marcher à distance du sol.

Je donne séparément le texte du passage, et sa traduction: il va m'être ainsi plus facile de souligner certains points qui doivent être éclairés si l'on veut comprendre le rôle du 'mutilé à la jambe unique'.

Remarquons tout d'abord les détails qui, formant un ensemble, doivent être expliqués pour que l'*eschacier* devienne un symbole clair. Car l'auteur n'a pas voulu lui donner un autre rôle dans la suite de son roman. Il apparaît, et il disparaît. Cependant il est ici devant le palais, et nous savons que ce palais est un Autre Monde. Mais, devant le château des Reines et des Demoiselles, il se contente d'être au pied d'un escalier, comme s'il était un mendiant; il n'a pas de siège, pas même un banc: il est assis sur des *glais*, c'est-à-dire des joncs. Ce mendiant, ce mutilé, a naturellement une jambe artificielle; et celle-ci ne prouve pas qu'il souffre d'une pauvreté quelconque; elle est faite d'un métal précieux, l'argent, et sa beauté est encore augmentée par l'or et les pierres précieuses dont elle est ornée: c'est là le plus grand mystère. Car il y en a encore trois autres:

a) Tout d'abord le mutilé tient un petit couteau, et cela lui suffit pour travailler le frêne, bois dur; pour Lucien Foulet, *doler* signifie 'appointer', 'aiguiser'.

b) A quoi peut, ou pourra, bien servir le *bastonet*?

c) L'homme à la jambe artificielle garde le silence. Pourquoi? Il ne dit pas un mot à Gauvain, et à son compagnon; mais l'explication donnée par celui-ci n'est pas immédiate; il veut d'abord savoir quelle est l'impression de Gauvain. Et le héros, s'il apprécie l'aspect luxueux de la prothèse, exprime son opinion avec humour, soulignant la dureté du métal par opposition au tremble, bois tendre et de peu de prix. Mais Gauvain apprécie le spectacle; il n'a pas peur; il admire.

La réponse du nautonier est très personnelle; elle révèle deux choses: que le mutilé a des revenus importants; et, chose plus inquiétante, en d'autres occasions le silence étonnant de ce portier de l'Autre Monde aurait pu être rompu. S'il n'a pas révélé ses terribles secrets, c'est parce que le nautonier sert à Gauvain à la fois de compagnon et de sauvegarde. Il est donc certain qu'il y a une sorte de complicité, ou tout au moins de connivence entre l'unijambiste et le nautonier qui a conduit, en traversant un rivière dangereuse, le protagoniste vers le château de l'Autre Monde.

Cinq éléments abstraits (la mutilation, l'immobilité, la richesse, le silence, la connaissance de secrets effrayants), quatre éléments concrets (les joncs, le couteau, le bâton, les métaux précieux), voilà les détails qui marquent la structure de ce bref épisode, unique dans le roman. Chacun d'entre eux a intéressé les commentateurs, mais ils ont choisi des interprétations variées, quelquefois contestables, rarement complètes.

Roger Sherman Loomis, dans son livre sur *La Tradition arthurienne et Chrétien de Troyes*[17], a avancé une hypothèse intéressante. Chrétien se souviendrait ici d'une situation présentée dans un conte gallois fameux, *Le Songe de Maxen Wledig*; placé dans un château de rêve, le seigneur Eudav, qui est très riche, est assis sur un *trône orné d'aigles*; dans la même salle deux jeunes gens jouent aux échecs, sur un *échiquier* d'argent *cerclé d' or*, et le vieux seigneur taille, dans une *baguette* d'or, des pions d'échecs. Chrétien aurait, selon R. S. Loomis, confondu *eschaquier*, qui désigne la table du jeu, et *eschacier*, qui signifie homme pourvu d'une jambe artificielle. C'est pourquoi chez le romancier l'*eschace* serait cerclée d'or. Trois manuscrits, *F* avec *eschaquier*, *P* avec *eskiekier*, *U* avec *eschequier*, enfin une forme *eskiés*, dans le ms. *P*, permettent à R. S. Loomis d'appuyer ses suppositions.[18] Mais il souligne lui-même que le riche personnage du conte gallois est assis sur un trône, dans un palais, et non à la porte, sur des joncs. *Trossel de glais* serait donc lui aussi tiré de l'expression 'trosne aorné d'egles'. Mais, outre que cinq manuscrits de Perceval conservent le mot *eschacier*, l'*eschace* est suffisamment commentée par Chrétien lui-même pour que l'on trouve l'hypothèse d'une erreur trop hardie, et, à mon avis, la supposition est peu convaincante. Car ce n'est pas l'*eschiquier*, mais l'*eschace*, qui est d'argent orné d'or. Et le nautonier, chez Chrétien de Troyes, sait que la vue du personnage de l'*eschacier*, en apparence si humble, mais visiblement si riche, peut intriguer et même inquiéter son compagnon. Tout ceci n'est pas dans le *mabinogi*.

Une seconde explication a été fournie par Mme Sheila Mac Finn, dans une note d'un article de la *Modern Language Review*.[19] Les personnages d'hommes a une seule jambe, rencontrés par J. Adhémar[20] dans la sculpture romane, sont souvent des païens: un bourreau martyrisant St Avertin, un victimaire sacrifiant un animal, représenté sur un chapiteau de l'église de Besse-en-Chandesse, ont une jambe de bois; et, dans l'église de Colombier (Charente), un homme baise la jambe de bois d'un autre personnage: le sculpteur aurait voulu ridiculiser l'idolâtrie.

Pour Mme Le Rider, qui approuve le commentaire de J. Adhémar, il s'agirait, dans ce passage, de représenter un païen, ou même un démon, comme 'un homme qui ne marche pas droit'. Et elle ajoute un grand nombre d'exemples où des démons sont figurés par des personnages à jambe de bois. En particulier une miniature de *L'Estoire de Merlin*, de Robert de Boron, au XIIIème siècle, dessine un démon à jambe de bois.[21] Or tous les exemples fournis offrent des mutilés, mais leur jambe artificielle n'est pas faite d'une matière précieuse. Chrétien insiste sur la richesse de l' 'eschacier'. Celui-ci est au pied d'un escalier, qui mène à un palais, où seuls peuvent entrer les chevaliers vertueux. Gauvain, malgré son caractère galant, n'est pas un païen; il invoque même le 'fils Damedieu'.[22] L' 'eschacier', connu du nautonier, est déjà, en quelque sorte, dans le parvis du temple; il est immobile, il ne menace pas, il ne cherche pas à entrer. Si l'on peut prendre, durant un certain temps, dans notre roman, la Male Pucelle pour une 'démone',[23] l'eschacier n'est ni un païen, ni un démon. Suivant une expression de Philippe Ménard, 'un païen n'a rien à faire au Château Merveilleux'.[24]

Sur deux points cependant, Mme Le Rider et Philippe Ménard se rapprochent: l' 'eschacier' est puissant, et il effraie. 'L'échasse d'argent', dit la première, 'semble matérialiser la puissance de celui que le texte dit "riche de bonnes et belles rentes"'.[25] Elle estime également que c'est un être effrayant.

Pour Philippe Ménard, il s'agit d'un être de l'Autre Monde . . . 'à l'aspect un peu inquiétant'.[26] Il ajoute: 'Chrétien semble sourire de ce bizarre portier, à la fois "béquillard" et menaçant, qui ressemble à un indigent, alors qu'il est richissime.'[27] Il estime donc que, riche comme Ploutos, l' 'eschacier' ferait plutôt penser à un dieu des morts, ou, du moins, à un dieu de l'Autre Monde. (Philippe Ménard cite le dieu Nuadu 'au bras d'argent', et le dieu Bran qui fut 'mehaignié' au pied). Dans le même passage de son livre, Philippe Ménard rapproche ce personnage d'un unijambiste qui, dans le roman d'*Humbaut*, placé sur une planche étroite, au-dessus d'un fleuve effrayant, est chargé d'empêcher les mortels aventureux d'accéder à l'Autre Monde; mais Gauvain, d'un coup de pied, jette cet adversaire dans les eaux: ce mutilé ressemble plutôt à un gueux qu'à un être surnaturel.[28]

Ces remarques originales me semblent, sur un point, coïncider avec celles que je voudrais présenter ici: elles font référence à des sources celtiques ou à des rapprochements avec les littératures celtiques.

La littérature galloise doit une partie de ses images à la mythologie irlandaise, et aux récits épiques des cycles guerriers de l'Irlande. Dans la *Bataille de Moytura*, le héros-dieu Lugh lutte contre une peuplade étrange, les Fomoré, dont la demeure est dans des îles de l'Océan; c'est une race terrible, 'dévoratrice, hostile'[29]. Durant la seconde bataille de Moytura, Lugh arrache l'oeil unique du roi des Fomoré avec une pierre que sa fronde a lancée; en tombant à travers l' 'arrière de la tête' du géant, elle anéantit un grand nombre de Fomoré; tous les autres pirates s'enfuient dans leurs navires; ces créatures, 'qui n'avaient qu'un oeil, qu'une jambe, qu'un bras', ne sont plus une menace. Ils sont refoulés dans des îles, comme s'ils appartenaient à un Autre Monde.[30]

Notre étonnement va être plus grand encore, en constatant qu'un conte gallois, *La Dame de la Fontaine*, parallèle au roman d'*Yvain ou le Chevalier au Lion*, présente un personnage assez effrayant, qui est le gardien des bêtes sauvages (parfois des bêtes féroces) de la forêt où se trouve la fontaine. L'hôte hospitalier explique à Kynon (qui correspond au Calogrenant de Chrétien de Troyes) l'itinéraire qu'il doit suivre, et lui parle de l'homme qui le renseignera. J'emprunte à Joseph Loth la traduction du passage:

'A quelque distance dans la forêt, tu rencontreras un chemin de traverse, sur ta droite, et tu chemineras jusqu'à ce que tu arrives à une grande clairière; et tu verras un tertre au milieu de la clairière, et tu verras un gros homme noir au milieu du tertre, qui est aussi grand à lui seul que deux hommes *de ce monde*. Et *il n'a qu'un pied*, et il n'a qu'un oeil au centre de son front; et il a une massue de fer, et tu peux être sûr qu'il n'y a pas deux hommes qui ne puissent dépasser leur charge en soulevant la massue. Mais son caractère n'est pas mauvais; cependant c'est un homme mauvais, et il est le gardien de cette forêt . . . Il te montrera un chemin par lequel tu pourras arriver à ce que tu es en train de chercher.'

Ce personnage, ce géant, n'appartient pas au monde des mortels, mais à un Autre Monde. Pour Arthur C. L. Brown, il devait se confondre avec l'Hôte Hospitalier, et il était chargé par une Fée de conduire le héros jusqu'au pays des Fées.[31]

Dans la *Destruction de la Demeure de Da Derga*, récit irlandais du IXème siècle, le roi Conairé, fuyant avec ses hommes la colère de l'Au-Delà, rencontre un personnage aux cheveux ras, à la main unique, à l'oeil unique et *au pied unique*.

Comme l'unijambiste signalé par Philippe Ménard dans *Humbaut*, comme les Fomoré après leur défaite, comme le géant à la massue de fer du mabinogi de la *Dame de la Fontaine*, comme le cyclope de la *Destruction de Da Derga*, le mutilé à la jambe d'argent est, chez Chrétien de Troyes, un personnage placé à l'entrée de l'Autre Monde (ce Monde qui, dans Perceval, est le Château des Demoiselles).

Cette double hypothèse: apparence physique monstrueuse (mais ici il n'a pas un oeil unique, comme dans les légendes irlandaises et dans le mabinogi gallois), et position entre le monde des hommes et l'Autre, permet d'expliquer les divers détails que nous avons énumérés tout à l'heure.

Supposons que l' 'eschacier' appartienne à l'Autre Monde; ceci explique que le nautonier, sorte de Charon rationalisé qui fait traverser la rivière à Gauvain, (et qui, pour sa récompense, reçoit en otage le prisonnier vaincu par le héros) n'a aucune crainte devant le personnage étrange: ils sont tous deux parmi les gardiens de l'entrée; quelqu'un a pu dire que l'unijambiste était le Cerbère de ce Charon. Mais d'autres détails sont également éclairés par notre hypothèse: le mutilé est assis sur une botte de *glais*: ces joncs sont les plantes des marais, et le marais, dans la mythologie celtique, comme dans la mythologie gréco-latine, est souvent placé autour de l'entrée des Enfers: il y a des marais près du Styx, il y en a aussi dans les voyages vers l'Autre Monde conservés par la tradition celtique.[32] Ces *glais* sont tout ce qui en reste, auprès de la rivière qui, dans les romans de Chrétien, sépare souvent la terre des mortels des châteaux de l'Autre Monde.

L'*eschacier* tient un *quanivet*, et il dole un *bastonet*; en principe, *doler*, c'était travailler le bois à la doloire; la doloire était, en termes de blason, une hache de guerre; et l'on se servait d'une doloire à manche très court pour décapiter les condamnés à mort. Avant le XVIème siècle, une lourde doloire attachée à une corde descendait, entre deux poteaux, sur le cou de condamné. Chrétien, dans

73

notre passage, a tout rapetissé: on ne parle pas d'une hache, mais d'un couteau, et même d'un petit couteau, un *quanivet*. En polissant un *bastonet* de frêne, le mutilé ne prépare pas une massue, mais une canne sans doute relativement fine. Remarquons malgré tout que le frêne est un bois dur et élastique à la fois; c'est un signe d'autorité que d'avoir, à la porte d'un palais de l'Autre Monde, un bâton de frêne.

L'*eschacier* ne parle pas; il n'adresse pas un mot à ceux qui passent devant lui; mais, dans les vers qui précèdent, on nous a dit[33] que nul chevalier ne pouvait durer ici, s'il était couard, traître, parjure, flatteur, avare; ceux qui ont de pareils vices meurent rapidement s'ils osent entrer. Gauvain passe, *on* le laisse passer, et il exprime sa pensée en disant: 'Mout m'est bel ce que je voi!' Il est admis au Palais: c'est donc qu'il est considéré comme un bon, comme un excellent chevalier. C'est là le sens du silence de l'unijambiste.

Gauvain a remarqué que la jambe artificielle est faite d'un métal précieux, l'argent, qu'elle est rehaussée d'or et de pierres précieuses; dans son livre *The Origin of the Grail Legend*, A. Brown avait parlé du demi-dieu Nuadu 'au bras d'argent'.[34] J'irai plus loin; dans ce que l'on nommerait volontiers aujourd'hui l'*imaginaire* de Chrétien, il y a certainement des souvenirs de ce qu'il a pu voir en diverses provinces, et particulièrement des reliquaires, en métal précieux, ou en bois recouvert d'argent.[35] On pouvait habiller d'argent ou d'or les parties du corps d'un saint, d'un martyr. Le reliquaire répétait la forme de cette partie; s'il s'agissait d'un crâne, on avait un *chef* reliquaire; mais il y avait aussi des *bras* reliquaires, des *pieds* reliquaires. L'église Sainte Foy de Conques (dans l'Aveyron) garde des pièces précieuses, et elle est ainsi devenue un musée de l'orfèvrerie religieuse médiévale, allant du IXème siècle (reliquaire dit de Pépin, ou de Charlemagne) jusqu'au XVème siècle (statue de Ste Foy). Les bras reliquaires sont assez nombreux: celui de St Georges, à Conques, en argent; celui de St Baudime à Saint-Nectaire, en argent. Il existe un bras reliquaire de St Judicaël à l'abbaye de Paimpont, au milieu de la forêt de Brocéliande; il y a un bras de St Gildas à Saint-Gildas de Rhuys; ceux-là sont en argent, ornés de pierres précieuses. Chose plus curieuse, on conserve aussi, à Saint-Gildas, un genou de St Gildas; le reliquaire, ciselé, et ajouré, a la forme allongée d'une partie de jambe, et il est en argent partiellement doré. Mais il date du XIVème ou même du XVème siècle. Toutefois, comme certaines reliques, ce genou peut avoir été placé dans un reliquaire avant cette date. Les pièces d'orfèvrerie religieuse sont quelquefois presque contemporaines de Chrétien. En Champagne, en 1201, le sarcophage du comte de Champagne Thibaut III, mort au moment où il allait partir pour la croisade, était de bronze revêtu de plaques d'argent; la statue du prince, en habit de pèlerin, était d'argent, le socle supérieur, d'argent enrichi d'émaux.

Pourquoi Chrétien de Troyes a-t-il représenté ainsi un personnage de l'Autre Monde? Sans doute parce qu'il y avait, dans certaines légendes celtiques qu'il connaissait, des dieux pourvus de membres artificiels en argent.[36] Placer à la porte de ce palais, peuplé d'héroïnes de la tradition arthurienne (comme Ygerne, mère d'Arthur, et la femme du roi Loth, mère de Gauvain) un héros à la jambe d'argent, c'est en faire un personnage de féerie; mais c'est aussi lui donner une puissance telle qu'il peut exiger un tribut: de là ces rentes 'grans et beles'[37] que le nautonier lui envie: car le nautonier est parfois avide de gain.[38]

Ainsi Chrétien de Troyes, qui a entendu des conteurs bretons bilingues, colportant des légendes celtiques, en particulier un lai ou un conte analogue à la *Dame de la Fontaine*, où apparaît un unijambiste au bâton ou plutôt à la massue puissante; Chrétien, à qui la vision des reliquaires permet la description des objets étincelants, argentés, cerclés d'or, ornés de pierreries, a campé devant nous un personnage qui conserve le silence et le mystère d'un dieu de l'Autre Monde celtique. Tout brillant et immobile qu'il est, l' 'eschacier' conserve encore quelque chose d'inquiétant: il possède les richesses de l'Autre Monde; il en est le gardien. C'est pourquoi Gauvain, chevalier pourvu de toutes les perfections morales exigées du héros que les damoiselles et les valets attendent, va pouvoir entrer, sans que le dieu lui dise un mot, dans le Château: il va y rencontrer le bonheur en revoyant sa mère et sa soeur Clarissant.

L'eschacier introduit le lecteur au monde du surnaturel, mais un surnaturel stylisé, où Chrétien joue, suivant son habitude, de son humour et de sa fantaisie artistique, en mettant le mystère au service de la narration romanesque.

A Process of Adaptation: the Spanish Versions of the Romance of Tristan

J. B. HALL

TOGETHER with other Arthurian material, the story of Tristan reached Spain from France in the closing decades of the twelfth century. It was about 1170 that the Catalan troubadour Guiraut de Cabrera composed his *Ensenhamen* in which he boasts of his familiarity with tales of Arthur, Erec and Gawain, as well as of Tristan and his love for Yseut.[1] Scattered allusions in the works of Catalan writers of the later twelfth century and of the thirteenth suggest a continuing but probably limited interest in Tristan.[2] Although largely confined to courtly and aristocratic circles, this interest became much greater in Catalonia in the fourteenth century as the impact of the French Prose *Tristan* made itself felt. Two manuscript fragments of a Catalan translation of the Prose *Tristan* have survived, both dating from the second half of the fourteenth century.[3] A *Romanç de Tristany* had been owned by En Joan Mitjavila as early as 1331, although the language is uncertain.[4] This text need not have been a translation, for many of the Catalan nobility could read French, and references to French Arthurian romances are frequent in the correspondence of the royal family throughout the century. The *Infant* Juan, for instance, writing to his wife in October 1383, mentions two French books owned by him of which one is 'de Tristany, historiat'.[5] Guillem Torroella's poem *La Faula* (1360–70) includes Tristan, Dinadan and Palamedes among a number of Arthurian characters depicted on tapestries in the palace of Morgane la Fée.[6] In the fifteenth century, allusions to Arthurian romance abound in the anonymous *Curial e Güelfa* (1443–60); however, alongside acknowledgement of the popularity of the adventures of Tristan and Lancelot, a degree of scepticism can be seen on occasion: the author, for instance, questions the veracity of the chroniclers and the severity of the tests that the heroes endured, since their feats of arms could be matched or surpassed by the knights of Aragon.[7] There are many references also in *Tirant lo Blanc* (ca. 1460), which *inter alia* describes a palace chamber in Constantinople decorated with paintings of scenes from the stories of Tristan and Yseut, and Lancelot and Guinevere; the two ladies even attend a festival held by the emperor, presumably as characters in a masque or pageant rather than in person, for a number of famous lovers of ancient times are also 'present'.[8] In the realm of spectacle and sport we find, for example, reference to a royal procession in Valencia in 1401 in which horses wore trappings bearing the portraits of Tristan and Yseut, while in 1424 contestants in a tournament in Barcelona carried shields adorned with what purported to be the arms of Tristan and Palamedes.[9]

In Castile, as might be expected, references to Tristan and other heroes of the Round Table appear later than in Catalonia. Alfonso X, the Wise (reigned 1252–84) alludes to Tristan, along with Arthur and Merlin, in his poems in Galician-Portuguese,[10] but the story does not seem to have been widely known before about the middle of the fourteenth century, when Juan Ruiz commented on its current popularity.[11] The Castilian lyric poets of the late fourteenth and early fifteenth centuries whose work was collected in the *Cancionero de Baena* refer time and again to the beauty of Yseut or the passion and musical skill of Tristan; some, in more moralizing vein, include them in lists of famous heroes and lovers subject, like all of mankind, to the inevitability of death.[12] A ballad describing Tristan's death at the hands of King Mark was very popular at the court of the Catholic Sovereigns, where several glosses were made upon it.[13]

There survives a long manuscript fragment of the late fourteenth or early fifteenth century, generally known as *Cuento de Tristán de Leonís*, written in Castilian and Aragonese.[14] This is similar but not identical to the version of the romance (to which I shall refer as *Libro de Tristán*) in the Castilian imprints of 1501 and 1528;[15] the fragment begins with their chapter iv and ends at chapter lviii. Another manuscript fragment, a single folio of the late fourteenth century in Castilian, is virtually identical to part of chapter lxxiii of the printed texts, suggesting that the *Libro* 'reflects an early state of the Castilian *Tristan*'.[16] The *Cuento* and the *Libro* would appear in fact to be separate renderings of a lost common source; Northup argued that this was in Italian, although more recent research has suggested a French or Catalan intermediary as likelier.[17]

However, it is not with the question of sources that I am concerned, but rather with the nature of the differences between the two Spanish versions of the romance. These involve more than the greater stylistic polish of the *Libro* and affect what may be called the tone or spirit of the story and the way in which it presents the characters and the whole courtly-chivalric way of life. I turn now to consider a selection of the more important differences in detail.[18]

The dignity of the knight-errant: Throughout the *Libro* one finds a concern to present the protagonists and their actions in a serious and uncritical manner. The occasional moments of humour or irony found in the *Cuento* – a feature of

Arthurian romance going back as far as Chrétien de Troyes, of course – tend to
be toned down or removed altogether.

> E anduvieron tres dias sin fallar ninguna auentura, nin tan solamente del
> agua non fallauan en estos tres dias. E desto fue mucho maravillado Godis,
> quando via que les convenia de dormir syn rropa en el monte e tan
> solamente del agua non fallauan, e dixo – Señor, yo so marauillado de vos
> que diziedes que en esta tierra se fallauan tantas aventuras, e yo veo que ya
> son tres dias que andamos por esta floresta, e tan solamente del agua non
> fallamos, nin vn lugar do albergar e ansi podemos nos aqui morir de fanbre
> e de set. Tristan começo a rreyr, e dixo – Hermano, pues non tenedes vos
> esto por vna aventura? Pues sabed agora que esta auentura podria bien ser
> puesta en el libro de las estorias: que onbre anda por vna floresta tanto
> tiempo e non falla do albergar nin do rrefrescar; e digovos que yo mesmo
> me maravillo mucho desta aventura.

(Cuento, p. 199)

> E agora dize la historia, que aquel dia anduuieron tanto Tristan e Quedin,
> fasta la noche, que no fallaron ninguna auentura, ni hallaron ningun lugar
> donde pudiessen refrescar, e dormieron aquella noche en el desierto; y
> otro dia, ellos se fueron por el camino e anduuieron fasta la ora de nona,
> que no hallaron refrescamiento ninguno. E Quedin dixo: mi amado
> Tristan, vos deziades que hauia muchas auenturas, mas a mi paresce que
> avn del agua no hallamos para beuer, ¿como fallaremos otras auenturas,
> que dos dias auemos andado que no fallemos ninguna cosa? E Tristan
> dixo: ¿pues parescevos que esta floresta no es de grande auentura?; por
> buena fe, a mi paresce de gran auentura.

(Libro, ch. xlii, p. 188)

Abandoning Yseut of the White Hands, Tristan has arrived in Britain; his
companion, the inexperienced Kaherdin, longs for adventure and so, leaving
Governal and Brangain for a while, they set out into the forest together. The
Cuento now stresses the harsher aspects of the knight's calling: the failure to
find water is mentioned three times, and there is the realistic touch of the need
to sleep 'syn rropa'; there is humour in Kaherdin's surprise that knight-
errantry can be at times a comfortless and tedious affair, with death from
hunger and thirst more likely than the prospect of winning honour and glory.
The *Libro*, on the other hand, minimizes the hardships which the two
companions encounter; Kaherdin addresses Tristan with greater courtesy ('mi
amado Tristan' instead of 'señor, yo so marauillado de vos'), and his remarks
reflect a serious concern to meet adventure rather than a naive anxiety at their
inability to find board and lodging. Tristan's reply is different as well: in the
Cuento he appears to be amused by Kaherdin's laments, and he jokingly plays
on the meaning of *aventura*; it is indeed an *aventura*, in the sense of an

uncommon experience, to be three days in the wilds without finding food and drink – something rare enough to be placed on record alongside accounts of more warlike incidents. In the *Libro*, however, this amusing justification of Tristan's belief that the forest was a place of 'adventure' vanishes completely: the pun is omitted, the humour vanishes, and Tristan's joke is transformed into a mere flat denial of what Kaherdin says: '¿pues parescevos que esta floresta no es de grande auentura?; por buena fe, a mi paresce de gran auentura'.

Later in the story Tristan and Yseut attend a tournament at Camelot, where he takes part in the jousting incognito and performs wonders. Anxious to discover the identity of this mysterious champion, Lancelot and Arthur come later to the tent where the two lovers are asleep:

E como los fallaron todos que dormian, Lançarote començo de saltar al derredor de la tienda. E como Brangel vio que saltauan al derredor de la tienda, ella salio fuera, e dixo – Señor cauallero, a mi paresçe agora que uos non sodes cortes como yo vi de otros asaz que vos andades saltando aqui çerca do duerme otro cauallero que por ventura ualle tanto como vos. E asy dios me de bien, que yo creo que vos andades buscando rruydo, e bien lo podredes fallar.

(*Cuento*, p. 269)

E ellos andauan al derredor de la tienda escuchando si era dentro alguno, e Brangel salio de la puerta de la tienda, tanto que los sintio, e quando vio a los dos caualleros, dixoles: de mala uentura soys, caualleros, que asi andays escuchando en derredor de la tienda; que si vos supiesedes quien es el cauallero que esta dentro, no podrian escapar vuestras personas si lo el supiese, e no esta en cortesia.

(*Libro*, ch. lviii, p. 251)

In the *Cuento*, Lancelot prances about outside the tent, presumably wishing to make sufficient noise to awake the occupants; Brangain rebukes him for discourteous conduct, insultingly compares him to the sleeping stranger inside, and warns him off in very blunt language. The scene is a comic one: the knight's undignified leaping is at once followed by the unflattering comments and threats uttered by an outspoken social inferior, and a pleasing sense of absurdity is created. In the *Libro* the atmosphere is totally changed: Lancelot and Arthur are merely walking and listening around the tent, and though Brangain does rebuke them, this is for being inquisitive rather than for allegedly seeking to provoke trouble; her speech is much less discourteous, with its use of the third person in 'no podrian escapar vuestras personas' and the impersonal 'no esta en cortesia' as opposed to 'uos non sodes cortes como yo vi de otros asaz' in the *Cuento*.

Noteworthy, too, are the ways in which the two versions show Yseut reacting at moments of crisis when her lover is in danger. At the Isla del Gigante, for instance, the *Cuento* describes Yseut as turning yellow and then black in her anxiety for Tristan during his fight with Bravor (p. 114); the *Libro* simply says that she pales, though it retains the more sophisticated description of her complexion taking on the colour of a rose when Tristan is finally victorious (ch. xxii, p. 90). Similar chromatic variations occur soon after in the *Cuento* as Yseut's complexion is transformed from rose-pink to grassy green in the course of Tristan's combat with Galehaut ('la color que auie como rrosa tornose tal como yerua' (p. 118)); the *Libro* omits this completely (ch. xxv, p. 96), and further enhances Yseut's dignity by making her wear her best clothes for the occasion (p. 95), whereas in the *Cuento* she puts on her worst.

The treatment of unworthy or dishonourable conduct: There are several striking differences here between the two versions, with the *Libro* commonly omitting, refining or otherwise modifying incidents in which the *Cuento* makes characters appear unpleasant or brutal. The adulterous love-affair between Tristan and Yseut is, of course, at the very heart of the story and presents a major problem. One solution found in the *Libro* is to play down the moral implications of the adultery by removing references to the lovers' sinfulness or the misfortunes which they bring upon themselves and others as a result of their illicit passion. In the *Cuento*, for example, Tristan decides to marry Yseut of the White Hands partly because she may help him forget Yseut the Fair, but also because 'bien es perder onbre el blasme e la mala fama e tornarse a lo mejor'; he recognizes that if he married, 'todas las gentes lo aurian a bien e non seria tanto blasfemado como era por la rreyna Yseo la Baça' (p. 185). The *Libro* refers to Tristan's desire to forget and his recognition of the fact that marriage to a princess will increase his personal honour; his frank admission of his present state of dishonour and sin has, however, vanished (ch. xl, p. 173). Dinadan's criticisms of Tristan's love have also been altered: in the *Cuento* he strongly condemns his friend's surrender to an unlawful love which can only do him harm: 'es perdido por el su loco amor, e non creo yo que algun dia su amor non le sea dañoso; e esto es grand pecado, ca mucho es cauallero de grand preçio' (p. 254). In the corresponding passage in the *Libro*, Tristan is simply referred to as being 'perdido por dueña', and Dinadan is making not so much a moral judgement as a comment on the physical danger which Tristan is incurring through his adultery with Mark's queen: 'creo que el perdera el cuerpo por Yseo' (ch. liv, p. 238). Tristan, then, might lose his life for his love, but spiritual perdition as well is not suggested.

When in the *Cuento* Tristan receives the poignant letter from Yseut the Fair and decides to go back to her, he takes a malicious pleasure in Brangain's deception of his naive young wife whom she assures of Tristan's prompt return once he has settled the 'matters' which require his presence in Britain: 'E Tristan començo a rreyr de las palabras de Brangen, por que ansi bien sabia componer sus dichos' (p. 197). This unpleasant trait is missing from the *Libro*, which instead describes Tristan's sincere attempts at comforting the girl; at this point the *Libro* also reminds the reader of the love potion which is the cause of Tristan's passion for Yseut the Fair and his consequent inability to be loyal to his bride: 'E Tristan la conortaua muy dulce e amorosamente, e hauia gran piedad della, mas tanto le destruyo el beuraje amoroso, que no podia estar de no yr alla' (ch. xlii, p. 186).

Elsewhere, one finds brutal or barbaric behaviour in the *Cuento* being modified in the *Libro* or omitted altogether. In the *Cuento*, for instance, Tristan slays Bravor, the giant who rules the Isla del Gigante, and then beheads his wife (p. 115); in the *Libro*, on the other hand, when the knights who guard the island tell Tristan that he must execute Bravor's wife, he refuses ('dixo que no haria tal villania'), and then, since she cannot escape execution, he orders one of the guards to behead her (ch. xxiii, p. 91). The *Libro* similarly changes the episode of the daughter of king Pharamont of Gaul: angry that Tristan does not return her love, she falsely accuses him of attempting to rape her, and he is condemned to death. The princess later repents, and persuades Pharamont to spare Tristan by threatening to kill herself with a sword unless he is allowed to live. In the *Cuento* she obtains the weapon by asking to be allowed to execute Tristan: 'Sseñor, pues datme la espada, e yo lo matare' (p. 82). Though only a ruse, this savage and unladylike request has been omitted from the *Libro*; there she asks her father for a gift, and when he agrees she demands the executioner's sword, but gives no reason at all for her unlikely choice of boon (ch. v, p. 23).

The revisions found throughout the *Libro* extend to what seem at first sight trivial points of detail:

E en esto dixo Tristan – Señor, sabed que yo non he voluntad de justar nin de combatir.

(Cuento, p. 209)

Por mi fe, dixo Tristan, no he voluntad de me combatir agora, que mi cauallo no es bien sano.

(Libro, ch. xliv, p. 198)

Tristan has just met Kay (El Rrey Senescal in the *Cuento*, Don Queas in the *Libro*), who has challenged him to a fight. Tristan declines, and the *Libro* makes it plain that what might seem reprehensible conduct in a knight-errant is the result not of cowardice but of his horse being unwell – a justifiable reason for refusing combat. There is an analogous situation later, when Lancelot turns down Arthur's request that he should fight a mysterious challenger (Tristan incognito) who has been defeating all the knights of the Round Table at a tournament:

Señor, dixo Lançarote, yo non se quien se es nin donde es venido, mas

81

bien paresçe que el es proboso cauallero e de grand afer; e bien lo ha
mostrado en este dia de oy.

(*Cuento*, p. 263)

E Lançarote dixo al rey: señor, si al cauallero yo fuese, no me seria honrra,
que tanto a fecho oy de armas, que bien se puede tener por buen cauallero.

(*Libro*, ch. lvii, p. 249)

The *Libro* seems to imply that it would not be honourable for Lancelot, himself
quite fresh, to challenge a knight who is doubtless weary after a day's fighting.

The character of Dinadan: In the French Prose *Tristan* Dinadan is a complex
figure: a critic of frivolous and belligerent knight-errantry with which he
prefers not to associate himself, he is nonetheless a man of courage and will
fight well if the occasion demands it. He is genuinely fond of Tristan and is
concerned lest his friend should come to harm through his passion for Yseut.
Dinadan perhaps over-reacts, the example of Tristan's experiences leading
him to conclude that love is generally destructive and thus always to be
avoided; nevertheless, he is a person of wisdom and sense, sometimes a
melancholy and unsettling character, but also amusing, with a sense of humour
which usually enables him to accept in good part the jokes and tricks with
which others avenge his verbal sallies at their expense.[19]

In the sole episode involving Dinadan which is common to both the *Cuento*
and *Libro*, Tristan and Yseut meet him while on their way to join Lancelot and
Guinevere at the Joyous Gard. Tristan does not at first recognize Dinadan and
issues a challenge which is refused:

Cauallero, tenetuos, si uos plaze, ca si el diablo es en vos, yo vos digo que
non es en mi; nin pensedes que vengo muerto por justar nin por batallar
como vos.

(*Cuento*, p. 253)

Cauallero, no fagays tal cosa, que no so diablo que me combatire con vos,
que yo no trayo dueña en mi compañia.

(*Libro*, ch. liv, p. 238)

The *Libro* lacks Dinadan's insulting comparison between himself and Tristan,
and gives him some degree of justification for not fighting – he has no lady to
defend. In the ensuing conversation, Dinadan's criticisms of Tristan are also
greatly toned down (see above, p. 80). Yseut alleges that Dinadan's hostility to
love stems not so much from the unhappy example provided by Tristan but
from his lack of a lady to call his own, and persuades Dinadan to take the lady of
the first knight whom they meet with an 'amiga' in his company. The first
knight encountered is Sagramor, and Dinadan is quickly unhorsed by him.

E començo de maldezir a sy mesmo, e deziendo estas palauras -Muchas graçias aya dios que agora aprende Dinadani a bollar! E maldito sea el dia de oy que yo esta conpañia falle! E maldita sea la puta falsa que en esto me puso, e avn aquel que lla trae en su conpaña, ca çiertamente el deuia ser algun onbre de poco saber!

(Cuento, p. 255)

E dixo Dinadan: ¡Gracias a Dios, que he aprendido a volar!; ¡mal aya la dueña y el que la tray, que por fuerça me fazen justar!

(Libro, ch. liv, p. 239)

Here the *Libro* turns to straightforward expurgation, cutting Dinadan's speech by about half and toning down his comments on Tristan and Yseut. At the close of this episode, when Dinadan parts from the lovers, the *Libro* adds a concluding judgement clearly aimed at removing any impression of his being an unworthy character; on the contrary, he is a skilled and courageous fighter, and his sense of humour – essentially harmless – makes him everywhere popular:

E Dinadan era cauallero saluaje, y era gran esgrimidor, y grande de cuerpo, e gran truhan, asi como hombre que anda por cortes de reyes; e auia sido buen cauallero, y era rico de moneda, que le dauan los reyes e los caualleros; e yua muchas vezes por mensajero de vna corte a otra, y escarnecia e burlaua con todos, asi que todos folgauan del e hauian plazer con sus palabras.

(Libro, ch. liv, p. 240)

The differences between the *Cuento de Tristán* and the sixteenth-century imprints of the *Libro* are no doubt the end result of successive modifications to the *Libro* over a long period of time. Some changes were made very late: Waley, for instance, indicated a number of passages in the *Libro* which are borrowed from *Grimalte y Gradissa*, Juan de Flores's sentimental romance of the late fifteenth century. They include the letter which the princess of Gaul writes to Tristan:

Donde el *Tristan* vaticano se limita a narrar lo acontecido sin elegancias retóricas, la segunda carta (i.e. that of the *Libro*) está construida sobre una base de hipérbole, antítesis, perífrasis, repeticiones, apóstrofe, preguntas retóricas y extravagancias sintácticas, del mismo tipo que se encuentra a menudo en las novelas sentimentales de Juan de Flores y de Diego de San Pedro.[20]

Similar differences of style distinguish the versions of the letter which Yseut the Fair sends Tristan after his marriage to Yseut of the White Hands;

83

although the highly rhetorical and passionate letter given in the *Libro* (ch. xli, pp. 179–80) seems not to reveal direct borrowings from Flores, it is nonetheless evidently a later recasting of the much simpler letter contained in the *Cuento* (pp. 191–2).[21] Presumably there must have been intermediate redactions of the *Libro* which have not survived, representing different stages in the evolution of the text as we know it today.[22]

Adaptations of the kind indicated above were still being made in the sixteenth century; in 1534 there appeared an edition of the *Libro* with a second book relating the adventures of the lovers' two children, named after their parents.[23] This sequel is prepared by a long interpolation in the first book: it tells how the young Tristan and young Yseut are born during the journey from Ireland to Cornwall, being left behind in the care of the people of the Giant's Isle when the parents continue their voyage. In his additional material the anonymous author deals with the problem of the adultery of Tristan and Yseut by frequent reminders of their accidental drinking of the love potion, and stresses their merits as parents and rulers in the course of their lengthy stay on the island; the fact that the children are illegitimate is ignored. As Eisele has shown, there is also a removal of any crudities missed by earlier redactors of the *Libro* text proper. For example, when Dinadan reluctantly agrees to act as Yseut's champion and is repeatedly unhorsed by knights who challenge him, he remarks that 'ya he bolado tres veces por la buena dama', whereas in the 1501 and 1528 editions he calls her 'mala puta' (ch. lix; the *Cuento* fragment breaks off shortly before this incident).[24]

This preference for a serious and favourable view of the courtly-chivalric way of life led to changes being made in other Arthurian texts which circulated in Castile; I have indicated elsewhere how *Tablante de Ricamonte*, based on *Jaufré*, turns a sometimes brutal and often ironical and slapstick romance into something much more refined, with the removal or rewriting of incidents in which Jaufré, Arthur and other heroes are made to seem cruel or foolish; even the villains become less unpleasant.[25] In the Castilian version of the *Roman du Graal*, the part known as the *Demanda del Sancto Grial* omits or tones down many passages (mostly, of course, deriving directly from the Vulgate *Queste del Saint Graal*) which stress the sexual immorality and the cruelty of members of Arthur's court who fail in the Quest as a result; the *Suite du Merlin* section, on the other hand, presents knight-errantry in an exalted and generally positive manner, and required few changes, as a comparison with the *Baladro del sabio Merlín* shows.[26] However, the most extensive modifications could not totally disguise the problems posed by the fact that Lancelot and Tristan, brave warriors and true lovers though they might be, were adulterers and guilty of disloyal conduct towards their respective monarchs. Though much influenced by Arthurian material, *Amadís de Gaula* avoids such difficulties, and the conduct of Amadís and Oriana is always exemplary.[27]

Translators and redactors in the Middle Ages commonly modified their material in order to cater for the tastes and prejudices of their readers; the spirit or ethos of a work might change considerably to take into account 'new stylistic modes, local social conditions and mores or political concerns'.[28] Some of the adaptations revealed by a comparison of the *Cuento de Tristán* with the *Libro* merely reflect the more sophisticated literary tastes of the late fifteenth or early sixteenth century: the letters are obvious examples. Others are more fundamental and would appear to stem from a desire to preserve and enhance the dignity of knighthood in order not to offend the susceptibilities of a public which, even more than in other European countries, held chivalry in high esteem. The fact of Moorish rule in southern Spain, though latterly posing a threat more apparent than real, gave until 1492 a seemingly convincing justification on sound military grounds for the existence of a class on which national survival and the defence of the faith could be seen to depend. In Castile the knight (or, indeed, his lady) was hardly to be censured on moral grounds, presented as a figure of fun, or even contemplated with irony, however gentle. The *Libro de Tristán* is only one of a number of romances which reflect the pro-chivalric ethos of Castilian society, and which may well have done something towards maintaining it.[29]

The Lion and Yvain*

TONY HUNT

Miror qua fronte quidam allegoriarum se doctores jactitant, qui ipsam
adhuc primam litterae significationem ignorant . . . Nos, inquiunt, litteram legimus, sed non secundum litteram. Allegoriam enim legimus, et
exponimus litteram non secundum litteram, sed secundum allegoriam
. . . Leo quippe secundum historiam bestiam significat, secundum allegoriam Christum significat: ergo vox ista, leo, Christum significat.[1]

Hugh of St Victor's gentle chiding of those who neglect the literal meaning in
their impatience to reach the mystery within stands as a useful corrective to
some interesting but speculative interpretations, in modern criticism, of the
meeting with the lion in the Yvain story.[2]

It is not, of course, possible to know where Chrestien got his lion from. The
story of Androcles and the lion immediately suggests itself as a partial parallel
to Yvain's adventure,[3] but the relentless ransacking of contemporary Latin
literature and Celtic legend has revealed not a few alternative points of contact
which simply serve to confirm the hazardousness of any attempt at a precise
location of Chrestien's source.[4] It is not putative source material which will
illuminate Chrestien's conception of the traditionally noble beast, but, rather,
close attention to the details of his initial presentation of the animal, a
procedure which yields results surprisingly inimical to the usual lines of
allegorical interpretation. There are at the outset five major features which are
antagonistic to a moral or spiritual interpretation of the lion's significance.
First, despite its legendary virtues, the *rex omnium animalium* is discovered in
undignified distress, clearly getting the worst of an encounter with a fire-
breathing serpent[5] which holds it by the tail (*Yv.* 3348–51): it is certainly in
desperate straits. Second, Yvain is motivated to assist it, not by any positive
recognition of its virtue, but simply by pity for its plight in contending with an

obviously evil and venomous creature (*Yv.* 3352–68). Furthermore, even as he prepares to attack the serpent he envisages the possibility of fighting against the lion afterwards (*Yv.* 3369–72), despite the compassion he feels for 'la beste jantil et franche' (*Yv.* 3375). Thus, whatever interpretations Chrestien's listeners may have availed themselves of, his hero certainly cannot be credited with an allegorical turn of mind. This is, perhaps, just as well in view of his next action, which is to release the lion by cutting off the tip of its tail (*Yv.* 3382–7) 'qu'onques mains ne pot'. Ever since Pliny the Elder wrote *leonum animi index cauda* (*Nat. Hist.* VIII, 19), medieval exegetes found particular allegorical significance in the tail of the lion. Like the first two, this third feature of Chrestien's treatment of the lion seems counterindicative of any trans-cendental significance.[6] The same may be said of a fourth feature, the reaction of the lion, which neither attacks Yvain (*Yv.* 3388–91) nor leaves him with mute relief, but weeps tears of gratitude in a pose which more readily recalls the bears in the *Ruodlieb* than a beast legendary for its ferocity. The fifth and final feature of the presentation of *nobilissimus bestiarum* is the portrait of *leo vigilans* lying beside his master. The medieval exegetes make much of the fact that the lion sleeps with its eyes open, but Chrestien playfully reveals that it is not its master that the lion keeps an eye on:

> Et li lions ot tant de sans,
> Qu'il veilla et fu an espans
> Del cheval garder, qui peissoit
> L'erbe, qui petit l'angreissoit.
>
> (*Yv.* 3481–4)

The five features of the narrative account of the lion which we have so far discussed appear to have been designed as warnings against an allegorical interpretation of the episode.[7] They are thoroughly in the manner of Chrestien and the last three closely resemble the procedures used by him in the other romances to 'block' the traditional connotations of names and motifs and thereby produce an ironic reversal or neutralization of expectations.[8] Chrestien himself was too learned to ignore the possibilities presented by the lion for allegorical exploration and commentary and took the opportunity, it might seem, to confound the *clergie* of some of his audience and prepare the way for a more 'immanent' interpretation, unencumbered by scholarly distractions, and more attentively focussed on what the narrator actually says.

That this approach to greater alertness to the letter, through humour and countersigns, is peculiarly Chrestien's is easily appreciated by comparing the versions of his redactors.[9] The motif of the lion's tail is given much less prominence, Chrestien's first reference to it being omitted by Hartmann, the Swedish author of *Herr Ivan*, and in the Welsh *Iarlles y Fynnawn*. In *Ywain and Gawain* the French has been misunderstood and the dragon is depicted as having wrapped its tail round the lion (*YG* 1981 ff).[10] The cutting of the tip of the tail is absent entirely from Hartmann (and the later German Ulrich Fuetrer), the Norse *Ivens saga*, and the Welsh account and is postponed in *Herr Ivan*. Clearly it was accorded no significance. The hero's motive in aiding the lion is also much less clear in the foreign redactions. In Hartmann, *Ywain and Gawain*, the *mabinogi* and Fuetrer, there is no suggestion of any desire on the part of the hero to assist the lion for a clearly deliberated reason.[11] In the *saga* Iven seems to understand that the lion was crying out to him for mercy (X, 28); in *Herr Ivan* merely that a serpent is always hateful (2705–6). The notion of pity overcoming fear in the hero himself is entirely lacking, the possibility of having to fight with the lion not being envisaged in *Ywain and Gawain*, the *saga* and *Herr Ivan* until the hero has actually freed the beast (though see *saga* X, 28). The lion's unexpected response, elaborated by Chrestien with poignant humour, is attenuated in the foreign versions, which display an attempt to accommodate the extravagant gestures of Chrestien's anthropopathic animal to the less eloquent repertoire of the 'dumb beast'. Whilst Chrestien is careful to restrict his hero to a simple acknowledgement that the lion wishes to thank him for his aid (*Yv.* 3402–7), the Scandinavian redactors anticipate future developments. Herr Ivan understood that the lion wished to serve him ('hon vilde honum thiana', 2742), whilst Iven 'þakkaði guði, at hann hafði sent honum slíkan fylgjara' (X, 31). Finally, the depiction of *leo vigilans*[12] is modified in such a way that Chrestien's significant suppression of any reference to its guarding its master no longer counts. In Hartmann and *Ywain and Gawain* the lion specifically keeps watch over both horse and master (H. 3911–6, *YG* 2055–6). In *Herr Ivan* the lion displays particular solicitude for its master's safety, for 'it held him so dear, that it spared itself no trouble to keep guard over him that night and to preserve him by its service, that no harm might come to him':

> Leonit haffde han swa kaer
> ok lot sik vara ther til ospara
> then nat ower honum at halda vara
> och gøma han medh sin froma
> at engen ma honum til skada koma.
>
> (2800–4)

In *Iarlles y Ffynnawn*, the *saga* and in Fuetrer the motif of the watchful lion is lacking completely, though it is a feature of a comparable story of a grateful lion related by Alexander Nequam and which we shall consider later:

> Cum vero miles somno artus recreavit, leo ad pedes eius quiescens custos domini sui fidelissimus est effectus.[13]

Against this background of the motif of the lion's vigilance Chrestien's remarks on the attention which it shows to the hero's horse is surely to be seen as a piece of pointed humour directed towards the allegorists.

In the Welsh tale and in the prose *Yvain* the whole meeting with the lion is handled differently. The *mabinogi* locates the lion and serpent in a cleft in a rock situated on a hillside in the middle of a forest. In the White Book text the lion is pure white (*purwyn*), according to the Red Book pure black (*purdu*). The serpent promptly attacks Owein who only observes the lion's reaction as he returns to the road and sees it 'ac yn gware yn y gylch ual milgi a uackei e hun' (670–1).[14] In the prose *Yvain* the hero's decision to kill the dragon first is a purely tactical one:

> Yuain dit a soi meisme qil les ocira andeus ci il onques pourra il dit quil ueut auant ocire le dragon por ce quil pourra miaus ocire le lyon quant il sera seul a seul o lui quil ne firoit le dragon. Et le dragon porra il miaus ocire a cestui point por ce quil a ha entendre au lyon quil ne firoit ce il fust seul a seul o lui.

After this intervention the lion exhibits a joyful response, but the hero still makes as if to attack it:

> por ce quant il uoit quil li uoloit doner (le) lespee il ne fuit mie ne ne fait semblant de soi defendre ne de maus faire ains encline sa teste et fait semblant de grant humilite.[15]

Yvain 'ha grant meruille' and resolves not to harm the lion, but shortly afterwards, when he sees the lion following him, he makes to strike it and the lion again 'fait semblance de grant humblece'. After this there is unfortunately a lacuna in the MS, folios 2 and 3 being lost.

What, then, is to be concluded from this consideration of the initial presentation of the lion in Chrestien and his successors? First, there is no evidence to support the identification of the lion with a moral principle or spiritual power which has special claim on the hero's conscience.[16] Second, Chrestien's handling of the episode is both more versatile and more comprehensive than that of the foreign redactors, whose treatment of detail is liable to be haphazard. Third, an essential part of the coherence of Chrestien's account lies in his ironical deployment of monitory signs or counterindications through which he attempts to frustrate an allegorical or too heavily spiritualized interpretation of the episode.[17] Like the literary virtuoso he is, he plays with the allegorical possibilities of the material whilst rejecting them. We must, therefore, accept that 'vox ista, leo, bestiam significat'.

If we recognize Chrestien's signals and refrain from a premature assessment of the lion's significance, we shall naturally wish to attend closely to the role of the lion in the hero's subsequent adventures, namely the Harpin episode, the rescue of Lunete, and Pesme Aventure. Before these adventures, however, there are already important indications of a significant dualism in the lion's nature. The beast's natural hunting instinct, its pursuit of *bestes sauvages*, its drinking of warm blood (*Yv.* 3416–55) are a reminder of its natural ferocity and anticipate its hostility to the series of uncourtly opponents which its master is called upon to confront.[18] On the other hand, its conduct at the fountain symbolizes a rare degree of *compassio*, the sight of its master's blood producing an entirely different reaction from that to the sight of its prey. Both its ferocity and compassion are unambiguously placed in the service of its master, its role, as we shall see, being to reinforce the power of the hero's own responses and aid the execution of his decisions. The autonomy of the lion is thus extremely restricted, limited in fact to the protection of its master when his courage exposes him to extreme danger. That the lion is not an allegorical figure is again suggested by Chrestien's manipulation of a detail from allegorical lore. Pliny the Elder had written of the lion 'vis summa in pectore est' (*Nat. Hist.* VIII, 19). The lion's attempt to pierce its own breast with the hero's sword (*Yv.* 3519, 3551),[19] thus clearly suggesting suicide, must surely 'block' any specifically Christian interpretation of its role, even though this radical degree of compassion may be felt to echo or reciprocate its master's earlier demonstration of *pitiez*. What emerges clearly from the transition to the Harpin episode is that the lion's service to its master accommodates both aggression and submission, strength and humility.[20] How, then, are these contrasting qualities illustrated in the three adventures in which the lion plays an active role?

The traditional ferocity of the lion is underlined by the initial reaction of the inhabitants of the castle at the beginning of the Harpin episode. They are frightened by the sight of the lion (*Yv.* 3789–93). Yet they are soon reassured by the hero's declaration of solidarity with his companion (*Yv.* 3794–801) and his apparent confidence that he can control the animal. The swing from *joie* (*annominatio* in *Yv.* 3813–25)[21] to *dolor/duel* (*Yv.* 3819, 3832) is reminiscent of the violent change of mood which the hero has just experienced at the fountain (*annominatio* on *joie* in *Yv.* 3532, 3542, 3554–8; *duel Yv.* 3819, 3832), as is the host's lament 'Nus miauz de moi ne se doit plaindre / Ne duel feire ne duel mener, / De duel devroie *forsener*' (*Yv.* 3860–2). That this parallel between hero and host provides a link between the two episodes is confirmed by the explicit association made by Hartmann's narrator:

> Swer ie kumber erleit,
> den erbarmet des mannes arbeit
> michels harter dan den man
> der nie deheine nôt gewan.
>
> (4389–92)

Another link is provided by the motif of *pitié*. As Yvain had been led by *pitiez* to aid the lion (*Yv.* 3373), so he is now moved by *pitié* (*Yv.* 3942/4070) to defend his host.[22] A third link may be seen in the fact that the *humilité* formerly displayed by the lion in the rescue scene (*Yv.* 3401, 3404) is now adopted by the hero himself, who will not suffer the host's family to kneel in obeisance to him (*Yv.* 3980ff), such a gesture of submission being called by Hartmann 'diu unzuht' (H. 4783). The potent alliance of courage and humility is recognized by the modified reaction to the knight and his lion:[23]

> Qu'an sa proesce mout se fïent
> Et mout cuident, qu'il soit prodon,
> Par la conpaignie au lion,
> Qui aussi doucemant se gist
> Lez lui, come uns aigniaus feïst.[24]
>
> (*Yv.* 4008–12)

The host's daughter and her mother would have prized the hero even more

> Se la corteisie seüssent[25]
> Et la grant proesce de lui.
> (*Yv.* 4022–3)

Strength combined with humility overcomes the giant Harpin, symbol of pride (*Yv.* 4137 and cf. *tors* in 4228),[26] and the hero appears as *li frans*, *li douz*, epithets already associated with the lion (*Yv.* 3375, 3393, 4011; Yvain also applies them to Gauvain in 3699). The hero's new qualities represent superior arms to the arrogance of Harpin 'qui a sa force se fioit, / tant que armer ne se deignoit' (*Yv.* 4209–10). Yet at a critical juncture the *nobilis ira leonis* manifests itself in its determined intervention: 'si saut par ire et par grant force' (*Yv.* 4221) and after Yvain has successfully dispatched the giant he significantly becomes *Li Chevaliers au lion* (4291, 4613).[27] Compassion, responsibility and humility are the salient qualities displayed by the hero in this episode. They are indications of his moral development and are reflected in the role of the lion. They are well conveyed in Hartmann's version, but seriously neglected by the other redactors. It should be noted that the lion always acts *in support* of decisions already taken. The juxtaposition of a series of prayers to God with a reference to the lion's presence (*Yv.* 4168–9: 'Mes aprés lui ne remassist / li lions an nule meniere'), a technique employed again in the subsequent adventure, may seem to justify Meng's observation concerning Hartmann, 'Es kommt dem Dichter also weniger darauf an, die Stärke und Überlegenheit Iweins im Kampfe zu zeigen, als vielmehr die Rechtfertigung seines Einsatzes zu zeigen, die Erfolgssicherheit des gottgefälligen Motivs'.[28] Furthermore, the lion's role underscores the belief that Right is Might,[29] as is clear from the beginning of Yvain's next adventure, the combat against the wicked seneschal:

> . . . buene fiance an lui a,
> Que Des et droiz li eideront,
> Qui a sa partie seront:
> An cez conpaignons mout se fie
> Et son lion ne rehet mie.
> (*Yv.* 4332–6)[30]

There is an important cluster of references to God, Justice and the lion here which constitute significant innovations. Although God is invoked in each of the adventures of the second part of the romance, this is the first occasion on which the hero himself affirms his trust in Him. The notion of *droit* appropriately appears, also for the first time, in the context of a legal trial. Equally without precedent is the explicit reference to Yvain's regard for his lion. On the other hand, continuity is assured by the reappearance of the theme of *pitié* (*Yv.* 4357). In the rescue of Lunete the lion's spontaneous and determined intervention is heightened by the fact that the hero makes a positive attempt to control his companion (*Yv.* 4472–4, contrast 4168–9), initially withdrawing it from the field of battle.[31] No less notable is the fact that the description of the lion's recognition of his master's need for help is interwoven with references to the prayers of the ladies for God's protection of the hero (*Yv.* 4509ff.).[32] Without seeing the lion as 'der verlängerte Arm Gottes', we may recall Meng's observation already cited, noting how the lion's ferocity and strength can be accommodated by the notion of moral right. The *nobilis ira leonis* is not to be rejected:

> . . . li lions sanz dote set,
> Que ses sire mie ne het
> S'aïe, einçois l'an aimme plus
> (4543–5, cf. 4453–8)

It is significant that, although the hero has already claimed that the two sides are evenly matched, since he has the twin supports of God and Right, it is the intervention of the lion which provokes the narrator's comment 'Or sont el champ tot per a per' (*Yv.* 4533).[33] This must encourage us to believe, with Adler, that the lion illustrates 'the claim of moral Goodness to be strongly, even ruthlessly equipped against Evil'.[34] It is made clear that the seneschal's brothers surrender on account of the lion (*Yv.* 4456–8), which spares them (as we shall see *parcere prostratis* is a traditional trait of the lion), their fate on the pyre being the result of human justice, specifically that of Laudine's court, not of the hero.[35] The rescue of Lunete also ends with Yvain's affirmation of his

92

new appellation 'Chevalier au lion' (*Yv.* 4613).[36] This time, however, both knight and lion are wounded and the hero demonstrates his devotion to the lion by carrying it on his shield.

There is, of course, no place for the lion in the legal formalities of the inheritance dispute and the combat of Yvain with Gauvain. The younger sister of Noire Espine successfully enlists the aid of 'cil qui ja n'iert / sanz un lion . . .' (*Yv.* 5020–1), but the episode is interrupted by Pesme Aventure. Here again the odds are uneven, the hero being forced to fight with the two *netuns*, and for the second time his opponents insist on the removal of the lion (*Yv.* 5537–46, 5552–63) whose participation is this time openly defended by the hero (*Yv.* 5551: 'Mout m'iert bel, se il m'aïe'). The mere sight of the *netuns* rouses the lion's *ire* (*Yv.* 5526–35) and the hero is forced to imprison it in *une chanbrete* (*Yv.* 5566, 5576–7). Pesme Aventure, as its name implies, is the most difficult of Yvain's undertakings[37] and it is no accident that it contains a striking innovation concerning the role of the lion. For the first time the beast's intervention in battle is carefully and explicitly motivated:

> Que de la grant bonté li manbre,
> Que cil li fist par sa franchise,
> Qui ja avroit de son servise
> Et de s'aïe grant mestier.
> Ja li randroit au grant sestier
> Et au grant mui ceste bonté,
> Ja n'i avroit rien mesconté,
> S'il pooit issir de leanz.
>
> (5596–603)[38]

The exemplary nature of Yvain's first gratuitous exploit – the rescue of the lion – is reaffirmed:[39] it is, indeed, paradigmatic in the ethical context of the second half of the romance. The theme of gratitude fittingly expresses the power which lies behind pity and justice and the lion's association with the motif of reciprocity is here renewed.

The adventure is concluded in a significantly different way from previous exploits. The hero disposes of one of the monsters and spares the other, a symbolic division of effort which has considerable importance, for the joint operation of power and pity through reciprocity is the fundamental theme of Yvain's collaboration with the lion. *Parcere prostratis* is here illustrated in the conclusion of the battle and the exchange between the combatants:

> '. . . qui merci prie et requiert,
> N'i doit faillir, quant il la rueve,
> Se home *sanz pitié* ne trueve
> . . .

93

> Veincuz sui maleoit gre mien
> Et recreanz, ce vos otroi'.
> 'Donc n'as tu mes garde de moi,
> Et mes lions te rasseüre'.
> (*Yv.* 5680–2, 5690–3)[40]

As always, the lion is not autonomous, but reflects, and gives effect to, the determination and compassion of its master. It is Yvain who takes the initiative in saving the second *netun*, even before he has been asked for mercy:

> Et maintenant a terre vient
> Par l'autre, que li lions tient,
> Que rescorre et tolir li viaut.
> (*Yv.* 5659–61)

The moral decisions remain with the hero, the lion serving to aid their execution.[41] It is striking that Yvain's most difficult adventure perfectly illustrates the themes of reciprocity, strength and compassion which run through all the adventures with the lion[42] and which are the basis of its significance.

The lion, associated with power and humility through the central notion of reciprocity, has been seen to represent the power of moral goodness, particularly when directed against the proud and in the service of the weak. It is, therefore, natural to enquire into the conditions which may have produced such a conception of the lion. The issue deserves to be examined in isolation from the hopelessly contentious question of the sources of the *Yvain* and its relationship to *Iarlles y Ffynnawn*, not least because the cultural determinants of Chrestien's lion have a much greater relevance to his audience's response than do his sources, about which they may be presumed to have known little or nothing. That the image of the lion was early present in Chrestien's mind may be inferred from an oblique indication in *Yv.* 31–2:

> Qu'ancor vaut miauz, ce m'est vis,
> Uns cortoiz morz qu'uns vilains vis.

This programmatic *sententia*, which contains *multum in parvo*, may be seen as an idealistic inversion of a verse from Ecclesiastes (IX, 4): *melior est canis vivus leone mortuo*. The conjunction of living – dead – lion is surely significant, for Chrestien has written a romance about a knight who transcends his initial moral *vilainie* (which leads to the burial of a *cortois morz* – Esclados) by undergoing a symbolic death (lament at the fountain following madness) and emerging with a new identity indicated by the companionship of a lion and the appellation *Li Chevaliers au lion*. The lion, saved from death by a knight newly *cortois*, crucially shares in the resolution of the problem posed by the two epigrams and is not the *leo ex machina* it is sometimes deemed to be.

At the fountain Esclados, who is described by his widow as a paragon of *cortoisie* (*Yv.* 1295), appears 'fiers par semblant come lions' (*Yv.* 488), reminding us of the lion as the common symbol of ferocious zeal.[43] On the other hand, this zeal is discriminating, as is revealed in the following account, which will lead us to the inspiration behind Chrestien's choice of his eponymous beast. In his *Chronica marchie trivixane* lib. X, c. 14 the thirteenth-century Italian writer Rolandinus of Padua describes how three hundred German soldiers fell on a camp of looters from Vicenza as they were dividing their spoil, killing some and capturing others (who were later massacred). He comments:

> Neque enim debet magnanimitas militum tollerare quemquam redditum vel vinculis alligatum, pro sue defensione persone in ore gladii deperire, si nobilitas attenderet, quod est dictum:
> *Parcere prostratis scit nobilis ira leonis* (var. leonum)
> *Pugna suum finem, cum iacet hostis, habet.*[44]

This quotation runs together two lines of distinct origins, both of which appear as *sententiae* in collections of proverbs and in medieval poetry. It is worth investigating their history.

The line *Parcere prostratis . . .* resumes an idea found in Isidore:

> Circa hominem leonum natura est ut nisi laesi nequeant irasci. Patet enim eorum misericordia exemplis assiduis. Prostratis enim parcunt; captivos obvios repatriare permittunt; hominem non nisi in magna fame interimunt.
>
> (*Etym.* XII, ii, 6)[45]

There already emerges here the crucial idea that the lion spares the defeated, which contrasts with Yvain's initial conduct at the fountain and his ruthless pursuit of the mortally wounded Esclados. Isidore's *Etymologiae* were, of course, commonly used in the schools and many passages were incorporated in later works, for example in the twelfth-century compilation *De bestiis et aliis rebus*:

> Quarta natura leonis est, quod nisi laesus fuerit, non facile irascitur. Patet enim eius misericordia, quod prostratis parcit. Unde versus:
> *Parcere prostratis scit nobilis ira leonis,*
> *Tu quoque fac simile quisquis dominaris in orbe.*
> Captivos homines sibi obvios repedare permittit, et non nisi prae magna

fame interimit. Ad cuius exemplum rationabiles homines respicere debent, qui non laesi irascuntur et innocentes opprimunt, cum eos Christiana lex dimittere iubeat liberos.[46]

The second line of the distich is different from that in Rolandinus and we will return to both later. For the present it may be noted that in *De bestiis* the basic Isidorean idea is accompanied by a moral *explicatio* as, indeed, it is in Alexander Nequam's account of the nature and significance of the lion in *De naturis rerum* c. cxlviii. He notes the fourth feature of the lion thus:

> Notandum est quod
> *Parcere subjectis scit nobilis ira leonis;*

and he explains in his *adaptatio*,

> Etsi enim fame acerrima agitetur et occurat ei homo prevolvens se ad pedes ipsius, parcit ei. Sic et regia nobilitas supplicibus veniam erogat. Nonne etiam et ipse Dominus superbis resistit, et humilibus parcit.[47]

To this is then added an exemplum about a soldier and a grateful lion!

There is thus no doubt that in the twelfth century the lion was often understood as showing mercy to the humble(d) (*prostratus / subjectus* might be interpreted literally as 'defeated' or morally as 'humble') and this derives from Isidore.

We are now left with the question of the two different lines which follow *Parcere prostratis . . .* in Rolandinus and *De bestiis*. In Rolandinus the second line is drawn from Ovid's *Tristia* lib. III, v. 33 where, in exile, he hopes for Augustus's forgiveness:

> quo quisque est maior, magis est placabilis irae,
> et faciles motus mens generosa capit.
> corpora magnanimo satis est prostrasse leoni,
> *pugna suum finem, cum iacet hostis, habet.*
> at lupus et turpes instant morientibus ursi
> et quaecumque minor nobilitate fera.
>
> (vv. 31–6)

We can now better understand how the introduction of the lion accords with a crucial change in the nature of Yvain's chivalry, a change which is important for the moral desiderata of a ruler, which Yvain, of course, becomes when he repossesses Laudine's lands. As an immature knight, Yvain hounds Esclados, but returns to the fountain at the end of the romance, ready to assume his responsibilities as lord of Laudine's territory and as vanquisher of the proud and defender of the weak. Claudian had already used the traditional self-control and *magnanimitas* of the lion to sing the praises of Stilico:

> obvia prosternas prostrataque more leonum despicias, alacres
> ardent qui frangere tauros, transiliunt praedas humiles.[48]

The lion, associated with humility, is contrasted with the bull, symbol of pride. We are reminded of the lion's attack on Harpin who:

> . . . bret et crie *come tors*;
> Que mout l'a li lions grevé.
> (*Yv.* 4228–9)

If we now consider the second line of the distich found in *De bestiis*, we are led irresistibly to the pseudo-Ovidian *De mirabilibus mundi*, a work of 126 leonine hexameters which seem to have been intended as rubrics for book illustrations or, possibly, wall paintings.[49] The poem is indebted to Isidore and Solinus and it has been conjectured that the author was Thierry, abbot of Saint-Trond from 1099 to 1107.[50] The 70th rubric runs:

> Parcere prostratis scit nobilis ira leonis;
> Tu quoque fac simile quisquis dominaris in orbe.

These two hexameters on the lion became extremely popular. They are found, for example, in a twelfth-century MS at Saint Omer which contains a group of epigrams devoted to the lion.[51] Another example of their use is found in Book 8 of Orderic Vitalis's Ecclesiastical History, where he discusses the treatment meted out by William Rufus to those (principally Odo of Bayeux) who had conspired against him and the pleas entered on their behalf by some of the people taking part with the king in the siege of Rochester:

> Decet nimirum ut sicut tumidos et vecordes vicisti fortitudine, sic humiliatis et penitentibus parcas mansuetudine. Severitatem regiam temperet clementia et gloriae virtutis tuae sufficiat celebris victoria . . . [there is then cited the example of David and his treatment of Shimei and Absalom] . . . In divinis voluminibus abundant exempla huiusmodi, a quibus non discrepat sagax poeta in libello de mirabilibus mundi,
> *Parcere prostratis scit nobilis ira leonis,*
> *Tu quoque fac simile quisquis dominaris in orbe.*[52]

It seems reasonable, therefore, to conclude from our study that, as Chrestien humorously indicates, no allegorical meaning is to be attached to the lion in

Yvain. On the other hand, its moral significance in the romance, which we defined as the representation of strength and humility through the notion of reciprocity, is entirely consonant with a tradition, derived from Ovid and Isidore and embodied in a popular hexameter in the *De mirabilibus mundi*, which was commonly associated with the moral attributes desirable in rulers. The lion was thereby supremely fitted to incarnate the theme of ferocity towards the proud and humility towards the oppressed which occupies such a major portion of the second part of the *Yvain*.[53] In such a view of chivalric service the knight achieves his apogee. The case of Yvain's lion may, therefore, serve to remind us that many details in Chrestien can be elucidated by reference to the Latin culture of his time, rather than by recourse to Celtic sources or scriptural exegesis.

The Arthurian Allusions in the Black Book of Carmarthen

A. O. H. JARMAN

THE Black Book of Carmarthen, a manuscript of a hundred and eight small pages, six and three-quarter inches by five, has been known by this title since the sixteenth century and is now kept at the National Library of Wales. It contains an anthology of some forty poems, consisting of 1,927 lines, and between ten and eleven thousand lexical items. Written in a liturgical script it has been described as a 'palaeographical freak', in that it combines certain archaisms, such as majuscule R's and N's, with a number of later features.[1] The letters exhibit a basically similar formation throughout the manuscript but they nevertheless tend to become progressively smaller, with the result that, while each of the first five pages contains only nine lines of text, the number increases to twelve, fifteen, sixteen, and then as many as twenty or twenty-one. It was perhaps on account of this characteristic that Dr Gwenogvryn Evans expressed the opinion in 1899 that the Black Book was written by 'several hands of the XIIth and early XIIIth centuries'.[2] The manuscript also contains a number of *lacunae*. Quires are missing in at least three places, with the result that the text of three or four of the poems is incomplete. This led Sir Ifor Williams to conclude that the Black Book consists of portions of at least three manuscripts bound together, with the implied suggestion that they were written by different scribes although, admittedly, they derived from the same scriptorium.[3]

The dating of c. 1200 proposed by Dr Gwenogvryn Evans and other contemporary palaeographers, such as Sir Frederick Madden of the British Museum and W. D. Macray of the Bodleian Library, was generally accepted and has held the field for many decades.[4] As a result the Black Book has enjoyed the prestige of being deemed to be the oldest surviving manuscript written entirely in Welsh. It has indeed been regarded as something of a national institution and the publication by Dr Gwenogvryn Evans of the Facsimile in

1888 and the 'Diplomatic Edition' in 1906 were exciting occasions. The latter, which is now a collector's piece, was issued by Dr Evans from his private press at Llanbedrog, near Pwllheli. It uses characters of various sizes to reproduce the text page for page and line for line, and most of the large initials are traced copies of the originals. The text of the manuscript contains certain ortho-graphical features, such as the use of *t* for *dd*, *d* for *d*, and *w* for *f* (= *v*), which appear quite uniformly, and as these differ both from the Old Welsh spelling (i.e. up to 1100) and from that of c. 1300, they have been taken as representing the orthography prevailing at about 1200. Modern Welsh scholars have used these features as a kind of yardstick or standard for dating, so that any text containing them is assumed to be derived from an original written close to 1200 even if it is only found in much later manuscripts. Some confusion of the issue, however, has been caused in recent years by the fact that two palaeographers, the late Drs H. D. Emanuel and N. Denholm-Young, have rejected the 1200 date for the Black Book and opted for the second quarter of the thirteenth century (1225–50).[5] Dr E. D. Jones, formerly National Librarian of Wales, has now completed a detailed palaeographical study of the manuscript and his conclusion is that 'none of it was written much before 1250 but that the writing of it continued for a considerable time after that date.'[6] He is further of the opinion that it was written by one scribe, but over a lengthy space of time and indeed at various periods during his life.

If we are asked where the Black Book was written, we are in no position to provide a satisfactory answer. Traditionally it is associated with Carmarthen, but the tradition is not known to be earlier than the sixteenth century. We possess no information concerning the history of the manuscript in the Middle Ages. It has been argued that it contains many references to places in south-west Wales, and it is certainly true that a Carmarthen association can be claimed on the basis of the inclusion within it of poems ascribed to Myrddin, or Merlin, who had very definite links with the town of Carmarthen. The earliest surviving item of information concerning its history is a statement that it was given, presumably in the 1530's, by a treasurer of St David's Cathedral to Sir John Prys, one of Henry VIII's commissioners for the dissolution of the monasteries, and that it had come originally from the Priory of St John's at Carmarthen.[7] Sir John Prys was an enthusiastic Welsh antiquary and preserved the manuscript. He was, in fact, the first to quote from it in print; this he did in his *Historiae Britannicae Defensio* (1573), written to defend the authenticity of Geoffrey of Monmouth's account of Arthur against the attacks of Polydore Vergil.[8]

There existed at Carmarthen an ancient Welsh religious house, the Priory of St John the Evangelist and Teulyddog, but this was taken over by the Normans in the twelfth century and converted into an Augustinian establishment. The ancient fort and town of Carmarthen went back to Roman times, and earlier, but in the period with which we are concerned it was a centre of Norman power. The Augustinian priory was small and enjoyed no great wealth. It has been argued that a manuscript like the Black Book of Carmarthen, which contains a central core of prophetic poetry of a very nationalist and anti-Norman character, is not the sort of product one would expect to emanate from such an institution. We have, however, little knowledge of the situation in the priory at the turn of the thirteenth century. Possibly Welsh and Norman influences alternated. After the death of Henry II in 1189 royal control over the priory appears to have weakened. In 1208 a certain Cadifor (presumably a Welshman) was prior, and pressures to oust him by a group of canons from Llanthony by Gloucester were resisted by King John. For eight years, from 1215 until 1223, Carmarthen was in the possession of Llywelyn the Great, prince of Gwynedd, and the Welsh element in the priory may easily have received reinforcement during this period. The process, however, was reversed during the long reign of Henry III (1216–72).[9] There exists a long religious poem, extolling the virtue of penitence, composed in Norman French in the mid thirteenth century and ascribed to 'Simun de Kermerthin',[10] but we do not possess a copy of it written at Carmarthen, and the Black Book is the only Welsh manuscript which can claim any association with the priory. It is perhaps permissible to envisage the scribe as a Welshman who had become a member of the religious community fairly early in the century and had learnt liturgical script although he was not a professional copyist. He had literary interests and over a period of years compiled his own anthology of verse. In spite of the progressive Normanization, his interest in Welsh poetry, which provided solace for him in his increasing isolation, was not discouraged. This, of course, is conjecture. Dr E. D. Jones accepts the Carmarthen tradition, but it has also been argued that the Black Book is the product of some other more Welsh-orientated religious house, such as Whitland (Hendy-gwyn), Talley (Talyllychau), or Strata Florida (Ystrad Fflur).[11]

The scribe's tastes in poetry were varied and the poems included in his anthology fall into four categories: (1) fourteen religious poems; (2) seven panegyric poems; (3) four vaticinations attributed to Myrddin; and (4) fourteen poems on various legendary themes. Only one poem, a collection of proverbs, fails to fit into any of these categories. There are no early heroic poems comparable with the sixth-century eulogies of Urien Rheged by Taliesin or the *Gododdin* of Aneirin. The entire contents of the Black Book belong to the period from the ninth to the thirteenth centuries and may be described as a mixture of late *hengerdd* ('old verse') and of some typically medieval poetry. The former contains many memories and echoes of the earlier tradition, including references to its North British setting, while the latter is well represented by four of the poems of Cynddelw Brydydd Mawr, who flourished 1155–1200. The latest datable reference in the poems is to King John's expeditions against Gwynedd in 1211, which involved the seizure of Degannwy and the sacking of Bangor, and the subsequent revolt of the Welsh under Llywelyn in 1212.[12] This is found in a prophecy probably composed soon after the event, though attributed to Myrddin. The scribe does not seem to have included any poems composed later than the early thirteenth century in his anthology. All the poems in the Black Book are anonymous, apart from the four by Cynddelw and three others ascribed to obscure poets named Elaeth and Addaon. The scribe, of course, probably believed that the vaticinatory poems were the genuine prophecies of Myrddin in the sixth century, but this view cannot now be sustained.

We are not here concerned with the religious poems. It may be noted in passing, however, that they deal with a considerable variety of subjects and that among them are found a Celtic nature poem of the type usually associated with the early saints, an example of the debate between the body and the soul, a penitential pilgrimage-poem, and a narrative poem recounting the legend of the Miracle of the Instantaneous Harvest. According to Professor K. Jackson the latter is the earliest known example in medieval literature of this legend, which is also found in France, the Netherlands, Ireland, as well as in the later folklore of many other countries.[13] Nor, with one exception, are we concerned with the panegyric poems. These are mostly laudations of twelfth-century princes, but one is a poem to the war-band or retinue of Madog ap Maredudd, prince of Powys, who died in 1160. It is by Cynddelw Brydydd Mawr who, at that date, was a young poet at the threshold of his career. In one line the sound of Madog's retinue is compared to 'the cry of the host of Arthur's war-band'. This admittedly does not tell us very much, apart from being evidence of the fame of Arthur in Powys in the mid twelfth century. In other lines similar comparisons are made with the war-bands of Benlli Gawr and Cynon. Benlli the 'Giant', or perhaps 'Champion', is at best a semi-historical figure, if as much. He appears in Nennius's *Historia Brittonum* as a wicked king and abominable tyrant who, presumably in early fifth-century Powys, refused to admit Saint Germanus to his fort to preach the Gospel.[14] He and his fort and its inhabitants were subsequently destroyed by fire from heaven. References occur in medieval Welsh verse to Benlli's valour as well as his tyranny. Cynon we may take to be Cynon ap Clydno Eidyn, a hero of the *Gododdin* and probably a historical figure although the evidence for him is found in sources of a poetic rather than a historical nature.[15] He appears in the Welsh romance of *Owain*, where he corresponds to Calogrenant in Chrétien's *Yvain*, and he is thus an Arthurian character. He was the only one of the heroes celebrated by Aneirin to achieve this distinction, which involved his being moved backwards in time some three generations from the end to the beginning of the sixth century. The mention of Arthur in the company of Benlli and Cynon in this poem shows that, as was common in the Middle Ages, Cynddelw thought of him as inhabiting the undefined borderland between history and legend.

The poems found in the third category, vaticinations ascribed to Myrddin, can claim to be within the Arthurian ambit, although their content is closer to the periphery than to the centre. Myrddin, or Merlin, was of course a most important Arthurian character, but in these poems we find substantial fragments of his legend in its pre-Arthurian form. The theme of vaticination, largely political but sometimes in more general terms, which Geoffrey of Monmouth introduced to the literary world c. 1134, and later incorporated into his *Historia Regum Britanniae*, under the title *Prophetiae Merlini*, was extracted by him from Welsh traditions associated with the names of Myrddin and Taliesin, to whom a large number of prophecies were attributed. Examples of these are the Black Book poems *Y Bedwenni* ('The Birch-trees'), *Yr Afallennau* ('The Apple-trees') and *Yr Oianau* ('The Greetings'). A fourth poem *Ymddiddan Myrddin a Thaliesin* ('The Dialogue of Myrddin and Taliesin') also contains some prophecy although it differs from the standard type.[16] All these poems contain two layers or strata, the legendary and the vaticinatory, which are related but best discussed separately.

The prophecies in the poems are uttered in the first person by Myrddin, who is portrayed as a wild man living in *Coed Celyddon* or the 'Caledonian Forest', whither he is represented as having fled after losing his reason in the battle of Arfderydd, or Arthuret, nine miles north of Carlisle. This battle was probably a historical encounter fought between rival chieftains c. 573 A.D. With his lapse into madness Myrddin acquired the gift of prophecy. Many of the predictions in the poems are couched in very general terms and merely foretell ultimate victory for the Welsh over their enemies. Myrddin's name had been cited as an authority for this kind of vaticination in the political poem *Armes Prydain* ('The Prophecy of Britain'), dated c. 930, but the tradition of prophesying a final Welsh or 'British' victory existed independently of Myrddin and is found attached to the legend of the two dragons in Vortigern's tower in the ninth-century *Historia Brittonum*. In 1136, in his own *Historia*, Geoffrey lifted this tale in its entirety from Nennius's compilation but substituted the name *Merlinus*, based on the Welsh *Merddin* (a variant of *Myrddin*), for that of the principal character, *Ambrosius*. He thus gave currency to a new legend of Merlin, which later was absorbed into the Arthurian complex. Although constructed out of previously existing materials, this legend was essentially Geoffrey's creation. But in his poem *Vita Merlini*, composed twelve years after the *Historia*, Geoffrey reverted to the original Welsh tradition and portrayed Merlin as a wild man of the woods. The discrepancy between the two portraits he explained by asserting that in the poem Merlin had lived on into a new age. The Myrddin of the Black Book of Carmarthen, however, has nothing in common with the Merlin of Vortigern's tower, apart from the power of prophecy which both possess. In the Welsh poems Myrddin grieves for the loss of his lord Gwenddolau and declares that he has himself been guilty of causing the death of his sister Gwenddydd's son. He lives in daily fear of capture by the men of Rhydderch, apparently the victor at the battle of Arfderydd, and he complains bitterly of the hardships he endures in the forest.[17]

The vaticinations found in these poems were used for propagandist purposes to strengthen the morale of the Welsh forces in their struggles against foreign invaders. Ultimate victory was promised in vague general terms, and the credibility of the promise buttressed by very specific prophecies referring to contemporary events. Thus, the first stanza of the Black Book text of the *Afallennau* states that there will be a 'Wednesday of blood' in the valley of the Machafwy in Elfael, when the English will be victorious. It adds that this will be followed, at an unspecified but later date, by a Thursday when the Welsh will overwhelm their enemies at Cyminawd, a place of uncertain location. There can be no doubt that the first prediction refers to the disastrous defeat suffered by the Welsh at the hands of the English at the battle of Machafwy on August the 12th, 1198, which fell on a Wednesday.[18] If Myrddin could foretell this event so accurately, so it must have been argued, why should he not also be believed when he prophesies that the tables will ultimately be turned in favour of the Welsh? In his *Prophetiae Merlini* Geoffrey does not reproduce details of this kind from the Welsh poems. It is not known how much Welsh he knew, but it was probably not sufficient for this purpose. One theme, however, deriving from Welsh verse occurs in both the *Historia Regum Britanniae* and the *Vita Merlini*, namely the prophesied return of the deliverers Cadwaladr and Cynan (*Cadualadrus* and *Conanus*) from the past to lead the Welsh to victory. Cadwaladr, a historical figure of the seventh century, was the son of Cadwallon who, with Penda of Mercia, devastated the north of England before he himself fell at Hexham in 634. The son is a shadowy figure compared with the father, but perhaps the qualities of the latter were transferred in popular memory to the former. There is less certainty as to who Cynan was, but recent scholars have taken him to be Cynan Meiriadog, 'the legendary founder of the Breton colony'.[19] In medieval Wales the two were coupled together as *meibion darogan* ('sons of prophecy'), and their return expected.[20] Cadwaladr is named five times in the Black Book poems, and Cynan three times. Both also figure in the poem *Armes Prydain*, in which their coming is predicted as leaders of a pan-Celtic-plus-Norse confederation to deliver the whole of the Island of Britain into the possession of the Welsh. This may have been the ultimate source of Geoffrey's information concerning them. It is clear too that, when he came to compose the *Vita Merlini*, he was aware of the content of the Myrddin legend as it is found in the *Afallennau* and the other Welsh poems which embody it, for his Guennolous, Rodarchus and Ganieda correspond to the Gwenddolau, Rhydderch and Gwenddydd of the poems. Similarly, the complaint of Merlinus in the forest in winter that his apple-trees have been taken from him can hardly fail to be related to Myrddin's addresses to the apple-tree in *Yr Afallennau*.[21]

It is also probable that Geoffrey was aware of the existence of the 'Dialogue of Myrddin and Taliesin', for he brings the two seers, whom he calls Merlinus and Telgesinus, together in the *Vita Merlini* and makes them engage in a lengthy conversation. The contents of the two dialogues, however, have nothing in common. It may be noted incidentally that it is in the first of the speeches of Telgesinus that we find the earliest account of the conveying of Arthur, wounded at Camlan, by ship to be healed by Morgen in the 'Island of Apples called the Fortunate Isle'.[22] There is none of this in the Welsh poems, but the name *Insula Pomorum* reminds us of the difficult and complex problems raised by the names *Afallach*, *Afallon*, *Avalon*, *Insula Avallonis*, etc., and we wonder what deeper significance attached to Myrddin's apple-trees in the forest.[23] The Black Book 'Dialogue' is concerned with two battles, one of which appears to have been fought in Dyfed early in the sixth century, while the other was the battle of Arfderydd.[24] One line refers to the death of three 'men of note' in the first of these battles. In the *Vita Merlini* Geoffrey ascribes Merlin's madness to his grief at the fall of three of his brothers in battle. This detail, thus adapted, may conceivably be derived from the Welsh poem, through an informant.

We now come to the fourth category, which consists of fourteen poems on legendary themes. Arthurian references occur in several of these, but for two or three a brief mention will be sufficient. The Black Book contains a fragment of *Trioedd y Meirch*, the 'Triads of the Horses', which actually is not a poem but merely a list of the horses of famous heroes.[25] Four of these have Arthurian associations, namely Carnaflawg ('Cloven Hoof'), the horse of Owain son of Urien; Gwinau Goddwf Hir ('Chestnut Long-Neck'), the horse of Cai; Ceingaled ('Hard Back'), the horse of Gwalchmai; and Lluagor ('Host-opener'), the horse of Caradog Freichfras. We cannot, however, be sure whether the reference to Owain is to the original northern warrior-prince, or to the hero of romance which he later became.[26] Ceingaled corresponds to Guingalet or Gringalet, the celebrated horse of Gauvain in *Erec*.[27] The relationship of the Welsh to the French forms has been the subject of some controversy, but the original name could have been *Gwyngaled*, 'Fair and Hard'. *Lluagor* is considered to have been the original of the name of the foal *Loriagort* or Lorzagor in the *Livre de Carados*.[28] The list does not throw light on the way the names found their way into French romance, but the occurrence of the name of Gilberd mab Cadgyffro ('G. son of Battle-Tumult') in one triad is suggestive of contact between the Welsh and Norman communities at, at least, some kind of a cultural level.[29] There were Gilberts of the Clare family in Ceredigion during the first half of the twelfth century.

References to Owain son of Urien also occur in another poem in this category, entitled *Mechydd ap Llywarch*.[30] This belongs to the body of saga-poetry associated with Llywarch Hen, which has been dated by Sir Ifor Williams in the ninth century. Parts of the poem are obscure, but in it a certain Pelis declares that he has been nurtured by 'Owain Rheged' and that he follows him on a white charger. The subject-matter is concerned with memories of conflicts in the sixth century among the Britons of the North but the poem is clearly too late to be classified with the Taliesin poetry in which the historical Owain figures. It is, on the other hand, probably too early to contain a reference to the Owain of romance.

Another Arthurian hero, Geraint, is the subject of a poem containing eighteen *englynion* entitled *Gereint fil' erbin* in the manuscript. It has recently been edited by Professor Brynley Roberts, who adopts the view that it is a eulogy rather than an elegy, as it has been interpreted by some critics.[31] It is, however, not contemporary with its subject and may probably be dated c. 900–1100. Geraint was a Dumnonian prince who is believed to have flourished about 580/600 A.D.,[32] which was also the period of the heroes praised by Taliesin and Aneirin in northern Britain. A reference occurs in the *Gododdin* to a Geraint whose 'battle-cry was raised in front of the men of the South' and Dr Rachel Bromwich has suggested that, as the army which Mynyddog Mwyn-fawr sent from Edinburgh to attack the advancing Angles at Catraeth c. 600 'was assembled from all parts of the British world', the two Geraints could have been identical.[33] Professor Jackson, on the other hand, has argued that references to 'the South' in the *Gododdin* need not necessarily be to southern Britain. They could very well, and perhaps more probably, mean areas such as Rheged or Elmet which, although much nearer to Mynyddog's court, were still to the south of Gododdin territory.[34] If the Dumnonian Geraint had in fact joined Mynyddog's war-band as a young man and fought at the battle of Catraeth until he fell (as did all the members of the war-band), it would indeed be difficult to explain the prominence accorded him in later south-western tradition. The Geraint of the Black Book poem is not, of course, the Geraint of the romance of *Geraint and Enid*. He is a chieftain or military commander who, valiantly supported by the men of Devon, fights against an unnamed enemy at a place called Llongborth, which could have been Langport in Somerset. One stanza in the poem states that Arthur was present at the battle:

> In Llongborth I saw Arthur –
> Brave men hewed with steel –
> Emperor, ruler of battle.

The description of Arthur as 'emperor' (*ameraudur*) may perhaps be taken as foreshadowing the portrayal of him found in Geoffrey's *Historia* and the romances. The 'imperial' character of the portrait should not, however, be overemphasized, for the strict meaning of the word is probably closer to 'general, commander', etc. We certainly have here an early instance of the intrusion of Arthur into the traditions of the South-west. It is, of course, anachronistic, for the 'historical' Arthur would have preceded Geraint by some three generations. There is in the poem no suggestion that the two were related, although in *Geraint and Enid* Geraint is described as Arthur's cousin. This has been attributed to the influence of Geoffrey.[35]

Several poems in the Black Book are in dialogue form and of these one is entirely Arthurian, while another contains a passing Arthurian reference. The latter is 'The Dialogue of Gwyddneu Garanhir and Gwyn ap Nudd', and is probably to be dated c. 900–1100.[36] Both Gwyddneu and Gwyn figure in early Welsh tradition, though not in an Arthurian context. At the end of the poem Gwyddneu (apparently) declares that he has been, presumably as a witness, at places where numerous heroes were slain. In one stanza he says:

> I have been where was killed Llacheu,
> son of Arthur, wonderful in songs,
> when ravens croaked over blood.

However 'wonderful' Llacheu was in the eyes of the poets, he is an obscure character. His name occurs a number of times in later verse (i.e. after c. 1150), and the thirteenth-century poet Bleddyn Fardd (fl. 1268–83) refers to his death 'below Llech Ysgar'. The Triads and the *Dream of Rhonabwy* mention him. The other Arthurian dialogue poem (discussed below) states that Cai and Llacheu 'fought battles'. In the Welsh version of *Perlesvaus* the name *Llacheu* is used for *Loholt*, whom Cai (Keu) treacherously kills, although there is some doubt as to how early the two names were associated. In view of these references we may no doubt endorse Dr R. Bromwich's opinion that 'Llacheu was a figure of considerable importance in early Arthurian saga, and . . . belonged to an early stratum of Arthurian tradition in Wales'.[37]

The other dialogue poem in the Black Book, mentioned above, is the 'Dialogue of Arthur and Glewlwyd Gafaelfawr'. It contains ninety lines but, unfortunately, breaks off in the middle of a very intriguing sentence, owing to a gap in the manuscript. In spite of some difficult textual problems it has been translated into English, fairly tentatively, several times, and edited recently by Professor Brynley F. Roberts.[38] Its probable date is, again, the tenth or eleventh century.[39] The actual dialogue is confined to the poem's first nine or ten lines, after which it becomes (for the most part, at least) a monologue spoken by Arthur. It opens with a series of exchanges between Arthur and Glewlwyd Gafaelfawr ('G. Mighty-grasp'), who is presented as the gate-keeper of a fortress to which Arthur, accompanied by a band of followers, seeks admittance. In reply to an inquiry by Arthur, Glewlwyd identifies himself and asks Arthur to do likewise. The latter declares that 'Arthur and Fair Cai' are at the gate, attended by 'the best men in the world'. Glewlwyd then informs Arthur that he will not gain admittance until he reveals who his men are. Arthur's monologue follows, consisting mostly of a list of characters in whom magical and fantastic powers are combined with the primitive heroic virtues. Here we have the earliest known assembling of Arthur's 'knights', many of whom are obscure but some well-known in later legend. Their milieu and associations and the atmosphere they bring with them are those of the earliest extant Arthurian prose tale, *Culhwch and Olwen*, and most of the names in the poem also occur in the tale. The first well-known character in the list is Mabon son of Modron, who is described as the 'servant of Uthr Pendragon'. In an episode in *Culhwch and Olwen* he appears as a prisoner, confined at Gloucester since he was three nights old, whose aid is required for the hunting of Twrch Trwyth and who is rescued from his captivity by Arthur, Cai and Bedwyr. The name *Mabon* is derived from that of the Celtic god *Maponos*, whom the Romans identified with Apollo, and to whom dedications are found in inscriptions in northern Britain. The name of his mother *Modron* is similarly derived from that of the Mother-goddess *Matrona*, which still survives in the French river-name *Marne*, as well as in the alternative Welsh form *Madrun*.[40] In no other Welsh text, however, is Mabon associated with Uthr Pendragon. In Geoffrey's *Historia* Uthr (Uther) is Arthur's father, and there are indications that this was so in earlier Welsh traditions.[41] Both Uthr and Mabon, of course, later appeared in Continental literature, but they were not in any way connected with each other.

A few lines further down Arthur names another Mabon, the son of Mellt (Ms. *Melld*). This name, which also occurs in *Culhwch and Olwen*, presents a problem. The two Mabons could be doublets. In Mabon son of Modron we have a matronymic, an example of the early practice of naming the mothers, rather than the fathers, of heroes. Could Mellt have been Mabon's father? In Welsh the name is also the common word for 'lightning' and T. F. O'Rahilly suggested that there existed 'a deity called *Meldos*, which may be interpreted as "thunderbolt, lightning-stroke"', and whose name survived as *Mellt*.[42] This, however, is not certain. Sir Ifor Williams made a case for deriving the name from a root **meldo-*, meaning 'gentle, mild, pleasant', which gave the second element in an Irish name for the Otherworld, *Mag Mell*, the 'Plain of Happiness', and possibly in the name of *Rhieinfellt*, a great-grand-daughter of Urien Rheged, apparently a gentle maiden who became the wife of Oswy of Northumbria in (or c.) 635 and thus helped to terminate a chapter of ancient enmities by a dynastic marriage.[43] It is therefore not clear whether Mellt in the Black Book poem is male or female.

Between the two Mabons Arthur mentions Manawydan son of Llŷr, whom he describes as 'profound of counsel'. Here we have a leading character from the Mabinogi. On the whole the medieval story-tellers succeeded in keeping the matter of the Arthurian cycle separate from that of the Mabinogi, and neither Arthur nor any member of his entourage appear in the Four Branches. Occasionally, however, characters from the one cycle obtrude upon the other. Manawydan must at one stage have been identical with the Irish sea-god Manannán mac Lir, famed for his cunning and the terror of seafaring men, but the exact relationship of the two is an intractable problem. As portrayed in medieval tales their characters are fundamentally opposed, although sagacity is a quality attributed to both. In the poem Manawydan is said to have 'brought shattered shields (*or* spears) from Tryfrwyd', a name which occurs in the list of Arthur's battles in the *Historia Brittonum*.[44] The Mabinogi, however, portrays Manawydan, not as a warrior, but as a long-suffering Christian gentleman (despite the story's pagan setting) and as a conscious advocate, and practiser, of conciliation.[45]

After mentioning two other characters possessing apparently superhuman or magical powers, Anwas the Winged and Llwch Windy-handed,[46] who are also named in *Culhwch and Olwen*, Arthur proceeds to a eulogy of his two most outstanding followers, Cai (Kay) and Bedwyr (Bedivere). The greater part of the remainder of the poem (some sixty lines) is devoted to praise of the two, and of Cai in particular. Bedwyr is said to be the steady leader of an army, dauntless in his use of sword and shield, whose enemies fell before him by the hundred. Cai, who is the principal hero of the poem, is described as one who cannot be slain, unless God wills it. He too strikes down his foes by the hundred and, as we have seen, has fought battles with Llacheu.[47] After killing nine witches he has gone to Anglesey to destroy lions and to fight against the man-devouring monster, *Cath Paluc*. The reference to 'lions' need not be taken too literally. Opportunities for the inhabitants of Anglesey even to know what a lion looked like were slim indeed in the early Middle Ages and the form *lleuon*, derived regularly from the Latin *leones*, would no doubt convey images of a wide variety of ferocious creatures of the imagination. *Cath Paluc* must have been one of these. *Paluc* has been explained as an adjective meaning 'cutting, lopping, scratching, clawing', etc., – thus the 'Clawing Cat', – although later, in the Triads, it was converted into the name of the Cat's owner.[48] The text breaks off just as Cai is coming to blows with the creature so that we are not made aware of the exact outcome of the encounter. The Cat makes its appearance again, however, in French romance. In the *Estoire de Merlin* Arthur fights victoriously against a monster cat near Lake Bourget in the French Alps and the memory of the occasion is still perpetuated in the area by the names *Col du Chat*, *Dent du Chat* and *Mont du Chat*. On the other hand, in the late twelfth-century *Romanz des Franceis* Arthur is himself slain by a monster cat called *Capalu*, which then crosses over to England, conquers the country, and wears the crown. Discussing this tale, Dr Bromwich has made the suggestion that it contains a genuine variant of the tradition of Arthur's end, which was later superseded by an account of his death in battle at Camlan conflated with another story telling of his removal to the island of Avallon.[49] This could no doubt have reflected a change in the tastes of audiences, a desire for a greater sophistication than was provided by the earlier and more primitive tales.

Apparently interpolated into the passage describing Cai and Bedwyr are eight lines which refer in the third person to Arthur himself. They reveal a weird and fantastic world reminiscent of that portrayed in some of the earlier Irish sagas. Arthur fights with a hag in the hall of Awarnach; he strikes Penpalach in the dwellings of Disethach; on the mountain of Eidyn he fights

109

with dogheads. Penpalach has been translated as 'Cudgel-head',[50] and the dogheads were presumably either weapons thus fashioned or 'a vague recollection of the fabulous Cynocephali'.[51] Some uncertainty, however, attaches to the text of this passage, for it has been argued that *arthur* is the scribe's misreading of *aruth(i)r* in his exemplar.[52] If this were accepted it would mean that the reference is to Cai rather than to Arthur. In favour of the reading *arthur* it may be pointed out that in *Culhwch and Olwen* Arthur does fight with a hag, or witch, though we are not told that this occurred 'in the hall of Awarnach'; on the other hand, in the same tale Cai enters the hall of the giant *Wrnach* and strikes off his head. The halls of Disethach are unknown and we can only presume that the mountain of Eidyn was at, or near, Edinburgh.

It is clear that the Arthur we meet in this poem is not the figure we are familiar with in early annals and medieval chronicles, or in the romances. He is rather a hero of folklore, the leader of a band of strange and wonderful characters derived from ancient Welsh and Celtic tradition. The view has been held that there had existed a 'mythological' Arthur, who was quite distinct from the military leader of the fifth/sixth century, and that the imprint of his memory is to be found in such works as *Culhwch and Olwen*, the poem we are now discussing, and another poem preserved in the Book of Taliesin entitled 'The Spoils of Annwfn', in which Arthur leads an expedition against the Otherworld.[53] If we reject this view, as being conjectural in the absence of hard supporting evidence, we have to note the complete transformation of Arthur, the historical or at least semi-historical 'leader of armies' of Nennius and other early sources, in a period of some four hundred years, by the interaction of popular memory and imagination, into the head of a company of folk-heroes who exercise marvellous and superhuman powers. Cai and Bedwyr belong to the same world as the Celtic hero *par excellence*, Cú Chulainn, who was able to go without sleep from the feast of Samain (November the 1st.) until the following harvest and whose powers of marksmanship were such that he could kill eight of a group of nine warriors with one cast of his javelin and leave the ninth unharmed. A wound inflicted by Cú Chulainn could only be healed by himself, and his innate ardour was such that, during an attempt made to calm him, he successively heated three vatfuls of cold water into which he was plunged.[54] In *Culhwch and Olwen* similar, though somewhat less spectacular, powers are attributed to the Welsh heroes. Thus, Cai was able to hold his breath under water for nine days and nine nights, and also to go without sleep for the same length of time; when he wished he could make himself as tall as the tallest tree in the forest; and no physician might heal a wound inflicted by his sword. So great was his natural heat that anything he held in his hand would remain dry for a handbreath before his hand and a handbreadth behind it, even when the rain was heaviest.[55] It should be noted that qualities such as these are not attributed to Arthur himself. As a warrior-hero in a folklore milieu he was, of course, invincible. But he was not so completely integrated into the world of marvels which enveloped him as to be dependent on the aid of magical powers rather than on the strength of his own right arm. This, no doubt, made it easier for Geoffrey in the twelfth century to depict him as a feudal monarch, rather than as a king of faery.

One other poem in the Black Book, 'The Stanzas of the Graves' (*Englynion y Beddau*), remains to be noticed. It consists of seventy-three *englynion*, mostly of three lines, recording the burial-places of ancient heroes.[56] They belong to the heroic saga tradition and were dated by Professor Thomas Jones in the ninth or tenth century. The heroes named, and sometimes celebrated in brief, pregnant phrases, belong to legend and folklore rather than to history, although a few were originally historical. Many are completely unknown from any other source. The names of a number of Arthurian personages appear, including Gwalchmai, Cynon ap Clydno Eidyn, Bedwyr and Owain ab Urien. The most interesting name, however, is that of Arthur himself, which occurs in the third line of a stanza rendered thus by Professor Thomas Jones:

> There is a grave for March, a grave for Gwythur,
> a grave for Gwgawn Red-sword;
> the world's wonder a grave for Arthur.[57]

The word translated 'wonder', *anoeth*, literally signifies something difficult, or even impossible, to obtain or achieve, and an alternative translation of the third line, based on a textual emendation proposed by Sir Ifor Williams, reads: 'Arthur's grave is something not to be found until the Day of Judgement'.[58] The import of the line, however, would not be affected by the emendation. The poet is saying that, although he can point to the graves of many other heroes, that of Arthur remains a mystery and is not to be found. It may be noted that another stanza specifically mentions the battle of Camlan at which, according to the *Annales Cambriae*, Arthur and Medrawd fell in 537.[59]

In his *Gesta Regum Anglorum* (c. 1125) the historian William of Malmesbury made the statement that 'the tomb of Arthur is nowhere beheld, whence ancient ditties fable that he is yet to come'.[60] This is very close to the Black Book *englyn*, but more specific, as it prophesies Arthur's return. The *englyn* is, in fact, the only example we possess of the so-called 'ancient ditties' (the phrase in the text is *antiquitas naeniarum*). There is, however, other evidence from this period of a belief in the survival or expected return of Arthur. When a party of canons from Laon came to Bodmin in Cornwall in 1113 they provoked a near riot because a local man maintained that Arthur still lived, a claim which the French visitors were so impolitic as to deny. In an account of the incident written in 1146 Hermann of Tournai comments that 'the Bretons are wont to quarrel with the French on behalf of King Arthur'.[61] Also, at the end of the Arthurian section of the *Historia Regum Britanniae*, Geoffrey asserted that Arthur 'was mortally wounded and was carried off to the Isle of Avalon, so that

111

his wounds might be attended to'.[62] This ambivalent statement was no doubt designed to satisfy both Norman and Welsh or Breton audiences. With it may be compared Geoffrey's more detailed treatment of the subject in his *Vita Merlini*, where Telgesinus recounts, as we have already noted, how the wounded Arthur was taken after the battle of Camlan to the *Insula Pomorum* to receive the ministrations of Morgen. The latter, we are told, 'put the king in her chamber on a golden bed, uncovered his wound with her noble hand', and at length said 'he could be cured if only he stayed with her a long while and accepted her treatment'.[63] After completing his account of this incident Telgesinus declares that, in view of the oppression of the Britons by the Saxons, a message should be sent to Arthur calling on him to return as leader 'to fend off the enemy and re-establish the nation in its old state of peace'. Merlinus, however, contradicts this declaration and asserts that the enemy will not be repelled in this way but that, after many years, Conanus will arrive from Brittany and join with Cadualadrus, the revered leader of the Welsh, to create an alliance of the Scots, the Welsh, the Cornishmen and the Bretons to 'restore to the natives the crown that had been lost'. We have already seen that here Geoffrey was using the tradition which was first given literary expression in *Armes Prydain*. To the names of Cynan and Cadwaladr, as expected deliverers, there was added in the fourteenth and fifteenth centuries that of Owain, a development which no doubt reflected the fame of Owain Lawgoch (c. 1330–78) and Owain Glyndŵr (c. 1354–1416). The concept of the *mab darogan* was therefore not exclusively associated with the name of Arthur. The importance which the authorities attached to the belief in his return in the twelfth century is, however, underlined by the reported 'discovery' of his body, together with that of his queen Guinevere, in a tomb at Glastonbury c. 1190.[64] The tomb was again opened by order of Edward I in 1278, a critical time in the king's relations with the Welsh, in order to demonstrate that the concept of *rex quondam, rex futurus* could at best only be a half-truth. It is strange that the only evidence for it in Welsh from the period is the one line in the *englyn* in the Black Book of Carmarthen.[65]

The Ideal of Queenship
in Hartmann's Erec

LEWIS JILLINGS

IN *Erec* Hartmann von Aue depicts the growth of an immature and aggressive young knight through self-knowledge to maturity and the status of a Christian *rex pacificus*. Decisive as stimulus to this royal progress is the selflessness and guiding influence of the knight's bride and queen, Enite. At the centre of his work Hartmann portrays the corresponding development of this beautiful but inexperienced noble girl from straitened circumstances through humiliation and self-sacrifice to recognition and royal dignity. Critics have in the main considered Enite in terms of her duty to Erec as his wife, asking whether she must bear any guilt for his neglect of his chivalric profession.[1] Less attention has been paid to the fact of Enite's own independent development to exemplary maturity.

As Arthurian romance is concerned to trace the path of the protagonist to self-recognition and maturity, so the role of the lady is to represent, symbolically or actually, both the stimulus to chivalric endeavour and its reward. It is regularly profitable in romance to examine the progress of the hero with regard to society and his ultimate re-integration into a position of honour in the community. When the romance is devoted specifically to the story of a marriage and is made the vehicle, as is Hartmann's courtly adaptation of Chrétien, of religious moralization, it is perhaps the more fruitful to consider to what extent the lady as well possesses a public, social aspect.[2] Given Hartmann's explicit advocacy of the ideal of 'erbärmde', *caritas*, in *Erec*, this approach certainly commends itself for Enite.[3] It is the aim of this essay to examine not Enite's wifely duty, but rather her formative contribution to her husband's development, and beyond this, the public role of the noble lady which Hartmann postulates as an ideal. This facet of the work may not claim to be dominant, but represents one possible identification model amongst others in a richly textured romance.

113

The hero and heroine of the *Vorgeschichte* are, despite their outstanding qualities, singularly unfitted for the responsibilities of the royal office which is their lot. In contrast to Chrétien's knight, Hartmann's Erec is still 'in den êrsten jâren' (2256), still to achieve his 'êrstiu ritterschaft' (1266). His immaturity is such that the blow from the dwarf's whip destroys his self-respect, unleashing in him profound suppressed anger and determination for revenge (97–137).[4] From his justified but violent punishment of the dwarf Maliclisier (1064–72), and throughout his growth to self-knowledge, anger and a tendency to violence characterize Erec's conduct: 'sînen grimmen muot' (858, 3221) he vents repeatedly upon his adversaries; his 'zorn' (3416 and passim) betrays the tempestuous emotions within his disoriented soul.

The partnership with Enite itself stems purely from Erec's need for a lady and chivalric equipment with which to pursue vengeance (488–515). Once he reaches agreement with the impoverished count Koralus, her father, neither man gives the girl a further thought; each subscribes to a notion of marriage which accords the lady little more than the status of a chattel. As the wedding approaches at Arthur's court, Erec is overwhelmed by sensual desire for his bride, an impatient, inordinate eroticism (1840–75) which anticipates the subsequent catastrophic 'verligen'. The love shared by Erec and Enite is an extreme and intense passion which remains on the level of sexuality. The marriage, contracted as a business arrangement and rooted in inordinate sensuality, has no basis in mutual regard and engenders in the partners no trust or reciprocal confidence.

Erec's susceptibility to violence and his unbounded sexual appetite are abundantly reflected in the deeds and words of his opponents before and after the crisis at Karnant – it is this pattern of motif-reflection which lends *Erec* its remarkable unity. One may indeed see in these recurrent, complementary forms of aggression a fundamental propensity to abuse the personal integrity of a fellow human being, and it is evident that the protagonist himself shares this same tendency to deny the individuality of his partner, to debase the personality of the other.[5] Moreover, Erec's proneness to extremes of behaviour is evident also in the inordinate appetite for chivalric combat and public acclaim which he displays in the tournament at Tenebroc, where he is even impetuous enough to risk fighting 'âne wâfen blôz' (2505) and without helmet, 'mit blôzem houbete' (2651, 2715). Inclined to disregard the integrity of others, and giving in the course of his exploits no thought to his bride, Erec is foolhardy enough to endanger his own life as well, a trait which later has nearly fatal consequences when after Karnant he overcompensates for his uxoriousness by an excessive zeal for chivalric feats. Despite his innate capacity for compassion (342), Erec lacks insight into his own volatile temperament, and cannot be deemed ready for the kingship conferred upon him at Karnant.

Enite is for her part a fitting companion. Young, inexperienced, living in poverty, the victim of armed violence, and isolated from courtly society, she, too, is ill-equipped for public position and responsibility.[6] Nonetheless she is possessed of a stunning beauty which belies her straitened circumstances and indicates her potential quality, which must be realized, made to bear fruit. At her first appearance she tends Erec's horse, a recurrent act of grooming which symbolizes her self-denying readiness to serve; she enjoys also the especial gift of perception and awareness of circumstances. It is this potential which Erec finally acknowledges after testing her 'als man daz golt sol / liutern in der esse' (6785f), and which Erec's father recognizes at the outset when he bestows the government of the realm upon the couple (2916–23).[7]

Whilst Enite rapidly gains insight into the defects of Erec's character, she has not the maturity to dissociate herself from a flawed and superficial social assessment. Informed of Erec's unparalleled daring in the tournament, Enite rejoices in his glory, but expresses concern for his safety:

> 2835 . . . si weste wol ir man
> in sô getânem muote . . .
> 2839 sô vorhte si in unlange hân,
> wan er den lîp ûf êre
> solde wâgen sêre,
> und wan erz versuohte,
> sô ein zage enruochte
> man spraeche im übel oder guot.

This episode occurs at the point where, in an Arthurian romance in the pattern of Chrétien, an apparent harmony is celebrated which shortly results in catastrophe. The court has likened Erec to Solomon, Absalom, Samson and Alexander, and drawn the wrong conclusion (2813–25); these comparisons are a familiar topos intimating that the man is shortly to succumb to the wiles of woman.[8] Despite her awareness of Erec's susceptibility to extremes, Enite concurs in society's shallow judgement (2833, 2844) and accepts unremarked the jeopardy of Erec's life in pursuit of acclaim (2845–51).[9] Enite is implicated in Hartmann's extensive relativization of the Arthurian court and its superficial insights at this point, and she misses an opportunity to mediate between Erec and those around him in a situation where his unmodified instincts or unaided perceptions endanger his survival.[10] Later, in the first duel with Guivreiz, Erec indulges in tactics which make him seem a 'zage' (4420), ill-advisedly refuses to respond to his opponent with blows, and is seriously wounded (4409–24);[11] Erec behaves there precisely in accordance with his dangerous conduct at the tournament, and suffers a wound which symbolizes the defects of his character and causes his apparent death; it is his recovery at Limors from this wound and *descensus* that marks also his attainment of insight, and reconciliation with Enite. Erec's very survival is intimately bound up with the capacity to modify his instinctive behaviour.

At Karnant the old king Lot confers the kingdom upon the newly-weds, who (in contrast to Chrétien's couple) from this point assume the social responsibilities of government (2918–23). For Enite this implies a function similar to that of Ginover at the side of Arthur. A consequence of Erec's kingship is that his failure has broader social implications. The 'verligen' has an extreme impact on society; the cohesion of the community breaks down, the court at Karnant disintegrates (2977–92). Even Erec's provision for his knights betrays his awareness of duty, the narrator's praise of such bounty having a decidedly ambiguous tone: 'ich lobe an im den selben site' (2965).[12] In the self-willed isolation of the lovers it is, characteristically, Enite who becomes aware of their public disgrace; acknowledging the courtiers' expectations of her, she recognizes immediately her responsibility to resolve the public's antagonism and mediate between Erec and society: '. . . gedâhte manegen enden / wie si möhte erwenden / alsô gemeinen haz' (3004–6, also 3007f). Her inability to act forthwith – itself a further default of her public duty – is grounded in her inexperience and in the complete absence of trust between the marriage partners: 'Erecke engetorste siz niht klagen. / si vorhte in dâ verliesen mite' (3011f). Betraying the truth *nolens volens*, she reluctantly explains, but only on condition 'daz erz âne zorn lieze' (3049).[13] In full cognizance of her husband's volatile temperament, and in contrast to her facile reaction during the tournament, Enite now acts to ensure her husband's welfare (compare 3012 and 2839).

Enite's experiences after the crisis may be seen to reveal progress and development on two fronts: Enite's conscious subordination of herself to her husband's survival; and the positive stimulus to compassion which Enite unconsciously, in her distress, instils in Erec's mind. After her youthful inexperience, Enite, her basic benevolence established, gains steadily in perception and maturity, and comes to recognize that her supreme function as wife and queen must be to promote her husband's fulfilment of duty. It becomes her priority to preserve his life when he is endangered, when his own unmodified instincts threaten his very survival. In this sense there is clear development in her resolution of the cruel dilemmas thrust upon her on the 'âventiure'-journey. Whilst the command to silence reflects Erec's disordered tendency to abuse the integrity of his partner, it is essentially also the formalization of Enite's initial fears in the bedroom at Karnant (3012, 3029–32).

The arguments which Enite adduces for defying her husband's threats when willing to sacrifice herself for his welfare show a gradual shift from her initial acquiescence in society's shallow acclaim at Tenebroc, to her partial self-pity at Karnant, towards some less self-centred focus, and ultimately to a clearly articulated awareness of her public responsibility as queen.

At the outset Enite is prompted to prevent the disintegration of the court at Karnant by self-pity as well as by public concern. Confronted by the first band of robbers she subordinates herself to Erec out of concern for the welfare of others who depend upon him:

> 3168 'bezzer ist verlorn mîn lîp,
> ein als unklagebaere wîp,
> dan ein alsô vorder man,
> wan dâ verlür maneger an.
> erst edel unde rîche:
> wir wegen ungelîche.
> vür in wil ich sterben
> ê ich in sihe verderben.'

Enite proclaims that it is 'triuwe' that underlies her concern for his 'lîbes gewarheit' (3260).[14] On the second occasion Enite is again conscious of her debt to Erec, who raised her to high rank:

> 3361 'sol ich den slahen sehen
> der mich von grôzer armuot
> ze vrouwen schuof über michel guot
> dâ von ich schône gêret bin
> (ich heize ein rîchiu künegin),
> daz sol mich geriuwen.'

The favours accorded by Erec to Enite herself here reflect the benefits which should accrue to others from his social position. That Enite is not motivated merely by her own good fortune is evident when she repudiates the similar favours and social enhancement proffered as inducements by the wicked count and by Oringles (3784–96 and 6469–79). Determining to preserve her husband's life in the face of danger from the wicked count, Enite accepts loyally that Erec's social obligations might require him to remarry after her death:

> 3985 'waz aber von diu, wirde ich erslagen
> unde nimt er mir den lîp?
> dannoch lebet manec vrum wîp.
> ich enbin ouch niht sô klagelîch:
> sô ist er edel unde rîch,
> mîn lieber herre.
> ê im iht gewerre,
> sô wil ich kiesen den tôt.'

Once more Enite defies her husband's threats in order to preserve his life (4134–8), once more the programmatic term 'gewarheit' indicates that it is her objective to ensure his safety, his survival (4259). In the first battle against

Guivreiz Enite witnesses the dangerous wound which Erec's hazardous tactics cause him to sustain, and offers herself in his stead (4421–8).

In her long lament Enite maintains this developed note of social awareness at three points which are peculiar to Hartmann. When Erec collapses before her apparently dead, Enite pours out her 'confused and contradictory'[15] emotions as she experiences the (apparent) loss of that which she had so selflessly fought to preserve, Erec's life. It is entirely in keeping with her earlier social sense that in imploring wild beasts to kill her Enite should note also the harm their ravages cause to the needy and unprotected whilst she is spared:

> 5844 'ir tier vil ungewizzen,
> nû habet ir erbizzen
> manec schâf unde swîn,
> armer liute vihelîn,
> die ius niht engunden
> noch überwinden kunden.'

Death itself she scolds for wilfully damaging society by sparing her life whilst claiming Erec's, for others are dependent upon him:

> 5925 'wan dû gâhes nimst daz leben
> einem sô gewanten man
> den diu werlt niht überwinden kan,
> und gebiutest einem an sîne stat
> dem ie diu werlt des tôdes bat
> unde lâst den werden alt.'

Bewailing the apparent futility of her marriage and her pretension, Enite likens herself to a lime-tree which is transplanted from poor soil to an orchard: even the best husbandry cannot make an infertile tree bear fruit (6008–41):

> 6021 'wan dâ enwürde niht an erzogen,
> swie vlîzic man ir waere,
> daz si bezzer obez baere
> dan ouch ê nâch ir art.'

Whilst the spiritual reference of this metaphor is clearly uppermost (*tilia dicitur mundi infecunditas . . . , falsa delectatio* without *utilitas*), for a courtly audience the lime-tree must betoken too the pleasures of requited love.[16] Enite understands that she, who held her husband in sensual thrall, has failed to maintain in him that social activity which is his duty, the fruit that she, now a lady of royal rank (6035), might have borne from his husbandry. The metaphor

118

reveals that self-denial which makes her consider herself sterile. Objectively Enite is wrong in her basic comparison with infertility, for she cannot know of course, with the audience, that Erec's apparent death is indeed the result of precisely such a social act of *caritas*, his first, the rescue of Cadoc; an act which is the fruit of his relationship with Enite.

The final intervention on Erec's behalf occurs after the reconciliation, as Erec, for the first time bettered, lies vulnerable before Guivreiz; Enite actually interposes herself between husband and opponent, her voice alerts the other party to the reality of the situation, indeed she now instructs the dwarf-king on the rights and wrongs of his conduct (6939–59). Such is now the capacity of the mature, proven queen Enite to mediate effectively between her husband and the hazardous world around him.

These cumulative conscious acts of mediation establish clearly an ideal model of marriage as a partnership in which the woman complements with her qualities the attributes of the man, compensates with her gifts for his shortcomings.[17] For Hartmann the woman has particular depths of emotion, suffers travail with copious tears and lamentation, and accepts obedience, renunciation and sacrifice as her ordained sphere.[18] Equally, however, she is possessed of greater sensibilities, has the capacity to see and hear what the man cannot. The mutual suffering of Erec and Enite shows that Hartmann posits an active and formative role for the woman in the resolution of conflict.

In the state of disgrace which Enite has revealed to him, Erec imposes upon his wife the sentence of silence. He is determined to resolve the crisis unaided; that is why she must accompany him in her finest array, as spectator. At each stage on the journey it is nevertheless Enite who first recognizes danger and permits the possibility of safety, which Erec's unaided perceptions would have forfeited (3123f, 3297f, 3348, 3967f, 4135f). This womanly quality of superior perception the narrator establishes in a fictitious exchange with his audience; Enite could see and hear better than Erec because his chivalric equipment encumbered him (4150–65):

> 4160 des was im warnunge nôt
> und vrumte im dicke vür den tôt.
> doch ez im solde wesen zorn,
> er haete dicke verlorn
> von unbesihte den lîp,
> wan daz in warnte daz wîp.

Beneath the literal meaning lies the obvious symbolic significance.[19] Erec's 'unbesiht' betokens the defects of his untutored temperament which were evident already at Tenebroc (2650, 2715f, 2835ff). Accordingly, when he recovers at Limors he is able fully to see and hear with recognition:

119

6600   und begunde mit den ougen sehen . . .
6608   als si in dô nande,
        zehant er si erkande . . .
6614   als er erkande ir stimme . . .

At the reconciliation the couple ride on a single horse, and Enite guides him on the way (6745–8); 'daz geschach durch gewarheit' (6749; see n. 10). Reconciliation is sealed when Erec bids Enite now to speak (6763ff). Her explanation brings the emotion to her seeing eyes: 'nu tete si im die sache / ir ougen zungemache / allez weinende kunt' (6768–70). The aim of the test imposed on Enite differs from that in Chrétien's romance, where Erec sought to establish whether his wife loved him 'parfitemant' (4887). Here Erec wanted to know whether she was the appropriate wife for him; that is, what he expected of her depended in part on what his position was.

Within the partnership of marriage the wife is able therefore to intervene consciously and complement the qualities of the husband. Can it be shown also that she is able unconsciously to effect changes within him, bring him to self-recognition, so that he is able to modify his own temperament?

Enite's beauty clearly works as a catalyst which draws out the inherent qualities of those who behold her. So Erec's propensity to extremes of behaviour leads rapidly to erotic desire for her, and in 'verligen', a consequence of that demonic power of 'minne' which afflicts others also and drives them to lust and treachery (3691ff). On the other hand 'minne' may be a force for good as well (3709–16). Enite's womanly qualities of grief and suffering touch the vein of compassion potential in Erec at the outset (342, 850ff) which asserts itself against his obsessive will. Following the escape which Enite effects from the wicked count, Erec feels able to relieve his wife of the burden of grooming by giving away the horses (4014f; contrast 3590–4). Although he persists in his misogynistic stereotype, failing to comprehend Enite's devotion (4122–32), his anger is confined to threats. There is a perceptible softening of his harshness towards her during the first duel with Guivreiz. Confronted by combat with the dwarf-king, Erec recognizes Enite's allegiance to him (4318f); when she cries out for grief at his wound, he acknowledges her worth openly (4431). When the combatants share chivalric fellowship afterwards, Enite is permitted to share in their mutual tending of wounds (4492ff). Her mixed feelings (4502–6) recall the moment of Erec's acclaim at Tenebroc (2830ff), although on this occasion Enite had intervened successfully to inspire him to modify his behaviour and ensure his survival (4432–8).

The decisive act of chivalry for Erec's social development follows the reluctant sojourn at Arthur's court, when Erec responds to cries of anguish from a lady in distress in the woods and rescues her husband from the violence of two giants. There is an essential analogy between the plight of the lady and Enite's own repeated grief as each bewails the loss of her husband:

5350   'weinens gât mir michel nôt
        herre, mir belîbet tôt
        der aller liebiste man
        den ie wîp gewan.'

In almost identical terms Enite had suffered on the journey:

3137   daz si vorhte werden weise
        des aller liebisten man
        den ie vrouwe gewan.

(Compare also 3976f and subsequently 6043f). As Enite had pointed out danger to Erec in the woods, so now Cadoc's lady points the way for him (5366). Similarly there are elements of suffering which Cadoc and Erec himself share; as Erec had suffered a blow from the dwarf Maliclisier's whip (97), so Cadoc suffers repeated lashes from the giants (5406–11). There is also chivalric solidarity between the knights, for the treatment meted out to Cadoc by the giants ('si brâchen vaste ritters reht/und handelten den guoten kneht' (5412f) recalls the wicked count's treachery against Erec: 'daz was doch wider dem rehte/daz er dem guoten knehte/sîn wîp wolde hân genomen.' (3678–80). It is therefore as a reflex of Enite's earlier suffering, and of his earlier chivalric response to it, that Erec hastens to aid one in distress and carry out a work of *caritas*. Enite may be said to have embodied for Erec the human qualities of a society around him which depends upon him, to have aided him in realizing in a social deed the compassion which had lain dormant in him. Erec's ultimate act of recognition, of seeing and hearing, occurs when he wakes at the sound of Enite's suffering (6587ff). At this stage the principal defects of Erec's character have been resolved in his work of compassion and his recognition of the partnership which is marriage.

It is a function of the final episode at Brandigan to resolve Erec's remaining fault, that excessive urge for chivalric combat which was itself intensified in reaction to the offence of uxoriousness. In Hartmann's account of Joie de la curt this is achieved in a radical heightening of the role of 'erbärmde', *caritas*. The introduction of eighty distressed widows here serves to reinforce Enite's formative role in distress as stimulus to compassion and social awareness in the knight.[20] Erec articulates most clearly Enite's beneficent influence upon him in his chivalric activity (8864–73):

8868   'swenne mich der muot iuwer mant,
        sôst sigesaelic mîn hant
        wan iuwer guote minne
        die sterkent mîne sinne . . .'

121

The superiority of their outwardly, socially directed love over the antisocial love of Mabonagrin and his lady is established, for the thought of Enite even in her absence can inspire Erec (9171–87). When Erec liberates Mabonagrin from the thrall of sensual love to a valid social existence he is essentially setting free a part of his former self (9413–38).

Enite herself plays an explicit public role at Brandigan when she comforts Mabonagrin's grieving lady, introducing her to the court (9699–743), and accompanies Erec to console the eighty widows (9816–25). At the end of the romance, when Erec's path to kingship is completed, the narrator concludes Enite's story with a clear statement of her proper influence as queen upon her husband:

> 10119 der künec selbe huoter
> ir willen swâ er mohte,
> und doch als im tohte,
> niht sam er ê phlac,
> dô er sich durch si verlac . . .

The king's duty to act honourably upon his wife's promptings does not detract from her counsel as a valid component of the exercise of kingship. King and queen alike attain the eternal crown which complements the proper discharge of their royal duties.

Comparison with the functions of Queen Ginover may cast light upon the duties incumbent upon Enite in her role as queen. On several occasions Ginover is active in recommending appropriate conduct for the court and its knights, including Arthur himself (1115ff, 4945, 144–9); at times she serves as point of reference for deeds of chivalry: vanquished or rescued knights are told to report to her (1080–5, 4981–3, 5691–709); repeatedly she gives comfort to the distressed or welcomes guests to the court (1523ff, 1698f, 5100–15, 5129–31, 9905–9). Significantly Ginover tends the injured Erec (5148–50, 5245f) to assist in the healing cure of his (symbolic as well as actual) wounds, a cure which Enite had initiated during her suffering (4492f) and brought to fruition in her maturity (7220–31). Further evidence of the active role of the queen may be found in the many occasions on which she acts as one with the king in public matters – *coniuncta manu*, as it were; her participation is implicit at times when only the king is referred to.[21] By this criterion Enite proves in her conduct at Brandigan that she also is a worthy embodiment of the dignity of queenship.

In view of the prevalent medieval notion that it is a wife's duty to be silent and not reprove her husband even if he is wrong,[22] can it be expected of Enite that she should as queen be aware of the impact of her married love upon society at Karnant and act upon this knowledge? 'This is of course a lot to expect from someone of such limited experience, but the fact remains that she gives much evidence of not being equal to her role.'[23] In contrast to Chrétien's romance there is no implication here that she should not have uttered her lament. Indeed the whole import of Enite's role and development to maturity in Hartmann's romance is to posit an identification model of the noble lady's active and socially responsible role within marriage, in which she helps enhance and direct her husband's fulfilment of his duty.

The principal duty of the queen in medieval Europe was to ensure the survival of the dynasty by providing children and by avoiding a disputed succession: certainly it was in this sphere that the dominant queens of the Merovingian period and in Anglo-Saxon England were most active.[24] The powers and influence of the queen consort are not easily defined. Writing to William the Conqueror's queen, Mathilda, Gregory VII reminded her of her duties and urged her to influence the king to *virtus*; further, the pope expected of her a chaste life, piety and concern for the poor and distressed.[25] In medieval panegyric the queen was regarded in a sense as a complement to the king who augmented his renown by her person, her participation in his duties, and her concern for the poor and needy.[26] Such a role, then, appears to be generally required of a medieval queen.

For the society and patrons for whom Hartmann wrote, however, there were profound undercurrents of change which must have lent his posited model of an active and socially responsible noble lady and wife much greater potential impact and topicality. In the late twelfth century, Germany (perhaps later than France) was experiencing most acutely that secular process of transformation in which medieval Europe passed from the archaic age to the high middle ages, with fundamental changes in social structure, economic patterns, religious expression, and intellectual horizons. '. . . Armut, Arbeit, Emanzipation waren sowohl Hintergrund der literarischen und menschlichen Bewegungen des 11.–13. Jahrhunderts als auch Inhalt des geschriebenen und gesprochenen Wortes wie des gelebten Lebens.'[27] Nowhere was this transformation felt more keenly than in south-western Germany where Hartmann worked. In a stimulating study of the Upper Rhine region B. Thum traces the impact on literature of the 'Krise der Virilität' of the old aristocracy, seeing in the ensuing cultural revolution in the relation between the sexes a release of social and political energy which amounted to the 'erste Frauenemanzipation der europäischen Geschichte' and freed women to vast creative achievements.[28]

In this period social mobility increased as a result of a new, positive evaluation of labour, the individual became less rigidly bound by the *familia* as the old high nobility weakened and new collective forms of association evolved. In the Church this change was reflected in the monastic reform movements and new pastoral activities amongst wider groups of a more disparate society, and in particular in the advocacy of the Augustinian ideal of *caritas*, of an active love and concern for all, especially the needy and powerless. By the end of the twelfth century, however, the spiritual aspirations of an evolving and volatile society were still not satisfied, especially in view of the wealth and power of the Church as an institution. There developed new religious forces, radical movements of lay preachers, mendicant orders, and groups soon branded by the Church as heretical: Waldensians and Cathars. It was in the preaching of a pure and total renunciation that these forces touched broad groups in society who were ready to regard themselves as *pauperes Christi*.

The Investiture Contest had cost royalty and aristocracy much of their former sacral legitimation, both became increasingly subject to the law, were obliged to seek new legitimation in the sanction of the Church and public, to show their *idoneitas*. Under the impact of the mass religious movements of now rising social groups, the nobility had to vindicate their authority by means of heightened exercise of social responsibility. One form which this took was the *pax Dei* movement, another the promulgations of territorial peace (*Landfrieden*) in order to defend those in need of protection (the poor, peasants and merchants) and to win the consent of subjects for military and financial levies. A further response of the nobles was to admit the new rising group of *ministeriales* into their ranks and their culture. Within the courtly cultural community all members shared an equality of status which took little account of distinctions of birth and rank, and all partook ideally of the spiritualized ethos of the *militia Christi*.

It is from the vantage point of these *ministeriales* that Hartmann wrote: 'dienstman was er ze Ouwe' (*Der arme Heinrich* 5). In a study of appellations in *Erec* R. Pérennec observed that the notion of kingship is subject to a process of spiritualization which is analogous to that undergone by the concept of knighthood in the work:[29]

> Pour être roi, il faut s'être montré parfait chevalier ou même: la vraie royauté n'est que l'accomplissement ultime de la chevalerie. . . . Chevalerie et royauté, indissociables donc, font ainsi l'objet d'une moralisation qui permet d'établir l'unité d'une aristocratie définie par la notion de mérite et de valeur intrinsèque.

Certainly Erec is designated 'künec' for the first time when at the moment of reconciliation with Enite he explicitly seeks guidance and information from her (6763); she is then designated 'künegîn' (6732). Similarly Enite is referred to as 'diu edel künegîn' (6507) when she displays supreme loyalty to her husband, whom she supposes to be dead, by repudiating the importunings of Oringles. Previous allusions to the couple's royal rank (3365, 5981; 6035?) indicate the social benefits which royal dignity can bestow. Subsequent allusions reinforce the exemplary character of the couple as they proceed to achieve the adventure of Joie de la curt and work the liberation of, and bring comfort to, others. The significant role of the dwarf-king Guivreiz may also be noted, for he alone of Erec's adversaries does not reflect the protagonist's intemperance, but rather accords the couple recognition and honour; this recovery of social respect is symbolized by the frequent allusions to Guivreiz's kingship.[30] It is therefore when they recognize their mutual interdependence in marriage and the true qualities of each that Erec and Enite come to merit, and make their own, the title and responsibility of royalty which had been conferred upon them at Karnant. Enite may be seen to have achieved this first. Whilst Pérennec's assessment is fully in accord with the aspirations of the *ministeriales* for acceptance, which Hartmann endorsed, it underplays the element of social beneficence which is incumbent upon those placed highest in society, for it is upon these that Hartmann's romance focuses specifically.

One of the most striking facets of the secular change in twelfth-century Europe was the part played by women, for in this *tempus muliebre* (Hildegard of Bingen) they served as 'Seismographen der Krise' of archaic society.[31] In south-western Germany women of various groups had a leading role in the ethical and religious activism of broad groups of the laity as they sought emancipation from the ambivalent status accorded them by the authorities. The noble women of the region (as well as upper groups of the towns) proved particularly responsive to the Catharist and Waldensian heresies widespread by the end of the century. As the establishment of territorial rule proceeded (in the south-west under the Staufens, Zähringens and Welfs) there was a levelling effect on the old nobility. From this subjection of an elite by greater forces, other social groups of unfree status – women and *ministeriales* – gained some relative equality. The reduced power of the kin-group allowed women more scope for manoeuvre; in Swabia inheritance through the female line was permitted in the twelfth century. One reflex of the aristocracy's new sense of social responsibility was the individual acts of renunciation; flight from marriage and wealth into communal living is a frequently recorded act of noble ladies.[32] Another is the emergence of women writers of note; Hildegard of Bingen and Herrad of Landsberg attained European importance. Both major cultural phenomena of the period which may be deemed to reveal a matriarchal current (adoration of the Virgin Mary and the cult of courtly love – where the woman represents the ideals and aspirations of the man) were richly nurtured in the literature of this period in the German south-west.

Hartmann gives abundant evidence in his works that he was aware of current social and religious developments, especially in the attention he accords to the dynamic potential of woman and the problems of rule and dominion. He declares matrimony to be the best, divinely ordained estate for mankind (*Gregorius* 2221–3) and emphasizes in *Erec* the indissolubility of marriage; nearly all of Erec's opponents aim to take his wife away from him, only for Enite to uphold the union even *in extremis* (5822–30). Hartmann was certainly critical of the feudal practice of marriage which often treated woman as little more than a chattel (the wicked count and Oringles, even initially Erec and

Koralus),[33] and he exposes ecclesiastical abuse when clerics connive in the enforced marriage of Enite to Oringles (6342–51). One consequence of the Church's success in establishing itself in the twelfth century as sole legislator in matrimonial matters was to bring about a relative improvement in the status of the wife vis-à-vis her husband, at least theologically speaking, by removing his sexual sovereignty, by imposing equal laws for both.[34] K. Smits is certainly right in seeing the community which is Hartmann's matrimonial ideal: 'In der Ehe gelangen, nach Hartmanns Auffassung, Mann und Frau zu einer Synthese, in der sich die Individuen, indem sie einander ergänzen, erst voll entfalten können.'[35] It may be contended, however, that greater weight should be given to the creative powers of the woman in contributing to the partnership and effecting change in her partner, even within the feudal dominance of the husband in marriage. Hartmann posits a high ideal of marriage in which the woman's emancipatory aspirations, the renunciation which many undertook at a time of widespread religious upheaval, might be expressed and given a social purpose within matrimony.[36]

The problems of the noble lady or consort are a recurrent theme in Hartmann's work, a natural fusion of his interest in woman's potential and the responsibility of rule. The mother of Gregorius has as duchess to ensure the succession in her realm, and after the incestuous marriage, to continue as sovereign (*Gregorius* 2212ff).[37] Laudine herself Hartmann raises to the rank of queen, in contrast to Chrétien's daughter of a duke, in order to confer upon her and Iwein equality with, and feudal independence from, Arthur himself.[38] This is in accord with Hartmann's emphasis in *Iwein* upon the just achievement of territorial dominion rather than the personal affirmation of a *chevalier errant*.[39] Moreover, the role of the queen as component of an effective monarchy is thrown into relief in the relativization of Arthur's court when he as king is powerless to prevent the abduction of his queen.

The closer the association which can be established between Hartmann's public and the radical religious movements in the south-west, the more readily one may expect his audience to respond to his postulated ideal of the active, socially aware noble lady. Hartmann's romances address themselves squarely to the interests of the territorial princes, and for this reason the Staufen court is considered unlikely to have offered him patronage.[40] Rather his patron is to be sought either at the court of the dukes of Zähringen,[41] or in the circle of the Welf court at Altdorf-Ravensburg;[42] arguments for the latter seem more convincing. H. Bayer has contended that the ethos of *Erec* is 'durch und durch waldensisch',[43] and ventures some bold identifications. His specific deduction, that Erec's counsel to Mabonagrin: 'bî den liuten ist sô guot' (9438) is an advocacy of the communal religious life appropriate to the Humiliati,[44] is less than conclusive, for this overlooks the socially active role expected of the knight within marriage: 'hin varn und wider komen / âne ir haz mac geschehen' (9427f; also 9589). Nonetheless, whilst some caution is in order, it would appear that Hartmann does stand close to the radical religious spirit of lay piety.

In the early 1180s, in a society where 'Armut, Arbeit, Emanzipation' were wreaking profound change, Hartmann addressed himself in the character of Enite to the question of responsible rule and the harnessing of woman's emancipatory potential. Abelard recognized the significance of woman's frailty: 'quo naturaliter femineus sexus est infirmior, eo virtute est Dei acceptabilior et honore dignior', and Hildegard of Bingen, writing to Emperor Barbarossa, deemed it the task of women and the laity to recall the rulers to their order and duty.[45] That the nobility of Germany needed prompting to duty is evident from the warning of Landgrave Ludwig II of Thuringia to his younger brother, a generation before *Erec*, that he should apply himself to the good of the realm:[46]

> Qua re, frater animo meo carissime, pacis tempore militaribus armorum ludis inutilibus; quibus iuveniliter sepenumero delectatus vite periculum incurristi, velim abstineas ac potius publicis regni negotiis virtutem tuam atque industriam, ut principem decet, enitescere facias.

That a noblewoman's radical spirit of penitent renunciation might be exercised by her remaining at court to work for the well-being of the realm was asserted early in the twelfth century by one of the pioneering itinerant preachers of *amor paupertatis ac solitudinis*, Robert of Arbrissel, in a letter to Countess Ermengarde of Brittany:[47]

> Non sis nimis sollicita de mutatione loci et habitus. In corde Deum habe, sive in civitate, sive in aula, sive in lectu eburneo, sive in veste preciosa, vel in exercitu, vel in judicio, sive in convivio fueris . . . Misericors esto pauperibus omnibus . . . suffere laborem propter utilitatem aliorum, non propter te.

It is Hartmann's achievement in *Erec* to make of Chrétien's pioneering romance and its treatment of the casuistry of courtly love, a profound analysis of sovereignty which is rooted in an awareness of the social responsibility and duty of the ruler. Whilst the kingship of the hero in *Erec* is generally held to be a camouflage for promoting the cause of the *ministeriales*,[48] it seems equally plausible to see that Hartmann is here commending to the nobility the service-ethos of that aspiring class.[49] Erec and Enite are required to gain anew that rank which was bestowed upon them and to show their fitness for it. By themselves experiencing hardship, powerlessness,[50] they achieve a true understanding of the ruler's responsibility to preserve the peace of society. It is the fragility of the lady which awakens in her husband awareness of the distress of others. In the figure of Queen Enite, who would rescue her king not for herself but for the sake of his subjects, Hartmann ennobles the lady's capacity for renunciation to the benefit of the kingdom:

> 3168 'bezzer ist verlorn mîn lîp,
> ein als unklagebaere wîp,
> dan ein alsô vorder man,
> wan dâ verlür maneger an.'

Rhyme, Reason and Repetition
in Erec et Enide

J. C. LAIDLAW

'He that hath ears to hear, let him hear'
Matthew, 11: 15

'Five hundred thousand volumes of indifferent
rhyme, and no reason'
Charles Dickens, *Uncommercial Traveller*

EIGHT hundred years after the first recitation of *Erec et Enide* it is impossible for us to tell exactly how a contemporary audience would have reacted on hearing the romance and particularly its prologue. However, we can assume that the members of that audience were accustomed to listening to narrative poems and more especially to poems in octosyllabic couplets. They would thus be acquainted with the works of poets earlier than Chrétien de Troyes, and would be familiar with the conventions which they followed in presenting their material and in setting it in verse. When modern critics have discussed the opening lines of *Erec et Enide* they have generally considered their content above all and have paid less attention to their style.[1] And yet a twelfth-century audience, hearing the prologue for the first time, would probably have been struck quite as much by its presentation as by its content. What Chrétien has to say is to a large extent traditional: the idea that talents and learning should be harnessed and not wasted has its source in Scripture and is found in the work of other contemporary writers. Equally, there is nothing especially novel about Chrétien's promise that his tale will make up a connected and coherent whole and will be remarkable for its great beauty; other writers of that period, indeed any period, have aspired to that ideal.

On the other hand, the audience would certainly have been struck and perhaps amused by the self-assurance of an author who twice named himself (lines 9 and 26) and who seemed to be nailing his literary colours to the mast.[2]

Through hearing the works of other writers, their ears had grown accustomed to hearing couplets with simple or sufficient rhymes above all, and to hearing the rhyme change regularly from one couplet to the next. Not that poets always employed exactly the same 'rhythm':[3] to give emphasis or to create variety, a poet might repeat a rhyme, using it in two, three or more successive couplets;[4] alternatively he might in adjacent couplets use rhymes which were phonetically linked;[5] again he might repeat a rhyme at a little distance from its first occurrence and thus create a rudimentary pattern.[6] As the audience listened to the prologue to *Erec et Enide*, however, they would have noticed that the rhymes were arranged in ways different from those to which they were accustomed; their ears would have caught the patterns in which the rhymes are set and the varying rhythms which they establish.

The Prologue (lines 1–26)

The prologue begins with a proverb which is set off by internal rhyme (*dit, respit*) in line 1 and by the use of leonine rhyme (*respit, despit*) in the couplet as a whole. While the second couplet has simple rhymes (*cuide, estuide*), the rhymes become more ornate in the next two couplets: rich rhyme (*l'ait, antrelait*) is followed by leonine rhyme (*teisir, pleisir*). Simple rhymes return in the next two couplets to be followed by a group of four couplets (lines 13–20) with 'ornate' rhymes:[7] a combination of rich (*d'avanture, conjointure*), equivocal (*savoir, savoir*), (*contes, contes*) and leonine rhymes (*n'abandone, l'an done*). Two couplets with simple rhymes then follow before the prologue ends with a final example of leonine rhyme (*crestïantez, vantez*). That final couplet is made the more emphatic by the use of *annominatio*, the play on words involving *crestïantez* and *Crestïens*. Earlier examples of that rhetorical figure had been the equivocal rhymes already mentioned in lines 15–16 and 19–20; the latter rhyme recalls line 13 and is echoed in line 22.

What effects does Chrétien achieve by using rhymes in this way? An obvious point to make is that the technique helps to guard against that repetitive monotony which might be induced by an unvarying sequence of octosyllabic couplets on simple rhymes. It gives the poet, or whoever related the poem, the opportunity to vary the rhythm of the text. More important, rhyme can also be used for emphasis: the importance of the proverb and the vaunt with which the prologue opens and concludes is underscored by the use of leonine rhyme; the internal rhyme in line 1 and the use of *annominatio* in lines 25–6 also contribute to that effect. Lines 13–20, where four successive couplets are built on ornate rhymes, are also among the most important lines in the prologue and have attracted considerable attention from modern critics:[8] in them Chrétien announces the subject of his tale and affirms that he will use his talents to create a work which is coherent and pleasing, and in those respects superior to the *conte d'avanture* from which it is drawn. Some of those ideas had been foreshadowed in lines 5–8 where the rhymes are also ornate and where stress is laid on the importance of *estuide* (lines 4 and 6).

In an article published in 1965, 'La Brisure du couplet dans *Erec et Enide*', Jean Frappier showed how much of an innovator Chrétien was in using that technique and concluded:

> Nul avant Chrétien n'a brisé le couplet aussi fréquemment que lui et, ajoutons-le, aussi adroitement.[9]

A similar conclusion can be drawn about Chrétien's use of rhymes: none of his predecessors had used them in so distinctive a way or combined them so effectively with other oral devices. It is not that earlier writers were unconcerned about the presentation or performance of their works. Repetition and variation play an important role in the *Chanson de Roland*, to take an obvious example: repetition of keywords, repetition and/or variation of lines and whole *laisses*.[10] Later writers were to use similar techniques. Benedeit in his *Voyage of St Brendan* used a high proportion of rich and leonine rhymes and often grouped them as Chrétien would do some decades later,[11] but his influence was limited, not least because his practice of counting the final unstressed *e* of a line as a full syllable did not find favour on the continent. When later poets wished to group couplets together to form runs or to create patterns, they generally used different methods. It is not uncommon to find consecutive couplets with the same rhymes: *tirades lyriques*, as they are called, are used regularly by poets such as Gaimar or Wace and in the *Roman de Thèbes*.[12] While editors generally highlight the presence of *tirades lyriques*, they have not always been aware of the ways in which consecutive couplets are linked by assonance or by vowel harmonies. Professor Johnston has made that point cogently in an excellent article on 'Sound-Related Couplets in Old French'; the examples which he cites show that this technique was also well established by the time that Chrétien was writing.[13] Where Chrétien differs from his predecessors is in his ability to see how those traditional devices might be developed, and might be combined with other techniques like *brisure du couplet* or the use of ornate rhymes; such techniques, although not strictly speaking innovations, had not been used by earlier poets to any consistent effect.[14]

The other extracts from *Erec et Enide* to be discussed here are all passages which, like the prologue, include a sequence of at least three couplets with ornate rhymes. Such sequences occur regularly throughout the poem and over one hundred examples have been found.[15] Three successive couplets constitute a convenient minimum figure, for it is unlikely that a sequence of that length would have gone unnoticed by the audience. It is also probable that the examples in question come from the pen of Chrétien himself, and not from a scribe or redactor: while the rhyme of a single couplet might have been enriched during the subsequent transmission of the text, the chances of two, three or more successive couplets being amended in that way are progressively reduced. Caution is the more necessary since the earliest surviving complete manuscripts of Chrétien's works date from the middle of the thirteenth century and, and as Mr Tony Hunt has recently pointed out, a satisfactory critical edition of the complete works is still lacking.[16]

To see how ornate rhymes are used elsewhere in the romance, all the sequences of at least three couplets in the first thousand lines will be examined; such sequences are often found in combination and the passages where this occurs will be treated as a whole. In that way it can be determined how consistently the technique is employed and what effects it creates. After those passages have been considered, two scenes from later in the romance will be examined to show how sequences of ornate rhymes are combined with other techniques, chief among them repetition.

Lines 81–114

The first passage to be considered after the prologue is also the scene in which Erec is introduced. King Arthur has persisted in his determination to revive the customary hunt for the white stag, despite Gawain's warning that dissension must ensue when one maiden is chosen to receive the victor's kiss. The hunt has set off, followed at a distance by the Queen and her maiden, who in their turn are followed by Erec. The passage is divided into three sections, each of which has a particular pattern of rhymes associated with it. The first section (lines 81–92) tells of Erec's standing at court, gives his age and stresses the handsomeness of his person. The style is straightforward and the tone neutral; the rhymes are simple and traditional, of the kind which the audience was accustomed to hear. The only detail which is singled out is Erec's beauty, emphasized in lines 87–9 where the epithet *bel* is thrice repeated.[17]

The rhetorical question in line 93 marks a change in rhythm, which is further emphasized by two couplets with leonine rhymes, followed by a couplet with rich rhymes (lines 93–8). The rhymes of the next three couplets (lines 99–104) look simpler but their effect on the ear will be different: the rhyme-words, *espee* excepted, are all forms of the past participle of verbs in -(i)er. These three couplets are a very clear example of what Professor Johnston has called vowel linkage and can also be seen as a variation on the earlier *tirade lyrique*. They are made even more insistent by the repetition of *chauces* and *chauciees* (line 99) and *chauciez* (line 102). In lines 105–14 the rhythm changes again, as couplets with ornate rhymes alternate with couplets with simple rhymes.[18] The repetition of *conpaignie* (lines 110 and 112) should also be noted.

The simple rhymes used in lines 81–92 constitute there and elsewhere the regular or basic rhythm of the poem, the norm from which Chrétien can depart by creating patterns which involve the use of more complicated rhymes. The arrangements vary: there may be a sequence of ornate rhymes, as in lines 93–8, or of related rhymes, as in lines 99–104; there may be an alternating pattern in which simple and ornate rhymes are combined, as in lines 105–14. Repetition is an associated technique, as can be seen from the examples of *bel* and *chauces*. The combined effect of these techniques is to emphasize particular details or phrases. Where they are first used, the ornate rhymes stress the richness or elegance of Erec's attire. These lines not only form a fitting conclusion to the portrait but they emphasize that Erec is dressed for leisure. The fact that he is not fully armed is further stressed by the couplets with linked rhymes. The alternating rhymes in the last section underscore the importance of Erec's decision to accompany the Queen, and help to make the audience wonder why so outstanding a knight should not have joined in the hunt. By using rhymes in this way, Chrétien has discreetly but skilfully prepared the audience for the scenes which will follow when Erec will be compelled to ride after the knight who has insulted the Queen; Erec cannot challenge him until he has found arms with which to fight.

Lines 189–246

The next passage where sequences of ornate rhymes are to be found occurs after the Queen, her damsel and Erec have encountered a knight in full armour, accompanied by a maiden and a dwarf. The Queen has sent her damsel to ask that the knight and his maiden come to her. That request is rudely refused by the dwarf, who strikes the damsel when she tries to push past him, and she comes back to her mistress in tears. In the lines in which these events are recounted (lines 138–88), simple rhymes predominate by far; there are only four examples of ornate rhyme. Thereafter the rhythm alters and Chrétien will again make use of techniques similar to those which have just been examined.

The damsel's distress and the Queen's dismay are the subject of lines 189–94, three couplets which are set off by leonine and equivocal rhymes. The Queen's speech to Erec, asking him to intervene (lines 195–204), starts with simple rhymes, but at line 199 the rhythm alters as rich and simple rhymes begin to alternate. The most marked change of rhythm is, however, reserved for lines 209–12 where the altercation begins between Erec and the dwarf. Line 209 is purely narrative; the couplet is then broken, marking the change from narrative to direct speech. The rhyme of lines 209–10 is both echoed and altered in lines 211–12, the simple rhyme of the first couplet being enriched in the second. Further ornate rhymes follow, combining with some internal rhyme to set off speeches which become ever shorter and more angry. The altercation ends in violence, and again that change is reflected in the verse: lines 217–18 are largely monosyllabic and end in a redoubled rhyme (*nus plus*). In the six lines immediately following Chrétien introduces different sound-effects. For a second time a ryhme is used in two successive couplets; in lines 219–22 as in lines 209–12, the rhyme of the second couplet is more ornate and is itself followed by a rich rhyme. The play on the words *colee* and *col* in lines 219–21 recalls similar examples of repetition in lines 188–9 (*retorner*), 193 and 197 (*bleciee*), 195 and 201 (*Erec, biax amis*) and 205–6 (*esperone*). The encounter ends with Erec's decision that discretion and retreat are the better part of valour, a decision which is conveyed in couplets with simple rhymes.

The beginning of Erec's long speech to the Queen (lines 234–71) shows how rhymes can be used in conjunction with other oral techniques. The change from narration to direct speech occurs within a couplet and is thus emphatic. Citing lines 231–4 as his example, Frappier wrote as follows:

> La brisure de couplet sert en général à souligner un changement dans le cours de la narration. Ce changement peut concerner la *forme* utilisée. C'est ainsi que la brisure ponctue le passage du *récit* au *discours*.[19]

The first four complete couplets have ornate rhymes (lines 235–42) and a similar couplet (lines 245–6) follows on closely. In the rest of the speech (lines 247–71) simple rhymes predominate and ornate rhymes are found twice only. However, those two occasions are interesting, for in the first example (lines 259–60) ornate rhyme is associated with some internal rhyme and with the repetition of *armes*, the equipment which Erec needs before he can fight. In the second example (lines 271–2) an ornate rhyme marks the end of the speech and is the more emphatic since the couplet is also broken and the rhyme is linked with that in the couplet following.

This examination of Erec's long speech shows that there is a clear association between rhythm and content. The use of ornate rhymes in the opening lines helps to convey Erec's anger and frustration; the last rhyme in the sequence of four is the more emphatic since it is literally outrageous. But Erec's anger subsides and gives way to calmer resolution as he decides to follow the knight; simpler rhymes match that quieter mood. The only exceptions have their purpose: the first to stress Erec's need to find arms, the second to mark the end of the speech with a flourish.

Lines 895–928

The next scene to be examined forms part of the contest for the sparrow-hawk. Before it is considered, however, intervening scenes in which sequences of ornate rhymes occur will be looked at briefly. The first is the passage where the vavassor, Enide's father, first describes the contest which is to take place the next day (lines 557–72). In the second (lines 727–32) Erec asks him to make preparations for his daughter to accompany him to the contest. In both those scenes ornate rhymes are used to created effects very similar to those in the prologue which were discussed earlier. The technique is also used at the beginning of the combat, and helps to convey the hostility of Erec's adversary when Erec invites Enide to take the sparrow-hawk (lines 827–46).

The battle between Erec and Ydier, as it will now be convenient to call him, is prolonged and towards evening Ydier suggests that they both pause for rest.[20] His speech begins simply (line 895) but moves to an emphatic conclusion: ornate rhymes are introduced in line 899 and continue to the end of the speech; repetition and internal rhyme also play their part. Thereafter there is a quieter section while both knights rest but, as Erec draws inspiration from Enide and as his strength is restored, so the rhythm changes. Ornate rhymes return, in a sequence of two couplets at first (lines 909–12) and then in a concluding group of three (lines 915–20). Linked rhymes are used in the two couplets which follow (lines 921–4).

There are two other points to note about this passage. Lines 915–16 explicitly recall lines 245–6, part of Erec's long speech to the Queen, and also line 332, part of the Queen's account to the court of the indignities which Erec and she had suffered; this striking use of repetition should make us alive to the part which it may play elsewhere in the romance.[21] The second point concerns love, for it is at this juncture that the audience, and perhaps Erec also, become aware of his love for Enide. A twelfth-century audience would have noted the way in which emphatic words like *amie* and *amor* are used in this scene. It is Ydier who speaks first of *amies*, in line 904, assuming that Enide's status is the same as that of his own maiden. The word *amie* is repeated three lines later at the rhyme and heralds the introduction of *s'amor* four lines later in line 911. It should be noted that the comments come from Ydier and from Chrétien. Erec will not himself describe Enide as his *amie* until line 1433 and then the reference is in indirect speech; it is in line 1535, when he is presenting Enide to the Queen, that Erec refers to her directly for the first time as 'ma pucele et m'amie'.[22]

Consideration of the functions of rhyme in this last scene has led to an examination of the part played by repetition, just as discussion of an earlier passage involved some assessment of the effects created by breaking a couplet to mark a transition. Chrétien is often at his most subtle when he uses ornate rhymes in combination with other techniques. Two examples from later in the romance will be used to illustrate the point: first of all, Chrétien's description of the wedding night.

Lines 2015–54

In the opening lines of the scene the sense of the rhymes is as important as their quality: to rhyme *delit* with *lit* in lines 2017–18 is perhaps predictable,[23] to associate and at the same time contrast *asanblee* and *anblee* as in lines 2021–2 is more subtle and more pleasing. The reference to Brangien in line 2023 is the third and last reference in the romance to the story of Tristan and Yseut:[24] in lines 424–6 the colour and lustre of Enide's hair was said to surpass that of Yseut; in lines 1241–4 the joy of the townsfolk at Erec's victory over Ydier surpassed that on the Isle of Saint Sanson when Tristan slew the Morholt. Now, finally, Chrétien emphasizes to us that no substitution took place on the wedding-night. These allusions to the Tristan legend are deliberate and are meant to point to the moral superiority of Erec and Enide and their married love.[25]

A literary allusion is followed by a biblical one. Lines 2027–8 recall the opening verse of Psalm 42 'As the hart panteth after the water-brooks'. From the stag and its thirst we move to the sparrow-hawk and its hunger. By extending the biblical text in that way Chrétien has skilfully and effectively combined both of the customs on which the first part of the romance is centred: the hunt for the white stag and the contest for the sparrow-hawk. Both involve a challenge or dispute and a prize; both are described as *costumes* and the word *desresnier* 'to challenge, to dispute' is used of both of them.[26] In that way Chrétien has forged a link between two apparently dissociated events, the chase and the contest, and has prepared for the time when he will finally bring them together. They are combined in successive couplets which themselves have linked rhymes. The *beisier du blanc cerf* is perhaps echoed in lines 2043 and 2047; lines 2037–40 specifically recall lines 1462–83 in which Chrétien had introduced a series of lyrical variations on *esgarder* and its near synonyms *remirer* and *regarder* to convey the delight with which Erec feasted his gaze on Enide and she on him. *Douz Regart* was not an invention of Guillaume de Lorris and the thirteenth century.

Lines 5319–6358

Rhymes and other oral devices play a substantial role in the presentation of *Erec et Enide*, and form an integral part of its *conjointure*. If the romance is to be fully understood, it must be read with an attentive ear, to use a paradoxical phrase. By blending simple and ornate rhymes in different proportions and by creating different patterns from them, Chrétien can vary the rhythm of his romance, can keep his audience's attention and can underscore the importance of a particular section of his text. Just as rhymes cannot be considered separately from other oral devices, so it is important not to consider the passages where they are used in isolation.

That point can be illustrated by considering the *Joie de la Cort*, that final test for Erec and also for Enide. Sequences of ornate rhymes play an important part in the episode taken as a whole: among the many examples which could be cited are the lines where the adventure is first named (lines 5411–20), the description of the enchanted garden (lines 5711–6, 5719–22 and 5725–32), Maboagrain's challenge and the ensuing contest (lines 5855–62 and 5939–48) and the joy which greets Erec's victory. The general delight at his triumph (lines 6112–39) is emphasized both by the choice of ornate rhymes (lines 6125–34) and by the repetition of *joie* and the use of associated words like *esjoie* and *lié*; only one person, Maboagrain's damsel, does not share in the rejoicing, being overcome by grief and tears (lines 6140–82). These contrasting reactions recall the explanation of the *Joie de la Cort* which had been given to Erec by King Evrain and the feelings voiced by the townspeople when Erec first arrived, and later when he set out to seek the Joy. Repetition was then used to emphasize the strangely contradictory nature of this Joy,[27] which seemed more likely to lead to death and sorrow than to honour.[28] One of the remarks addressed to Erec by the townspeople is especially significant: 'Mar i fus' (line 5666).

All these elements bring to mind passages earlier in the romance. Erec and Enide's departure 'en avanture' (line 2763) had been most immediately provoked by Enide's remark 'Con mar fui' (line 2492), a remark twice echoed in that particular scene.[29] The departure was for Enide the occasion of grief and tears, emphasized there by the repetition of words like *duel* and *plorer*.[30] Enide's mood then contrasted markedly with the joy which had been stressed on several previous occasions: when Erec and Enide were betrothed, when Erec defeated Ydier,[31] on the couple's wedding-night[32] and on their arrival at the court of Erec's father.[33] That first scene is the most important in this connexion for it is there that Chrétien begins to prepare for effects which will be fully achieved only later. Joy is the keynote of lines 679–85 which immediately follow the speech of one line in which Enide's father signifies his consent. There is thus no doubt that the *Joie de la Cort* is an integral part of the romance and that Joy and Sorrow are important elements in the *sen*, the sense of the work as a whole.[34]

Repetition, like ornate rhyme, will be heard by those who have ears to hear. Whatever the justice of the reference in the *Uncommercial Traveller* to 'five hundred thousand volumes of indifferent rhyme, and no reason', no similar criticism can be made of Chrétien de Troyes.[35]

La Mort le Roi Artu:
an Interpretation

FAITH LYONS

IN attempting a fresh evaluation of the prose romance, I have used the indispensable works of the late Jean Frappier, his edition of the text[1] and his literary study.[2] My first paragraph summarizes briefly those parts of the narrative which receive most attention in the course of my task. At the outset of the *Mort Artu*, the main characters are in residence at Camelot; soon Arthur presides over the Winchester tournament which is later followed by joustings at Taneborc and then at Camelot. Lancelot is detained by illness near Winchester so that a jealous misunderstanding alienates Guenevere from him and his kinsmen. At last the queen becomes wholly isolated after she offers a deadly poisoned fruit to Gaheris, brother of Mador. By a sudden reversal, she and Lancelot are then reunited until events, based on the *Tristan* romance, overwhelm them. The fateful, unending war breaks out in which Arthur and his kingdom must perish. The survivors perform what duties they can for themselves and for the noble dead.

Alongside traditional Arthurian themes, the first third of the *Mort Artu* contains two new episodes: that of the Maid of Escalot and that of the Poisoned Fruit. These finally overlap with one another, the second episode breaking into the first just before a boat carries the damsel's corpse to Arthur's palace. Other fictional elements also intrude to form an interwoven narrative known as *entrelacement* or interlace. Arrivals and departures at court of Arthur's knights are framed and boxed in by the episodes of the Maid of Escalot and of the Poisoned Fruit. She is buried soon after the interment of Gaheris, dead by poisoning. Together with her testamentary letter accusing Lancelot, the maiden's death constitutes a trigger signal, a time bell for his return to court. He then rescues the queen by his victory in judicial combat. Guenevere has handed a gift of fruit to Gaheris, an unsuspecting knight. This highly sensational incident inculpates the queen for homicide; now she must find a

138

champion for a trial by combat. Contrived as it is, this expedient serves to reunite Lancelot and his lady. The subterfuge which connects the Maid of Escalot to Lancelot's story is an equally fortuitous expedient. This is the rash boon, the granting of a promise without knowing what will be required of one. By this means, the damsel tricks Lancelot into wearing her sleeve at a tournament, ostensibly for love of her. In an important communication,[3] Jean Frappier cites the above instance from the *Mort Artu* as the example of a strange custom, Celtic in origin, common enough in the Old French romances to be termed the Arthurian boon, 'le don arturien'.[4] For readers of Chrétien de Troyes there are parallels to the above fictional elements, notably in *Yvain*: the rescue of Lunete by her champion from burning at the stake; or in the *Conte de Graal*, the wearing by Gawain of a silk sleeve as a love-token at the Tintagel tournament. By contrast, the *Mort Artu* uses in a more sophisticated way similar material to make an impact on the characters.

After fighting incognito, Lancelot lies wounded in a house near Winchester. Returning from the same tournament, Gawain lodges with the vavassor of Escalot and enjoys flirtatious conversation with his daughter (26, 17–71). Recognizing Lancelot's shield, he informs the love-sick damsel that her knight has no sentimental attachment at court (28, 16–19). He then leaves, believing wrongly that Lancelot is enamoured of her (29, 7–11). Absent from Winchester at Arthur's request, Guenevere learns little from the king and his nephew who respect Lancelot's anonymity (31, 5–9). Some scanty information reaches her by a device I have called 'cross-linking.' A day or so after the tournament, there occurs at Camelot the first important linking with the absent Lancelot. Gawain speaks of the victor of Winchester, an unknown knight with a red shield, and on his helmet a sleeve (31, 9–16). Guenevere feels, but cannot say, that her lover would never wear another's token (31, 16–19). Then Girflet blurts out that he has identified Lancelot as the knight of the sleeve (32, 1–11). At this the queen withdraws to weep in secret (32, 20–30). A second important 'cross-linking' follows between the absent knight and Arthur's court two weeks later. Pledging the king to secrecy, Gawain reports on the Maid of Escalot's love for Lancelot which he believes to be reciprocated (35, 24–45). Arthur himself thinks his absence is due to the wound inflicted at Winchester (36, 10–14). Overhearing all that is said, Guenevere questions Gawain about the damsel – she is the beautiful daughter of the vavassor of Escalot. Their conversation confirms the sorrowing queen in her fears (36, 20–4). These events reported by what I call 'cross-linking' are reinforced by a 'knock-on' or 'domino' effect. For example, the queen gives Bohort news of his cousin's supposed faithlessness. At each successive report from Gawain, she summons him. In the first interview, Bohort confirms that he himself wounded the knight of the sleeve (34, 14–19). Guenevere complains of her lover whose faithlessness Bohort steadfastly denies (34, 28–40). Two weeks of misery at court follow for the kindred of Ban because of the queen's anger and Lancelot's silence. She then summons Bohort again to inform him that his cousin is dallying with a damsel at Escalot (36, 27–9). Guenevere says she will never be reconciled with Lancelot (36, 45–7). Bohort retorts that her knight has loved her truly (36, 64–6). He will leave court at once to quest for him (36, 50–2). In conclusion, these successive interviews reveal the romance-writer's intentions. He distances the characters from one another. Near Winchester his hero lies in a retreat, at Camelot his heroine withdraws into growing isolation, while Bohort abandons her to search for his elusive lord. This situation will be resolved by the final drawing together of all three characters for the judicial combat.

To maintain Lancelot in isolation from court, his incognito and his wounding are the devices used by the prose writer. Favoured by Chrétien de Troyes, the incognito can be found in *Erec*, *Yvain* and *Cliges*. In the *Mort Artu*, treatment of the device is wider in interest than in the verse romances. Indeed Lancelot's disguise at Winchester may even reflect in part a religious scruple, according to Jean Frappier.[5] He argues that, alongside fearfulness for his knightly renown, Lancelot may feel reluctant to seek worldly glory openly so soon after his return from the Grail quest. This is surmise indeed, since the text does not support any religious slant to the hero's incognito. To quest for adventure secretly, Yvain in Chrétien's romance steals away from court.[6] To attend a tournament unidentified, Lancelot slips out of Camelot. Chrétien's hero dismisses his squire before attempting any feat of arms. Lancelot acts in similar fashion lest his squire's presence betray his own identity (16, 57–63). Later Arthur observes that Lancelot came secretly to Winchester in order to avoid any refusal to joust with him if his identity were recognized (30, 43–6).[7] In the *Mort Artu*, the stratagem does permit him to test his martial skill against his own kinsmen. Throughout the first third of the prose romance, Lancelot remains attached to his incognito for many weeks. For example, he warns the two brothers of Escalot that in future he will often depart alone, giving no news (56, 16–18). He insists upon continuing his incognito when confronted by Guenevere's unyielding hostility after Taneborc (60, 70–6). His return to court waits upon the death of the Maid of Escalot which will end the queen's mistrust of him. He cannot appropriately resume his identity until after his defeat of Mador, her accuser (75, 54–6). In this respect, his attitude is dictated by the narrative context of the romance.[8]

Alongside the incognito, Lancelot's isolation is maintained by his woundings. At Winchester he is wounded because disguise hides his identity from Bohort and Hector. In Chrétien's romance also, friends fight because of non-recognition. Examples are fights in *Erec* and *Yvain* where non-recognition excuses the combatants. Medieval writers find piquancy in such incidents. In the *Mort Artu*,[9] Hector wishes death to an unidentified victim (24, 35–40). The latter in turn vows death to an unknown assailant (40, 17–21). Of Lancelot's initial wound, Jean Frappier suggests that it may begin for him a religious type of expiation: 'L'expiation de Lancelot commence; il est en danger de mort.'[10] One must object that Bohort, who inflicts the wound, seems an unlikely instrument of divine punishment. After Taneborc, Lancelot's friends meet and jest about the wounding. Bohort excuses his error because of his cousin's disguise as a new knight, a novice (46, 23–30). If it is intended to give the wound a deep significance, this light-hearted treatment seems inappropriate. Nevertheless, immobilized by wounds, Lancelot is excluded from two successive tournaments. To motivate Lancelot's absence at Taneborc, Albert Pauphilet puts forward a novel explanation: this mishap usefully prevents his open conflict with the Round Table. Countering Pauphilet's argument, Jean Frappier points out the lack at this stage of any aggressive rivalry between the kindred of Ban and the lineage of Arthur.[11] A month or so later, Lancelot misses the contest at Camelot when he is accidentally wounded by a huntsman in the forest. Commenting on the above incidents, Jean Frappier raises a question: 'donc, par deux fois, Lancelot est écarté cruellement des tournois auxquels il brûle de prendre part: n'y a-t-il point là un avertissement céleste?'.[12] It is true that for Lancelot enforced absences through his wounds appear as misfortunes. Yet the resulting delays have in fact a positive and beneficial aspect, unbeknown to him. Because he is absent from Taneborc, he does not confront Guenevere's hostility too soon, before his full recovery. Because he misses the contest at Camelot, he does not risk the discovery of his identity, jeopardizing his incognito before the important judicial combat. The above interpretations are implicit in the text. Moreover it seems incongruous to describe wounds in practical and worldly fashion, while using them to warn Lancelot on heaven's behalf. This fact surely militates against an extra-terrestrial view of the woundings. Before Taneborc, the doctor treats Lancelot's relapse in a common sense way (40, 26–9). Before the Camelot tournament when he is wounded accidentally by the huntsman (65, 35–9), a hermit advises timely prudence.[13]

Jean Frappier claims that Lancelot at Taneborc attempts to conceal his whereabouts and state of health without justification, 'sans raison valable'.[14] But the fact is that he then exercises discretion, because he no doubt feels too ill to meet his friends. After his full recovery, they proceed to Camelot together where Guenevere's hostility compels him to return to isolation. One may fairly say that his anonymity persists right through from Winchester to the coming judicial combat. Yet Lancelot reassures Bohort by promising to attend the Camelot tournament within a month (61, 8–15). In advance, he orders his squire to prepare a white shield such as would identify him to his kinsman alone (64, 8–10). These preparations are realized in an unexpected way. On the day fixed for the judicial combat he appears at court, after recovering from a wound in a hermitage. Helmeted, he carries the selfsame white shield (82, 3–13). The attitude of other knights also foreshadows Lancelot's victory over Mador. In a recent article on the structure of the Poisoned Fruit episode,[15] a

141

ɪʳench scholar censures the conduct of Gawain when he first refuses to champion the queen, and then belatedly recognizes her innocence. I quote her judgement as follows: 'cette volte-face survient trop tard; Gauvain, par son manque de générosité, a laissé, au profit de Lancelot, échapper une occasion d'augmenter son honneur'.[16] Surely the situation here is in reality different. After the death of the Maid of Escalot, Guenevere is able to exonerate her knight. Completely healed, he is ready to combat Mador. Gawain cannot usurp the role of queen's champion, once we are aware that Lancelot is at hand. It is not Gawain's egoism that decides who defends the queen. The narrative situation determines attitudes and not the reverse.[17] Bohort's conduct furnishes a parallel. Jean Frappier censures his cruel revenge for Guenevere's harshness to Lancelot.[18] But he may be undeserving of blame when he refuses to act as her champion (77, 34–43). By this refusal, he opens the way for Lancelot whose incognito he is careful not to betray. The narrative context forces him to play a part here that is enigmatic rather than cruel. Subsequently he intimates a champion, other than himself, may come forward, without naming Lancelot. He thus reassures the queen, and maintains suspense (80, 17–23). Will this champion appear in time? If so, it must be Lancelot. Unable to guess his identity, Arthur observes: 'I do not know this knight, but I believe he will gain honour in victory and so be it.' (83, 14–16). Above all, there is surprise at the way the queen's knight formulates the exculpatory oath, saying that she never entertained any thought of false wrongdoing (83, 4–5). Guenevere is thereby exonerated, her fault being unpremeditated and involuntary. She then repeats verbatim her champion's oath, applying it to herself (84, 12–13). Jean Frappier has already remarked on the form of Lancelot's oath, but without noting how Guenevere reinforces it.[19] With right on his side, the victor of the Winchester tournament overcomes Mador in single combat. After enforced absence, Lancelot, the best of the brave, now reaches the height of his career at court. (85, 11–17).

Coinciding with the use of interlace or *entrelacement* the introductory part of the *Mort Artu* (1–84; 85, 1–32) concludes with the judicial combat. A tale of misunderstanding and mishap, its achievement is to create, by the skilful use of surprise, an absorbing interest for the reader in preparation for the plot and characters of the *Mort Artu* as a whole (85, 33–204). Once our attention is won, the excitement of the opening prepares us for the greater tension and suspense of Arthur's downfall. Between the initial tournament and the combat with Mador, concealment and secrecy dominate the atmosphere. Disquiet and confusion result. These various aspects of the narrative are best illustrated by examples. The maid of Escalot makes a second avowal of her love to Lancelot, accompanied by the threat of her own death (57, 7–20). Yet he remains silent about their relationship, only betraying unaccustomed sadness to his companions (57, 42–7). Bohort also has remained silent, saying nothing about Guenevere's unyielding animosity (47, 8–12). Yet, to the reader, if either friend breaks silence, the queen's misunderstanding may be dissipated. Everything waits, however, upon an event unexpected even by Lancelot. Only the maiden's death can restore the queen's trust, and so permit Lancelot's return to court. It constitutes for the narrative what I have called a trigger signal, a time bell for a chain of events to begin. The judicial combat is at hand, heralding the reunion of the lovers and the disaster of their discovery. In the meantime, the circumstances of the death establish for Guenevere Lancelot's fidelity. Despite this, 'cross-linking' between him and Camelot has by now ceased. Lacking a champion, Guenevere despairs of her own rescue from death. She fears that Lancelot will arrive too late to save her, and so he will die of grief (72, 15–23). In actual fact, it is uncertain when or how he can learn of her predicament. Almost immediately, in a good instance of 'cross-linking', he meets by chance a witness of the Poisoned Fruit episode who reports to him that the queen is in danger and at fault (74, 34–63). Lancelot decides that she must be defended (74, 87–98). He himself will save her, whatever her disposition towards him (75, 33–42). He and his kinsmen are unaware in what way Guenevere has changed or how the Maid of Escalot's death has affected her. In confidence and joy, she herself welcomes Bohort back to the court, wrongly expecting his help (76, 12–21). He torments her at first. Yet when she appeals in Lancelot's name for help, he reassures her at once (80, 6–10 and 20–6). Tension falls with restored hope. One cannot justifiably look on this first part of the romance as a mere introduction or preliminary to the main body of the work. Jean Frappier, who calls it a 'mise en train du roman', also indicates its distinctive quality.[20] To the reader, twists and turns in the plot are unexpected, and promote a lively interest. The behaviour of the characters appears at times enigmatic, even disconcerting, when they act in the way the narrative context dictates, and not as autonomous beings. The main theme here is that of separation, arousing suspicion and anxiety. The whole beginning can be enjoyed in its own right, as complete, independent and self-contained.

Immediately following the judicial combat, another episode, the discovery by Agravain of the lovers, opens the main part of the *Mort Artu*. Already, before these two events, the kindred of Ban experience the greatest concern for the missing Lancelot. In their unshared knowledge of Guenevere's jealousy lurks the fear of his possible suicide for love (60, 42–51). Faced by disquiet, Hector warns Bohort of a future war against Arthur over Lancelot's love for the queen (66, 51–4). His prediction occurs after the tournament which their prestigious kinsman expected to attend. To Arthur's inquiry for news Bohort replies ominously. Yet Hector's talk of a great war is premature. Such a danger does not emerge until the episode of the lovers' discovery. However Hector's isolated prediction of conflict does serve to link the introductory part of the *Mort Artu* with the rest of the narrative. Such must be its purpose here. It is an anticipatory pointer, and a surprising one.

In the earlier part of the *Mort Artu*, one group at court is singled out, the kindred of Ban, Hector, Bohort and Lionel. As foreign knights, they are not vassals of Arthur (79, 45–9). At court, they occupy guest accommodation (33, 3–5 and 80, 28–30). They are favoured by the king and above all by the queen (36, 90–3). At important moments, attention is fixed on them, particularly on their spokesman. Faced by Guenevere's jealous denunciation of her knight, Bohort speaks plainly. After the Grail quest, he and his kinsmen tarry in Logres because of Lancelot's attachment to her (36, 59–66). One must infer that they accept his adultery on sufferance (36, 77–80). Bohort has also spoken of their future withdrawal to some great seignorial household, or to their own lands overseas (36, 52–8). He puts this same plan to the approving Hector and Lionel. They will find peace in Gaunes or Benwick (Benoïc), if Lancelot can leave her (36, 81–6). Bohort surely displays here no indulgence for the adultery. If he pleads with Guenevere, it is because he believes her cruelty endangers his kinsman's very life (59, 24–6). Jean Frappier appears over-severe when he castigates him for making such pleas, pleas that the French scholar deems to favour the cause of adultery.[21] But, for example, if at Joyous Guard Bohort argues against restoring the queen to Arthur, he fears that Lancelot's sacrifice will prove an unbearable burden (118, 45–54). Earlier the kindred of Ban have experienced cruel uncertainty in the dread that Lancelot cannot live on, unreconciled with Guenevere (60, 32–51). Within a month, concern is so great that Bohort curses the hour which saw the adulterous love begin (66, 46–9). This is the clearest inditement of Lancelot's affair, and it comes from his own kinsman and friend. Thereupon Hector makes a first prediction of war.

In the *Mort Artu* predictive warnings are specific and repeated. After the Camelot tournament, Hector's isolated threat of war with Arthur is a precursor of similar warnings. Following on the judicial combat, Bohort takes up Hector's presage, and Lancelot is warned against unending war with Arthur, on the eve of Agravain's plot. He persists in visiting Guenevere, and makes good his escape (90, 81–4). Bohort then announces the outbreak of the war he has just predicted (90, 85–92). In this way, timely warning frames an ill-fated episode, the discovery of the lovers. Upon hearing of Gaheriet's death, Lancelot will forecast war with Gawain as well (96, 11–15). In the course of this war, direct warnings come to the king's nephew from messengers at Joyous Guard and at Gaunes. These recall the prophetic vision he has formerly witnessed in the Adventurous Hall of the Rich Fisher King.[22] The pointers here are therefore both retrospective and anticipatory. It is foretold that the siege of Gaunes will leave Arthur without success and Gawain without health (131; cp. 110, 34–55). On his death-bed, the king's nephew seeks too late to prevent the worst of the prophecy, that concerning the battle with Mordred (172, 11–15). In the *Mort Artu* Fate is well represented by that aspect of Fortune which includes lost opportunity, ill-timing and ill luck.

The prose-writer skilfully points to the future departure of the kindred of

Ban overseas, as we have seen. In the end they are exiled to Gaul by Arthur himself. On arrival, Lancelot gives to Bohort the kingdom of Benwick (Benoïc), and to Lionel the kingdom of Gaunes (125, 7–10). Jean Frappier suggests that this gifting of two earthly kingdoms is a deliberate renunciation of temporal might. The French scholar asks whether Lancelot has not thereby rejected earthly power because he craves for spiritual honour, and wishes to win the kingdom of God.[23] However a contrary view may see this territorial distribution as foreshadowing certain events in this world. After the last battle, Bohort is able to return to the two kingdoms (201, 24–5). At Lancelot's death, he disposes of them to his people (204, 1–5). Moreover, after rewarding his faithful kinsmen, Lancelot retains his military power, able to command troops and to direct operations. There can be no effective renunciation by him of his chivalric world, until it disappears with the deaths of Gawain, Arthur, Guenevere and Lionel. Earlier, to save him from despair, Bohort has recommended tournaments, to be followed by Lancelot, not alone, but with a goodly company.[24] After all, his cousin has his own household or 'mesniee' (60, 65–7). This retinue will go wherever required. Nonetheless, Lancelot persists in isolation, retaining his incognito until the combat with Mador. Thereafter, in order to rescue the queen from death by burning, he will need a number of followers. Some eighty knights are killed by them (95, 3–4). They themselves number thirty-two (94, 14–15). Later the queen's escort numbers some five hundred mounts (119, 13–19). Leaving for Gaul, Lancelot commands four hundred knights, not counting the squires and other armed men (122, 8–12). At Joyous Guard eight hundred men fight in his army (115, 32–5). At Gaunes, he is accompanied by ten thousand combatants (149, 35–8). Finally to fight Mordred's sons, twenty thousand men assemble (196, 21–5). It is noteworthy that, in proportion to his needs, Lancelot's company of armed followers continues to grow. A good part of the *Mort Artu* describes warfare at length. It has been claimed by a modern critic that accounts of battles in the romance are wearisome.[25] Yet a non-specialist reader may enjoy the timing which gives pattern and shape to successive conflicts in the *Mort Artu*. Before a battle, preparations begin about prime, or 6 a.m., until hostilities are in full swing by tierce, or 9 a.m. The issue of victory or defeat is often decided about none, or 3 p.m. Fighting normally ends at vespers. Despite the huge numbers engaged, the battle of Salisbury itself follows marked phases.[26] In single combat the time-scale may differ. Lancelot is able to overcome Mador before midday (84, 36–45). To defeat Gawain, he has to fight until vespers (157, 42–5). At Gaunes a day's battle is interrupted prematurely (132, 46–59). The fighting divisions are fully engaged by 9 a.m., or tierce. But when Arthur grievously wounds Lionel, the battle will cease before vespers. At the last and post-Arthurian battle, both sides are evenly balanced by none, or 3 p.m. Then the enemy are routed when Lancelot enters the field, killing Mordred's younger son. After vespers, victorious but lamenting Lionel's death, he rides away alone (199,

22–5). Thus ends his knightly career. Jean Frappier[27] emphasizes how he has just experienced a crisis of hatred against transgressing enemies (198, 8–9 and 26–8). The French scholar believes that this paroxysm of vengeful fury brings disgust and despair, preparing him for final repentance. However one cannot assert that hate in battle is new to Lancelot. Already at Joyous Guard he leads the fight, a carnage in which Gawain's forces encounter deadly hatred (113, 7–13). Shortly before, he spares Arthur's life, in an act of great generosity. Lancelot is besides, at an early stage, confident of personal victory. To Bohort's concern for his safety, he answers that he has ever proved victorious with God's help (60, 80–4). Later he claims that God is on his side when he escapes from Agravain (90, 83–4). He remains undefeated at Joyous Guard, at Gaunes and in the post-Arthurian battle. The name of Lancelot strikes terror in those who expect his onslaught (94, 17–19; 196, 41–2). He is a mighty warrior whose reputation is inseparable from his knightly career. On the other hand, the epilogue interrupts this tale of war to speak of his ascetic life (201, 28–50) and of his saintly death (202, 8–38).

Despite some scenes of fighting, the earlier part of the *Mort Artu* is relatively peaceful. It reveals Lancelot at the outset as a worthy Christian knight. At Escalot, he rises at dawn to hear mass and recite his prayers, as befits such a knight (16, 25–31). Great-hearted, spirited and noble, Lancelot appears throughout as steadfast and faithful. Accused by Gawain of wrongfully killing Gaheriet, he has circumstances in his favour. The king himself orders his nephews to prevent by force Lancelot's rescue of Guenevere. When the queen's allies attack first, some of those present run away because they recognize Lancelot. The alarm is thus raised (94, 17–19). Bohort is surely correct to refute the charge of treacherous killing (145, 53–8). Lancelot's nature is stable despite the stresses of war. He is able to save Guenevere, to spare Gawain, and to rescue Arthur. His habit is to remember with gratitude services and benefits bestowed by others. Even if the queen continues to hate him, he will never see her dishonoured as long as he lives (75, 33–8). In his duel with Mador, he deliberately sacrifices any advantage because he cannot harm a former companion at arms (84, 45–9). He dismounts to fight on foot, and will not kill his defeated opponent who readily kneels before the greatest of knights to surrender his sword. His adversary's generosity enables Mador to identify him. When Lancelot's peace overtures are rebuffed, he laments because the king has bestowed on him many past favours (111, 21–3). By saving Arthur from death in battle, he forces him to regret the war between them (116, 6–13). Lancelot admits to Bohort that he is unable to return Gawain's hatred (145, 75–7). He spares his life without humiliating him. Thereupon Arthur praises Lancelot as the most courteous of knights (157, 50–4). When Lancelot at Gaunes leads on foot an embassy to parley for peace, the king praises his lineage as most chivalrous. He adds to this a prayer for reconciliation (147, 17–26). Lancelot's exemplary virtue finally touches Gawain who relents on his death-bed (172, 16–24). His virtue is the same in kind as ever it was, only the war forces him to exercise it to a greater degree. Changing situations require a moral response that is ever more extraordinary. We have here a feature commonly found in medieval romance, *la surenchère*, the outbidding process by which the hero vies with himself to win ever greater renown. It is as part of a literary convention that his heroism flourishes and dominates. It is difficult to speak here of character development since that would suppose the hero's autonomy and independence. Any development is apparent rather than real.

Jean Frappier has written of the tragic senility present in the Arthurian world. He stresses its mood of bitterness, of retrospection and of doom.[28] Yet the Arthurian heroes are able to display great strength and dexterity in handling arms. At the siege of Joyous Guard, King Arthur fights better than any knight of his age. Indeed he fights better than any knight old or young on his side, so the *estoire* asserts (115, 106–07). Arthur is able to kill in battle the young emperor (161, 49–52). He also displays extraordinary strength when his grasp stifles life in the disarmed Lucan (192, 8–11). When Lancelot is disguised as a new knight, his blows also prove him to be more vigorous than a youth (19, 12–17). Later he kills Mordred's younger son with a great blow (198, 13–18). In her relations with Mordred, Guenevere herself appears as a woman of decision and energy. She has the Tower fortified, as a senior knight might have done (141, 36–46). Lancelot faces trials with fortitude; in the end both Arthur and Gawain respond positively to his generous spirit (165, 15–19, 21–34; 166, 23–31). These examples belie decay and decline among great Arthurian figures. The failure of their world arises more from ill-timed misfortune and tragic accident.

Jean Frappier allots to the goddess Fortune the domain of fallen earthly kingdoms. He quotes from Wace's *Brut* passages which may have suggested the theme to the prose-writer.[29] Yet, there is another medieval commonplace, equally concerned with the downfall of empires, which is more positive, and is itself found in Wace. In the *Roman de Rou*[30] he writes of the death of past civilizations, the disappearance of cities like Babylon and Nineveh (ll. 85 –102). Chronicles preserve past deeds, keeping alive dead conquerors like Alexander and Caesar (ll. 102–30). He concludes that universal death may be overcome by the writings of the clerks (ll. 141–2). It is noteworthy in the *Mort Artu* that, after the Maid of Escalot's death, Arthur orders the circumstances to be inscribed on her tomb so that 'those who come after us may have her in remembrance'. Similarly Lancelot bequeaths his shield to St Stephen's, Camelot, as a memorial of his deeds in Logres. Such gestures symbolize the way in which the romance itself recalls the great and noble men of Arthur's kingdom who deserve to be remembered. Indeed the writer uses *li contes* or *l'estoire* to designate his own narrative (39, 23–4; 57, 40–1). In some instances, he seems to appeal from his own narrative to *l'estoire*, as if to a written authority which supports some detail, for example 'encore l'aferme l'estoire' (115,

147

106–7). No doubt, one should give full credence to what the prose-writer sets down in his narrative, for example in relation to Lancelot. The adultery theme is attenuated in the *Mort Artu* by the threat of death to the lovers and by their separation. Gawain's excessive fault is redeemed when he at last relents, attempting vainly to make amends. His tomb records his sole responsibility for his own destruction. The overall effect is to diminish Lancelot's guilt. Within his own tale of Arthur and Lancelot, the *Mort Artu* author alludes to the earlier part of the prose Lancelot. His 'pointers' are both retrospective and anticipatory, as exemplified in the warnings directed at Gawain. Besides this type of brief retrospective 'pointer', there is the more extended type represented by the Morgan episode where scenes are portrayed of Lancelot's past life. The effect here of proof of adultery is neutralized, as it were, by the Maid of Escalot theme which seems at times to confirm Lancelot's infidelity to Guenevere. The Morgan episode[31] is what one may term a 'marker' or 'weight' which anchors us retrospectively in the time when Lancelot is a new knight. In a sequence of past events painted on the walls, Galeholt, Lancelot's early friend, is portrayed (52, 4; 53, 1–20). This acts as an anticipatory 'pointer' to Lancelot's later burial with him in a shared grave.[32] The *Mort Artu* introduces into Lancelot's death a dichotomy since his soul is lifted up by angels in a heavenly vision, while his bodily remains are removed to Joyous Guard for an earthly funeral. With his eyes on the worthy and spiritual death, Jean Frappier thinks that Bohort misunderstands when he weeps openly for his late lord.[33] However Bohort's role here is surely to witness the fulfilment of the prophecy that Galeholt and Lancelot would one day share the same grave. Eugène Vinaver cites Lancelot's burial as an example of the way in which the recurrence of a theme may convey new meaning. For him, this 'symbolic ending' to the prose romance 'brings home but only to those whose memory can retain it' a group of events culminating in Galeholt's death, 'as if the mind's eye could absorb simultaneously all the scattered fragments of the theme in the same way as our vision can absorb the development of motif along the entire length of an interlaced ornament'.[34] Lancelot's poverty as a hermit is manifest when the bier carrying his body is dragged painfully by hand, in contrast to the horse-drawn bier escorted by knights that transports Gawain's corpse to Camelot (202, 41–5). Yet in all other respects Lancelot's funeral is a seignorial one, with loud lamenting over the body as it rests in the principal chapel, where it receives the honour due to so great a knight (202, 46–53). Laid to rest in Galeholt's rich tomb, and in the presence of King Bohort, Lancelot experiences what is a fitting end to his own story and to the tale of the kingdom of Arthur.

The River Humber in French Arthurian Romances

CEDRIC E. PICKFORD

THE part played in Arthurian romance by a major natural geographical feature of the island of Britain may throw an interesting light on the function of geographical realism for both the readers and writers of some of the romances of the Round Table. At the beginning of his *Historia Regum Britanniae* Geoffrey of Monmouth, in his description of Britain, mentions the three principal rivers: 'tria nobilia flumina, Tamensis videlicet et Sabrinae, necnon et Humbri, velut tria brachia extendit, quibus transmarina commercia ex universis nationibus eidem navigio feruntur' (éd. Faral, § 5, ll. 15–18, p. 73).[1]

Brief descriptions of the islands of Britain are to be found, of course, at the beginning of Bede's *History of the English Church and People*, and in a more precisely Arthurian context in Gildas's *De excidio et conquestu Britanniae* and in the historical miscellany usually described as the *Historia Britonum* of Nennius. Bede does not mention the rivers at all, and Nennius and Gildas refer only to the Thames and the Severn. Geoffrey, and following him Wace, develops two points in particular concerning this estuary: the first is of minor importance, the second is to have fascinating consequences in terms of romance.

According to Geoffrey, the estuary derived its name from that of Humber, King of the Huns, who, after his defeat by Locrinus and Kamber was drowned therein (éd. Faral, ch. 24, p. 93), or as Wace expands it:

> E en une eue s'enbati
> Ki de sun nom Humbre est nomee
> Pur Humbro fu Humbre apelee;
> Humbre cest non l'eue reçut
> Pur Humbro que dedenz morut.
> (*Le Roman de Brut*, éd. Arnold,
> vv. 1310–14)[2]

149

But this great estuary is more than a geographical feature whose name is explained by this not very striking anecdote, it is a great natural waterway and a barrier or frontier as far as a non-seafaring race was concerned. It is used as a dividing line. Naturally that which is to the north of it is Northumberland, but more strikingly, in Geoffrey, that which is to the South in Loegria (éd. Faral, ch. 72, p. 145). Wace condenses his version at this point (vv. 5237 et ss.) and suppresses here Geoffrey's precise statement: 'Subjacuit metropolitano Eboracensi Deira et Albania, quas magnum flumen Humbri a Loegria secernit'. This silence on Wace's part is curious. On the one hand he does regard the Humber as one of the extremities of Arthur's realm:

> Arthur le set, forment l'en peise;
> Tute s'ost manda des qu'al Humbre,
> Grand fut li pueples, n'en sai numbre;
> (*Brut*, vv. 13242–4)

and on the other hand he does adapt Geoffrey's explanation of the name of Logres:

> Locrin, cil qui esteit ainz nez,
> E plus fort et plus senez,
> Out a sa part la region
> Ki de sun nun Logres out nun.
> (*Brut*, vv. 1267–70)

(Locrinus, qui primogenitus fuerat, possedat mediam partem insulae, quae postea de nomine sua appellata est Loegria, *Historia Regum Britanniae*, éd. Faral, ch. 23, p. 93). The delimitation of the northern frontier of Logres as the Humber is also the object of a note by Joseph Loth, who in his translation in the *Mabinogion* of the story of *Manawyddan, Son of Llyr*, observes: 'Lloegr ou Lloegyr est le nom que les Gallois donnent à l'Angleterre proprement dite, au sud de l'Humber' (*Mabinogion*, trans. J. Loth, tome I, p. 153, n. 1).[3]

This use of the Humber as a boundary is a historical one and is referred to by Bede on more than one occasion:

Confinium usque Humbrae fluminis maximi, quo meridiani et septentrionales Anglorum populi dirimuntur.
(*Historia Ecclesiastica Gentis Anglorum*, I, XXV, p. 45)[4]

is a typical example. Bede does not of course refer to the Southern region as Logres. The other references to the Humber in the Welsh Arthurian tradition include the reference in the Triads to the three great rivers of Britain; the other two being the Thames and the Severn (*Mabinogion*, trans. J. Loth, tome II,

319–20) and to the fact that of the three principal invaders of Britain one, the Corraniaid, from the land of Pwyl, settled on the banks of the Humber (Loth, trans. tome II, pp. 298–9).

The same pseudo-historical function of the Humber is to be noted in all the other references to that estuary which are to be found in Wace's *Brut* as well as in the Anglo-Norman *Brut* (ed. Alexander Bell, *ANTS, 21–22*, 1969)[5] where the river is crossed and recrossed in different military campaigns.

Thus, to pause and take stock, up to the time of Chrétien de Troyes, and somewhat later, the Humber, in Arthurian romance, is correctly described – in very general terms – as one of the three major estuaries of Britain, playing a key role in military campaigns – whether fictional or historical – and because of its size, location and strategic importance, forming an important natural frontier. The tradition is straightforwardly geographical and historical, stemming from – among others – Orosius and Bede, and cannot in any way be described as particularly Arthurian.

Although Chrétien de Troyes sets his Arthurian romances in Britain, he nowhere refers to the boundary of the Kingdom of Logres as being the Humber. In fact the estuary is not mentioned at all in any of Chrétien's romances, though he does of course mention other places in Britain, e.g. Carlisle, Chester, Windsor or London; and the River Thames is mentioned, though not the Severn.[6] Chrétien was not particularly interested in geographical realism, and the absence of the name of the Humber is not surprising; furthermore Chrétien never refers to the land north of the river. What is perhaps less expected is the fact that, according to G. D. West's *Index of Proper Names in French Arthurian Verse Romances*, the Humber is not mentioned at all, except for the single reference in the second continuation of the *Perceval*:

> Li Ombres d'autre part coroit,
> Qui toz estoit plains de saumons,
> De luz, de barz et d'esturjons.
> (ed. Roach, Vol. IV,
> ll. 22580 et ss.)[7]

The salmon and the sturgeon have long since gone, alas. According to this romance, the river is close by the castle of Biau Repaire.

Now this solitary reference is a fascinating case. The name clearly meant little to the scribes who copied the manuscripts for only two seem to recognise it, one reading *Li Ombres* and a second *Li Hombres*. The others deform the name to *Li ambres* or *Li lombres*, two replace the proper name by either *Li havres* or *Le havre*, and one, in despair (?!), writes *une aigue*. For these copyists the name clearly meant little or nothing, and certainly they did not associate it with a geographical reality in eastern England. At the same time the river is associated with the castle of Biau Repaire, a site which, far from having a geographical reality, has, if the expression may be used, an Arthurian reality, for it is introduced by Chrétien in his last romance as the castle of Blanchefleur. From this first slight link with one of Arthur's knights, the River Humber is to become a prominent feature of the prose romances.

It is in the *Lancelot en prose* that the River Humber plays a part in the narrative, and acquires characteristics in which the Arthurian element dominates the geographical. When the young Lancelot comes to Arthur's court for the first time he is known as 'le vallet' or 'le chevalier' even though, at the beginning of the *Lancelot* proper the author has made it very clear that the name of the hero is:

> Lancelos en sournon, mais il avoit non en baptesme Galaaz et chou pour coi il fu apeleis Lancelos, che devisera li contes bien en avant.
>
> (éd. Micha, tome VII, ch. 1 a § 1, p. 1)[8]

Lancelot in fact does not, in the first instance, know his own name. This is revealed to him in the course of his first major adventure, the capture of the castle La Dolorouse Garde. He there lifts up a tombstone, and sees an inscription which reads:

> 'Chi gerra Lancelos del Lac, li fiex au roi Ban de Benoÿc'.
>
> (éd. Micha, tome VII, ch. XXIV a § 32, p. 332)

He keeps this secret for himself, asking the damsel who is with him not to reveal it, and continuing to be known for some time longer as 'le blanc chevalier'. The adventure of the castle of Dolorouse Garde is thus not only the first major adventure of the new hero, it marks an important turning point, the revelation to the hero of his name and of his destiny. It is therefore necessary to ascertain in what way Dolorouse Garde may be seen as being more important and symbolic than other castles. To take the castle, an attacker had to overcome ten knights who in succession replaced each other as they became exhausted, thus forcing their ever more weary opponent to face a challenger who was fresh (éd. Micha, tome VII, ch. XXIV a, § 3, p. 313). This human defence was complemented by a mechanical one – a huge knight, cast in copper and armed with a mighty axe, was positioned over another portal: as soon as any attacking knight looked at it, it would fall down to the ground – and doubtless crush him.

The route which the young 'blanc chevalier' takes in order to come to La Dolorouse Garde is as follows: he sets out from Camelot (éd. Micha, tome VII, ch. XXIII a, § 1, p. 287) and after resting for a while on account of the heat, he leaves the main track and, in a narrow forest path, is struck in the face by a branch. At nightfall he sets free a damsel who is imprisoned on an island meadow in a lake, and is thereby enabled to free another damsel who had been guarded in a tent by a jealous knight, whom the young 'blanc chevalier' defeats in a joust. When the news of this exploit reaches the queen, she sends a sword to Lancelot (whom the storyteller will henceforth describe as a knight and not a valet, since he has received a sword) (éd. Micha, tome VII, ch. XVIII a, § 16, p. 298). The new knight travels on to Nohaut and there, with the help of Keu, overthrows the two champions of the King of Northumberland, who have been oppressing the Dame de Nohaut. A few days later – 'un lundi matin' – the young knight leaves Nohaut (éd. Micha, tome VII, ch. XXIII a, § 25, p. 304). He travels for a day through the forest, and passes that night in a house which is thirty English leagues from Nohaut where there is the tomb of Leucan, a nephew of Joseph of Arimathea (éd. Micha, tome VII, ch. XXXIII a, § 28, p. 306). Thence the new knight leaves the land of Nohaut and comes to a river after travelling for several days. The river crossing is guarded by Alibon, whom the new knight overthrows. Alibon is sent to Arthur's Court, and we learn that the river crossing was called the 'Gué la Reine' after a combat which took place there when Arthur was sojourning by the Humber, 'il s'estoit logiés sur Hombre' (éd. Micha, tome VII, ch. XXIII a, § 32, p. 308). Thus the land of Nohaut was situated within reach of the Humber. The descriptions so far have not had the detailed precision which enables the reader to visualize either the geographical situation or the physical appearance of the places mentioned. When the young knight approaches the Dolorouse Garde the narrator sets the scene with precision and clarity:

> . . . . toute la fortereche siet en une haute roche naïve et si n'est mie petite, car ele a de toz sans plus c'une arbaleste ne trairoit. Au pié de la roche de l'autre part cort li Hombres et d'autre part cort .I. grant rix qui vient de plus de .XL. fontaines qui toutes sourdent a mains d'une archie del pié de la tor.
>
> (éd. Micha, tome VII, ch. XXIV a, § 2, pp. 312–3)
> (éd. Kennedy, p. 183, ll. 12 et ss.)

After describing the defences and the enchantments we learn that:

> Et par desos estoit li bors assés aaisiés, ou l'en pooit trover toutes les choses qui mestier eussent a nul chevalier errant; si avoit non li bors Chanevinche et seoit tres desus la riviere de Hombre.
>
> (éd. Micha, tome VII, ch. XXIV a, § 4, p. 314)
> (ed. Kennedy, p. 184, ll. 5 et ss.)

Two other references to the river Humber are made in the account of the taking of Dolorouse Garde. Gauvain and nine companions are tricked into entering a castle as guests: they take off their armour, and shortly afterwards

153

they are attacked and imprisoned, together with other companions of the Round Table. This castle is:

> un castelet petit qui estoit en une ille dedans le Hombre sor une roche grande, la plus fort de son grant que nus seust.
> > (éd. Micha, tome VII, ch. XXVII a, § 3, p. 345)
> > (ed. Kennedy, p. 203, ll. 10 et ss.)

Towards the end of the episode of the Dolorouse Garde, Lancelot pursues an adversary whose horse:

> s'adreche vers le Hombre qui d'autre part del castel coroit.
> > (éd. Micha, tome VII, ch. XXIX a, § 7, p. 359)
> > (ed. Kennedy, p. 211, line 27)

To what extent is the river Humber, as it is described here, a geographical reality? The fact that it is an estuary into which several rivers flow may be reflected in the reference to the forty springs which feed streams that run into it, but this seems, to say the least, doubtful. There are no islands in the Humber on which castles like La Dolorouse Garde ever existed, nor is there any site remotely like that of Dolorouse Garde. The area is not noteworthy for its rocky headlands – quite the reverse. But to jump to the conclusion that the author could have no knowledge whatsoever of the region is perhaps too simple a judgement. The possible links between the abbey of Fontevrault and the Vulgate Cycle have been described by Neale Carman[9], and the Plantagenets certainly do seem to have shown interest in the Arthurian prose romances. They, like many of their contemporaries, were widely travelled, and did indeed cross the Humber. Let one example suffice: the itinerary of King John between 26th November 1200 and 12th March 1201 has been described by Lady Stenton.[10] On 23rd January he was travelling north from Lincoln and spent that night near Grimsby, at Great Coates. He crossed the Humber the next day – the exact crossing point is not known (it could have been near Immingham) and he spent that night at Cottingham (on the northern edge of modern Hull) before travelling on to Beverley, thence via Driffield, Scarborough and Guisborough to Durham, Newcastle and Alnwick which he reached on 12th February. For him, and for his retinue, the Humber was a reality, not just the name of a great arm of the sea separating 'Northumberland' from the southern part of England. Similarly the now vanished port of Ravenspur was much used by travellers to and from the Low Countries.

It is not therefore lack of knowledge of the region which made writers present the Humber in the way they do in the romances. Indeed it may be precise knowledge that this great estuary had been a frontier, often an impassable barrier, marking the northern edge of the Kingdom of Logres, which encouraged them to place Dolorouse Garde on its banks. For it was in the adventure of Dolorouse Garde that the great hero Lancelot learns his own name, gains a sword, and also acquires that shield by which he is to become recognised – a white shield with three red bends, which has the power to give him the strength of three knights (éd. Micha, tome VII, ch. XXIV a, § 15, p. 321). It is through the conquest of Dolorouse Garde that Lancelot is made known to the whole court:

> – Qui fu, fait li rois, li chevaliers qui nous fist entrer en la Dolerouse Garde? – Che fu, fait il [Gauvain], Lancelos del Lac, li fiex au roi Ban de Benoÿc, et che fu cil qui venqui l'assamblee del roi d'Outre les Marces, quant il porta armes vermeilles. Et cheste dont nous venons ra il vencue et je parlai a lui: si sachiés que ch'est .I. des plus biax chevaliers del monde et le miex tailliés de tous menbres et si est uns des millors qui ore soit; et s'il vit longement, il sera li mieudres." Tant est espandue la novele que tout le sevent et chevaliers et dames par laiens, et chi fu premierement conneus a cort li nons Lancelot del Lac, li fiex au roi Ban de Benoÿc.
>
> (éd. Micha, tome VII, ch. XLII a, § 2, p. 428)

Lancelot's conquest of the castle on the river Humber becomes therefore a symbol of his entry into his career of greatness as a knight – as an Arthurian knight. And Lancelot in his turn transforms this castle from an enchanted place of terror into a symbol not of the frontiers of hatred, but of the power of friendship, love and adventure. The name of the castle is changed to Joyeuse Garde, and it is thither that Lancelot had conveyed the body of his great friend Galehault, 'le seigneur des Loingtaines Isles', and there Galehault was buried. It is at this point in the narrative that the change of name is noticed:

> il vindrent a la Dolerose Garde, et neporquant cil d'entor le païs l'ape-loient la Joiuse Garde.
>
> (éd. Micha, tome II, ch. L, § 56, p. 252)

Joyeuse Garde is the castle to which Lancelot takes Guenevere after having rescued her from the stake, and it is as a dwelling for lovers that Joyeuse Garde features in the prose *Tristan*. Lancelot takes Tristan and Yseult to Joyeuse Garde and there enjoys the sport of the rivers and the woods (Löseth, *Analyse critique du Tristan en prose* § 344). The terrible castle of Carados has become virtually a *locus amoenus*. Arthur wishes to meet Tristan and Yseult and in order to facilitate the meeting arranges a splendid tournament, which lasts for three days and is the major chivalric event before the Pentecost of the Grail is introduced into the *Tristan*. This tournament takes place at Louverzep, a castle situated on the banks of the Humber and but half a day's journey from Joyeuse Garde (Löseth § 352). Before the tournament proper begins there is introduced the story of the King of the Red City whose body is borne on a ship which comes to rest on the bank of the Humber:

> Tout ainsi come ilz parloient si voient venir parmi le Hombre ung vaisseau tout couvert de soye vermeille. Le vaisseau arriva devant le tref du roy Artus.
>
> (Löseth § 366; *Tristan*, édition publiée par A. Vérard, Paris, 1489, sig. ll, iiii & 2 verso, col. i)[13]

The tragic tale of the murdered King, whose death is to be avenged by Palamède, is brought to King Arthur by 'Humbir bank' (according to Sir Thomas Malory.[14]) Despite the colour and the splendour of the tournament of Louverzep on the banks of the Humber, that estuary retained in the prose *Tristan* something of the sinister atmosphere it had in the *Lancelot*. Earlier in the romance, Tristan and a maiden arrive at the 'Chastel criminel' where knights errant are ill-treated. This takes the form of having to remain in that castle until they have fought against, and vanquished, a knight who challenges them to combat on an island, which is situated in the Humber and linked to the castle by a bridge built of iron (Löseth § 187) (Shades of the Humber Bridge in the thirteenth century!!). The outcome is a happy one, for Tristan's challenger turns out to be his fellow knight Lamorat. And so another potentially mortal combat ends in triumph for the hero Tristan and the reconciliation of Lamorat with his companions.

The use of the name Humber to describe a river by which important, or indeed any, adventures take place becomes detached from any semblance of geographical reality, especially in the later romances. Sometimes, as in the *Roman de Palamède* or *Guiron le Courtois* it is not simply a convenient name to attach to a river, it acquires in addition a fictional location which contrasts starkly with the fictional geography of, for instance, the prose *Lancelot*. In one episode of the *Palamède* it is the name given to the river which flows by Camelot! Meliadus, having waged war against Arthur, is imprisoned in a dungeon at Camelot. Arthur is prevailed upon to allow his royal prisoner to enjoy less harsh conditions and Meliadus is placed in a room 'en la mestresse forteresse de la tour' which, though it is made secure by a strong, heavy iron door, nevertheless has windows giving a fine prospect of the countryside and Meliadus enjoyed this view:

> Le roy se reconforte moult: et combien qu'il soit en selle prison si est il plus lyé qu'il ne souloit: car il avoit leans deux grans fenestres de fer moult fortes. Par ces deux fenestres povoit il veoir par toute la prison, ne homme ne povoit venir dedans Kamaalot a cheval qui passast le Hombre que il ne veist tout clerement.
>
> (*Meliadus de Leonnoys*, éd. D. Janot, Paris 1532, fol. CLVJ recto, col i;

Löseth p. 446, note; R. Lathuillère, *Guiron le Courtois*, § 44, p. 230).[15]

There is clearly no allusion here either to the real river, or to the concept of the Humber as the northern frontier of Arthur's Kingdom. Among later prose romances which ignore these points is the *Suite du Merlin* of the 'Huth' manuscript where it is a river close by which Arthur defeats the armies of the Five Kings:

'Il est voirs que li rois Artus est logiés prés de chi seur l'Ombre a l'entree d'une forest que on apiele Marsale'.

(*Huth Merlin*, tome II, p. 161)[16]

It is a large river: 'Quant il vinrent au Hombre, il le troverent moult profont et moult orgilleus' (Idem, tome II, p. 163) but it is not impassable, the queen indicates a ford:

Et quant il regardent viers Hombre, il voient que la roine l'avoit ja passé et estoit de l'autre part de l'iaue. Et il se voelent ferir dedans, et la roine lour crie: 'N'entrés mie par illuec, mais par de la' si lour monstre le gué.'

(Idem, tome II, p. 164)

This clearly is romancer's licence or ignorance – for a queen to make herself heard across a river which is more than a mile wide is a remarkable feat! A more striking instance of inventiveness is the account of the Humber in the so-called *Histoire de Grimaud*, a part of the *Saint-Graal* as edited by Eugène Hucher, where the Humber is described as a river which: 'se feroit en Saverne desous la montaigne reonde' in a region which is near 'la citeit de Norgales'. (Tome III, p. 454)

Tempting though it may seem to argue that the earlier romances based their references to the Humber on the early historians, and later romances treated the name in an increasingly unreal, even fanciful manner, such an assertion is not supported by the texts themselves, for it is in one of the later Arthurian prose romances that more precise geographical references are again introduced. The *Perceforest* opens with a description of Britain which draws upon Orosius and follows Geoffrey of Monmouth very closely where we read that the island:

si est arrousee de lacz et de rivieres plaines de poissons, et sans ce que la mer la clot par devers midy, par laquelle on navie par devers Gaulle, elle estend en maniere de trois bras trois nobles fleuves, c'est assavoir la riviere de Tamise, de Labruche et de Hongre. . . .

(*Perceforest*, éd. Jane H. M. Taylor, p. 62, ll. 50–5)[17]

C. E. Pickford

As in Geoffrey, or Wace, the Humber is a frontier:

> Depuis ilz partirent le royaume en deux, duquel celle partie qui du fleuve de Hombre se tourne vers Occident elle eschey en la part Ingenii, et l'autre partie avecques toute Albanie a Pereduro;
>
> (Idem, p. 118, ll. 1944–8)

and it derives its name from 'Humber, le roy des Hungres' (Idem, p. 87, l. 889).

Much more novel is the account of the source of the romance given in *Perceforest* itself. The 'author' worked from an ancient book which had been found in an old tower. A wall fourteen feet thick had been pierced by workmen who had discovered an arch beneath which was an altar where lay a 'livre de croniques' (Idem, p. 122, l. 2027). This old book, written in Greek, had been translated by a clerk who had arrived from Greece in a ship which berthed at Hanstonne (Idem, l. 2080) – doubtless Southampton. These remarkable events foreshadow the accounts of sources beloved of more modern novelists, such as Jules Verne whose tale *Journey to the Centre of the Earth* has as its starting point an old book from the shop of Hevelius of Hamburg in which was discovered a parchment inscribed with runic characters. Moreover, the realism of the modern novelist who situates his discovery in Hamburg echoes the realistic detail that the discovery of the source of *Perceforest* took place in the abbey of Wortimer:

> une abbaye qui seoit dessus la riviere de Hombre.
>
> (Idem, p. 121, ll. 2045–6)

The part played by this great estuary is once more a major one: it serves to add realism and authority to the account, but once more is a symbol of the region where wondrous discoveries are made. It seems hardly necessary to add that the Abbey of Wortimer is quite fictitious and no place name on the banks of the Humber can be adduced as a source.

The Humber is a symbolic, yet at the same time quasi-real, starting point of one of the last great prose romances, just as it had earlier presaged the ending of Arthur's kingdom. It is by the banks of the Humber that the duel between Lancelot and his life-long companion Gauvain was fought: Arthur and his companions take a vow to continue the war against Lancelot, and as an army they advance from Camelot to Joyeuse Garde, whither Lancelot has fled after having rescued Guenevere from burning at the stake: 'et s'apareillent d'aler en la terre qui est close del Hombre' (*La Mort le Roi Artu*, éd. J. Frappier, § 105)[18] and Arthur and his army pitch their camp 'seur la riviere del Hombre en paveillons, mes ce fu moult loing del chastel (éd. cit., § 108). A pitched battle follows:

Et cil qui furent assemblé es pres desus la riviere del Hombre commencie-
rent des le matin la mellee qui dura jusqu'a ore de vespres en tel saison
comme en esté; si ne veïstes onques, ne vous ne autres, si cruel bataille ne
si felenesse comme cele fu le jour, car molt i ot d'ocis et de navrés d'une
part et d'autre.

(Idem, § 115)

This great slaughter is the opening episode of the civil war which is to
culminate in the great battle on Salisbury plain where the chivalric world of
Arthur is to come to an end. And at the conclusion of the Vulgate Cycle we
learn that Lancelot, who dies after living the last few years of his life as a
hermit, is taken to be buried in his castle of Joyeuse Garde on the banks of the
Humber.

The part which this river plays in the romances is quite different from that of
the other two sister rivers, the Severn and the Thames. These two were never
to have the symbolic value which the Humber acquired. They do not mark the
limits of Arthur's kingdom, no great Arthurian castle is situated nearby.
Throughout the *Lancelot* – even to the very end – the Humber marks key
moments in the narrative – it is the setting of moments of triumph, of tender
love, and of the resting place of great heroes. And is it too hazardous to suggest
that the Arthurian links of the Humber are still remembered, thanks to the
father of that 'Roy Edouard d'Angleterre' of the *Perceforest* (éd. Taylor, p.
120, l. 2019) namely Edward I, himself an Arthurian enthusiast, whose King's
Town, founded by him in 1299 by the banks of the Humber, has borne over the
centuries on its coat of arms the three gold crowns on a blue field which, as we
see in so many illuminated manuscripts, was the blazon of King Arthur
himself?[19]

Le Lai d'Yonec est-il une allégorie chrétienne?

JACQUES RIBARD

VOILÀ bien des années que nous hantons la 'forêt aventureuse' des lais de Marie de France. Ces petits poèmes, si envoûtants sous leur apparente sécheresse, n'ont cessé d'exercer sur nous une véritable fascination.[1] C'est l'un d'entre eux qui nous retiendra encore aujourd'hui – l'un des plus beaux sans doute: nous voulons parler du *lai d'Yonec*.

Les quelques réflexions que nous voudrions présenter ici, les quelques perspectives que nous souhaitons ouvrir n'ont pas la prétention, il faut le dire d'emblée, d'emporter la conviction générale et nous savons qu'on pourra y faire bien des objections parfaitement légitimes et recevables. Fidèle en effet à un tour d'esprit et à une méthode d'interprétation des oeuvres médiévales dont nous avons donné dans le passé quelques témoignages,[2] nous voudrions nous interroger sur le sens profond qu'on est en droit peut-être de prêter à ce poème passablement mystérieux qu'est le *lai d'Yonec*.[3]

Le point de départ de nos réflexions et de notre tentative trouve en effet sa justification, à nos yeux du moins, dans un certain nombre de difficultés auxquelles on ne peut manquer d'être sensible quand on prend un peu de recul pour examiner cette oeuvre maîtresse de Marie de France.

Le premier problème est lié à la structure même du lai, assez étrange de prime abord, puisque le récit, après avoir suivi un déroulement somme toute assez classique et qui n'est pas sans rappeler celui du *Laostic*, rebondit soudain, en une cauda surprenante, avec l'entrée en scène du personnage d'Yonec. Plus des quatre cinquièmes du lai sont consacrés aux aventures de Muldumarec et il faut attendre le vers 459 pour que le récit bascule et que l'attention se porte enfin sur Yonec. Et c'est pourtant ce personnage, à l'arrivée fort tardive, qui donne son nom à l'oeuvre tout entière. Il y a là, on en conviendra, une originalité dans la facture qui ne peut être sans signification et doit nous mettre en alerte.

Surprenante aussi et non moins significative à nos yeux est l'importance assez remarquable donnée par Marie de France à l'aspect proprement religieux de la longue scène où l'auteur s'attarde à souligner le caractère très chrétien du mystérieux oiseau-chevalier (v. 135–192). On ne peut lire cet important passage, où l'étrange personnage justifie de sa foi dans un credo très orthodoxe avant de recevoir la communion, sans s'interroger sur sa signification. A moins de taxer Marie de France de maladresse – et la maîtrise qu'elle manifeste tout au long de son oeuvre l'exclut d'emblée –, on ne peut rendre compte, nous semble-t-il, de cet épisode sans y voir une intention délibérée de l'auteur, une invitation au lecteur à dépasser le cadre proprement féerique pour y déceler quelque projet caché et plus ambitieux, une invitation évidente à 'gloser la lettre' pour lui conférer un 'surplus' de sens.[4] N'y aurait-il pas, autrement, quelque chose de sacrilège et de profanatoire à nous présenter un amant recevant le 'corpus domini' (v. 186) avant de s'abandonner sans remords aux plaisirs de l'adultère? Rien n'obligeait Marie de France à 'christianiser' de façon si accusée son récit si elle n'avait pas eu quelque intention cachée. Faut-il ajouter encore que la véritable crucifixion de l'oiseau-chevalier ne pouvait manquer d'éveiller à l'esprit d'un lecteur médiéval l'image de cet autre Crucifié qui, à cette époque de foi vivante et militante, était comme une présence constante et obsédante?

Ainsi mis en alerte, à tort ou à raison, il ne restait plus qu'à lire et à relire l'oeuvre en s'attachant à suivre le fil d'Ariane ainsi repéré et à se lancer, à nos risques et périls, dans une interprétation délibérément chrétienne du poème. C'est ce que nous nous proposons de faire, sans ignorer pour autant que d'autres éléments ne cesseront d'interférer avec ceux que nous allons nous efforcer de mettre en lumière. Nous pensons, par exemple, aux apports proprement mythiques qui rattachent ce lai à une tradition folklorique dont le conte de *l'Oiseau bleu* est une manifestation parmi d'autres.[5] Et nous n'oublions pas non plus tout ce que Marie a pu emprunter aux genres littéraires de son temps, depuis les chansons de mal-mariée jusqu'aux romans de Tristan dont son *Chèvrefeuille* montre assez l'influence qu'ils ont exercée sur elle. Faut-il rappeler ici tous les thèmes littéraires dont on retrouve la trace dans son lai: la mal-mariée et le vieillard jaloux, le rôle des 'losengiers', la nécessité du secret et de la mesure, et ce lien amour, souffrance et mort auquel le mythe de Tristan a donné son expression la plus parfaite?

Cela dit, Marie a pu, a dû – c'est du moins notre conviction – utiliser ces motifs pour servir un dessein d'une tout autre ampleur et d'une tout autre signification, comme nous allons essayer maintenant de le montrer.

A laisser de côté les quelques vers du prologue sur lesquels nous reviendrons ultérieurement, le récit s'ouvre, comme bien souvent chez Marie de France, sur ce qu'on pourrait appeler une situation de blocage. Blocage affectif, spirituel, dont l'emprisonnement n'est que la manifestation symbolique – cette tour, cette chambre, où la dame est 'enserrée' (v. 27). Cette dame, disons-le d'emblée, est à nos yeux la figure de l'homme ou, pour mieux dire, de l'âme humaine[6] – une âme humaine véritablement assoiffée d'amour, comme en témoigne la violence de ses plaintes. Et elle nous est présentée comme la prisonnière, d'ailleurs aimée, notons-le (v. 24), d'un couple de vieillards, personnages allégoriques dans lesquels nous reconnaissons la figure de la Synagogue. Ce vieillard 'jaloux' – comme le Dieu qu'il prétend servir –, cette femme porteuse d'un 'psautier' dont elle ne cesse de méditer les versets (v. 59–60), se caractérisent l'un et l'autre d'abord par la vieillesse: lui 'vielz e antis' (v. 12), 'trespassez en eage' (v. 17), elle plus encore puisqu'elle est sans cesse désignée par le vocable de 'la vielle' (v. 55, 59, 169, 177, 190, . . .). Mais – et c'est plus significatif encore – ils sont aussi placés sous le signe de la stérilité: elle 'vedve' et 'sanz seignur' (v. 30), lui incapable d'avoir d'enfant, malgré son désir de transmettre un héritage – ce 'bon heritage' dont parle Marie de France (v. 18) et qui n'est autre que celui de la révélation chrétienne. Vieillesse, stérilité d'un rituel sclérosé que n'anime plus comme autrefois le vent vivifiant du large: 'jadis i ot de nes trespas' (v. 16); qui s'enferme frileusement sur lui-même: 'e aprés lui fermer les hus' (v. 56); qui ne se survit que dans le cadre légaliste et désséché des 'comandements' (v. 36, 57). Prison étouffante où l'âme humaine se débat en vain, en attente d'une libération, où se trouvent impliquées les autres âmes, ces 'autres femmes' enfermées elles aussi 'en une autre chambre par sei' (v. 33–34), figures des justes en attente de la venue du Sauveur, car, de façon significative, il est interdit à la dame, et pour cause, de se rendre à l'église, 'al mustier', pour y entendre le service divin (v. 75–76).

D'où l'évocation nostalgique de ce paradis perdu – 'Mut ai sovent oï cunter / Que l'em suleit jadis trover / Aventures . . .' (v. 91–93) –, de ce temps de l'innocence originelle où l'on pouvait aimer librement – 'Si que blasmees n'en esteient' (v. 99) – avant que le péché ne soit entré dans le monde et avec lui le Décalogue, la loi – cette loi mosaïque dont saint Paul montre bien les liens étroits qui la rattachent justement au péché et à la mort.[7] D'où cet appel aussi à un renouveau spirituel, à un envol, que symbolisent la reverdie et le chant des oiseaux (v. 51–52) et qui viendra arracher l'âme humaine à cette impuissance de l'ancienne loi, qui est prise de conscience du Mal – le 'flum d'enfern' du vers 88 – mais à laquelle manque irrémédiablement le souffle libérateur de l'amour.

L'appel sera entendu. Et c'est l'apparition, au travers de l'estreite fenestre' (v. 107 – ouverture minuscule, mais toujours offerte au fol espoir de l'homme – de ce 'grant oisel' (v. 106), de ce messager ailé, divin, qui n'attendait pour se manifester (car Dieu respecte la liberté de sa créature) qu'un acte de foi et de désir, car lui, de toute éternité, a aimé l'homme:

> 'Jeo vus ai lungement amee
> E en mun quor mut desiree . . .
> Mes ne poeie a vus venir
> Ne fors de mun paleis eissir
> Si vus ne m'eüssez requis.'
> (v. 127–131)

Figure de Messie, attendu, espéré, appelé, être tout de noblesse – 'gentil oisel ad en ostur' (v. 122) – et de beauté – 'kar mut esteit de grant beauté' (v. 141) –, le voilà prenant corps d'homme, s'incarnant sous les yeux d'abord surpris, craintifs, puis rassurés de l'âme humaine en quête de son Sauveur. Et, pour que nul n'en ignore, Marie de France met alors dans la bouche de cet étrange personnage une sorte de rappel du plan divin sur le monde, évoquant en quelques vers très denses la création, la chute et la rédemption:

> 'Jeo crei mut bien el Creatur,
> Ki nus geta de la tristur
> U Adam nus mist, nostre pere,
> Par le mors de la pumme amere;
> Il est e ert e fu tuz jurs
> Vie e lumiere as pecheürs;'
> (v. 149–154)

insistant aussi sur le rôle proprement salvateur de l'Eucharistie:

> 'Si volez aveir le servise
> Que Deus ad el mund establi,
> Dunt li pecheür sunt gari.'
> (v. 158–160)

Puis l'auteur nous fait assister à cette communion qui est comme la manifestation concrète de l'amour de Dieu pour sa créature, la condition même de l'union mystique que vont vivre la dame et son mystérieux amant (v. 192).

Mais ce n'est là encore qu'une manière d'anticipation – car il faut se garder de lire de façon linéaire et chronologique un récit où l'Eternité et le Temps se côtoient et s'interpénètrent constamment. Pour avoir pris un moment forme humaine, le Sauveur n'en reste pas moins fondamentalement un être de l'Autre Monde vers lequel il retourne sans l'avoir jamais vraiment quitté:

> Li chevaliers ad cungié pris:
> Raler s'en voelt en sun païs;
> (v. 195–196)

– ubiquité non moins caractéristique du monde spirituel dans lequel s'inscrit cette sorte de condensé symbolique de l'aventure humaine. Dieu n'est pas venu arracher l'homme au monde d'ici-bas – ce qui est peut-être le cas de Lanval –, mais il l'y laisse délibérément avec la responsabilité de ses actes, lui annonçant seulement, dans une série de futurs prophétiques, les dangers et les souffrances qui le menacent et l'attendent. Cet amour extraordinaire qu'il est venu apporter à l'homme ne peut être que méconnu, incompris, persécuté, et il conduira inévitablement le Sauveur à la mort, redoutée et nécessaire:

> 'Ceste vielle nus traïra
> E nuit e jur nus gaitera;
> Ele parcevra nostre amur . . .
> Ne m'en puis mie departir
> Que mei n'en estuce murir!'
> (v. 203–210)

Pour l'heure l'homme s'abandonne à la joie de la révélation de l'amour et il s'en trouve entièrement changé – 'Esteit tuz sis semblanz changiez' (v. 227). Véritable transfiguration, métamorphose intérieure, spirituelle, qui est comme l'écho et la conséquence de celle du messager divin. L'être ailé – Dieu – s'était fait homme et voilà l'homme qui, à son contact, comme illuminé de l'intérieur, devient un objet d'étonnement et de scandale aux yeux de ceux qui n'ont pas connu, qui n'ont pas voulu, pareille transformation. Le prisonnier, la prisonnière, par son épanouissement spirituel, se rit désormais de sa prison matérielle, de ces 'huis' qu'on ne cesse de refermer inutilement sur elle (v. 190, 246, 262. .).

Mais le Mal n'est pas vaincu pour autant, ce Mal qui est aveuglement volontaire de celui qui ne veut pas voir, qui ne veut pas comprendre. Et puisque les portes, les 'huis', sont impuissantes à retenir le prisonnier, c'est la fenêtre qu'il faut clore. Ce sera alors le thème – largement développé et qui fait écho à celui déjà rencontré dans le lai du *Laostic* – de la ruse, du piège, de l' 'engin' (v. 256, 284), de la trahison – ce thème de la trahison qui connote si fortement celui de Judas:

> Deus, qu'il ne sout la traïsun
> Que aparaillot le felun!
> (v. 295–296)

Et l'oiseau-chevalier, le Messie, viendra s'empaler, se déchirer sur les broches de fer – véritable crucifixion d'amour:

> 'Pur vostre amur perc jeo la vie;'
> (v. 320)

que souligne l'évocation insistante du 'sanc' et de la 'plaie' (v. 317).

Mort d'amour, mort qui féconde aussi – avec peut-être en arrière-plan l'image traditionnelle du pélican, cet autre oiseau divin, nourrissant de son sang ses petits.[8] Cette femme, cette âme, restée désespérément stérile pendant tout l'Ancien Testament – ce cycle de sept ans, écho du chandelier à sept branches:

> Issi la tint plus de set anz.
> Unques entre eus n'eurent enfanz;
>
> (v. 37–38)

voici qu'elle va concevoir un fils auquel on donnera le nom d' Yonec. Véritable 'annonciation', s'exprimant en des termes qui, à l'évidence, font écho à des formules évangéliques bien connues:[9]

> Un fiz avra, pruz e vaillant. . .
> Yönec numer le ferat.
>
> (v. 328–330)

Mais nous nous réservons de revenir tout à l'heure sur ce passage-clef.

Pour l'heure, avec la dame, suivons plutôt l'oiseau blessé au long de son chemin sanglant, véritable calvaire. Fécondée et rachetée dans une sorte de douloureux baptême de sang:

> Devant la dame el lit descent,
> Que tuit li drap furent sanglent;
>
> (v. 315–316)

elle peut maintenant se lancer à la suite de son sauveur – 'a la trace del sanc s'est mise' (v. 342) –, après s'être dépouillée de tout ce qui l'alourdissait et l'attachait encore à la terre – 'ele esteit nue en sa chemise' (v. 341) –, après avoir osé, comme Tristan ou Lanval, le saut dans l'inconnu d'un autre Monde (v. 338–340), ce saut de la foi et de l'amour. Long et douloureux itinéraire, où elle connaîtra les épreuves de la 'porte étroite' – l'entrée sous la 'hoge' (v. 347) –, l'obscurité aussi de ce tunnel ténébreux, cette sorte de nuit spirituelle, 'petite mort' des mystiques:

> Ne pot nïent avant veeir. . .
> El n'i trovat nule clarté.
>
> (v. 349–353)

Mais, au sortir de cette épreuve quasi initiatique, elle verra enfin apparaître, sur un horizon soudain dégagé (v. 356), une cité de rêve, la cité 'tute d'argent'

165

(v. 363), figure de la Jérusalem céleste, une cité que de toutes parts environne l'eau vivifiante – 'curt une ewe tut envirun' (v. 368) –, une cité dont on nous précise qu'elle est comme frémissante du passage des vaisseaux (v. 369–370), [10] à la différence, significative, de la cité terrestre du début du lai, la cité morte qui ne connaissait plus le passage des nefs. Et, à la différence de l'autre encore avec ses huis fermés, cette cité-là est largement ouverte – 'la porte aval fu desfermee' (v. 371) – car elle est tout attente, tout accueil. Alors, dans le silence et la solitude mystiques (v. 376), elle franchira le triple seuil de ces trois chambres successives pour atteindre cette figure de 'saint des saints' où sur un lit-autel, environné d'or pur – symbole de souveraineté – (v. 388) et de cierges enflammés – symbole de divinité – (v. 390–391), est étendu le Sauveur agonisant qui l'attend et qui l'aime: 'cil la receit ki forment l'aime' (v. 397). Un sauveur qui prédit sa propre mort 'en mi le jur' (v. 403) – à la troisième heure, serions-nous tenté de gloser.

Mais l'âme humaine n'a pas encore mérité de rejoindre définitivement son Dieu dans l'Au-delà. Elle doit retourner, rester plutôt – car ce pélerinage sanglant est tout intérieur et quasi onirique – parmi les hommes, ses frères: son itinéraire à elle n'est pas encore achevé. Elle n'est déjà plus 'du monde', mais elle est encore dans le monde. Elle repartira donc, mais en emportant avec elle trois talismans. Un anneau d'abord, anneau qui scelle la nouvelle alliance (au sens biblique du terme) qui la lie désormais et à jamais à son nouveau Maître – signe d'une aventure intérieure qui ne peut que rester parfaitement incompréhensible à l'homme de l'Ancien Testament qu'elle va bientôt retrouver (v. 415–420). Une épée aussi, l'épée en forme de croix de la vengeance de Dieu.[11] Une précieuse tunique enfin – 'un chier bliaut' (v. 438) – qu'il lui ordonne de revêtir et qui, en écho au dépouillement de ses vieux vêtements, fait d'elle un être nouveau – 'revêtez l'Homme Nouveau', a dit l'apôtre Paul.[12] Le Messie peut alors mourir, sa mission est accomplie: l'homme, pour être revenu dans le monde d'ici-bas sans l'avoir peut-être jamais quitté, n'en est pas moins fondamentalement différent, renouvelé – définitivement sanctifié.[13]

Et le récit pourrait s'interrompre ici, comme s'interrompt de façon tout à fait similaire le lai du *Laostic*. La dame est retournée auprès de son mari et nous voilà revenus, semble-t-il, à la situation initiale:

> Si s'en reveit en sa cuntree.
> Ensemblement od sun seignur
> Demurat meint di et meint jur.
> (v. 454–456)

Comme si rien ne s'était vraiment passé, comme si cette aventure intérieure n'était qu'un gigantesque rêve.[14]

C'est alors que le récit rebondit soudain, mettant en scène ce qui avait été annoncé, prédit – toujours ce jeu d'annonces et de rappels qui est la négation même du temps événementiel et chronologique – par le Messie agonisant, qui présentait lui-même sa mort comme encore et toujours 'renouvelée':

> Par une tumbe k'il verrunt
> Orrunt renoveler sa mort . . .
> (v. 430–431)

L'enfant naît et, comme dans les formules évangéliques déjà mentionnées, on lui donne le nom d'Yonec: 'Yönec le firent numer.' (v. 461)

'A la feste seint Aaron' (v. 469) – et on sera sensible aux connotations vétéro-testamentaires de cette dénomination – et selon 'la custume del païs' (v. 474) – traduisons: selon les usages de l'ancienne loi – le vieillard va prendre l'enfant et sa mère pour s'engager 'od ses amis' (v. 473) dans ce qu'il croit être un pélerinage traditionnel – 'mes il ne seivent u il vunt' (v. 478), ajoute curieusement le poète. Et, de fait, un mystérieux 'meschin', envoyé de la Providence, va les dérouter et les conduire 'le dreit chemin' là où ils devaient aller.

Où sommes-nous donc exactement? Encore dans ce monde ou déjà dans l'Autre? On comprend l'embarras des érudits, incapables et pour cause de tracer des frontières précises entre ces mondes qui s'interpénètrent inextricablement.[15] Car cet autre monde où les pèlerins vont arriver est le monde des esprits qui ne connaît pas de frontières géographiques. Les prédictions vont alors s'accomplir: la 'grant tumbe' est là, nouvel avatar de l'autel, avec ses cierges enflammés, ses chandeliers d'or pur et ses encensoirs d'amétiste' (v. 500–508) – l'améthyste, cette pierre de couleur violette, symbole de la Passion.[16]

Et ce sera la révélation finale, cette 'novele' (v. 527) qui est la 'bonne nouvelle': le Christ-Roi – 'de ceste tere ot esté reis' (v. 519) – a accepté de mourir par amour pour l'homme – 'pur l'amur d'une dame ocis' (v. 522). Mystérieux projet de Dieu sur l'homme, dont la dame se fera elle-même l'interprète en déclarant: 'avez oï / Cum Deus nus ad menez ici?' (v. 529–530).

C'en est fini désormais de l'Ancien Testament symboliquement décapité en la personne du vieillard pour faire place à la 'nouvelle alliance', elle-même scellée dans le sang du Christ-chevalier.[17] La dame, l'âme humaine, va s'abîmer définitivement en Dieu dans une union d'amour qui ne connaîtra plus les limitations de la vie d'ici-bas (v. 540–543). Et ce sera le règne d'Yonec, un règne promis et longtemps attendu – 'ainz avum atendu meint jur / un filz qu'en la dame engendra / si cum il dist e cumanda.' (v. 524–526) – qui s'établira alors sur le monde: 'lur seignur firent d'Yönec' (v. 553).

Mais qui est donc en définitive cet Yonec qui donne son nom au lai? Et pourquoi intervient-il si tard et comme par raccroc, telle une pièce rapportée, faisant pâle figure auprès du véritable héros qui semble bien être Muldumarec?

Marie l'a laissé entendre dès le prologue de son lai et elle est restée fidèle à son projet: Yonec est bien l'aboutissement de toute l'histoire. Ce qu'elle a voulu rapporter, ce sont les circonstances de sa naissance, qui était son père et comment il fut engendré dans sa mère (v. 6–8). Qu'est-ce à dire au juste?

A prendre un peu de recul et si l'on veut bien admettre notre hypothèse de travail, le jeu allégorique – si jeu allégorique il y a – se présenterait, pour l'essentiel, de la manière suivante. Le personnage-pivot du lai serait la dame, figure de l'âme humaine, aspirant à vivre un amour spirituel fécondant, épanouissant, auquel font obstacle le vieillard jaloux et sa soeur, la 'vieille', représentants d'une conception archaïque, sclérosée et étouffante de la religion – la Synagogue. Muldumarec serait la figure du Messie, un Christ souffrant, crucifié, dont le sacrifice permettrait à l'âme d'atteindre enfin à cet amour mystique, absolu, qu'elle appelait de tous ses voeux.

Or le Christ-Muldumarec, au moment de mourir, annonce en ces termes à la dame la naissance d'Yonec:

> Un fiz avra, pruz e vaillant;
> Icil la recunforterat.
> Yönec numer le ferat.
> (v. 328–330)

Ces paroles ne sont pas sans rappeler, de façon très nette, la promesse faite par Jésus à ses apôtres dans l'Evangile de saint Jean, quand, au cours de la dernière cène, il leur annonce la venue du 'Paraclet', de l'Esprit Saint, dont il leur précise d'ailleurs qu'il demeure avec eux et en eux et dont il dit encore qu'il confondra le monde 'en matière de péché, en matière de justice et en matière de jugement'[18] – ce qui explique sans doute et justifie le don et l'usage de l'épée dans notre lai. Pour nous, Yonec n'est rien d'autre que le nom que Marie de France donne au Paraclet.

On remarquera d'ailleurs que ce nom d' 'Yonec' est en quelque sorte glosé par Marie elle-même dans le vers: 'icil la recunforterat.' On sait assez que les auteurs médiévaux recourent volontiers à ce procédé quand ils veulent orienter leur lecteur dans le sens qu'ils souhaitent donner à un nom propre à première vue de signification obscure. C'est ainsi que pour notre part nous avons glosé le nom de 'Logres' dans le *Conte du Graal* en nous appuyant notamment sur le vers 'qui jadis fu la terre as ogres'.[19] Somme toute, Marie déclare ici sans ambages qu' Yonec sera 'le Consolateur'. On sait que c'est une des traductions traditionnelles que propose l'Eglise pour ce terme assez obscur de 'Paraclet' qui ne se rencontre, à notre connaissance, que dans l'*Evangile de Jean*. Curieusement d'ailleurs, si l'on en croit U. T. Holmes, le nom celtique d' Yonec reprendrait un terme breton qui signifie précisément 'qui récon-forte'.[20] Il y a là, à défaut de preuve, un faisceau de présomptions, une conver-gence de témoignages, qui méritent pour le moins examen et réflexion.

Dans cet esprit, on comprendrait que Marie ait souhaité donner à son lai cette conclusion qui n'a désormais rien de postiche: après le sacrifice rédemp-teur du Christ, mettant fin à l'ancienne loi, s'ouvrirait pour l'homme le règne de l'Esprit – 'lur seignur firent d'Yönec' –, cet Esprit envoyé par le Père pour poursuivre ici-bas l'action du Fils et en révéler à l'homme toute l'importance et toute la signification. Sous un habillage romanesque, la poétesse développerait ainsi une large fresque allant de l'Ancien Testament, temps de l'attente et de l'espoir, au règne de l'Esprit Saint, en passant par la venue et le sacrifice du Christ.[21]

C'est peut-être, pensera-t-on, prêter à notre gentille poétesse une largeur de vue et un projet littéraire d'une singulière et presque vertigineuse ambition; les lais de Marie de France ne sont pas *la Quête du saint Graal*. Et pourtant il n'y a là rien de si extraordinaire quand on pense au climat chrétien dans lequel baigne notre Moyen Age, quand on se rappelle aussi combien le jeu symbolique, allégorique, est familier aux auteurs et au public de ce temps. Peut-être est-ce nous qui sommes trop timorés, trop déformés aussi par nos habitudes et nos étroitesses modernes, au point de refuser à tort aux grands auteurs du Moyen Age une vigueur de pensée et d'écriture qui déconcerte nos petits esprits.

The Welsh Romance of the
Lady of the Fountain (Owein)

BRYNLEY F. ROBERTS

CRITICS have been slow to follow the lead given some forty years ago by Saunders Lewis[1] who saw in the three Welsh 'romances', *Gereint*, *The Lady of the Fountain* (or more briefly *Owein*) and *Peredur*, the pinnacle of the Welsh prose tradition in the Middle Ages. This neglect was due, in no small measure, to the constraints placed upon Welsh scholarship by a lack of primary research aids and of well-edited critical texts. Remarks on the excellence of the prose tales rarely involved more than general comments on their style, and the matter of their literary composition was usually ignored. On the other hand, the development of the material of the stories became a major area of research, since much of the scholarly interest in these tales developed in a period of source criticism and comparative mythology. The result was that when native narratives were approached from a non-linguistic standpoint, it was usually in terms of a folkloric or mythological interpretation based on a study of more or less analogous material, and the search for a hypothetical 'original' or 'pure' version. This attitude, which owed much to the theories of the nineteenth-century comparative linguists, had special relevance to the study of the Welsh 'romances' which became dominated by the question of their possible relationship with the corresponding romances of Chrétien de Troyes. The discussion was important for the light it threw on the origins of the narrative material of the romances and had relevance for any study of Chrétien's innovating originality, but nevertheless the *Mabinogionfrage*[2] had a specially stultifying effect on any literary discussion of the Welsh stories. They were read, not for their own sakes, but for the light they might shed on the composition of the French poems and for the evidence they might provide for the priority of one version over the other. An analysis of structure aimed to show by listing or rearranging episodes and motifs that the one version was 'purer' or 'more logical' or 'reflected the original more faithfully' than the other. Literary qualities became part of the argument and the assumed virtues were not always those of their own tradition. The Welsh tales were criticized for lacking the sophistication of the French, Chrétien's romances were faulted for not having the narrative qualities of the Welsh. Changes in attitudes allied to good editions have allowed emphases to shift and have enabled readers to deepen their appreciation of Middle Welsh prose writing, so that the tales can be read for what they may reveal not only of their origins but also of their authors' skills and intentions. *Owein* is one which repays such study.

There has always been agreement on the essentially native character of the style of *Owein* and it has been generally recognized that this reflected, in a literary form, the skills of the *cyfarwydd* or reciter of tales. Dr Rachel Bromwich in a valuable study[3] drew attention to many of these characteristics, and more recently Mr Tony Hunt[4] has used Max Lüthi's work to reveal the folktale elements in the Welsh story. The influence of oral recitation on written tales like *Owein* is of two kinds. The *cyfarwydd* tradition must be considered a major stylistic source but there is in much medieval literature an oral influence of a different kind, arising from the common custom of audible reading in both private and public situations and of the same method in copying a text from an exemplar. Variant readings, laboriously gathered by editors as they collate texts, are frequently nothing more than the result of a copyist unconsciously altering the syntax of a phrase or sentence or exchanging one word for another as he mouthed the text. Similarly, modern editors, bound to grammatical logic, 'correct' and re-edit sentences the meaning of which is perfectly clear, though they may lack the syntactical consistency which grammatical analysis demands. Reading the text with a class is the closest one gets to an oral recitation of *Owein*, but it seems to confirm that there is no need to emend a sentence such as this which has no main clause:[5]

A gwedy gwisgaw vy arueu ac adaw vy mendyth yno a dyuot hyt vy llys vy hun;

or this:

Ac ef a welei morwyn benngrech uelen, a ractal eur am y phenn a gwisc o bali melyn ymdanei, a dwy wintas o gorwal brith am y thraet ac yn dyuot y'r porth.

A sentence clumsy and ill formed on the page:

A honno [the portcullis] a'e medrawd odis y pardwgyl y kyfrwy yny dorres y march yn deu hanner trwydaw a throelleu yr ysparduneu gan y sodleu

171

> Owein ac yny gerda y dor hyt y llawr, a throelleu yr ysparduneu a dryll y
> march y maes, ac Owein y rwng y dwy dor a'r dryll arall y'r march;

becomes, when told, a vivid expression of a sudden breathtaking moment of
drama which can be fully exploited only on film. At the other extreme, it is
difficult not to sense that the formal balanced rhythms of other sentences also
derive from oral reading.

More easily recognized as oral elements are the delight in glowing colours
and the descriptions of courtly appurtenances and costly dress, features which
the author of the *Dream of Maxen* used as lovingly as the author of *Owein* and
which, though taken to satirical extremes by the author of the *Dream of
Rhonabwy*, were nevertheless designed to evoke a sense of awesome wonder as
being not of this world. Our author, like those responsible for the other tales
and 'romances', has the same respect for direct untrammelled expression of a
kind which has no waste words but which never becomes curt, and for him as
for his fellow writers the essence of narrative lay in an account of a series or
sequence of events and actions rather than in an analysis of motives and
emotions or descriptions of character. His descriptive passages are brief and
stereotyped as he draws on his knowledge of the oral tradition for the familiar
adjectives, the proven comparisons and the tried collocations. But from the
same tradition comes his ability to catch the cadences of real conversation and
the ability to switch effortlessly from *oratio recta* to *obliqua* and back again. Nor
is this a mere formal or acquired skill, for his ear unerringly tells him at what
point the change needs to be made, precisely on the significant words which
bear most emotional stress:

> Ac y dywawt Owein gwbyl o'e gerdet idaw, 'ac yn ymgeissaw a'r
> marchawc yssyd yn gwarchadw y ffynnawn y mynnwn vy mot';

or:

> A datkanu eu kyfranc a orugant idaw mal y datkanassei y uorwyn y nos
> gynt, 'ac Owein a pallwys idi, ac am hynny y illosgwn ninneu hi'.

The words which most clearly convey the drama and personal feelings are the
point of change. Throughout, the characters speak with an ironic air which
must derive from an urbane, slightly cynical environment. Owein, overcome
by love for the widow of the knight whom he has slain, cries 'God knows that
she is the woman I love most', which evokes little sympathy from Luned, 'God
knows she loves you little or none'; the vainglorious Cynon seeking an
adventure is offered one by the black man who, one senses, has heard it all
before, 'and if you don't find trouble there you need not look for any any more.'

The use of triadic repetition to create tension is a common enough narrative
technique employed by oral storytellers as by modern raconteurs. It is seen in

Owein in its most elementary form in the account of Owain's fight with his friend Gwalchmai: they attack and strike each other on the first day, on the second they strike each other 'with lances' but on the third they fight 'with keen strong and stout ('kadarnuras') lances'. The incremental repetition, the use, first of an adjective, and then of a compound adjective with the suggestion of a rhetorical device, brings the account to the expected climax. But the way the author makes use of traditional techniques reveals him as being something more than an experienced craftsman. His style is based on accepted usages and these are what gives confidence and fluency to his writing, but he is a conscious writer who can extend the techniques even as he uses them. Owain has wounded the knight of the fountain, and from the upper chamber where he himself is being sheltered by Luned he hears 'wailing in the castle'. 'What crying is this?' 'Anointing the nobleman whose castle it is', replies the maiden. At midnight they hear 'fearful wailing', and the maiden explains, 'the nobleman whose castle it is has died now'. The following morning they hear 'wailing and immeasurable crying', and it is explained that 'they are taking the body of the nobleman whose castle it is to the church'. The threefold rhetorical development in the style is here linked with the threefold development of real events surrounding the knight's death, – the sacrament of extreme unction, the death and burial, so that the narrative device becomes absorbed into the patterns of the story.

A similar development is seen in the use of formulas. Dr T. J. Morgan showed some years ago[6] that the phrase 'pa hyt bynnac y bydant ar y ford' ('however long they were on the way') is a stylistic device denoting the passage of time when nothing relevant to the development of the plot took place, so that the author has no need to pad out his account with irrelevant detail. The author of *Owein* uses this type of formula to avoid detailed descriptions of encounters and fights, but he can also change these linking formulas so that they become significant without the addition of any details. Thus where the author of the Four Branches writes 'and they spent that night', *Owein* has 'That night seemed long to me,' a development of an accepted narrative device which reveals that the interest of Welsh story-tellers was beginning to turn away from purely external actions to the feelings and mental condition of their heroes. Our author used common formulas to open his tale and to denote his 'chapters' ('The emperor Arthur was at Caerlleon on Usk', 'And as Gwalchmai one day . . .'), but he is not bound by these and Cynon's tale opens with a new, self-confident approach, 'I was the only son of my mother and father, rash and arrogant.' Where the traditional opening formula named the hero and gave his status, this is a wholly literary, i.e. written, opening owing nothing to oral tradition and laying stress on those personal traits which motivate the adventure. It is too soon to speak of the personal analysis or emotional investigation associated with courtly romance but *Owein* has begun to avoid the characteristics both of the folktale and of purely oral narrative.

173

But by its nature and the circumstances of performance, oral recitation has a dramatic quality which is apparent in this tale. The author has the dramatist's visual imagination which sees events happening before him so that he succeeds in structuring a scene and presenting it to his readers as though on stage, by means of skilful dialogue and by the significant movements of the characters.

Owain, from the window of Luned's chamber, sees the funeral procession of the knight whom he has killed. The scene is described in detail, and centres upon the bier carried by four barons, but Owain's eyes are soon drawn to the fair-headed lady dishevelled and grief-stricken. He is filled with love for her and turns to Luned to enquire who she is. Her reply is deliberately framed to twist the knife in his wound:

God knows, a lady one could claim as the fairest of women, the most chaste, most generous, wisest and most noble.

Owain's feelings for her are confirmed. Luned continues:

That is my lady.

His hopes rise for he has a love messenger at hand. But he is cruelly disillusioned:

and she is called the Lady of the Fountain, the wife of the man whom you slew yesterday.

Luned has arranged the facts in a way which will cause Owain greatest discomfort.

The focus changes immediately from the window to the room itself. There is no further word spoken, but Luned's swift abrupt movements fill the stage as she flits here and there carrying out her tasks with an air of urgency:

And thereupon the maiden rose up and lit a charcoal fire and filled a pot of water and set it to heat, and she took a towel of white linen and placed it round Owain's neck, and she took a bowl of elephant bone, and a silver basin, and filled it with the warm water and washed Owain's head. And then she opened a case and took out a razor with an elephant bone handle and two golden grooves on the razor, and she shaved his beard, and dried his head and neck with the towel. And then she set up a table before Owain and brought him his dinner.

The reason for the maiden's excitement and purposeful activity is made clear in her first words:

Go to sleep here, and I'll go to woo on your behalf.

The possibility of accommodating her lady's as yet unspoken problem and Owain's apparently hopeless love came to her as she stood beside Owain. A plan was born, but it is conveyed to the reader by a series of actions, a minimum of dialogue and no explicit explanation.

The scene that follows, Luned's interview with her lady, could be presented on a modern stage with almost no alteration. The contrast between the two is marked from the outset. Luned's unfeeling, coldly practical attitude deeply wounds the Lady who had expected sympathy. The two friends quarrel bitterly, vowing that they will never speak to each other again. Head in air, Luned stalks out, reaches the door, and the Lady 'coughs loudy. Luned looked over her shoulder and the Lady nodded to Luned'. Her first words are those of a mother who scolds her child and then embraces her, 'By God, you are perverse!'. Luned has taken an enormous risk but it has paid off. By her 'shock therapy' she has compelled the Lady to reassess her position, and by taking their relationship to the very brink she has released the tensions and emotions which now enable her to present her plan. The author seeks his motivation of events in naturalistic terms, and he realized that a situation which required the grieving widow to marry her husband's slayer must be fraught with emotion. A highly charged dramatic presentation would be the only convincing one.

The narrator's perspective changes according to the focus of events. Owain is usually the central character, but when the scene shifts again to Arthur's court at the beginning of the Emperor's search for his missing knight, the narrative is told from the viewpoint of the searchers. Owain is not named throughout the account of the journey, and when he appears as the defender of the fountain he can be referred to only as 'the knight'. His identity is concealed from the audience because it must be concealed from the searchers until the moment when his closest friend Gwalchmai fights with him. The view from Arthur's host merges back into that of the audience precisely where it should, as Gwalchmai's visor opens and Owain realizes who his opponent is:

And with that the knight struck Gwalchmai a blow so that the helmet turned up from his face with the result that the knight recognized that he was Gwalchmai. And then Owain said, 'Lord Gwalchmai. . . .'

Changes in focus enabling the audience to know more than the characters are full of possibilities for ironic comment which are not lost on the author, for example in his treatment of the box of healing ointment 'wasted' on the emaciated Owain.

The author displays his ability to develop the structural techniques of the oral tale in a number of ways. The repeating of incidents is an often-used device in Welsh stories. In the story *Lludd and Llefelys*, for example, the advice on how the land may be rid of magical oppressions is given first, and then followed by an account of how the directions were successfully carried out. A favourite device of the author of *Owein* is to describe an adventure before it is undertaken by the hero or another character. Cynon comes to the court of the yellow-haired man who reveals the stages of the journey which lie before him; these then become parts of his progress to the glade where the black man describes what awaits him at the fountain. Throughout the narrative the reader knows what is to come and the pleasure lies in awaiting the crucial difference which makes the present account of the adventure significant. As the first part of the *Dream of Maxen* is structured around a journey undertaken three times by different groups of travellers, so is the pattern of the first part of *Owein* based on similar repetition. Cynon relates his journey and adventure at the fountain, Owain follows, and finally Arthur and his men trace his footsteps as they search for him. The dangers of this method of composition are obvious, but the author avoids monotony by changing the tempo of the narration of successive journeys, by stressing different details and by constantly referring to his previous accounts, Thus throughout Owain's journey it is assumed that the reader can recall Cynon's description of the wonders which he saw so that the mere mention of them will be enough to produce a response:

> And at last he came upon the valley which Cynon had told him about so that he knew certainly that it was that one;

or even more succintly, 'he saw the maidens'. Repetition in these terms is effective in evoking a sense of wonder only to the extent that the imagination of the audience is sufficiently vivid or active. The author's more usual and safer method is to convey the sense that the characters find the wonders even more striking than the description had led them to expect. A constant comment, therefore, is 'Hoffach oed genhyf' (*or* 'gan Owain' *or* 'gan Arthur') ['I – *or* Owain *or* Arthur – marvelled more at . . .']. Cynon's account of the black man of the clearing contains such a comparison in every sentence, each expressed in a different form and revealing a subtle use of syntactical patterns. These rhetorical devices succeed in giving the narration of current happenings in the story, though it is less developed than the previous account, more of an impact on the reader than the adventures of minor characters. The variation in detail and tempo, together with the back references, retain the reader's interest in each account, but another danger inherent in this method is that he may become absorbed in the references and lose sight of the 'real' story. Cynon's tale is a self-contained episode, but the narrator of the story never usurps the role of the author because the speaker is made to address a member of his audience by name throughout the account, and the reader is never unaware that this is a tale within a tale. Similarly when Owain has achieved his position as the knight of the fountain, the reader is reminded that this is merely the beginning of the 'romance'. Owain's adventure must now be placed in the context of the whole: the scene shifts to Arthur's court, and the setting is re-stated. Owain is relocated in his true environment, his sojourn at the fountain cannot be permanent, and thus, by returning to the opening scene of the tale, the author has opened the way to the next development.

The tale is a well-balanced composition of two similar but contrasting parts. The opening paragraphs set the scene at Arthur's court where the three knights, Owain, Cynon and Cei, bicker as to who should entertain the court with a diverting tale. Owain's authoritative voice decides the issue and Cynon's reply reveals Owain's standing at court, 'You are an older man than I and a better raconteur, and you have seen more marvels'. The hero is placed in the centre of the stage as an experienced successful knight. He it is who has called for the story which will bring about his own adventure; from the start he has motivated the tale. The two knights follow the same adventure but their characters and motives are different. Cynon is moved by pride and self-esteem and it is right that he should be humbled, but Owain, moved simply by the news of an unheard-of wonder, succeeds and wins his place as knight of the fountain; 'and he was thus for three years'.

The story returns to its opening scene where Arthur's conversation with Gwalchmai reminds us that though we have accompanied Owain on his quest, for Arthur these have been a long three years. Owain is discovered and he makes welcome his colleagues: 'And the feast which took three years to prepare was consumed in three months', his return to Arthur's court is noted contrapuntally, 'And when he had come to his own kindred and fellows he remained three years instead of three months'. By this bridge passage the author not only underlines the passage of time and the enormity of Owain's neglect of his wife, but he also makes clear that his story is not at an end, for his hero must make amends and retrieve his status. All that has gone before is revealed simply as the setting for the true theme of the 'romance'.

The second part opens violently. The maiden who comes to Arthur's court and takes Owain's ring insults him ('shame on your beard', one of the three wrothful words of the legal codes) to his face with impunity. He returns disconsolate to his quarters 'and he grieved much that night', a sad echo of his eagerness to undertake the same journey three years previously. His grief overcomes him and he goes out of his mind, a wild man wandering the hills. The theme of the wild man of the woods who has lost his sanity because of some traumatic experience is well-known, but here it is used allegorically. Owain's clothing wears out, hair covers his body and he walks and eats with the wild beasts. His treatment of his wife is literally inhuman, with the result that Owain has lost not merely his knightly status but his claim to humanity itself. The rest of the 'romance' will describe his restoration, physically and morally, to his former state. He must return to the fountain, and regain his position, but now a renewed and purified personality. He descends, symbolically, from the mountain to the valley where men live, to the countess's park. That she is a widow is a clear enough sign of what is to be expected, for in the genre of courtly romance the knight is to defend the helpless. But the technique of laying out the path which the adventure will take, which we saw in the first part, is now used to denote stages in Owain's restoration. The first of these is his recognition of his sorry state, 'and he was ashamed when he saw the condition he was in', for the ability to blush and to be ashamed, the recognition of self-respect and of moral standards, are of the essence of the human, rather than of the animal, condition. The irony of the precious ointment links this to the second stage in his return which is his regaining of his chivalrous standards. He is fit, as man and knight, to journey to the fountain.

The pattern of the first part is again echoed but with the roles of the protagonists reversed, for now it is he who releases Luned from the prison, as she had him in the earlier episode, and she again becomes the medium of his adventure. The narrative structure of romance is frequently no more than a series of episodes placed within the frame of the journey or quest. They may be as loosely connected as the author chooses and there need be no logical or inescapable conclusion. The author of *Owein*, aware of the pitfalls of a non-thematic progression, here no less than throughout his story, has kept a close rein on his material and has attempted to link Owain's adventures one with another by means of the lion.

As he prepares to sleep in the forest, while the lion hunts for him, he encounters Luned and hears of her plight. The lion helps him in the adventure in which he defeats the giant threatening the earl's family, and upon his return the lion helps him to free Luned. The lion is used as a connecting link to bind together adventures only one of which is directly involved with Owain's story. The balanced structure is completed with the maiden's release, for all that remains is the statement of the hero's reconciliation with his wife. A detailed description of the scene would be superfluous as the whole 'romance' has been progressing to this point and we have observed Owain's maturity developing. The climax of the first part, his return to Arthur's court, is echoed now in his return again, but this time in the company of his wife. The first part, satisfying in simple terms of a quest achieved, is now seen to have been the prologue to the true theme of the 'romance', the loss and regeneration which occur in Owain's personality. The two parts, the two journeys to the fountain, complement each other, and the adventures are seen to have a deeper significance than the events themselves. The Du Traws episode following upon the 'natural' conclusion of the tale seems out of place in such a tight schema. It may be, as Mr Hunt[7] suggests, a folktale characteristic releasing tension and taking the tale back to 'the more conventional channels of military prowess'. It may have been an episode already connected with the hero, for as the reference to 'the three hundred swords of the Cynferching and the raven flock' suggests, other adventures were traditionally told of Owain, so that an oral story-teller would well have been tempted, indeed would not have considered it a fault, to add material relevant to his hero after the artistic conclusion of the tale. The *Dream of Maxen* is another obvious example. Nevertheless, the events at the court of Du Traws are a misfortune which strikes married couples and Owain's adventure here may have occurred while he and his wife were en route to Arthur's court. The oppressor's words, 'it was prophesied that you would come here to overcome me', seem to be an attempt to restructure an episode recognized as being, if not misplaced, certainly incongruous. That such a need should have been felt is interesting but the motive is unconvincing and may have been borrowed from *Peredur* (where it is however no mere device but basic to the vengeance theme).[8]

The theme of the romance is Owain's coming to know himself, and to recognize the immaturity in his character which led him to spend three years at the fountain unmindful of Arthur and the court, and three further years at court forgetful of his wife. He achieves *moderatio (mesure)* when he keeps in balance the delights and responsibilities of his calling as knight, companion and husband. The author of *Owein* has created a vehicle to express his theme, however traditional his materials may have been. He was well versed in the skills and techniques of the oral story-teller, and his stylistic virtues, tempered indeed by the opportunity afforded by the written medium, stem from the long tradition of the Welsh *cyfarwydd*. He was not the only author to respond to the challenge of giving a written form to what was essentially an oral tradition, but apart from the author of the *Four Branches*, who is the most atypical of all the Middle Welsh prose writers, the authors of the Welsh 'romances' alone appear to have discovered the possibilities of using narrative stories consciously to express contemporary attitudes or to investigate human behaviour, in this case chivalric themes.

Owein, Gereint and *Peredur* have normally been regarded as standing apart, though not in any way which can be well defined, from the rest of the Middle Welsh prose narratives. The distinction drawn between 'native' tales and 'romances' reflects the claim of readers to sense a change in atmosphere in the latter, notwithstanding their traditional stylistic features. Their special charac-teristics are usually identified as, for example: Arthur, *le roi faineant*; the courtesy and social customs of the court; the logical structure of the 'romances' and their imprecise topography;[9] but more important, though less specific, are the unreal fairy-like quality of the setting, the literary function of the court as an opening scene for adventures, the theme of knight errantry (a loosely linked series of adventures), and the motif of love service, none of which is character-istic of the 'native' stories. A comparison of *Yvain* and *Owein* reveals 'the similarity in incident and detail of the two texts' (in spite of a number of differences noted by critics),[10] but nevertheless the most striking resemblance resides not so much in the episodes themselves, as in the theme and genre characteristics.[11] What is novel in the Welsh 'romances' are largely those features of the form peculiar to the romance, not in its structure but in its milieu,[12] and there must be doubt whether the author of *Owein* could have conceived a narrative with the sophisticated chivalric themes of the tensions arising from the topos of courtly love and the hero's self-knowledge,[13] had he not been aware of the developed forms of French romance.

A comparison of *Owein* and *Yvain* reveals significant changes in the ethos of the two texts and in the narrative methods. *Owein* consistently plays down explicit chivalric features. Thus Calogrenant's story opens as he was making his way 'in search of adventure', whereas Cynon is more naturalistically motivated by arrogance and pride, subsequently however Yvain's journey is motivated by the desire to avenge Calogrenant's disgrace as a knight and the theme of vengeance becomes a dominant thread, while Owain is again more simply moved by Cei's taunts and the desire to discover a marvel (though the words 'adventure' or 'marvel' are not used here). *Owein* does not refer to the flirtatious behaviour of Arthur's knights and the ladies, and has not reported the discussion on the dangers of marriage to the knight, which Gauvain and Yvain have before their return to Arthur's court, nor does the Welsh note Yvain's and Gauvain's excursions from the court to tournaments and jousts. The element of judicial combat in Lunete's search for a champion is absent in the Welsh version where it is more simply explained, and the latter's account of the motif of the wild man is both more logical and more implicitly symbolic (though lacking the literary symbolism of the five arrows[14]).

It is, therefore, to be expected that *Owein* is less conscious of social mores and has nothing corresponding to the self-questioning analysis of motives and propriety which preceded Yvain's marriage to Laudine, and that the Welsh knight never regards himself as the captive either of Love or the Lady, and he does not suffer a love wound. The whole episode of the marriage of the knight and the Lady is, as already noted, passed over more swiftly and simply in Welsh. Though the problems posed by the alliance are not avoided, they are viewed more in human than in social terms. The changes in ethos reflect the codes of social behaviour with which the different audiences of *Yvain* and *Owein* might be expected to be familiar and which they could accept in a literary context. The demands of these audiences necessarily affected the narrative methods of the two authors.

The most obvious of these demands is, paradoxically, that the Welsh text has no reference to its audience, for traditional Welsh prose tales are simply, but in no derogatory sense, narratives which function under their own impetus (as it were). The presence of the audience must be assumed, but it is never addressed and there is normally only one narrative voice. There are no authorial comments on the significance of events or situations, there are no formal rhetorical passages to amplify the material or to explore the emotions. It follows that there can be no soliloquies, descriptive monologues or imaginary debates. The only narrator is the anonymous author who never intrudes or intervenes. *Owein* follows this 'epic' convention of the Welsh prose tradition. As we have seen, it is, of course, possible for a character to hold the stage for such an extended period that he becomes the narrator, leading the audience to confuse the two voices, protagonist and author. Instances of such extended speech occur in the native tales, e.g. Rhiannon's explanation to Pwyll of her plot to capture Gwawl, but it is significant that the most elaborate example occurs here in Cynon's tale-within-a-tale, which is handled more carefully than Calogrenant's story in *Yvain*.

Equally marked is the difference in the narrative line of the two texts. Once Yvain embarks on his quest the narration is strictly linear. The hero leaves the court knowing that Arthur will seek the same adventure within a fortnight, so that there can be only a few days between his marriage, the king's arrival, and his departure. *Owein* however follows a pattern found in other Welsh texts. The author's fondness for a repetitive structure whereby events are foreshadowed, either by virtue of their having occurred before or by being described by a guide, has already been noted, but here he makes use of a technique also employed in *Pwyll* to describe two contemporary sequences merging at a single point. Owain leaves for the fountain, and his adventure ends with his marriage. He is left there for three years while the scene returns to Arthur's court and the Emperor, worried by his long absence, sets out to look for him. His quest ends at the fountain: the two narrative strands join and the story can progress to the next significant event. As R. L. Thomson remarks, the time scale in Welsh is 'very different (and more plausible)',[15] but it is the established technique of 'back at the ranch' which makes this possible.

Owein, of course, cannot be a translation of *Yvain*. R. L. Thomson's comparison of the two texts has established that the degree of difference between them is far greater than between, for example, the Welsh *Ystorya Bown de Hamtwn* and the corresponding Anglo-Norman *Boeve de Haumtone*[16] which may be taken to represent a norm. It is not easy to find the precise word which can convey the process by which a text or literary genre is transmitted from one culture and linguistic environment to another, or to judge what the result of such transplanting into the alien soil of a different socio-political group might be. One such word is *translatio* which is used for translation, transmission, paraphrase, but which may also refer to the broader process of adaptation both to a new language and a new culture. Translating here will mean the choice of texts judged to be relevant to the receiving culture and the modification they undergo to become acceptable in whatever their new role may be. Hans Ulrich Gumbrecht has used the term 'reception' for 'a process by which a certain number of texts from the general supply are selected in accordance with the needs of society, and are then used in the traditional way or adapted to new uses by means of the above techniques of translation.'[17] Chrétien's romances, *Yvain, Erec, Perceval,* were the ones selected (unconsciously) for putting into Welsh because they were the only ones which could be accommodated (in varying degrees and ways) within the Welsh tradition. They were not simply Arthurian (rather than ancient or Ovidian), but their heroes were recognizable (in a way that Cligés and Lancelot were not), and these romances were therefore 'receivable' and significant. Their 'receivability' is the element which made their presentation in Welsh different in nature from the translation given to the old French epics and the Grail romances, which remain translations in the modern sense. Their immediate and obvious foreign origin, and their incompatibility within the tradition prevented the full absorption which the romance achieved.[18]

The result of such wholehearted adaptation was a new genre in Middle Welsh prose. The authors follow Welsh narrative techniques, styles and usages, but introduce new techniques, like the interlacement of the first part of *Peredur*. They introduce the scenario associated with romance, and they take Welsh narrative away from those 'pure narrative values . . . without the weight of moral and ethical commentary' wherein 'personages exist for the sake of the story, functioning only in terms of the action' which the late Helaine Newstead[19] discovered in *Culhwch and Olwen*. The structures of these tales has a thematic significance and the sequence of events is given meaning, but they are implicit and naturalistic rather than specific and chivalric in motivation, suggestive rather than rhetorical in their exploration of character, still revealing the objectivity of narrative rather than the personal voice of the author. Slimmed down and in miniature, these 'romances' are nevertheless not trivial. The fruit of the meeting of two cultures and two narrative forms, they are the most sophisticated examples of imaginative writing in Middle Welsh prose.[20]

Traditional Material in
Artus de Bretaigne

S. V. SPILSBURY

THE prose romance *Artus de Bretaigne*,[1] also known as *Le petit Artus de Bretaigne* and *Artus le Restoré*, was composed, probably during the period 1296–1312, by an anonymous author who had connections with John II, Duke of Brittany, or with his son, Arthur II.[2] It was Professor Loomis's contention that the work contains a significant proportion of authentic Celtic material, and this in a form more primitive than that which is to be found in other, earlier, literary works.[3] Loomis was basing his claim mainly on conclusions drawn from an analysis of one of the most striking episodes in the romance: the hero, Artus, son of the Duke of Brittany, after overcoming various obstacles and assailants, puts an end to the enchantments of the revolving castle of Porte Noire. Loomis's suggestion that *Artus* contains a complete and authentically primitive version of the inconsequential episode of Hugon's palace in the *Voyage de Charlemagne* and also of Chrétien's rationalized version, recounting Gauvain's adventure in the Chastel de la Roche de Canguin, in the *Conte de Graal* is an attractive one. The difficulty lies in the fact that the *Artus* version is far from being clear and simple. It is extremely long and complicated, and is packed with incidents and details, most of which can be found individually or variously combined in a wide variety of texts. So is the Porte Noire adventure merely a gigantic literary conflation which sheds no more than a delusive light upon earlier versions from which, in fact, the *Artus* author has borrowed? Or is it an admittedly expanded and embellished version of a complete and genuinely early tradition? And if the latter, is it really possible to identify the particular features which formed part of the original narrative? And what, in any case, do terms such as 'early' and 'primitive' mean when referring to Celtic tradition? Perhaps in the end the best one can do is examine generally the sources and nature of the material used by the romancer, and thus estimate the importance of literary borrowings as against popular tradition.

183

A study of the proper names occurring in *Artus* is quite revealing in this respect.[4] The most interesting of the place-names is Orcanie, which Arthurian tradition identifies with the Orkney Isles.[5] In the *chansons de geste* and works dealing with the Alexander legend it is a Saracen land or town; more precisely, the thirteenth-century *Florence de Rome* and the *Jeu de saint Nicolas* identify it with Hyrcania. In *Artus* Orcanie is 'un royaume qui estoit ou costé de Babiloine et s'estent jusques a la Rouge Mer' [Ms A f. 11r°]; Flutre tentatively indentifies this also with Hyrcania, although obviously, if this is the case, the author had no more than a very hazy notion of where the land was situated. The important point is that the romancer, in placing Orcanie in the Middle East, is following a tradition different from the Arthurian one. The land of Sorelois which, apart from its use in *Artus*, is exclusive to Arthurian literature where it is in or near Wales, has also been transported to the Middle East 'ou costé d'Inde la Major sus la Mer Betee entre Perse et Mesopotame' [Ms A f. 11r°]. If the mysterious 'Mer Betee' is the Caspian Sea (and the only other possibility is that it is the Persian Gulf), then Sorelois is exactly on the site of ancient Hyrcania.[6] Greek names also figure in *Artus*: Athenes is where the clerk-magician Maistre Estienne learnt his arts; Corinte (correctly depicted as an archbishopric) and Macidoine are cities belonging to Queen Fenice; so also are Phelase, which seems to correspond with Phylaca in Thessaly,[7] and which figures in the *Roman de Troie* as Pilace or Pilache, and Commenie. The latter appears to be identical with Conmenie or Orcomenie, also in the *Roman de Troie*, which is Orchomenus in Bœotia. Another city, Pancaponne (also Pancaphone, Pantaponne), may, as Flutre suggests, be a deformation of Pentapole. From Asia Minor come the names of Ermenie, Galacie and Arsire (for Ancyra, capital of Galatia?).

Among the personal names in *Artus* few are specifically Arthurian; Artus himself was named after King Arthur, who, together with Gauvain and Lancelot du Lac, is just mentioned in passing. Gouvernaus, in his role as tutor and companion to Artus, obviously derives his name from Governal in the various versions of the Tristan legend; Hector, Artus's cousin, bears a name which has Classical as well as Arthurian associations. Most of the remaining characters who are of any importance have rather ordinary names: Jaquet, Bauduin (which Loomis saw as a corruption of Gauvain), Estienne, Phelippe, Gace, Raoul Brisebarre. Brisebarre occurs only in *Galien* and the name of the squire Tiecelin is attested only in *Aubri* and the *Mort Garin*. In *Artus* Clamados is a Saracen king, and the name occurs regularly, in that form, in the *chansons de geste*, attached to a Saracen. West indicates[8] that in Arthurian romance the usual forms of the name are Clamadeu, Clamadé and Clamadas, rather than Clamados. In addition a number of more or less exotic names are found in *Artus*, all absent from early Arthurian tradition: Emenidus and Perdicas (who were also two of the peers of Alexander), Pamenion, Cliçon and Gadifer, for example. Many of these are in the *chansons de geste*, denoting Saracens or Eastern rulers, and the *Artus* author's debt to that genre is certain, since the name Malegrape (in *Artus* the monster of Mont Perilleus) appears to be attested only in *Li Covenans Vivien* and in *Aliscans*, in both cases as a Saracen; also Afilé (the name of Artus's horse) is also a horse in *Anseïs de Carthage, Gaufrei* and *Mainet*. Mesire Ysembart, the arch-villain of *Artus*, seems to be a reincarnation of the traitor of *Gormont et Isembart* and of *Hugues Capet*.

In conclusion one can say that the proper names of *Artus* reveal that the author was strongly influenced by the *chansons de geste* and the *romans d'antiquité*. The absence of Arthurian names is striking but probably due to the fact that in the author's mind these were too closely associated with individual heroes and their homelands to be transferred to the latter-day Arthurians and the lands of the East, even when the countries are clearly fictitious. Loomis contended[9] that *Artus* shows traces of an abduction myth involving a vegetation goddess, and that the author reveals his understanding of this underlying theme by naming the queen of the fairies Proserpine. However, the role of chief allotter of destiny in the *chansons de geste* was often played by Morgan, and it is probable that the author has replaced the British goddess by the more 'appropriate' Classical one.

The first section of the romance, dealing with the childhood and youth of Artus, contains one episode whose theme, the Forgotten Bride, was originally an independent folk-tale. Artus falls in love with Jehanete, daughter of an impoverished gentlewoman. Unable to marry her because of her lowly status, Artus is betrothed to a noblewoman of doubtful virtue, Peronne of Austria, whose mother enlists the aid of Jehanete in order to conceal from Artus the fact that Peronne is not a virgin. Jehanete is substituted for Peronne on the wedding-night but subsequently reveals the deception to Artus. The disgraced Peronne is sent away and dies shortly after, while Jehanete wins the gratitude but not the hand of Artus. The best-known literary analogue in Arthurian romance occurs in the Tristan story, and given that Artus de Bretaigne's tutor and friend has the name of Gouvernaus, it might well appear that the author of *Artus* has adapted the Substitute Bride theme as he found it in *Tristan*. But this is not the case, for the Tristan version is a later and much altered version of a story which Miss Schoepperle outlined as follows:[10]

A girl who cherishes the hope of regaining a lover who has forgotten her, seeks advice with a woman to whom he is about to be married. The bride, who has lost her virginity, begs the servant to take her place on the marriage night. The youth discovers that his bride has deceived him and recognizes in the maidservant his lost betrothed.

On the three main points the *Artus* version coincides with the original: namely that it is the substitute bride who is the heroine, that she and the bridegroom are the real lovers and that the deception attempted by the intended bride is discovered. On all these points the *Tristan* version differs.[11]

The second section of the romance deals with the birth and upbringing of the heroine Florence. The motivating theme of the story is the Swearing of a Destiny: Queen Fenice went to Porte Noire, abode of Proserpine, to give birth to her first child. The baby girl was taken to the Mont Perilleux to be given a name and a destiny. At first doubts had been expressed as to the wisdom of this, 'quar l'en ne set comment les destinees se porteront', but King Emenidus declared that it should be done. A solemn charter was drawn up by him and his peers, promising that whatever destiny the child was given they would not seek to pervert it. The baby was taken to the Mont Perilleux, placed on a stone slab, and all withdrew. Four fairies, led by Proserpine, duly appeared and pronounced the destiny: she should be called Florence; she should receive the castle of Porte Noire, the sword Clarence and the White Shield; she should be 'bele, gracieuse et amiable'; she should marry the best knight in the world, who would take possession of her sword and shield and put an end to the enchantments of Porte Noire; and should another try to take Florence, he would die 'de male mort sanz nul respit'.

Stories of the supernatural beings who are present at the birth of a mortal child to whom they allot a destiny are part of the common corpus of popular folk-tale, and are found from India to Ireland. Known under the names of Parcae (or 'Birth Spirits'), Moirai, Norns, Wyrds, these allotters of destiny are usually three in number, and though they have passed into literature, they have an independent existence, even today, in folk-memory.[12] In French romance they are fairies rather than goddesses, though they fulfil the same function. As far as Arthurian tradition is concerned, one must look to the late twelfth-century *Brut* of the Englishman Layamon to find an analogue. In this work the elves appear at the birth of Arthur and grant him gifts: that he should be the best knight in the world, that he should be a rich king, that he should live long, and that he should be the most generous among men. In French literature, however, it seems once more to be the *chansons de geste* which make a commonplace of the tradition: at the birth of Garin de Monglane three fairies appear, of whom one, Morgan (how futile is the attempt to separate epic from Arthurian?), prophesies that Garin will be the father of a glorious race;[13] at the birth of Ogier six fairies appear, of whom five grant him gifts and the sixth, Morgan, decrees that after a long hard career, he should come and live with her in Avalon;[14] and traditionally Galien, son of Olivier, was given his name by the fairy Galienne who was present at his birth.[15]

The closest analogue to the version in *Artus* occurs in the surviving fragment of the fourteenth-century verse *roman d'aventures* called *Brun de la Montaigne*. The nobleman Butor de la Montaigne takes his newly-born son to the forest of Broceliande in Brittany, the poet explaining that 'en vielle ancesserie' the nobility would take their infants to places known to be the haunts of fairies, 'Afin que leur enfant amandassent leur vie, Par destinee qui fust a aus otroïe'.[16] The version in *Artus* shows signs of a non-literary origin: medieval literature tends to be hero-oriented and therefore in most cases it is a boy child, the future hero, whose destiny is sought. The quotation from *Brun de la Montaigne* indicates that the folk-belief related to children of both sexes; indeed in a modern survival of the folk tradition it is specifically a girl who is involved, the Moirai decreeing that she shall become the bride of Charos (the Angel of Death and modern equivalent of Charon); in other words, she will die young.[17] Also, the folk-belief called for the child to be taken, as in *Artus*, to a place known to be frequented by the allotters of destiny, while most of the literary analogues have the fairies arriving unsolicited and unexpectedly, often with the complication of having one of the fairies proving unfavourable towards the child. A further point worth mentioning, given the *Artus* author's apparent debt to the *romans d'antiquité*, is that, as Faral has pointed out,[18] the Parcae, when they appear in early French romance, are clearly recognizable in their Classical role of spinners or weavers. This literary tradition is not followed in *Artus* which appears to enshrine ancient popular belief, little influenced by literary sources.

Structurally *Artus* begins with a bi-partite introduction dealing with the respective births and upbringings of Artus and Florence, and in these the episodes of the Forgotten Bride and the Swearing of a Destiny play a large part. Each theme has an independent existence, the first as a folk-tale, the second as a folk-belief or superstition, but both were current over a wide geographical area.

As to the Turning Castle itself, though it is thought of as an Arthurian theme, analogues can be found over the whole Indo-European area.[19] Turning Castle adventures come in two forms which are worth distinguishing: the first, as in the *Voyage de Charlemagne* and in the fourteenth-century romance of *Berinus* (and, if Loomis is correct, in the *Conte del Graal*), describes how the hero is inside the castle when it begins to whirl round at great speed; in the second, as in *Perlesvaus* and *La Mule sans frein* (and, if Loomis is correct, in *Yvain*), the hero has difficulty entering the castle because it is already revolving. The Porte Noire episode in *Artus*, discussed at length by Loomis, is of the first type and will be further examined later in this article. Loomis made no mention of another episode in *Artus*, which involves the second type of Turning Castle adventure, albeit in somewhat disguised form. The Tour Ténébreuse, whose location and description mark it out as a typical Other-world castle, lies in the middle of a Waste Land, and it is Artus's task to restore the land to its former prosperity. The one unique feature about the castle is that, as Artus approaches it, he sees that it is surrounded by 'un grant environnement de moeles de molin, qui estoient l'une sus l'autre si comme il sont au molin; et tournoient aussi roidement comme se il fussent sus un molin par enchantement que nulz n'i passant sanz morir' [Ms A f. 57v°]. Curoi's fortress in *Fled Bricrend* turned 'as swiftly as a mill-stone', Hugon's palace in the *Voyage de Charlemagne* 'cum arbre de molin', and the castle in *La Mule sans frein* 'con muele de molin'.[20] It is clear that in *Artus*, by accident or design, the usual comparison which accompanied the description of the Turning Castle has been taken as being literally true, a phenomenon for which there is an interesting precedent: Hugon's palace is described also as turning 'cumme roe de char',[21] while Porte Noire revolves 'comme une roe trop fort' [Ms A f. 37r°]. In the *Chevalier du Papegau* and the German *Wigalois*, both deriving from similar twelfth-century sources, the corresponding castle, though stationary, has its entrance blocked by a rapidly turning wheel, and, in common with the episodes of the Tour Ténébreuse in *Artus* and the Chastel de Grant Defois in *Perlesvaus*, it is a well-directed blow from sword or lance which breaks the mechanism, stops the movement and enables the hero to enter the castle. That the castles in the *Chevalier du Papegau* and *Wigalois* are manifestations of the Turning Castle has never been in doubt; nor can it be doubted that the Tour Ténébreuse is another such. The evidence suggests that they were not purely arbitrary rationalizations and that, in the case of the Tour Ténébreuse at least, there was a genuine misunderstanding: a castle surrounded by whirling mill-stones is, after all, scarcely more believable than one which revolves 'as swiftly as a mill-stone'.

As Artus attempts the difficult approach to the Tour Ténébreuse, beset by monsters and armed knights, he meets a servant who explains to him the origin of the total blackness which covers the land:

– Sire, ele vient d'une grant fosse qui est en cele tour ou l'en avale par degrés. Si a ou milieu de cele fosse un grant feu fait d'errement et de ne sa[i] quel chose. Si est si lais, si noirs et si hideus et si obscurs, et gete par .iiii. bouches qui sont entour cele tor si laide fumee et si noire comme vous veez, qu'i n'est solel ne lune ne clarté nule ne nule chose qui esclarcir la peust. Et dure bien .v. lieues, si conme je vous ai dit, si que tous cilz pays en est gastez et s'en sunt toutes les gens fuies [Ms A f. 58v°].

The tower was the work of an enchanter, servant to Mesire Ysembart. This latter had decreed that it should be built as a punishment for the monks of Grâce-Dieu who, on a particular occasion, had refused to interrupt their solemn Palm Sunday celebrations in order to provide him and his followers with refreshment. As a result the abbey lands were enveloped in darkness and left untilled, and all religious worship ceased.[22] Artus's task was thus to enter the tower, descend into the earth down a dark passage, through heat, smoke and invisible assailants, and extinguish the fire with the waters of a magic fountain to be found nearby.[23]

Although there are distinct echoes of the Waste Land theme here, the two details which the author particularly stresses are the fact that no religious services are held and the total darkness. Porte Noire and the Tour Ténébreuse are linked by more than their names and the fact that they are both manifestations of the Turning Castle: the Porte Noire episode, which on the surface seems no more than a testing adventure to find a chosen hero, hints at the involvement of a 'bringer of light'.[24] When the palace begins to whirl round, a noisome black smoke is blown in through a window, only to disappear when the castle comes to rest, 'si fist leens aussi cler comme il soloit' [Ms A f. 37v°]. A servant appears and announces to Artus that a further enchantment remains, and is to be found in the path which links the palace to the castle courtyard, 'mais portons y du feu qar l'alee est si obscure que l'en n'i voit goute' [Ms A f. 38r°]. Two copper statues beat the air with flails, barring the entrance; these Artus overturns with a door-bar, 'lors failli li enchantemens, si vit on par leens moult cler' [Ms A f. 38r°]. The next day Artus is taken by the clerk Maistre Estienne to the tent of Florence (or of Proserpine, for they are identical) where he takes possession of the sword Clarence and the White Shield, which will light his way to the Tour Ténébreuse.

References to darkness and light abound: one remembers that the palace of Ysopés in *Berinus* turned one complete revolution each day at a certain hour;[25] that the entrance to Curoi's fortress could not be found after sunset;[26] that regarding the two comparisons used to describe the Turning Castle, the wheel is a solar symbol[27] (and the phrase 'roe de char' recalls the chariot of Helios), while Loomis unearthed an Old English reference which, describing the firmament, said, 'It turneth ever about us swifter than any mill-wheel'.[28] If solar mythology is at the root of the Turning Castle theme, as seems likely, the version in *La Mule sans frein* is particularly interesting in that there is no question of Gauvain halting the motion of the castle, which turns unceasingly; rather he can only enter at the precise moment when the gate appears opposite him. One may speculate that that moment represents sunset, when the sun is seen to come in contact with the earth, and that the hero's task is to enter the realm of darkness and ensure the return of light the next morning. Day and night, summer and winter, life and death: the primeval themes are all interlinked, and the seasonal myth is a parallel to the solar myth, involving the alternation of the fertility and the barrenness of the earth.[29]

Two further examples complete the record of what might loosely be termed 'Otherworld castles' in *Artus*. La Broche is a 'castle with a custom' of a familiar type. Each passing knight must challenge and fight with its lord; if he defeats him, he himself becomes lord of the castle and must defend it against all-comers until he in turn is defeated. The La Broche episode also has some unique features: Artus and his companion Gouvernaus part company, and it is Gouvernaus who is met and detained by a group of knights. They tell him that he must strike upon a shield suspended from a pole as a challenge to the lord of the neighbouring castle. If Gouvernaus is defeated in single combat with the lord, he will lose his arms, be publicly shamed and 'mené à la justice'; if he wins, that same fate awaits his opponent, while he himself must become lord of the castle and of its owner, the lady Blancheflor. The explanation given is that Blancheflor's father, Nevelon le Rous, was slain by the monster Malegrape, and the 'custom' was instituted in order to find a champion to avenge Nevelon's death. But this semi-rationalization hardly accounts for the fact that the successful combatant becomes Blancheflor's consort, 'sire de la dame de leens', nor yet why the defeated knight should be so harshly treated, perhaps put to death (the precise meaning of the phrase 'mené à la justice' is not made clear). Chrétien uses the same situation in *Yvain*, with Yvain as victor, Esclados le Ros as the defeated champion (was Nevelon le Rous originally not Blancheflor's father, but her former 'champion'?), and Laudine as mistress of the castle, though here Yvain's succession as husband of Laudine is persuasively argued as a feudal 'marriage of convenience'. The theme occurs in other Arthurian works, not without retaining a degree of mystery: for example, in the *Roman de Balain* the lady of the tower has a knight with her who fights with all-comers, the victor of each encounter taking the lady;[30] and in the prose *Tristan* a battle takes place at the Pont sur l'Ombre, with the victor guarding the bridge for the following year.[31] Both Chrétien and the *Artus* author have attempted to adapt a traditional theme to fit in with their own story, but the latter at least has not entirely erased the faint image of a seasonal myth in which the consort of Earth is replaced each year by a younger, more vigorous god.

Finally there is Proserpine's castle of Hurtebise: as Artus tries to enter it a great wind arises which nearly blows him off his feet, and so much rain falls that he finds himself up to his thighs in water. He has been sent to fetch a healing ointment for the Chevalier Navré, who describes his wounding in these terms:

> – Il est bien voirs que je amoie moult fort une damoisele moult haute dame et gentil, qui orendroit est en cest chastel la amont. Si aloie moult volentiers a lui quant je pooie, si le sorent si ami, si lor anuia tant qu'il me fist (*sic*) guetier une journee que j'estoie avecques li, si me pristrent, et m'atournent, ensi comme vous poez veoir, de coutiaus envenimez, si que je n'en peusse avoir santé [Ms A f. 80v°].

Miss Weston points out that it was one of the tasks of Gauvain as Grail hero to bring a special herb to heal the Maimed King;[32] and in *Sone de Nansai*, in the Grail section, the king is said to have been maimed as 'a punishment for sin, he had conceived a passion for a pagan princess'.[33] The details in *Artus*, however, are so sketchy and vague that they need only be literary borrowings.

The general framework of *Artus* has been compared by Miss Schlauch to a fourteenth-century Icelandic saga, the *Rémundar Saga Keisarasonar*, in these terms:[34]

> Obviously both tales are constructed on the same formula: the mutual dream, the quest for the far-away Princess, tests and adventures on the way, battle against a rival wooer, ultimate success. This is also the formula

of a number of Oriental tales with which our romances are no doubt
ultimately connected – notably the Hindustan *Adventures of Kamrup*, the
Sanscrit *Daçakumāra-Caritam* by Daṇḍin (sixth century?), the Sanscrit
Vāsavadatta, and a number of Arabian and Persian tales. In all of these the
interest is derived from the dream which causes two young people to fall in
love with each other without having met.

Certainly there are Irish tales, too, which are thematically related, as Miss
Schlauch points out; and Welsh ones for that matter, like *Culhwch and Olwen*.
The young Culhwch refused to take as his wife the daughter of his step-mother,
which latter then swore a destiny upon the boy that he should have no wife but
Olwen, daughter of the giant Ysbaddaden. At the mere sound of her name
Culhwch coloured, 'and love of the maiden entered into every limb of him,
although he had never seen her'.[35] The rest of the tale relates Culhwch's search
for Olwen and the various tasks which he has to perform in order to win her
hand, which he eventually does. Parry has pointed out[36] that this is a common
folk-tale, the Giant's Daughter, known in many areas, in which the giant is to
die when his daughter marries. The later Welsh *Dream of Macsen Wledig*
furnishes the theme of the hero who sees and falls in love with his future wife in
a dream, and who then sets out upon a journey to find her. In *Artus* many of the
themes of the two Welsh tales are reflected: the refusal of the mother's choice of
a bride; the Swearing of a Destiny upon hero and heroine; the dream in which
the hero sees his future wife; the hero's love which is engendered before he
meets his beloved; the many tasks which he must perform to win his bride; the
marriage; the death of the bride's father after his daughter's marriage.

Not only does one find the general framework of *Artus* occurring in Welsh
tales, but there are small details and individual incidents which indicate some
sort of connection, albeit a tenuous one. One example of this is in the Fourth
Branch of the *Mabinogion*, *Math vab Mathonwy*: Gwydion, nephew of Math,
goes on his uncle's behalf to Pryderi to ask for the swine of Annwn as a gift:[37]

'Lord', he said, 'will anyone do my errand to thee better than I myself?'
'Not so,' he answered, 'a right good tongue is thine.' 'This then lord, is my
errand: to beg of thee the animals that were sent to thee from Annwn.'
'Aye,' he replied, 'that would be the easiest thing in the world were it not a
covenant between me and my country concerning them.'

Compare this with the exchange between the Emperor of India and King
Emenidus, Florence's father:

Li roys Emenidus li demanda qu'il avoit, et por quoi il pensoit tant; si
respondi li empereres:
– Sire, jel vous dirai, quar message n'i puis je envoier que vous deussiez

miex croire . . . Je sui jones homs et a marier, ne miex ne me porroie metre
que en Florence avoir, si que je la voz demant a bouche.

– Ha! sire, dist li roys , ele ne puet avoir mari fors que celui qui li est
destiné, ou autrement seroit cilz perdus et mors qui la prendroit. Et
d'autre part je l'ai juré et seelé et toute ma court a garder [Ms A f. 14r°].

Three similar details emerge here: the remark that no-one is better able to
make the request; the request itself; the refusal because of a previously made
promise. In both cases the ruler is persuaded to grant the request; in both war is
declared between the two sides as an eventual consequence. The parallels are,
if nothing else, curious. In *Manawydan vab Llyr* a magic mist falls over the
land, the seven cantrefs of Dyfed become barren and desolate, and mention is
made of the one 'who cast a spell over this land' and who built the magic caer.[38]
This suggests instantly the enchanter of Mesire Ysembart who brought
desolation to Argençon and built the Tour Ténébreuse. Again in *Math vab
Mathonwy* Gwydion conjures up a fleet to surround the castle of Aranrhod, and
makes it disappear suddenly when it has served its purpose.[39] In *Artus* Maistre
Estienne conjures up a huge army to advance upon the castle of La Roche, and
makes it disappear when all the enemies have fled.[40]

In a similar fashion one could comb the romances of Chrétien and his
contemporaries and find more such analogues. But what conclusions is one
justified in drawing as to the connections between the various versions and as to
their ultimate sources? Loomis's claim concerning the Porte Noire episode in
Artus was categorical: the source was Celtic, the material was primitive. The
'Arthurian' Turning Castle has been identified as a Celtic solar palace.[41] All this
may be so: the Celts seem to have had gods with solar attributes; they may well
have had a complete solar mythology. It has to be said, however, that the
evidence does not suggest that they had solar gods as such,[42] and even in
Ireland, where it is considered that Celtic culture was best preserved, there is
no archaeological evidence of a cult of the sun. Furthermore the major festivals
of the Celtic year are known to have coincided with the important events in the
pastoralists' life, the beginning and end of the grazing season, rather than with
the solstices and equinoxes, as one would expect among a people for whom the
sun was of great importance.[43] The Celts may well have invented the revolving
castle (as distinct from the Russian revolving hut[44] or the Jewish revolving tent
door[45]), though there is no reason to suppose that there is anything very
primitive about it; that the traditions of the turning mountain[46] or the turning
island[47] were not conflated at a comparatively late date with descriptions of the
wonderful Oriental palaces seen by the Crusaders, and which themselves seem
to have been man's attempt to build a sky palace on earth. The case for the
ancient Celtic solar palace remains not proven, and we cannot do better than
quote the words of Miss Schlauch:[48]

To me it seems very likely that the palace of Bricriu and the palace of Hugon are both modified Regiae Solis, or Abodes of the Sun, and they may be Celtic for all I know, but I do not think they are therefore primitive.

The same may be said of Porte Noire.

As to the rest of the material in *Artus*, it no doubt has its vestiges of vegetation myths, nature rituals and the like, along with many other works composed at a time when it was accepted that writers should use traditional themes rather than create their own 'matière' out of their imaginations. Loose ends and puzzling details remain, indicating the author's debt to a narrative which was originally quite other than the adventures of a medieval knight errant. Nevertheless, the episodes concerning Porte Noire, the Tour Ténébreuse, Hurtebise, the Chevalier Navré among many others, cannot be demonstrated to have a source more remote than the literature of the twelfth and thirteenth centuries.[49] Themes such as the Forgotten Bride and the Swearing of a Destiny do show signs of a non-literary source, but these are not specifically Celtic. The influences on the *Artus* author were various: vernacular French literature, especially the *romans d'antiquité* and the *chansons de geste* (for both names and themes), *romans bretons* (for certain themes), folk-tales from some source, folk superstition of a very general kind, and possible even, an element not previously discussed, fairly recent historical events.[50] *Artus*, like the *Voyage de Charlemagne*, poses the Celtic-Oriental problem over sources: the conclusion can only be that the romancer was not drawing heavily on any single homogeneous corpus of knowledge.

On Birds and Beasts, 'Death' and 'Resurrection', Renewal and Reunion in Chrétien's Romances

KENNETH VARTY

A CATALOGUE of all the birds and beasts which appear in Chrétien's works together with a critical survey of the pages scholars have devoted to them would alone provide ample material for a monograph – pride of place going to white stags, sparrowhawks and lions. Much has also been written on the way Chrétien's heroes grow up in – or away from – society, how they are shaped and reshaped by their experiences, how they become new men. As I have chosen to write about some aspects of both these subjects, and in particular some of the links between them, I hope that I may be excused from acknowledging in any detail the immense debt I owe to the many who have written on either Chrétien's animals or his heroes.

I have come to the ideas and arguments presented here in a roundabout way. I once read and re-read Chrétien's romances many times a year as I taught undergraduates to appreciate their various qualities. Then I deserted him for other authors and genres – the lyric, the epic, the beast epic, fable and fabliau. Eventually I found myself more and more intrigued by the ways in which the renewal of life, even resurrection, was treated in these genres – comically, tragically, lyrically; metaphorically and literally.

It is not of course in the least surprising that a literature which was largely the product of men formed within the walls of Christian institutions, often the product of priests and clerics, destined largely for a Christian public, should reflect the belief (and sometimes doubts about that belief) which is at the heart of Christianity, the resurrection of Jesus, and therefore the resurrection of the faithful who died repentant and forgiven. As St Paul says (I Corinthians 15, vv. 16–17): 'if the dead rise not, then is Christ not raised: and if Christ be not raised, your faith is in vain, ye are yet in your sins. Then they also which are fallen asleep in Christ are perished . . .' In addition to this belief in the life to come is that in the need to lead a new life in Christ, to renew life here on earth (Ephesians, 4, vv. 22–4, etc.).

Once one begins to look for the artistic treatment of these beliefs in medieval French literature, one finds a truly rich variety; and in many a work, the literary artist makes magnificent capital of them, producing some of the most powerful, moving, memorable speeches, actions or images that have come down to us. Truly comic exploitation of these beliefs is relatively rare. One readily recalls that outburst of Aucassin's when he says he would rather go to Hell than Heaven provided he can have his sweet Nicolette; and those much longer, mini-epic movements in the *Mort et Procession Renart* (Martin's 17th branch) which begin with the fox being nailed to a chessboard by the testicles (surely the ultimate penalty a man may have to pay to clear off a gambling debt!) and end with him jumping out of his grave and seizing the leading mourner by the neck. For an artistically serious, solemn and powerfully dramatic, poetic treatment of both a feigned death and resurrection and a 'real' death and resurrection, the author of the *Roland* is unsurpassed. The feigned sequence concerning the pagan is admirably juxtaposed with the real thing, with Roland's death agony and spiritual ascent. In *La Mort le Roi Artu* we find, at the story's climax, artistic exploitation of both those fundamental aspects of Christian belief to which I have referred. The renewal of self in Christ is depicted at the very end in the portrayal of Lancelot, who is also seen (in a dream) to be resurrected after death; but the most impressive death and resurrection sequence (a curious mixture of pagan and Christian elements) is reserved for Arthur where – if we follow the narrative sequence – it seems as if we are first shown the translation (or 'resurrection') of his soul into a kind of Paradise, when he is taken off in the boat crewed by beautiful women, before his body is taken for burial by them to the Black Chapel. (A similar sequence is in effect shown in the *Roland*, with the Angel Cherubin, St Michael del Peril and St Gabriel receiving the warrior's soul into Heaven, and Charlemagne and his men taking his body back to France for burial.)

Images of renewal and resurrection are present in most of Chrétien's romances, woven with great skill into the main narrative, always at a critical and sometimes at the culminating point. Furthermore – and here he is, I believe, unique in medieval French literature – he frequently employs animal imagery not only to embellish but to reinforce and, in a way, comment on the renewal and resurrection sequence.

It is in *Cligés* (the second of Chrétien's romances) that a death and resurrection sequence is most obviously brought into focus by animal imagery – and this is drawn primarily from the bestiaries. Chrétien himself brings this to our attention when he introduces his heroine:

Fenyce ot la pucele a non:
ce ne fu mie sanz reison,
car si con fenix li oisiax
est sor toz les autres plus biax,
ne estre n'an pot c'uns ansanble,
ice Fenyce me resanble:
n'ot de biauté nule paroille.

(2685–91, ed. Micha)

In fact the exceptional beauty of the phoenix is mentioned in only one or two of the bestiaries which have come down to us (it is not, for example, in Pierre de Beauvais, nor in Guillaume le Clerc, nor is it mentioned by Richard de Fournival, nor by Brunetto Latini; nor is it referred to in Thibaut de Champagne's *chanson* (XX, strophe 4); nor was it normally portrayed by artists who depicted the phoenix in paintings, stained glass, etc.). The only place I know where the bird's beauty is stressed is in the collection of Vatican manuscripts concerning the *Physiologus* published in 1587 by Consali Ponce de Leon (chamberlain to Sixtus V). There we may read:[1] 'The Phoenix is a bird more beautiful than the Peacock, for the Peacock indeed has golden and silver wings, but the Phoenix has wings of jacynth and emerald, and is adorned with the colours of all costly precious stones . . .' and these are, also quite exceptionally, the first words of this particular version. It seems obvious to me that Chrétien knew this apparently rarer bestiary tradition concerning the phoenix, and that he makes his comparison with this imaginary bird as soon as he introduces Fenice quite simply because he is looking forward to the 'death' and 'resurrection' sequence to follow, still some 2,500 lines ahead. (Incidentally, nowhere in any bestiary I know is this bird attributed *virtuous* qualities, though some scholars imply that it is. Recently, for example, Deborah Nelson[2] asserts: 'even the choice of the name of Fenice is deceptive since it leads the audience to expect in this young woman virtue which equals her beauty.' This I doubt. I imagine it would have led audiences in the twelfth century to think first and foremost of a bird which was resurrected through fire, a bird which burnt itself and rose, renewed, out of the ashes.)

A typical bestiary account of the Phoenix reads thus:

Now there is a bird in India called Phoenix. And at the end of five hundred years he comes to the trees of Lebanon, and fills his wings with pleasant odours, and he makes known his return to the priest of Heliopolis early in the month of Nisan or Adar (= April or May) . . . And the priest, when he hears the tidings . . . fills the altar with wood . . . And the bird comes to Heliopolis laden with odours of pleasant spices, and settles on the altar, and kindles a fire and burns himself. And on the following morning the priest searches through the ashes on the altar and finds therein a small worm. And on the second day, behold! it achieves feathers and becomes a young bird. And on the third day they find it even as before, the Phoenix, and it salutes the priest, and flies away and returns to its old dwelling place.

(Carlill, pp. 222–3)

The bestiary author-commentators were quick to draw parallels between the bird's death and resurrection and Jesus Christ's: 'Christ suffered death and parted his soul from his body, as also the Phoenix lays himself down on his back and burns himself to death . . .' (Carlill, p. 224), and this comparison is made in all the bestiaries. It is from this common reference to the bird's burning that Chrétien clearly draws when he has the three doctors try to make Fenice talk by burning her:

> Or endroit la metront an rost
> tant que ele iert tote greslie . . .
> (5928–9)

> Ja la voloient el feu metre
> por rostir et por graïllier . . .
> (5932–3)

> . . . au charbon et a la flame
> li feisoient sosfrir martire . . .
> (5940–1)

The detailed account of the search for and construction of Fenice's sepulchre, her feigned illness and the intervention of the doctors from Salerno is, of course, far removed from *any* bestiary account of the Phoenix. But the burning derives undoubtedly from the traditional account, as do one or two other details – mostly to be found in the later stages of this death and resurrection sequence. Amongst them are the sweet-scented qualities of the Phoenix, especially on the funeral pyre; these are transferred to Fenice's tomb:

> et por ce que soef li oelle,
> espant desus et flors et fuelle.
> (6031–2)

Especially interesting is the role of the sun and sunlight. It is the urge to see the sun as spring draws to its climax that finally brings Fenice out of the underground world in which she happily lives with her lover:

197

Quant Fenice vit l'uis ovrir
et le soloil leanz ferir,
qu'ele n'avoit pieça veü,
de joie a tot le san meü,
et dit c'or ne quiert ele plus . . .
(6305–9)

Thus she rises, like the phoenix, from the fire which threatened death to the life-giving light and warmth of the sun; for in many bestiary traditions it is said that once the bird is on the pyre, it turns towards the sun and fans the fire by the beating of its wings. As Florence McCulloch points out,[3] 'for the Egyptians the phoenix was a symbol of the rising sun and this linked with the idea of a resurrection.' No doubt that is why, in the commonest bestiary tradition, the phoenix goes to Heliopolis (i.e. City of the Sun) to perform this rite of renewal.

I would not for one minute argue that Chrétien tries to draw parallels between Fenice and Christ; nor that he tries to Christianize her, even slightly, nor the Tristan and Iseut story which he is, in a way, in part, retelling, and of which Fenice is very much aware:

'Se je vos aim, et vos m'amez,

(this is Fenice speaking to Cliges)

ja n'en seroiz Tristanz clamez,
ne je n'an serai ja Yseuz,
car puis ne seroit l'amors preuz
qu'il i avroit blasme ne vice'.
(5199–203)

But Chrétien does make it sound as if Fenice's chief concern is the preservation of chastity and fear of fornication because of her Christian faith; and he does this by having her say:

'Qui chaste ne se vialt tenir,
Sainz Pos a feire bien anseingne
si sagement que il n'an preingne
ne cri, ne blasme, ne reproche.'
(5266–9)

And he does have Cliges himself and the faithful servant Jehan view Fenice, after the unforeseen and terrible tortures inflicted on her by the three doctors, as a kind of saint. For Cliges she suffers *martire* (5972); and Jehan tells Alis that he had constructed a tomb in which he had thought only a *cors sainz* (6008) would be laid; and Chrétien has Alis declare her to be a *molt sainte chose* (6012). Chrétien's readers, however, know all this to be false. Furthermore, if they know their St Paul as well as Chrétien thought they would, they will know that what he said to the *unmarried* (and widows) is: 'if [you] cannot contain . . . *marry*: for it is better *to marry* than to burn.' (I Corinthians 7, vv. 8–9). Now Fenice clearly abhors the idea of running away with Cliges not because it is wrong according to a Christian code of conduct as laid down by St Paul, but because:

> 'quant nos an serïens alé,
> et ci, et la, totes et tuit
> blasmeroient nostre deduit'.
>
> (5254–6)

What she wants, and what for a while she gets, by *her* phoenix-like decision to 'die' (does she, one wonders, recall one bestiary-commentator who, developing the comparison Phoenix/Christ, argued: 'Christ is your coffin . . . your faith is your coffin . . . fill it with the good spices of your virtues which are chastity, compassion and justice, and thus enter safe into the sweet innermost chambers . . .'?)[4] – what Fenice wants is peace and quiet to enjoy an illicit sexual relationship without public criticism of either herself or Cliges. She may argue, of course, that she is not really married (one recalls the argument of lines 3117–24); but she does go on to enjoy a sexual union with Cliges for fourteen months at least without being married to him, and St Paul clearly did not have that kind of union in mind any more than Fenice had Christian marriage in mind! Indeed, the only God Fenice acknowledges is Love in the form of Cliges:

> De Deu cuident que ele die,
> mes molt a male entancion,
> qu'ele n'antant s'a Cliges non:
> c'est ses Dex . . .
>
> (5642–5)

In short, the closer one examines Fenice's words and conduct, the more one becomes convinced she was utterly selfish and unchristian.

It is, it seems to me, a nice touch that it should be the song of a bird, the nightingale, that makes Fenice long for the garden in which she and her lover are eventually discovered; and that it should be another bird, a lark, which brings about their discovery – first the bird most commonly associated in folklore and poetry with lovers at night is referred to by Chrétien as Fenice and Cliges embrace in their subterranean world; then the bird most commonly associated in folklore and song with lovers in daylight is referred to as Fenice and Cliges sunbathe and embrace, nude, in their walled garden. The ornitholo-gical imagery and links are even more intricate, for Cliges's explanation of his comings and goings to the place where Fenice hides is that he has a moulting falcon there (Chrétien's version of the bestiary's Phoenix 'worm' in the ashes? – certainly a bird *renewing* its feathers!); and it is the wayward flight of Bernard's hawk which misses the lark and lands inside the lovers' walled garden that reveals the lovers' deceit to the world.

Their discovery is, of course, necessary to bring about their return to the world, to fulfil Fenice's implied hope that she will one day be the empress with Cliges at her side as rightful emperor:

> '. . . ja mes ne serai d'empire
> Dame, se vos (= Cliges) n'en estes sire'.
> (5293–4)

Their discovery is also necessary to show how false Fenice's reasoning and motives have been, for the public, whose blame and criticism she had feared for herself and her lover, does not in fact blame either of them. On the contrary, after her lawful husband Alis is out of the way, dead through the grief and shame she caused him, that very public receives Cliges and Fenice with great joy (6629). It is, in fact, Chrétien who criticises, if anybody does – but gently, good-humouredly, recounting how, in the closing lines of his story, there has never since been an emperor who did not stand in fear of his wife lest he should be deceived by her upon hearing the story of how:

> Fenice Alis deçut,
> primes par la poison qu'il but,
> et puis par l'autre traïson
> (6649–51)

– the *traïson* of the Phoenix-like Fenice.

In *Cligés*, one sees how Chrétien uses a death-and-resurrection sequence which is centred on one bird image, and embellished at the end by other bird images, not only to bring about a happy-ever-after dénouement full of dra-matic twists and turns, but also to show his heroine from several viewpoints and, with gentle irony, to bring the knowledgeable reader (especially the one who knows his Bestiary and his St Paul) to a definite but mildly critical view of her.

It is not a feigned but an accidental death and resurrection sequence that we find in Chrétien's first romance. It comes shortly after Erec rescues Cadoc de Cabruel from the two evil giants. Returning to Enide whom he had left alone while he effected the rescue, Erec collapses in front of her from loss of blood, and she thinks he is dead. Erec:

> . . . chiet pasmez con s'il fust morz;
> (4569, ed. Roques)

and Enide is so convinced he is dead that she prepares to commit suicide using Erec's sword (4617–32). At that moment the Comte de Limors chances by. He tries to comfort her, and, impressed by her beauty, offers her marriage on the spot. She of course tells him to go away, but he persists. At his command, Erec's 'body' is placed on a bier:

> 'Feisons tost une biere,
> sor coi le cors an porterons';
> (4678–9)

and carried in what develops into a kind of funeral procession to the Chastel de Limors where:

> 'sera anfoïz li cors'.
> (4682)

The symbolism of the proper names is transparent: the Count of Death has a body taken for burial in the Castle of Death. In this castle's great hall Erec's 'body' is laid upon a round table. The Count promptly consults with his barons about his wish to marry Enide. They acquiesce, and a marriage ceremony takes place, Enide protesting all the while. They then proceed to a wedding feast, apparently in the great hall where the 'body' of Erec is still laid out on a table. The Count gets angry because Enide, instead of enjoying her wedding feast and tucking in heartily, goes on weeping. He says to Enide (clearly inviting Fate and Chrétien to take a hand in the matter):

> 'Certainnemant poez savoir
> que por duel nul morz ne revit'.
> (4758–9)

Shortly after uttering these words and knocking Enide about (just to add to the tempting of Fate and author), the Count witnesses Erec recover from his swoon . . . but to him who is the Count of Death, who had led a funeral procession into his Castle of Death, and subjected Enide to Hellish torment, Erec rises from the dead; and with sword in hand rushes around creating havoc. The Comte de Limors becomes *mort* indeed:

> (Erec) fiert par mi le chief le conte
> si qu'il l'escervele et esfronte . . .
> li sans et la cervele an vole.
> (4827–30)

201

Pandemonium is let loose, and all flee from the hall, leaving Erec alone with
Enide . . .

> car ne cuidoient pas qu'il fust
> nus hom, qui chacier les deüst,
> mes deables ou enemis,
> qui dedanz le cors se fust mis.
>
> (4853–6)

For the onlookers there, this was a resurrection with a difference, a diabolic
resurrection.

Although this incident was almost certainly meant to cause some amusement, Chrétien introduces it at a pivotal point in his romance, for throughout
the middle third of the story, from the marriage-bed scene until the Comte de
Limors scene, Erec and Enide have not been the happiest of husbands and
wives, with Erec clearly doubting Enide's love for him. What he heard and
witnessed as he came out of his deep swoon, as he 'came to life', convinced him
of her love (4815–21) and they are at last reconciled (4879–97). Though very
brief, this particular incident neatly parallels that earlier incident in the story
when, in bed with Enide, Erec came out of a deep sleep only to overhear her
talking to herself and saying the very things which caused him to doubt her
love. Thus, retrospectively, one can see the earlier episode as a kind of death
and resurrection in reverse – an Erec who has been very much alive and
honoured becomes, to all intents and purposes, dead; where the chivalric
standards that had meant so much to him are concerned, he falls into a kind of
mortal sloth; he then goes through a kind of limbo in which he seeks and gains
rehabilitation; and as he returns to life on the round table in the great hall of the
Chastel de Limors, so is he fully restored to the chivalric life, and he goes on to
prove abundantly that this is so in the final third of the story.

The fact that Enide recalls for us, at the beginning of the Limors episode,
those words she uttered as Erec awoke in their conjugal bed, words which
caused him to doubt her love, proves, surely, that Chrétien meant us to see this
parallel. Enide recalls these words so vividly and so emotionally that she
imagines she is directly responsible for Erec's 'death':

> 'Ha! fet ele, dolante Enyde,
> de mon seignor sui omecide;
> par ma folie l'ai ocis:
> ancor fust or mes sires vis,
> se ge, come outrageuse et fole,
> n'eüsse dite la parole . . .'
>
> (4585–90)

Then, soon after the 'resurrection', Erec in turn recalls these fateful words, but only as he reassures Enide of his love for her, and enjoys her embrace:

> 'et se vos rien m'avez mesdit,
> je le vos pardoing tot et quit
> del forfet et de la parole.'
>
> (4891–3)

He 'died' when their mutual trust and love seemed to him to be at an end; and he was 'resurrected' when it was clear to him that that love and trust was restored.

How then is this death and resurrection sequence embellished by – even reinforced by – animal imagery? It is so, it seems to me, through the use Chrétien makes of that most ordinary but important animal, the horse. And it begins and ends with special emphasis on Enide's horse. When Erec takes Enide from her home with the intention of marrying her, Chrétien makes much of the horse she is given – the only gift Erec allows her to be given – as they leave (1364–99). As Erec and Enide approach Arthur's court, deeply in love, they ride side by side on their horses (1469 and 1497); but when they leave Lac's court, divided by a profound misunderstanding, they ride in a single file, Enide forced by Erec to lead the way (2770). The first thing the 'resurrected' Erec does after scattering his enemies is to recapture his horse on to which he leaps and then lifts Enide up so that the couple are re-united on the one horse. On this one horse they are not only re-united but reconciled. On the one horse he forgives her and she accepts his forgiveness. On that horse they embrace and kiss as they make their escape from the darkness of the Chastel de Limors – a darkness broken by the light of the moon, so dear to lovers (4898–900). It is as if Love resurrects them, and that they are resurrected *to* Love, who breaks the darkness of division and of the land of Limors. And this happens on a horse which, in long-lived folklore, is above all a symbol of virility and sexual power, a life-creating symbol.[5]

The couple's first encounter is with Guivrez who helps Erec to recover fully physically and Enide morally so that the happiness they once had in marriage is also fully restored (5196–211). Chrétien emphasizes the fact that the 'resurrection' is now complete with a final flourish of his horse imagery. As the happy couple prepare to leave Guivrez's castle, Erec has his faithful steed returned to him but Enide is given a new one. For the 'new' Enide, a new horse – for the one she had ridden right from her parental home, the one which brought her to Arthur with Erec, and on to Limors divided from him, had stayed behind in that dark place. Now she has bestowed upon her a horse which glows with colour: it is for the most part:

> . . . sors,
> mes la teste fu d'autre guise:

> partie estoit par tel devise
> que tote ot blanche l'une joe
> et l'autre noire come choe;
> antre deus avoit une ligne
> plus vert que n'est fuelle de vingne
> qui departoit del blanc le noir . . .
>
> (5274–81)

It is difficult to account for these colours. The bestiaries tell us that the sorrel horse is the noblest. Perhaps the one black and the one white cheek are to remind us of the dark sadness left behind, and of the lightness of the joy newly rediscovered. As green has always been one of the symbols of hope, of renewed life, the meaning of the green which divides black from white is fairly obvious. The unusual colour-scheme of this unusual horse must be meant to draw attention to its unusual owner. Nor are the colours all that make it appropriate, for on its ivory saddle-bows are carved scenes from the story of Dido and Aeneas – in particular those of the lovers in bed, and Dido's suicide. It is as if Chrétien wishes to emphasize still further the nature of the joy now known by his hero and heroine – a joy due largely to the fidelity of his heroine who had indeed contemplated suicide. And all this is achieved through the introduction of this horse.

In this death and resurrection sequence is one other moment made specially memorable by an animal image. This is when Erec, angry and hurt, has a Limoges rug laid before him, a rug depicting a leopard on which he sits in order to be armed for the series of adventures through which he is to put Enide's love to the test. A strange and curious detail. The bestiaries, however, tell us that the animal 'is very swift and strongly inclined to bloodshed.' (M. R. James, p. 13). It is perhaps therefore intended to emphasize Erec's fury, his fierce temper, and would suggest to Chrétien's contemporaries that swift and bloody actions are to follow. The picture of an angry Erec on his leopard rug contrasts nicely with that of a contented Enide on her multi-coloured palfrey at the end of the death and resurrection sequence – but it is not a contrast clearly willed by Chrétien. The one he clearly wills is between the inexperienced Enide we see set out from the parental home on one splendid horse with the experienced Enide setting out from Guivrez's castle on a yet more splendid horse. As Chrétien says, this latter:

> . . . palefroiz fu biax et buens;
>
> (5271)

and it:

204

> ne valoit pas moins que li suens
> qui estoit remés a Lymors . . .
>
> (5272–3)

and which, appropriately 'estoit noirs' (5274).

We cannot leave *Erec et Enide* without a brief word about white stags and sparrowhawks, if it is only to point out that whatever truth there may be in the arguments which have been advanced about the links between the white stag and Enide and her distant otherworldly origins, Chrétien seems deliberately to eschew here the possibility of a metaphorical passage from 'this' world to 'the other' world. Nor does he draw, as he might have done, on any of the lore he and his contemporaries would know well about the stag's longevity, its ability to renew its life so that it was, to all intents and purposes, immortal. Most of the many variants of this lore (recently treated so well by Michael Bath[6]) seem to have been deliberately set aside by Chrétien, and this is curious in a writer who exploits as much as he does images and metaphors about the renewal of life, of self. There *is* a moment when he might have given a hint of his knowledge of this lore: as Erec and Enide go to bed after the wedding ceremony, Chrétien writes:

> Cers chaciez qui de soif alainne
> ne desirre tant la fontainne,
> n'espreviers ne vient a reclain
> si volantiers quant il a fain,
> que plus volantiers n'i venissent,
> ençois que il s'antre tenissent;
>
> (2027–32)

and here, he and his contemporaries *could* have thought (with the first two lines) of the bestiary stag which, when fifty years old, put its nostrils to the entrance of a snake's hole and held its breath, causing the snake to rush out and enter the stag's jaws, and be swallowed. The stag then rushed to a stream for, unless it drank water within three hours, it died; but if it found water, it lived for another fifty years when the cycle would be repeated. But what Chrétien *does* here, is use two common animal images (in both literature and art) in a way which reminds his readers of the two interlocking adventures of the first part of his story, the one centred on the *hunted* white stag, the other on the *hungry* sparrowhawk, adventures which brought Erec and Enide together, and to the marriage bed.

There is no death and resurrection sequence in the *Lancelot* comparable with either of those in *Erec* or *Cligés*. What one finds are fragments of metaphors which suggest such a sequence. The first fragment occurs at the point where

Lancelot and Gauvain have spent the night at the Castle of the Flaming Lance.
They are at windows overlooking a meadow and a river beneath the Castle
when:

> an virent porter une biere;
> s'avoit dedanz un chevalier,
> et delez ot duel grant et fier
> que trois dameiseles feisoient.
> Aprés la biere venir voient
> une rote, et devant venoit
> uns granz chevaliers qui menoit
> une bele dame a senestre.
> Li chevaliers de la fenestre (= Lancelot)
> conut que c'estoit la reïne . . .
>> (552–61, ed. Roques).

Clearly, this is some sort of funeral procession of which Guenievre is a member.
Lancelot and Gauvain give pursuit, but lose sight of the procession. A passing
maiden guides them, telling them that it is heading for that kingdom:

> don nuls estranges ne retorne
>> (641).

The land of the dead? She tells them of the two bridges which cross into this
land, an underwater bridge, and a sword-bridge. Gauvain chooses the former,
Lancelot the latter, and the two knights part company in their efforts to rescue
the queen. After numerous adventures encountered on his way to the sword-
bridge, Lancelot comes upon a cemetery where some tombstones bear inscriptions which, in effect, predict that one day some of the most famous of Arthur's
knights will be buried there. One, bigger and heavier than all the others, covers
a particularly splendid marble tomb, and on it is written:

> 'Cil qui levera
> cele lanme seus par son cors
> gitera ces et celes fors
> qui sont an la terre an prison,
> don n'ist ne clers ne gentix hon
> des l'ore qu'il i est antrez;
> n'ancors n'en est nus retornez:
> les estranges prisons retienent;
> et cil del païs vont et vienent
> et anz et fors a lor pleisir.'
>> (1900–09)

Again we read of this land which seems to be the land of the dead; and Lancelot proves that he is to be the messianic saviour and liberator of those held in this land by lifting alone that tombstone. The descent – if descent it be – into this mysterious other world/underworld is finally made, many adventures later, accompanied by imagery which recalls Christ's death and suggestions of survival after death. Firstly, the river crossed by the sword-bridge is described as if it were part and parcel of Hell itself:

> l'eve felenesse,
> noire et bruiant, roide et espesse,
> tant leide et tant espoantable
> con se fust li fluns au deable . . .
> (3009–12).

Secondly, in order to cross this formidable bridge, Lancelot removes the armour from his hands, legs and feet – to get a better grip, some commentators say! But Chrétien expresses wonderment at this action:

> (Lancelot) fet molt estrange mervoille.
> (3096)

No, Chrétien clearly wanted his hero to bleed in his hands and feet to recall some of Christ's wounds on the cross: for a little further on, after Lancelot has crossed the sword-bridge, Bademagu (who witnesses Lancelot's agony, especially the pain of the wounded hands and feet – 3323) offers to find him:

> de l'oignemant as trois Maries.
> (3358)

Thirdly, Lancelot braves this encounter with the evil forces at what seems, metaphorically, death's frontier, with a declaration of faith in God which recalls the faith of many a saint:

> 'mes j'ai tel foi et tel creance
> an Deu qu'il me garra par tot'.
> (3084–5)

It is here that Chrétien brings to bear animal imagery which emphasizes both the strength of the hellish powers now braved by his hero, and the nature of the victory – a victory over Hell's powers, over death; a kind of resurrection. For, adding to the terror which the river and bridge strike into the hearts of Lancelot's companions is the sight they (and Lancelot himself) see, or think they see, at the other end of the sword-bridge of:

> dui lÿon ou dui liepart . . .
> . . . lïé a un perron.
>
> (3035–7)

Leopards, we know, were thought of as fiercely bloodthirsty creatures. And lions, if they were not the lions of Judah, were the Devil incarnate and symbolized the Devil who 'goeth about like a roaring lion, seeking whom he may devour.' Since these lions might be leopards, they are clearly devilish (and lines 3061–5 make it pretty clear they are bloodthirsty!). But when Lancelot has undergone his test of faith and reached the other side of this Styx-like river:

> . . . nul des deus lÿons n'i trueve.
>
> (3126)

Although Lancelot is to experience further set-backs, he does bring about Guenievre's release and return (along with that of many others) to Arthur's kingdom. Also, in the process, he is united for one night with his beloved. In spite of the fact that crossing the sword-bridge was as impossible as re-entering a mother's womb and being born again (3056–7), Lancelot achieves the impossible. Thus, a fragmented metaphorical death and resurrection sequence brings about, ultimately (in a kind of underworld which vaguely recalls that of Cliges and Fenice), the union of two divided lovers – but only briefly, for they are not free to marry and live happily ever after: Arthur is too great an obstacle even for a Chrétien de Troyes and the miracle of a metaphorical death and resurrection to overcome!

When Yvain pursues his opponent through the palace gate and there has his horse cut in two by the portcullis (and only just avoids death himself) it is implied that – for a moment at least – the place is like an entrance to Hell:

> si con li deables d'anfer
> descent la porte . . .
>
> (944–5, ed. Roques)

There he is trapped and, as Lunete tells him, when Laudine and her followers have recovered sufficiently from their grief at the sight of their mortally wounded lord, they will come and kill him there:

> '. . . vos voelent ocirre ou pandre:
> a ce ne pueent il faillir . . .'
>
> (990–1)

For a moment it seems as if Yvain is a good as dead, as if this palace gate is to be his tomb. But he is made invisible from his would-be killers by the power of Lunete's magic ring. Vaguely this compares with the remarkable effects of the potion taken by Fenice which protects her from discovery by those from whom she must escape as she lies on her 'death' bed – for here Yvain is told he is safe as long as he stays put on a certain bed (1063–6); and just as Fenice was beaten on her bed, so eventually is Yvain (1191–2). The room in which Yvain hides serves as a kind of resting place for the dead – indeed, referring to her late lord, Lunete warns Yvain:

> '. . . il aporteront
> par ci le cors por metre an terre . . .'
> (1070–1).

And when Laudine's followers come to take Yvain but fail to find him they are convinced his body must be there –

> 'morz ou vis est ceanz li cors'
> (1120).

They reinforce a little the idea that this is a Hell-like place in which a devil-inspired resurrection may have taken place when they say:

> '. . . ancor est il ceanz . . .
> ou nos somes anchanté tuit,
> ou tolu le nos ont maufé'.
> (1129–31)

Laudine herself, as her husband's body is brought through the gatehouse, addresses the unseen Yvain as a *fantosme* (1226). Then we are told that Yvain is in effect mortally wounded in that place – by Love:

> Cele plaie a mes sire Yvains,
> dom il ne sera ja mes sains,
> qu'Amors s'est tote a lui randue . . .
> (1379–81)

Thus, as Yvain sees (from his palace-gate 'tomb') Laudine left alone by the grave of her dead husband, he is metaphorically mortally wounded and, at the same time, the seeds of a metaphorical resurrection are sown.

Exceptionally no significant or memorable animal imagery is used here. We find instead just a few bird or beast comparisons and similes which help make some relatively minor points just a bit more vivid, as when Laudine's followers express their amazement at Yvain's apparent disappearance from the gate-house. 'How can this be?' they ask themselves, 'for there is no door or window here through which anything could escape unless it be a bird, a squirrel or a marmot, or some other even smaller animal . . .' (1111–16). And afterwards, Lunete observes that they have poked about in all the corners more diligently than a hunting dog goes ferreting for a partridge or a quail (1264–7).

Metaphorically Yvain seems to die and to be restored to life a second time in the romance, after his marriage to Laudine; and this time Chrétien makes much use of animal imagery. I refer, of course, to Yvain's bout of madness, his recovery and eventual reconciliation with Laudine.

It all begins when the damsel envoy from Laudine comes to Yvain at Arthur's court, riding on a black palfrey with white forefeet (2709), accusing him of disloyalty, treachery and hypocrisy (2721–3) and takes from him Laudine's ring. Yvain has 'killed' Laudine (2744) and is quickly overwhelmed by a sense of guilt. He thinks of hiding in a wild and desert land (2787), in an abyss (2791) and considers himself dead:

> ne set a cui se confort
> de lui qui soi meïsme a mort.
> (2793–4)

Naked he becomes as a beast among beasts in the woods:

> les bestes par le bois agueite,
> si les ocit; et se manjue
> la venison trestote crue . . .
> (2826–8)

and he responds to a hermit's kindness rather like a half-tame animal, bringing him game and being fed in return. Resurrection from this metaphorical death, recovery from this animal-like state begins with the care provided by the damsel with the ointment from Morgue la Sage. As she applies the ointment she hopes that 'cil se ravoie' (3009), a passage (or a variant of that passage) being translated by W. W. Comfort with the words 'if God calls him back to life' (p. 219 of the Everyman's Library translation; but a word for God does not appear in any French text I know!). In no time at all he excels in battle to defend the damsel's mistress (the Dame de Norison) against Count Alier's attacks, and is compared, among other things, to the falcon descending on the teal (3191) and the lion among the fallow-deer (3199). It is after this first battle and act of service that the 'resurrected' Yvain meets the lion which is henceforth to be associated with him. He finds it locked in mortal combat with a fantastic, bestiary-inspired serpent that breathes fire (3744–5), a serpent which is winning the struggle, having the lion's tail in its jaws and having badly burned its hind quarters.

To anyone who has examined twelfth- and thirteenth-century sculptures, stained glass and paintings in France and England (especially on sculptured capitals) the frequently-depicted struggle between the lion which represents Christ or the forces of Good and the serpent which represents the Devil or the forces of Evil is immediately brought to mind by the first glimpse Chrétien gives of these two creatures. It has to be admitted, however, that this particular variation of the theme is nowhere to be found. Nevertheless, Chrétien's description makes it clear that the serpent *is* evil (*venimeus* and *felon* – 3353), the lion noble (*gentil* and *franche* – 3371) – and therefore good?; and Yvain chooses to attack the serpent, even though he fears the lion may turn on him once it is freed of the serpent. To Chrétien's contemporaries Yvain clearly chose the better part; he sides with personified or rather symbolical good in the form of the lion, which then becomes his 'man' (3391–2), his attribute, and helps Yvain through the rest of the adventures before his successes are crowned with the joy of reunion with his beloved Laudine. In this way an extended animal image underlines Yvain's chivalrous and spiritual renewal and progress till it culminates in the resurrection of marital bliss.

Each of Chrétien's first two romances has an easily perceived metaphorical death and resurrection sequence, and each one is framed, embellished and partly conveyed by bird or beast imagery. Furthermore, both these sequences are employed at critical points in the story. In the next two romances this kind of metaphorical sequence is less easily perceived, is more fragmented and less regularly aided by bird or beast imagery. It continues, however, to be used at critical, even pivotal points in the story. In the first two romances a fair amount of good-humoured irony is discernible; but in the next two, though irony and comic touches are not unknown elsewhere, there seems to be little if any in connection with these sequences. In all four these metaphors are used primarily to portray the coming together, or reunion, of lover and beloved. *Perceval*, though clearly the story of a man who, whether he knows it or not, seeks spiritual growth and fulfilment, is singularly different from the other romances given the viewpoint adopted in this essay. It contains no significant bird or beast imagery, no clearly definable death and resurrection sequence, and no compelling all-powerful sentimental relationship to which either imagery or sequence can be applied. Looked at from this angle, then, it is *Perceval* and not *Cligés* which is so different from the other stories. Nevertheless there are two implied death and resurrection themes in *Perceval* – one in that of the Waste Land which would prosper again if its Fisher King were healed, a theme which is only touched upon; another in that of Perceval's pilgrimage through life in which he forgets God but is brought back to Him and to spiritual rebirth on Good Friday in Spring. Here, in *Perceval*, the two themes are admirably interwoven since it is in the desert of the Waste Land that Perceval forgets God, but is brought back to Him at the time of Nature's renewal. Thus Perceval's 'death' and 'resurrection' become part of a cosmic image of death and resurrection.

Although his use of this particular imagery is always complex, Chrétien moves through his romances from a relatively narrow to a wide and profound application of it, at first supported by fairly precise bird or beast imagery, then vaguer use of it, to more general, universal nature imagery.

Notes on Rhythm in Chrétien's Yvain

B. WOLEDGE

WE do not normally hear Chrétien de Troyes' romances read aloud, and when we read them silently what we hear in our heads is apt to be rather blurred. Perhaps it is for this reason that we do not often talk about Chrétien's skill in organizing the rhythm of his sentences and paragraphs or his ability to build harmonious syntactical structures. Yet he was, to my mind, supremely successful in writing lines whose rhythmical cadences give pleasure to the ear, as well as being a means of suggesting his own attitudes and the feelings and actions of his characters.

Some aspects of Chrétien's skill as a poet have of course already been studied; it is well known that he handled the octosyllabic line, and the couplet, with great freedom and sensitivity, putting long or short pauses wherever he wanted them; his mastery of natural and expressive rhyme is also well-known, as is his occasional use of onomatopoeia. Frappier went further than anyone else in analysing Chrétien's versification; he did not neglect questions of rhythm, and what he wrote on this topic shows his usual critical sensitivity.[1] If I am venturing to glean after Frappier, it is because he mostly discusses single lines and short sections of text, while I am more particularly interested in long sentences and in paragraphs.

A difficulty here is that, although we have a fairly precise idea of how Chrétien pronounced vowels and consonants, we know very little about such things as intonation, sentence stress and the position or duration of pauses in 12th-century French, so that what I am going to say is bound to be impressionistic, hypothetical and tentative. It may perhaps be said that I am merely a 20th-century Englishman posing as a Champenois of the 1170's, or the reader may shrug his shoulders and say he doesn't feel what I feel. But perhaps it is time that we at least mentioned the things I shall try to describe.

I shall quote mostly from M. Roques' edition,[2] which gives the text of

BN fr 794, copied by Guiot, but I shall also refer to Foerster's editions; these give a composite text based on a comparison of the seven manuscripts of *Yvain* known to Foerster.[3] An unusual feature of BN 794 is that Guiot makes use of dots from time to time to indicate syntactical breaks; I shall refer to some of these later; unfortunately from my point of view, they mostly mark places where the break is obvious to a careful reader.

Yvain starts off with a splendid complex sentence, followed by a very ordinary short one:

> Artus, li boens rois de Bretaingne,
> la cui proesce nos enseigne
> que nos soiens preu et cortois,
> tint cort si riche come rois
> a cele feste qui tant coste
> qu'an doit clamer la Pantecoste.
> Li rois fu a Carduel en Gales.
>
> *Yvain* (ed. Roques) 1–7

We see that Chrétien begins in a very straightforward way by giving us the subject of the sentence; we recognize *Artus* as the nominative form, the oblique case being *Artu*;[4] he then isolates the subject by means of a short pause; it is to be picked up and given its verb later; meanwhile Chrétien proceeds to build up his sentence first with a phrase in apposition, then with two subordinate clauses; this takes him to the end of the third line. At the beginning of the fourth line, just at the right moment from the point of view of balance, we get the main verb, linking up with *Artus*. Two more subordinate clauses follow, and we reach the end of the sentence with the feeling that its various components balance each other perfectly. This is reinforced by the way the rhymes are handled in these six lines: the first two rhymes are unobtrusive, with little or no pause at the end of the couplets, but the end of the third couplet coincides with the end of the sentence, and here the rhyme is more prominent (*coste*: *Pantecoste*) and is part of the 'conclusive' effect. Musically speaking, we have reached a perfect cadence.

Chrétien's second sentence is of one line only: *Li rois fu a Carduel en Gales.* This certainly does not balance the first sentence in the sense of having similar weight, but the contrast that it provides is, to my ear, very satisfying. And if Chrétien had continued with a second sentence of the same kind as the first, he would have set altogether too solemn a tone for the sort of work he was setting out to write. This simple sentence strikes a different note: it clearly brings us nearer to the story that we are going to hear and at the same time it has a faintly off-hand tone that makes it the first step in the personal, spoken relationship that Chrétien is going to build up between narrator and hearer.

The opening lines of *Yvain*, then, can be seen as a short paragraph that makes excellent rhythmical sense. Naturally, not all the lines of the romance lend themselves so readily to this kind of analysis, as will be clear when we look at the next few lines. Here Chrétien first gives us a simple four-line sentence and then plunges us into something much more complicated.

Here first are the four simple lines:

> Aprés mangier, par mi ces sales
> cil chevalier s'atropelerent,
> la ou dames les apelerent,
> ou dameiseles ou puceles.
>
> *Yvain* 8–11

It would be easy to dismiss this last line as a fill-up, but it is not just that. A regular feature of Chrétien's technique is the addition of extra subjects at the end of the sentence; by this means he keeps his narration relaxed, both from the point of view of the sense and from the point of view of rhythm. This construction is in fact part of Chrétien's way of being friendly with his audience.[5] We notice that these four lines cut across the rhymes; this prevents them from being too conclusive; perhaps one reason for the presence of *ou dameiseles ou puceles* is that here Chrétien wanted a half couplet sticking out towards the next sentence.

We come now to a more complicated passage, in which Chrétien contrasts his contemporaries, who he says look upon love as a mere amusement, with the men and women of Arthur's time, for whom love was something like a religion:

> Li un recontoient noveles,
> li autre parloient d'Amors,
> des angoisses et des dolors
> et des granz biens qu'orent sovant
> li deciple de son covant,
> qui lors estoit molt dolz et buens;
> mes or i a molt po des suens
> qu'a bien pres l'ont ja tuit lessiee,
> s'an est Amors molt abessiee,
> car cil qui soloient amer
> se feisoient cortois clamer
> et preu et large et enorable;
> or est Amors tornee a fable
> por ce que cil qui rien n'en santent
> dient qu'il aiment, mes il mantent,
> et cil fable et mançonge an font
> qui s'an vantent et droit n'i ont.
>
> *Yvain* 12–28

215

This passage, and especially the later part of it, seems to me to be written with a good deal of feeling, but it is difficult to say how far this impression comes from what is said and how far it comes from the way in which Chrétien says it. Roques' edition, which I have followed here, with its sparing use of punctuation and no full-stop before we reach l. 28, may suggest the speech of a man who feels strongly and speaks forcefully, but this is superficial. The absence of any punctuation before *que* meaning *car*, as in l. 19, is a frequent feature of Roques' edition, which I suspect was due to his going to press before he had decided between the rival claims of comma and semicolon in this construction. Foerster certainly hesitated over the punctuation of these lines, and his last edition shows more marked pauses than his first.[6] We certainly cannot dogmatize either about how Chrétien intended performers to read these lines or how in fact they read them. Line 23 for example (*et preu et large et enorable*) could be said quickly and smoothly, or the three adjectives could be detached and emphasized: *-et preu -et large -et enorable* 'Yes, and they were valiant, and generous, and honourable.'

An important rhythmical element in these lines is the emphatic *mes or* of l. 18, coming after the pause at the end of the previous line; the effect is repeated with the equally emphatic *or* at the beginning of l. 24; together, these two help to give these lines a coherent shape.

There are two rhyme-words here that stand out as particularly emphatic, and it may be that Chrétien chose them because they contributed something to the expression of his feelings:

> qu'a bien pres l'ont ja tuit lessiee,
> s'an est amors molt *abessiee*
>
> 19–20

> . . . et preu et large et enorable;
> or est amors tornee a *fable*
>
> 23–4

abessiee gives a leonine rhyme, the word is rather unexpected, and it is followed by a pause; these things seem to make *abessiee* strike home. The effect with *fable* is rather similar; the word is unexpected, a contemptuous dismissal of contemporary values and a good contrast with *enorable*. Though the rhyme is not rich, the *-ble* ending gives it body. There is effective repetition of *fable* in l. 27, joined with *mançonge*, which picks up and emphasizes the *mantent* of l. 26.

It would obviously be a mistake to lay much stress on such features, but there does seem to be some evidence for the idea that Chrétien was here expressing himself with a certain amount of vigour and feeling. I am not sure that I agree with Frappier when he says of this passage:

'[Chrétien] oppose, ou fait semblant d'opposer, la décadence morale de son siècle à la perfection du passé, à l'âge d'or arthurien de la chevalerie et de la courtoisie. Dans ce contraste, on a voulu voir de l'amertume, de la mauvaise humeur, un accès de pessimisme. C'est, je crois, beaucoup forcer les choses . . . Regretter le *bon vieux temps* des loyales amours est une manière de badinage où il entre plus de grâce et de sérénité que de tristesse ou de dépit.'[7]

Line 19 (*qu'a bien pres l'ont ja tuit lessiee*) exemplifies another difficulty that we meet with in judging the details of Chrétien's versification, namely the complexity of the manuscript tradition. I have quoted the line as it stands in the Guiot manuscript; it is less tightly packed in some other copies, which do not contain the word *ja*. Foerster prints *Que a bien pres l'ont tuit lessiee*, and from the information he gives us it looks as if four manuscripts include *ja* and three do not.[8] The relationships between the different manuscripts of *Yvain* are complex, and in a case like this it is impossible to be sure of the authentic reading, but it seems to me that a scribe was more likely to miss out a *ja* that was in his model than to add one if it was not there. I therefore think it probable that Chrétien wrote *qu'a bien pres l'ont ja tuit lessiee*. The difference between the two versions is certainly not great, but perhaps the reading with *ja* is more forceful than the other, since it has a stressed *ja* in place of an unstressed *que*. Whether this is so or not, the example certainly illustrates how variant readings complicate the task of judging the details of Chrétien's rhythms.

It was a characteristic of Old French that a very large proportion of its words were of one or of two syllables; in addition of course some words, like *que*, could lose their vowel and so not take up a syllable. An octosyllabic line can have nine or ten words in it. If it had not been for this predominance of short words in the language, a writer of the stature of Chrétien could hardly have accepted the octosyllabic line, in spite of its shortness, as a suitable vehicle for long and serious narratives. But once 12th-century writers had got beyond the stage of treating octosyllabic couplets as units and had learnt the free use of overflow, of any kind, at any point, they had created the Old French equivalent of English blank verse. The metre was then just what a writer of Chrétien's sensitivity needed: it was light, flexible, capable of keeping close to the rhythms of familiar speech, but also capable of dignity. And in spite of the frequency of short words, Chrétien knew very well how to use the weightier rhythm of long words when he felt they were needed:

> Felenessemant s'antr'espruevent,
> *Yvain* 835

This line throws some light on the way in which Chrétien constructed paragraphs. It comes from the description of the fight between Yvain and

Esclados le Roux, and it follows a lively (and very typical) series of phrases
made mostly of short words used without big pauses:

> Li uns l'autre a l'espee assaut
> si ont au chaple des espees
> les guiges des escuz colpees
> et les escuz dehachiez toz
> et par desus et par desoz,
> si que les pieces an dependent,
> n'il ne s'an cuevrent ne desfandent;
> car si les ont harigotez
> qu'a delivre, sor les costez,
> et sor les piz, et sor les hanches,
> essaient les espees blanches.
> Felenessemant s'antr'espruevent.
>
> *Yvain* 824–35

The last line forms an effective contrast with what goes before, and it is
tempting to see it as a kind of summing-up, a short pause in which Chrétien
surveys the fight so far; but things are more complex than this, as we see when
we read the next few lines. Neither Foerster nor Roques puts a full-stop after
s'antr'espruevent, and we have:

> Felenessemant s'antr'espruevent,
> n'onques d'un estal ne se muevent
> ne plus que feïssent dui gres;
> einz dui chevalier plus angrés
> ne furent de lor mort haster.
> N'ont cure de lor cos gaster, etc.
>
> *Yvain* 835–40

We see that the line in question is more than a summing-up of what goes
before; it seems to look both ways, forming a kind of peak between two
passages made up of shorter words; it perhaps deserves a semicolon rather than
the comma given to it by Foerster and Roques. Apart from anything else, a
slight pause here will underline the point that Chrétien makes in the next two
lines: that the two knights never shifted their ground in spite of giving and
receiving such terrible blows. Once again, we realize that Chrétien's verse
deserves a sensitive reciter.

Many passages in *Yvain* are worth looking at from the point of view of the
different rhythms used by Chrétien. As an example of the way in which he
varies his verse to fit different characters and situations, here are two contrasting speeches, one from Calogrenant and one from Yvain himself. As Frappier

pointed out, the characters of these two cousins are very different; it is only natural that this should be reflected in the way they talk.

First, Calogrenant; Frappier describes him as follows:

> Chrétien, cherchant à établir un contraste entre son impétueux Yvain et le héros malheureux du premier voyage à la fontaine merveilleuse, a fait de Calogrenant un chevalier discret, réservé, un grant seigneur 'honnête homme', modèle d'urbanité, capable de se moquer de lui-même et de parler de son échec avec un mélange de modestie et d'ironie
>
> (op. cit., p. 146)

Calogrenant's account of his journey to the fountain is in fact one of the most delightfully written parts of the romance, and the easy rhythms fit his character perfectly. Here are the opening lines:

> Il m'avint plus a de set anz
> que je, seus come païsanz,
> aloie querant aventures,
> armez de totes armeüres
> si come chevaliers doit estre;
> et tornai mon chemin a destre
> par mi une forest espesse.
> Molt i ot voie felenesse,
> de ronces et d'espines plainne;
> a quelqu'enui, a quelque painne,
> ting cele voie et ce santier;
> a bien pres tot le jor antier
> m'en alai chevalchant issi,
> tant que de la forest issi,
> et ce fu en Broceliande.
> De la forest en une lande
> entrai, et vi une bretesche
> a demie liue galesche;
> se tant i ot, plus n'i ot pas.
>
> *Yvain* 173–91
(Foerster 175–93)

And so on. The smoothly flowing effect of these lines seems to be due to several factors. Overflow is relatively little used, and a number of the lines are self-contained units of meaning; the sentences are mostly simple, and the three subordinate clauses do not cause interruptions (*il m'avint . . . que; si come chevaliers doit estre; tant que de la forest issi*); there are no climaxes and no complex constructions such as we saw in the opening lines of the romance;

219

yet there is no monotony because the couplet is not treated as a unit and the lines fall into groups of varying length. The result is something quiet and harmonious, a kind of *andante piacevole*.

Compare the spiky rhythms and the strong climax that Chrétien uses for Yvain's first conversation with Laudine:

> '. . . Mes seez vos, si me contez
> comant vos iestes si dontez.
> – Dame, fet il, la force vient
> de mon cuer, qui a vos se tient;
> an ce voloir m'a mes cuers mis.
> – Et qui le cuer, biax dolz amis?
> – Dame, mi oel. – Et les ialz qui?
> – La granz biautez que an vos vi.
> – Et la biautez qu'i a forfet?
> – Dame, tant que amer me fet.
> – Amer? Et cui? – Vos, dame chiere.
> – Moi? – Voire voir. – An quel maniere?
> – An tel que graindre estre ne puet;
> an tel que de vos ne se muet
> mes cuers, n'onques aillors nel truis;
> an tel qu'aillors pansser ne puis;
> en tel que toz a vos m'otroi;
> an tel que plus vos aim que moi;
> en tel, s'il vos plest, a delivre
> que por vos vuel morir ou vivre.

Yvain 2015–34
(Foerster 2013–32)

Chrétien did not have to invent the rhythms he uses here; he has simply combined two conventions used by his recent predecessors: the jerky dialogue with lines divided between different speakers was a feature of *Eneas*, and anaphora was one of Wace's favourite devices. But if Chrétien was here using two familiar technical devices, his way of combining them was new, and the climax reveals his personal touch:

> . . . an tel qu'aillors pansser ne puis;
> en tel que toz a vos m'otroi;
> an tel que plus vos aim que moi;
> en tel, s'il vos plest, a delivre
> que por vos vuel morir ou vivre.

Chrétien's care over the detail of his verse shows here in the series of single lines

220

leading to the final couplet with its prominent rhyme *delivre*: *vivre*. Altogether, these sixteen lines are a brilliant piece of rhetoric in which rhythm has a part to play.

This passage also gives us a good example of Guiot's use of punctuation marks. In l. 2021 he wrote:

> Dame mi oel. et les ialz qui

and in ll. 2025–6:

> Amer. et cui. vos. dame chiere
> Moi! voire voir. an quel maniere.

This is fairly typical of his method. The punctuation marks would help a reader to sort out the syntax quickly, but they do not provide us with much information about speech rhythms which we should not otherwise have. The dots often show overflow, as in:

> Mes ce fu seul a seul. et cele
> Li a la mançonge retreite
>   3106–7

> Et dautre part. autre destrece
> Le retient. la granz gentillece
> Mon seignor Gauvain son ami
>   4077–9

> Et lautre dist que ele iroit
> A la cort le roi Artus. querre
> Aide a desresnier sa terre
>   4708–10

The dot is also used before *et* in phrases where we might not expect a break:

> La honte. et le mal en avomes
> Qui onques ne le desservimes
>   5258–9

> Qui deust son cuer. et santente
> Metre an pucele bele et gente
>   5719–20

> Les merites. et les desertes
> Ne lor an seront ja rendues
>   6156–7

In such cases, which are fairly frequent, the reader hardly needs any help with the construction; can it be that Chrétien (or Guiot) recommended a short rhetorical pause in such lines?[9]

Nearly a hundred years ago, Foerster drew attention to a feature of Chrétien's verse that deserves a place in any discussion of rhythm: the non-elision of a final -*e* that would normally be elided. We are not concerned here with monosyllables (the well-known *que on* as an alternative to *qu'on* etc.) but with words of more than one syllable, as in:

> . . . Mes lués es granz galos se mist;
> Que l'anbleüre li sanbloit
> Trop *petitë*, et si anbloit
> Ses palefroiz de grant eslés.
> Einsi galope par les tes
> Con par la voie igale et plainne.
> *Grosse Ausgabe* 5034–9

'But immediately she put her horse to a quick gallop, for an ambling pace seemed too slow, – and yet the horse was doing a very fast amble. She gallops through the mud as though it were a smooth, level road.' With typical exactitude, Chrétien here describes the messenger's haste to catch up with Yvain, who is urgently needed to champion the cause of the dispossessed daughter of the Seigneur de la Noire Espine. Though Foerster did not print a tréma on *petite*, he intended it to be pronounced in three syllables, as he made clear in a note (p. 279, l. 212). This reading is not found in all the manuscripts, but it occurs in four out of seven, and I think Foerster was right in attributing it to Chrétien. If Chrétien did write this and other similar things, this is another example of his sensitivity: although elision was usual in such cases, he felt free to elide or not as he wanted, and since non-elision implies (I assume) a slight pause, this made his rhythm more flexible and allowed him to give a twist to the way his verse was to be recited. In the lines I have just quoted, the pause shown by non-elision corresponds perhaps to a dash in modern punctuation: '– and yet the horse was going quite fast.' Such things are to me a part of Chrétien's skill in talking to his audience.

Foerster first drew attention to this feature in his edition of *Cligés*, which forms the first volume of the complete works; in his *Grosse Ausgabe* of *Yvain*, he listed 18 examples found in this romance.[10] They may not all be authentic readings, but almost all of them can be interpreted as deliberate exploitation of the option of non-elision. I have not space to discuss them all, but here are some of the most significant ones.

Laudine forbids her maid Lunete to refer again to the subject of finding a second husband; Lunete goes away, but later returns and reopens the conversation with:

> *Damë*, est ce ore avenant
> Que si de duel vos ociëz?
> Por Deu, car vos an chastiëz,
> Sel leissiez seviaus non de honte.
> A si haute dame ne monte
> Que duel si longuemant maintaingne.
>
> *Yvain, Grosse Ausgabe* 1666–71

I suggest that *damë* may be an invitation to the reciter to dwell on the word, slowing down the line and giving it the appropriate tone of voice used by Lunete.

Again, an expressive pause seems to be present in the list of items that Lunete gives to Yvain when she is preparing him to appear in the presence of Laudine:

> Si le fet chascun jor beignier
> Et bien laver et apleignier.
> Et avuec ce li aparoille
> Robe d'escarlate vermoille
> De ver forree atot la croie.
> N'est riens qu'ele ne li acroie,
> Qui covaingne a lui acesmer:
> Fermail d'or a son col fermer,
> Ovré a pierres precïeuses
> Qui font les janz mout gracïeuses,
> Et *ceinturë* et aumosniere,
> Qui fu d'une riche seigniere.
>
> *Yvain, Grosse Ausgabe* 1881–92

Ceinturë without elision makes the items of the list a little more detached and seems to invite a more expressive intonation, perhaps stressing Lunete's generosity or her thoroughness.

Arthur politely greeting Laudine:

> 'Vostre janz cors et vostre chiés,'
> Fet li rois, 'bele criature,
> Et *joïë* et buene avanture!'
>
> ib. 2382–4

Gauvain to Lunete:

> 'Ma dameisele, je vos doing
> Et a mestier et sanz besoing
> Un tel chevalier con je sui.

223

Ne me changiez ja por autrui,
Se amander ne vos cuidiez.
Je sui vostrë et vos soiiez
D'ore an avant ma dameisele.'

ib. 2433–9

Yvain to the crowd who are insulting him:

'Janz sanz enor et sanz bonté,'
Fet mes sire Yvains qui escoute,
'Janz *enuieusë*, et estoute,
Por quoi m'asauz, por quoi m'aquiaus?
Que me damandes, que me viaus,
Qui si aprés moi te degroces?'

ib. 5136–41

Chrétien was by no means the only Old French poet who used non-elision of -*e* at the end of polysyllables. It is an occasional feature in a number of 12th and 13th-century poems and as such is mentioned in the standard works on versification[11] and in editors' introductions to texts; the fullest treatment, however, is in G. Rydberg's *Geschichte des französischen ə*.[12] Rydberg gives a rich collection of examples, in which we note quite a large number from Wace and the author of *Eneas*, two poets whose works were familiar to Chrétien. One particular type that occurs rather frequently in *Eneas* and which may have appealed to Chrétien shows two verbs linked by *et* and denoting an idea of violent activity or restlessness. Thus the sleepless Dido is described in these terms:

else se *pasmë* et s'estant,
sofle, *sospirë* et baaille;
1230–1[13]

and when she knows of Aeneas' departure:

S'amor l'*arguë* et destraint;
1958

and when she is dying:

sa blanche char et bele et tendre
contre lo feu ne peut deffandre;
ele art et *brullë* et nercist.
2121–3

We can compare with this Chrétien's use of non-elision in:

> Lors se *pasmë* et se descire
> Trestot quanque as mains li vient;
>> *Yvain, Grosse Ausgabe*
>> 1300–1, var. of *P*

> Ne vuel pas sanbler le gaignon
> Qui se *hericë* et regrigne
> Quant autre mastins le rechingne.
>> ib. 646–8

And again, but without any idea of violence:

> Qui mout la *prisë* et mout l'ainme;
>> ib. 2419

> Si les *saluë* et enore.
>> ib. 5834

Some critics consider non-elision to be a 'licence' used by writers as a convenient way out when they get stuck.[14] Whatever may be said of medieval literary hacks, the idea of a poet as skilful as Chrétien being unable to manage octosyllables without having recourse to a 'licence' seems unacceptable.

Yet some medieval people, at least in the 13th century if not in the 12th, appear to have disliked this kind of rhythm when they met it in *Yvain*: variants strongly suggest that some copyists got rid of non-elision by means of 'corrections'. Among scribes whose copies have been preserved, Guiot went furthest in this direction: not one of the eighteen examples found in other manuscripts of *Yvain* appears in his copy.[15] The manuscripts that contain most are *V* with 14, *G* with 10 and *F* with 9. Some examples will illustrate the situation (see the Table, p. 226).

Not surprisingly, Foerster, when he was constructing his critical texts, was very much worried by these and the other examples. He did not suggest any aesthetic reason for non-elision; he noted that it sometimes followed a group of consonants and that in most examples it was followed by an *et*, which word he claimed might have passed unnoticed without the hiatus.[16] In his later editions he changed his mind about some of these lines, becoming less tolerant of the *-ë*. It seems to me that the evidence strongly suggests that some if not all of these instances of non-elision go back to Chrétien, though I may well be wrong in guessing at his reasons for using them. The question is worth pursuing, looking not only at Chrétien's other works, but also at the usage of other 12th-century writers.

Line nos. (CFMA in brackets)	Text of *Grosse Ausgabe* (tréma added by B. W.)	Non-elision: mss. with -ë acc. to *Gr. Ausg.*	Elision: Guiot (CFMA) and variants given in *Gr. Ausg.*	
5036 (5028)	Trop petitë et si anbloit	AGV	estre petite et si anbloit	Guiot
			trop petite estre. . .	PS
1666 (1670)	Damë, est ce ore avenant	AGV	Ha! dame, est ce ore avenant	Guiot
			Ah! dame . . .	P
			Dame, est ore bien avenant	F
			Dame, ce est ore avenant	S
1891 (1893)	Et ceinturë et aumosniere	AFGPSV	et ceinturete et aumosniere	Guiot
2384 (2386)	Et joië et buene avanture	AV	ait joie et grant boene av.	Guiot
			ait joie et la b.av.	
			ait grant joie et b.av.	FS
5138 (5132)	Janz enuieusë, et estoute	GV	gent enuieuse, gent	P
			estoute	Guiot
			maleüreuse *for* enuieuse	A
			maleüree *for* enuieuse	P
			trop estoute *for* estoute	S

I am very conscious of the fact that in these notes I have done nothing more than touch the fringes of a vast and complex subject. I have said nothing about many passages in *Yvain* that might repay this kind of approach, nor have I mentioned Chrétien's other romances.[17] More serious is the fact that I have not tried to compare Chrétien with other writers of the 12th and 13th centuries. To mention only one: Jean Renart was supremely skilful in handling octosyllables in something like the same way as Chrétien. But I have not been trying to pass a final judgment on Chrétien or to assign him a place among great narrators. All I have tried to do here is to point out some features of his verse which are not often discussed and which give me pleasure.

Notes

'The Treson of Launcelote du Lake'; Irony in the Stanzaic Morte Arthur
FLORA M. ALEXANDER

1. See D. H. Green, *Irony in the Medieval Romance* (Cambridge, 1979), pp. 326–58.
2. *Le Morte Arthur*, ed. J. D. Bruce (E.E.T.S.), London, 1903, ll. 2200–1. All references to *Le Morte Arthur* are to this edition, but punctuation has, when necessary, been altered to agree with that in *Le Morte Arthur*, A Critical Edition, ed. P. F. Hissiger (The Hague, 1975).
3. ll. 2824–5; 2922–37.
4. ll. 2876–81.
5. ll. 622–3; 784–7.
6. ll. 57–66; 728–35; 1760–71.
7. ll. 1679, 1683.
8. ll. 1878–9.
9. ll. 2936–7.
10. *La Mort le Roi Artu*, ed. J. Frappier, third edition (Paris, 1964), § 146, 1. 9 – § 146, 1. 65. All references to *La Mort le Roi Artu* are to this edition. The work is hereafter referred to as *Mort Artu*.
11. § 109, 1. 20–49.
12. ll. 2654–67
13. ll. 2683–91.
14. ll. 1088–95.
15. ll. 1736–43.
16. § 51, 52, 53.
17. § 30, ll. 67–70.
18. ll. 704–19; 784–815.
19. This interpretation is adopted by K. H. Göller, *König Arthur in der Englischen Literatur des Späten Mittelalters*, (Göttingen, 1963), p. 70, and by A. V. C. Schmidt and N. Jacobs, *Medieval English Romances* Part Two (London, 1980), p. 147.
20. ll. 834–51.
21. ll. 1339, 1371.
22. ll. 544–54.
23. ll. 3216–21.
24. ll. 3325–7.
25. § 89, 1. 20 – § 90, 1. 4.
26. See D. C. Muecke, *The Compass of Irony* (London, 1969), pp. 102–4.
27. ll. 213–6; 560–3.
28. § 14, ll. 1–19.
29. § 27, 28.
30. ll. 1934–41.
31. § 93, ll. 60–77.
32. § 129.
33. ll. 2955–7.
34. ll. 3048–9; 3006–7.

35. e.g. ll. 123–7; 704–7; 532–5.
36. 'The Theme and Structure of the Stanzaic *Morte Arthur*', *P.M.L.A.*, 87(1972), 1079–80.
37. ll. 121–36; 464–87.
38. § 176, ll. 64–75.
39. § 178, ll. 10–29.
40. op. cit., p. 1075.
41. See J.A. Burrow, *Ricardian Poetry* (London, 1971), pp. 93–129.
42. 'The Problem of the Hero in the Later Medieval Period', in *Concepts of the Hero in the Middle Ages and the Renaissance*, ed. N. T. Burns and C. Reagan, (New York, 1975), p. 40.

The Ambivalence of Adventure: Verbal Ambiguity in Sir Gawain and the Green Knight

W. R. J. BARRON

1. This paper is based on a lecture first given in the University of Warwick in November, 1981.
2. *Sir Gawain and the Green Knight*, ed. J. R. R. Tolkien and E. V. Gordon (revised N. Davis), Oxford, 1967.
3. See R. A. Waldron, ed. *Sir Gawain and the Green Knight* (York Medieval Texts), London, 1970, p. 31.
4. *MED lai* n.², (a) A short narrative poem of love, adventure, etc. to be sung and accompanied on instruments, especially the harp; (b) A song, lyric.
5. 'The term "romance" in the early Middle Ages meant the new vernacular language derived from Latin, in contradistinction to the learned language, Latin itself. *Enromancier, romançar, romanz* meant to translate or compose books in the vernacular. The book itself was then called *romanz, roman*, romance, *romanzo*. Then the meaning of the word extended to include the qualities of the literature in these tongues, in contrast to Latin literature or works composed in Latin.' (G. Beer, *The Romance*, London, 1970, p. 4).
6. Witness the pseudo-chronicle *Roman de Brut*, the beast fable *Roman de Renart*, the psychological allegory *Roman de la Rose*, the social satire *Roman de Fauvel*, the sporting manual and moral handbook *Roman des Deduis*.
7. Jean Bodel, *Roman de Saisnes*, ed. Fr. Michel, Paris, 1839, line 7.
8. 'It is doubtful whether the romance can be indeed regarded as a genre at all. . . . The romance is in origin merely a narrative in the vernacular and the texts that we call romances merely a somewhat arbitrary selection from medieval narrative. . . . It seems preferable to speak of a romance mode.' (P. Gradon, *Form and Style in Early English Literature*, London, 1971, pp. 269–70).
9. '. . . the concerns of medieval romance are fundamental and permanent . . . these concerns create and re-create the conventions – of plot, image and character – essential to their expression. . . . Medieval romance deals indeed with "experience liberated" . . . However, in the Middle Ages there are many kinds of fiction which meet this demand. In fact, one is tempted to say that there are none which do not.' (J. Stevens, *Medieval Romance*, London, 1973, pp. 17–18).
10. R. Hoops ('Der Begriff "Romance" in der mittelenglischen und frühneuenglischen Literatur', *Anglistische Forschungen*, 68 (1929), 1–46) finds that in Middle English the term could mean a work in or translated from French, a work in or from Latin, a narrative poem, any sort of narrative or an authoritative source, and was applied to works as varied in character as *Beues of Hamtoun, The Myrour of Lewed Men, St Gregory*, and *Meditations on the Passion of Christ*.
11. I have outlined some of the problems underlying the conventional classifications in 'Arthurian Romance: Traces of an English Tradition', *English Studies*, 61 (1980), 2–23.
12. For a more detailed analysis along these lines see my forthcoming article 'Alliterative Romance and the French Tradition' in *Middle English Alliterative Poetry: Studies in Context* (ed. D. A. Lawton), Cambridge, 1982.
13. See P. Strohm, '*Storie, spelle, geste, romaunce, tragedie*: Generic distinctions in the Middle English Troy narratives', *Speculum*, 46 (1971), 348–59, p. 355 and p. 350.
14. Ibid., p. 348.
15. Lexical material throughout is drawn from *The Middle English Dictionary*, ed. H. Kurath,

S. M. Kuhn, J. Reidy, Ann Arbor, Mich., 1952– (*MED*), and *The Oxford English Dictionary*, ed. Sir. J. A. H. Murray, H. Bradley, Sir W. Craigie, C. T. Onions, Oxford, 1933 (*OED*). The complexity of *aventure* in contemporary French usage is well illustrated in the glossary of Elspeth Kennedy's monumental edition of *Lancelot do Lac*, 2 vols., Oxford, 1980.

16. See N. Frye, *Anatomy of Criticism: Four Essays*, Princeton, N.J., 1957, p. 186 and p. 34.

17. J. A. Burrow (*Ricardian Poetry*, London, 1971, p. 26) cites these instances to exemplify the too easy use of such phrases amongst other deficiencies in the handling of their medium by poets of the Alliterative Revival. The high poetic skill and verbal control of the *Gawain*-poet suggests that when he echoes the conventional excesses of the Alliterative School he does so deliberately for a particular expressive purpose – as when he uses a superfluity of alliteration to suggest the insincerity of the tears shed for Gawain at his departure from Camelot (684), and haphazard verbal choice in the breathless catalogue of his wayside adventures which mocks the glibness of conventional romance (718–23). (See my *'Trawthe' and Treason: the Sin of Gawain Reconsidered*, Manchester, 1980, pp. 18–19).

18. See above, note 3 and W. R. J. Barron, ed. and trans. *Sir Gawain and the Green Knight* (Manchester Medieval Classics), Manchester, 1974.

19. *MED merveille* n., 1(a) A thing, act, or event that causes astonishment or surprise; a wonderful feat; an unnatural occurrence or circumstance; a wonder of nature or art; a monster or monstrosity. 1(b) A miracle. 2 A written account or spoken report of a marvelous thing or event. 3(a) Cause for wonderment or surprise. 4(a) Wonderment, astonishment, surprise.

20. M. W. Bloomfield, *Essays and Explorations*, Cambridge, Mass., 1970, p. 106.

21. It is, perhaps, significant, in a poem so strongly marked by numerological patterns (see A. K. Hieatt, 'Sir Gawain and the Green Knight: pentangle, *luflace*, numerical structure', in *Silent Poetry: Essays in Numerological Analysis*, (ed. Fowler), London, 1970, pp. 116–40 and H. Käsmann, 'Numerical Structure in Fitt III of *Sir Gawain and the Green Knight*', in *Chaucer and Middle English Studies in Honour of Rossell Hope Robbins*, (ed. Rowland), London, 1974, pp. 131–9), that it occurs at line 250, suggestive of the five pentads of its central image, the pentangle, symbol of *trawþe* whose imperfect observance in the world of Camelot is extended through all human history when line 2525 echoes the opening line of the poem.

22. For the evidence on which this ambiguity rests, see my edition of *Sir Gawain*, note 18 above.

23. J. Leyerle ('The Game and Play of Hero', in *Concepts of the Hero in the Middle Ages and the Renaissance* ed. N. T. Burns and C. Reagan, Albany, N.Y., 1975, pp. 49–82) distinguishes six categories of meaning in the Middle English use of the word which together 'present a remarkably complete summary of the poem in all its complex, interlocked structure and also illustrates how *gomnez* are the focus of the centripetal forces arising in the elements of the poem's narrative' (p. 50). As such they constitute the nucleus or nodal point around which, according to Northrop Frye (op. cit., pp. 73–82), the manifest structures of a narrative poem are organized, the meaning of the events arising from their centripetal force focused upon it as the inner core of poetic deep structure.

24. If the poet intended a pun on *croun* – *MED coroune* n., 5(a) Royal status or authority; 10(a) The top of the head, crown, skull; also, head – the threat to the head of state under the terms of the beheading game is ironically underlined.

25. See Tolkien and Gordon, op. cit., p. 87; the editors assume a word-play emphasized by the fact that Arthur speaks *gaynly*, 'appositely'.

26. See Waldron, op. cit., p. 30.

27. *OED wonder* n., I Something that causes astonishment. 1 A marvellous object; a marvel, prodigy; (b) An extraordinary natural occurrence, esp. when regarded as supernatural or taken as an omen or portent. 3 A marvellous act or achievement. 5(a) Evil or shameful action; evil; (b) destruction, disaster; (c) great distress or grief. II 7 The emotion excited by the perception of something novel and unexpected, or inexplicable; astonishment mingled with perplexity or bewildered curiosity. M. W. Bloomfield (op. cit., p. 133) suggests that the opposed sense 'marvel', 'crime' may be intended to relate to the poem as a whole.

28. P. B. Taylor, '"Blysse and Blunder", Nature and Ritual in *Sir Gawain and the Green Knight*', *English Studies*, 50 (1969), 165–75, p. 166.

29. 'The poem is both a lay of marvels and a moral tale; its hero is both a superior romantic figure, capable of prodigies of courage and endurance, and an Everyman figure, "one of us". This is the basic "modal counterpoint" which gives rise to much of our sense of the subtlety of the

poem.' (J. A. Burrow, *A Reading of Sir Gawain and the Green Knight*, London, 1965, p. 184)
30. See N. Frye, op. cit., pp. 50–52 and p. 305. On the inherent ambivalence of Romance see also D. Brewer, 'The Nature of Romance', *Poetica*, 9 (1978), 9–48, pp. 9–11.
31. C. Muscatine (*Poetry and Crisis in the Age of Chaucer*, London, 1972, p. 60), commenting on the interrelated verbal ambiguities of the first two stanzas, suggests they imply 'that the marvellous adventure to be narrated is not only historical (a forgivable poetic stance), but will constitute a comment on history and on the alternation between those two forces of history, *blysse and blunder*, that is between order and confusion. In a general sense the variational style in *Sir Gawain* supports and expresses a sense of variation – vicissitude – in human history.'

Celtic Elements in Arthurian Romance: a General Survey

RACHEL BROMWICH

1. Ifor Williams, *Canu Aneirin* (Cardiff, 1938), line 1242; K. H. Jackson, *The Gododdin* (Edinburgh, 1969), 112. See p. 54 below. As Jackson remarks of the reference: 'if authentic it dates from a time when people who remembered Arthur would still be alive.'
2. These and a number of the Welsh personal names mentioned in this paper have received detailed discussion in my book *Trioedd Ynys Prydein: The Welsh Triads* (Cardiff 1961; new edition 1978) (henceforth TYP). For Cai, TYP, 303–7; Bedwyr, 279–80.
3. See below pp. 45–6 and note 26.
4. For Arthur and his name see TYP, 274–6; Additional Note TYP^2, 544–5.
5. H. M. and N. K. Chadwick, *The Growth of Literature* (Cambridge, 1932) I, 162^n. For the genealogies see P. C. Bartrum, *Early Welsh Genealogical Tracts* (Cardiff, 1966).
6. As interpreted by Melville Richards, 'Arthurian Onomastics', *Trans. Hon. Soc. Cymmrodorion* 1969, 257. See also TYP, 380–5.
7. TYP, 369–75; 488–91.
8. TYP, 329–30; *Studia Celtica* xiv–xv (1979–80), 55–6.
9. TYP, 469–74.
10. From *Adsiltia* (cf. Welsh *syllu*) 'she who is gazed upon', K. Jackson, *Language and History in Early Britain* (Edinburgh, 1953), 709; TYP, 349–50. For the earlier form *Etill* in an early genealogy, see D. S. Evans, *Historia Gruffud vab Kenan* (Cardiff, 1977), 39.
11. TYP, 479–83.
12. Jones and Jones, *The Mabinogion* (Everyman), 100, 143, 239; R. S. Loomis, *Arthurian Tradition and Chrétien de Troyes* (New York, 1949), 19, 491–2 cites refs. to *Yder* in Chrétien's *Erec* and *Charette*. J. R. F. Piette, 'Yr Agwedd Lydewig ar y Chwedlau Arthuraidd', *Llên Cymru* 8 (1965), 186 indicates that the form *Isdernus* on the Modena Archivolt could as well come from the name *Edern* in Breton as from Welsh.
13. Jones and Jones, *Mabinogion*, 55; Ifor Williams, *Pedeir Keinc y Mabinogi* (Cardiff, 1930), 67, 76, 252; Loomis, op. cit. 483–4, citing *Erec* and *Graal*.
14. TYP, 520–3.
15. TYP, 299–300.
16. Piette, op. cit., 187.
17. TYP ciii–vi, 106; Loomis, op. cit., 156–9. *Guin* 'white, fair' is easily intelligible as a corruption or variant of *kein* 'back'; similar variants occur frequently in the 'Triads of Horses.'
18. TYP, 484–7. References to Arthur's contest with *le Capalu* were collected by E. Freymond, *Festgabe für Gustav Gröber* (Halle, 1899); see also *Romania* xxix, 121–4.
19. TYP, cvi, 98; cf. 188.
20. As pointed out by I. Ll. Foster in R. S. Loomis (ed.) *Arthurian Literature in the Middle Ages* (Oxford, 1959) (ALMA), 39. Cf. TYP, 98.
21. TYP, 414–6.
22. TYP, 353–4.
23. Piette, loc. cit., 185–7.
24. J. G. Evans, *The Black Book of Carmarthen* (Pwllheli, 1907), 94–6.
25. TYP, 361–3.
26. A revised version of a translation I contributed to Richard Barber, *The Figure of Arthur* (London, 1972), 69–71. The most recent edition of the poem is by Brynley Roberts,

Astudiaethau ar yr Hengerdd, ed. R. Bromwich and R. B. Jones (Cardiff, 1978), 296–301, to which I gratefully acknowledge my indebtedness, though my interpretation departs from his in a few details. See also K. Jackson in ALMA, 14–15; Jones and Jones, *The Mabinogion*, xxiv; Thomas Jones, 'The Early Evolution of the Legend of Arthur', *Nottingham Medieval Studies* viii (1964), 16–17.

27. Alternatively, perhaps 'enumerate them.' One of the meanings of *gwaredu* (*gwa* + *rhed*) is 'run under.' Many years ago Sir Ifor Williams suggested to me (in conversation) that in this context *gwaredu* might have the sense of 'run through', hence 'enumerate' or 'list (them)'. An analogous suggestion, 'vouch for, speak for(?)', is made by P. Mac Cana, *Ériu* xx (1966), 220.

28. The meaning of all three names – or words – is obscure. All may be adjs.: *syw* 'wise'; *Eléi* (3 sylls.) occurs as a river name, if its meaning were e.g. 'fierce, boisterous' this would be intelligible also when applied to a warrior; *gwytheint* (without -n-) is 'anger,' *wytheint* 'vultures.'

29. In all other instances *ap Modron*, i.e. the god Maponos son of Mātrona; TYP, 433–6.

30. TYP, 520–3; 'Head of Dragons', i.e. 'Leader of Warriors.'

31. Listed in *Culhwch* among the warriors at Arthur's Court; *The Mabinogion*, 104.

32. TYP, 441–3, 427–9. The characteristics here attributed to Manawydan are interestingly similar to those attributed to him in the *Mabinogi* which bears his name.

33. This is the name given to one of Arthur's battles in the list of these in the *Historia Brittonum*. Alternatively it may be an adj. 'bloodstained (or 'battered') shields.'

34. Like Gwyn Godyfrion above, both Anwas and Llwch are listed among the names of heroes at Arthur's Court in *Culhwch*, Jones and Jones, *The Mabinogion*, 102 (*Henwas* for *Anwas*), 104. On Llwch's epithet see I. Ll. Foster in ALMA, 34.

35. i.e. Edinburgh. K. Jackson suggests that the 'border' concerned is that between the Britons and Pictland; ALMA, 15.

36. *mynei ymtiwygei*. Ifor Williams suggested (in conversation) that *mynei* here is a corruption of *myn y(d)*, an oblique case of *man y* 'the place where.' One of the meanings of *diwygio* is 'recompense.'

37. *Celli* means 'woodland, a grove.' But it is tempting to interpret it here as an abbreviated form of *Celliwig*, Arthur's Cornish capital in *Culhwch* and in the Triads.

38. Unless *cuelli*, 'fury, savagery' is, like *Celli*, a place-name now forgotten.

39. Perhaps to be identified with the *Wrnach Gawr* ('W. the Giant') of *Culhwch*; cf. TYP, 362 and n. 1.

40. The 'mountain of Eidyn' must be either Arthur's Seat or the Castle Rock. 'Dog Heads' have been explained as the mythical *Cynocephali* of St Augustine; *Y Cymmrodor* xxviii, 110 n.; ALMA, 15. They may more appropriately be compared with the mythical *Coinchenn* who figure in a number of Irish sources; cf. G. Murphy, *Duanaire Finn* (*Irish Texts Society*, vol. xliii), 91 n. J. Lloyd-Jones renders *pen palach* as 'cudgel-head', *Ériu* xvi, 123 (possibly a nickname). *Dissethach* is unknown.

41. On Bedwyr's epithet see TYP, 279.

41a. *Traith Tribruit* is the name given by Nennius to one of Arthur's battles; see K. Jackson, 'Once again Arthur's Battles', *Modern Philology* xliii, 51–2.

42. *Garwlwyd* 'Rough Grey' is perhaps the monster *Gwrgi Garwlwyd* of the Triads; TYP, 391.

43. Or 'a hostage was given' (*disguistlad*).

44. This suggests the *Emrys Wledig* (Ambrosius) of the *Historia Brittonum*. But it is difficult to see the relevance, unless his name is here employed symbolically, with some such meaning as 'the lords of Britain (?)'.

45. *Hir* 'long, tall' is an epithet borne by Cai in the romances; TYP, 304, n.

46. A son of Arthur named in the Triads, TYP, 416–8. His name renders *Loholt* in the Welsh version of *Perlesvaus*.

46a. Ystafngwn is an unknown place-name.

47. 'Lions' is here a conjectural interpretation of *lleuon*, as the customary pl. of *llew* 'lion' is *llewod*. 'Lions' is however accepted by Jackson, ALMA, 15, and by Jones, *Mabinogion*, xxiv. It is not inappropriate for a monster-cat such as the *Cath Palug* of the next line, who appears in a triad as 'one of the Three Scourges of Anglesey.' Cf. n. 18 above.

48. *Palug* probably originally meant 'scratching, clawing', but came to be taken as a personal name. Cf. J. Lloyd-Jones, *Ériu* xvi (1952), 123ff.

49. Loomis, *Arthurian Tradition*, 238–9; B. Roberts, *Astudiaethau*, 298.
50. In 'The Second Battle of Moytura', Cross and Slover, *Ancient Irish Tales* (London, 1936), 35–6.
51. TYP, lxxxi, 16, 172; on Llywarch Hen, 430–3 and refs. cited.
52. TYP, 480.
53. For Urien Rheged see TYP, 516–20; *Owain*, 479–83; Ifor Williams (trans. J. E. Caerwyn Williams), *The Poems of Taliesin* (Dublin, 1968).
54. *Hist. Reg. Brit.* xi, i.
55. J. Loth, *Revue Celtique* xiii, 483–4; xliii, 424. Cf. TYP, 348. Cf. L. Fleuriot, *Le Vieux Breton* (Paris, 1964), 45; TYP, 348. On Middle Breton *Guerec* see K. Jackson, *A Historical Phonology of Breton* (Dublin, 1967), 138–9.
56. In Irish *Manannan mac Lir*, a god of the sea, particularly associated with the Isle of Man. Cf. TYP, 442.
57. J. G. Evans and J. Rhys, *The Text of the Book of Llan Dâv* (Oxford, 1893), 181.
58. *Descriptio Cambriae* i, ch. vi.
59. J. Loth, *La Métrique Galloise* (*Cours de Littérature Celtique*; Paris, 1902) vol. xi, 182–3, 188–91, 202–3; Roparz Hemon, *Trois Poèmes en Moyen Breton* (Dublin, 1962).
60. Léon Fleuriot, 'Old Breton Genealogies and Early British Traditions', *Bulletin of the Board of Celtic Studies* xxvi (1974), 1–6.
61. J. Marx 'Monde Brittonique et Matière de Bretagne', *Études Celtiques* x (1963), 478–88.
62. R. Bromwich 'Celtic Dynastic Themes and the Breton Lays', *Études Celtiques* ix (1961), 439–74.
63. From *Guihomarch* 'horse-worthy', J. Loth, *Chrestomathie Bretonne* (Paris, 1890), 176.
64. Emyr Llydaw is commemorated in the 'Stanzas of the Graves', ed. Thomas Jones, *Proc. Brit. Acad.* liii (1967), verse 38. 'Howel vab Emyr Llydaw' renders Geoffrey of Monmouth's Duke *Hoelus* in the Welsh versions of his *Historia*, TYP, 407–8.
65. According to Fleuriot's discussion of the 'Livre des Faits d'Arthur', incorporated in the *Life of St Goevnovius*; see his *Les Origines de la Bretagne* (Paris, 1980), 245–6, 277 and *passim*.
66. Poets travelled freely over the whole of Ireland and Gaelic Scotland, sharing in a cultural community which transcended political barriers.
67. On the movement of legend from the 'Old North' see my paper 'Scotland and the Earliest Arthurian Tradition', BBSIA 15 (1963), 85–95. Northern heroes transferred to Wales who do not re-appear in Arthurian Romance include Llywarch Hen, Huail son of Caw, and Gwyddno Garanhir.
68. R. Bromwich 'Some Remarks on the Celtic Sources of *Tristan*', *Trans. Hon. Soc. Cymmrodorion* 1953; on *Fomóire/Morholt*, pp. 39–40 and n.; TYP, 329–33, etc.
69. Cf. ALMA, 531, and the sources there listed in n. 4.
70. Tolkien and Gordon, *Sir Gawain and the Green Knight*, 2nd. edn. edited by Norman Davies (Oxford, 1968), 128–9.
71. K. H. Jackson, *The International Popular Tale and Early Welsh Tradition* (Cardiff, 1961), 123–4; TYP, lxv; P. Mac Cana, *The Mabinogi* (Cardiff, 1977), 19–20.
72. Mac Cana, loc. cit.
73. R. Bromwich 'The Celtic Inheritance of Medieval Literature', *Modern Language Quarterly* xxvi (1965), 203–27.
74. R. Bromwich 'Celtic Dynastic Themes and the Breton Lays', *Études Celtiques* ix (1961), 439ff.
75. As first pointed out by Deutschbein, *Beiblatt zur Anglia* xv, 16ff.; R. Bromwich, 'Some Remarks on Celtic Sources of *Tristan*', 38–9.
76. Cf. my remarks in *Études Celtiques* xi (1967), 11.
77. M. L. Sjoestedt, *Dieux et Héros des Celtes* (Paris, 1940).
78. Cf. Ernest Renan, *Essai sur la Poésie des Races celtiques*, first published in the *Revue des Deux Mondes* for 1854.
79. Thomas Jones, 'The Early Evolution of the Legend of Arthur', *Nottingham Medieval Studies* viii (1964), 11.
80. In the episode of the canons from Laon who visited Bodmin in 1113; E. K. Chambers, *Arthur of Britain* (London, 1927), 18.

81. Thomas Jones, 'A Sixteenth-Century Version of the Arthurian Cave Legend', *Studies in Language and Literature in Honour of Margaret Schlauch* (Warsaw, 1966).
82. For a survey of speculations concerning the site of Celli Wig, see now Oliver Padel 'Kelli Wic in Cornwall', *Cornish Archaeology* 16 (1977), 115ff.; cf. TYP, 3–4.
83. Cf. note 1 above for refs., and p. 42.
84. *Early Evolution*, 13.
85. *Early Evolution*, 5–6.
86. *The Gododdin*, 63–7, and *passim*.
87. Cf. my paper 'Concepts of Arthur', *Studia Celtica* x–xi (1975–6), 163–81.

L'Autre Monde celtique et l'élément chrétien dans les lais anonymes
JACQUES DE CALUWÉ

1. 'L'élément chrétien dans les *Lais* de Marie de France', in *Mélanges Jeanne Lods*, Paris, 1978, t. I, pp. 95–114.
2. Cfr. J. De Caluwé, 'La conception de l'amour dans le lai d'*Eliduc* de Marie de France', in *Le Moyen Age*, 77 (1971), pp. 53–77, Marie-Noëlle Lefay-Toury, 'Pluralité des structures et des sens dans les *Lais* de Marie de France: quelques exemples', in *Le récit bref au Moyen Age*, Amiens, 1979, pp. 25–44.
3. C'est le titre du fameux article de S. Foster Damon, in *P.M.L.A.*, 44 (1929) pp. 968–996.
4. Jean Frappier, 'A propos du lai de *Tydorel* et de ses éléments mythiques', in *Mélanges de linguistique française et de philologie et littérature médiévales offerts à Paul Imbs*, Strasbourg, 1973, pp. 561–587; cit. p. 567.
5. P. M. O'H. Tobin, 'L'élément breton et les lais anonymes', in *Mélanges de langue et littérature françaises du Moyen Age et de la Renaissance offerts à Charles Foulon*, t. II, Liège, 1980, pp. 277–286; cit. p. 277.
6. P. M. O'H. Tobin, *Les lais anonymes des XIIe et XIIIe siècles*, Genève, 1976; index, pp. 375–378. Toutes les citations sont extraites de cette édition.
7. Cfr William Allan Neilson, 'The Purgatory of Cruel Beauties', in *Romania*, 29 (1900), pp. 85–93 et René Comoth, 'Le Châtiment des Cruelles – Antécédents médiévaux d'une nouvelle du Décaméron', in *Marche Romane*, 30 (1981), 3–4 (sous presse).
8. R. C. Johnston et D. D. R. Owen, *Two old French Gauvain Romances: 'Le Chevalier à l'épée' and 'La Mule sans Frein'*, Edinburgh and London, 1972, p. 110.
9. Cfr Jean Frappier, art. cit.
10. Cfr François Suard, '*Bisclauret* et les Contes du Loup-Garou: essai d'interprétation', in *Mélanges . . . Charles Foulon*, t. II, pp. 267–276.
11. 'Le projet narratif dans *Lanval*, *Graelent* et *Guingamor*', in *Etudes de langue et de littérature françaises offertes à André Lanly*, Nancy, 1980, pp. 357–369; sur *Guingamor*, voir aussi Sara Sturm, *The Lay of Guingamor: a study*, Chapel Hill, 1968. L'auteur de cette étude s'attache notamment aux thèmes de la fée maîtresse et du voyage dans l'Autre Monde ainsi qu'à un traitement particulier du mythe de la Femme de Putiphar.
12. 'L'élément chrétien dans les *Lais* de Marie de France' pp. 98–99.
13. Index, p. 376 et note p. 122.
14. *Le Coeur mangé, Récits érotiques et courtois*, Paris, 1979, p. 29.
15. *Deux lais féeriques bretons: Graelent et Tyolet*, Bruxelles, 1979, p. 9. Comme Herman Braet ne se fonde pas sur l'éd. P. Tobin mais sur celle qu'il prépare en collaboration avec Willy Van Hoecke, il s'agit pour lui des vers 99–101.
16. Loc. cit.
17. Cf. Jean Subrenat, 'L'aveu du secret d'amour dans le *Lai de Désiré*', in *Mélanges . . . Charles Foulon*, t. I, Rennes, 1980, pp. 371–379.
18. Je crois, comme Jean Subrenat (art. cit., p. 379), que la 'teinte religieuse' de *Désiré* est volontaire et 'suggère une remise en cause de la vision à la fois sociale et religieuse de l'amour et du mariage à son époque.' Mais il me semble que cette remarque pourrait s'appliquer à *Yonec*, *Eliduc* ou *Fresne*, même si le motif religieux n'y est pas aussi développé.
19. 'L'Autre Monde celtique dans la littérature française du XIIe siècle', in *Bulletin de la classe des Lettres et Sciences morales et politiques de l'Académie royale de Belgique*, 46 (1960), pp. 584–597, cit. p. 591.

20. Art. cit., p. 591.
21. 'Le Bâton et la Belette ou Marie de France devant la matière celtique', in *Melanges . . . Charles Foulon*, t. II, pp. 157–166.
22. *Les Lais de Marie de France*, Paris, 1979, p. 186.
23. Cfr Omer Jodogne, 'La conversion dans le lai d'*Eliduc*', in *Mélanges de langue et littérature françaises du Moyen Age offerts à Pierre Jonin*, Aix-en-Provence, 1979, pp. 347–354 et Charles Foulon, 'L'éthique de Marie de France dans le lai de *Fresne*', in *Mélanges Jeanne Lods*, t. I, pp. 203–212.
24. Danielle Regnier-Bohler ('Figures féminines et imaginaire généalogique: étude comparée de quelques récits brefs', in *Le récit bref au Moyen Age . . .*, pp. 73–95) distingue soigneusement l' 'être faé' féminin de l' 'être faé' masculin. 'L'être féminin', écrit-elle, 'venu de l'Autre Monde présente toujours la plus parfaite normalité et jamais dans son être même, la fée n'accuse l'opposition entre les deux mondes.' L'exemple du lai de *Désiré* ne me paraît pas compatible avec cette distinction: comme le père de Yonec, la fée porte en elle les traits mythiques qui la rendent suspecte pour les esprits chrétiens.

Un Personnage mystérieux du Roman de Perceval le Gallois: *l'*eschacier *dans la Seconde Partie du* Perceval

C. FOULON

1. Numérotation de l'édition Félix Lecoy, *CFMA*, 1973.
2. Editions S.E.D.E.S. 1978.
3. Vv. 4959 et 5381.
4. Vv. 5762–5765.
5. Vv. 6872–6885.
6. Vv. 7094–7113.
7. V. 6362.
8. V. 6367.
9. Vv. 6384–6385.
10. Vv. 7917–7919.
11. Vv. 7304–7312.
12. Vv. 7341–7344.
13. Vv. 6954–6960.
14. Vv. 6961–6962.
15. V. 8690.
16. Vv. 8694–8701.
17. R. S. Loomis, *Arthurian Tradition and Chrétien de Troyes*, New York, Columbia University Press, 1949, pp. 445–447. *Le Songe de Maxen Wledig* se trouve dans les *Mabinogion*, éd. J. Loth, I, pp. 215–222.
18. *F*: Florence, Riccardiana 2943; *P*: Mons, 331/206; *U*: Paris, F. fr. 12577.
19. 'The "Eschacier" in Chrétien's *Perceval* in the light of Medieval Art', *Modern Language Review*, XLVII (1952), pp. 52–55.
20. J. Adhémar, *Influences antiques dans l'art du Moyen Age français. Recherches sur les thèmes d'inspiration*, Londres, 1937, pp. 204–205, cité par Mme Le Rider.
21. *Le Chevalier dans le Conte du Graal*, p. 270 et note 23.
22. Supra, Cf. note 16, v. 8696.
23. 'Pire que Sathenas' (Vers 7206).
24. P. Ménard, *Le Rire et le sourire dans le roman courtois en France au Moyen Age*, p. 396 et note 55.
25. Vers 7419.
26. Op. cit. page 396.
27. Même page, note 55.
28. Op. cit. p. 396.
29. J. P. Marx, *Les Littératures celtiques*, P.U.F., Coll. 'Que sais-je?', 1959, p. 50.
30. *Celtic mysteries*, par John Sharkey.
31. J. Loth, *Mabinogion*; G. et T. Jones, *The Mabinogion*, p. 158.

32. Voir, dans Anatole Le Braz, *La Légende de la Mort chez les Bretons armoricains*, l'histoire du Yeun Elez.
33. Vv. 7304–7312.
34. *The Origin of the Grail Legend*, New York, Harvard, 1943, page 145.
35. 'Nus orfevres ne doit faire ouvrage de keuvre ki soit dorés ne argentés, se ce n'est ouvrage d'eglise'. (Tailliar, *Recueil d'actes des XIIème et XIIIème siècles*, p. 245. – cité par Littré).
36. Les *eschaces* (pour mutilés) se faisaient couramment en bois au moyen âge; il en est question dans certaines chansons de geste, comme *Aliscans*: 'Fetes eschaces de fresne ou de seü' (*Aleschans*, vers 1520).
37. *Perceval*, vv. 7417–7419.
38. Vv. 7128–7167.

A Process of Adaptation: the Spanish Versions of the Romance of Tristan

J. B. HALL

1. Ed. M. de Riquer in *Les chansons de geste françaises*, trans. I. Cluzel (Paris, 1957), pp. 342–51. The reference is at ll. 185–6.
2. The troubadour Guilhem de Berguedan addressed a poem to Tristan in about 1190; see M. de Riquer, 'El trovador Guilhem de Berguedan y las luchas feudales de su tiempo', *Boletín de la Sociedad Castellonense de Cultura*, XXIX (1953), 219, 247. See *Libro del esforçado cauallero don Tristan de Leonis y de sus grandes fechos en armas (Valladolid, 1501)*, ed. A. Bonilla y San Martín (Madrid, 1912), xxvii–xxviii, for allusions to Tristan in the work of Guillem de Cervera (fl. 1259–82) and Serverí de Gerona (ca. 1270).
3. A manuscript fragment of the second half of the fourteenth century has been edited by R. Aramon i Serra: 'El *Tristany* català d'Andorra', *Mélanges offerts à Rita Lejeune* (Gembloux, 1969), I, 323–37. It describes Tristan's marriage to Yseut of the White Hands, his receipt of a letter from Yseut the Fair asking him to return to Britain, and his arrival with Kaherdin. A fragment of the late fourteenth century has been edited by A. Duràn i Sanpere: 'Un fragment de *Tristany de Leonis* en català', *Estudis Romànics*, II (1917), 284–316. It relates the story of Tristan's birth.
4. See Duràn i Sanpere, op. cit., p. 314.
5. A. Rubió y Lluch, *Documents per l'historia de la cultura catalana migeval* (Barcelona, 1908–21), I, 314. In the inventory of the library of the Príncipe de Viana (d. 1461), published by R. Beer, *Handschriftenschätze Spaniens* (Vienna, 1894), item no. 38 is given as *Tristany de Leonis*; the language of the text is not stated.
6. Ed. J. Massó Torrents, *Repertori de l'antiga literatura catalana. La Poesia* (Barcelona, 1932), I, 501–11. There is also in *La Faula* a description of a horse with the story of Tristan and Yseut represented on its harness; its bells play the melody of one of Tristan's lays.
7. Ed. R. Aramon i Serra (Barcelona, 1930–1), II, 184–5.
8. Ed. M. de Riquer (Barcelona, 1947), pp. 309, 588. Elsewhere, the empress sings a ballad describing how Tristan was fatally wounded by the jealous Mark (p. 753; see also Riquer, 'Sobre el romance, Ferido está don Tristán', *Revista de Filología Española*, XXXVII (1953), 225–7).
9. See *Libro del esforçado cauallero don Tristan de Leonis (1501)*, ed. Bonilla y San Martín, xxx, for the Valencia procession. For the Barcelona tournament, see *Llibre de solemnitats de Barcelona*, ed. A. Duràn i Sanpere, J. Sanabre (Barcelona, 1930), I, 28–9.
10. See W. J. Entwistle, *The Arthurian Legend in the Literatures of the Spanish Peninsula* (London, 1925), p. 14.
11. *Libro de buen amor*, quatrain 1703.
12. See, for example, *Cancionero de Baena*, ed. P. J. Pidal, 2 vols. (Buenos Aires, 1949), nos. 38, 149, 226, 234, 249, 301, 305, 400, 572.
13. See Riquer's article mentioned above, n. 8.
14. Ed. G. T. Northup, *El cuento de Tristán de Leonís* (Chicago, 1928). In his prefatory study Northup notes that the other Castilian Tristan text (see below) 'refines away many barbaric elements' in the *Cuento* (p. 44). However, he does not discuss most of the differences between them, and fails to see the significance of those which he does mention. His observations are at times incorrect or misleading; see, for example, his comments on Tristan's departure from his

wife and arrival in Britain (pp. 66–7), and his meeting with Dinadan (p. 74).

15. For the 1501 imprint, see above, n. 2. That of 1528 was also edited by A. Bonilla y San Martín, *Libro del esforzado caballero don Tristan de Leonis y de sus grandes hechos en armas*, in *Libros de caballerias*, Primera parte: *Ciclo artúrico–Ciclo carolingio* (Nueva Biblioteca de Autores Españolas, VI, Madrid, 1907), pp. 339–457. An edition with a sequel giving the adventures of the lovers' children appeared in 1534; see below, n. 23.

16. H. L. Sharrer, *A Critical Bibliography of Hispanic Arthurian Material* (Research Bibliographies and Checklists, III, London, 1977), I, 30.

17. For a good account of recent work on the question of sources, see H. L. Sharrer, 'Malory and the Spanish and Italian Tristan Texts: The Search for the Missing Link', *Tristania*, IV (1979), 37–43.

18. References in the text are to Northup's edition of the *Cuento* and to Bonilla y San Martín's edition of the 1501 *Libro*.

19. For Dinadan see, for example, the following: E. Vinaver, 'Un chevalier errant à la recherche du sens du monde: quelques remarques sur le caractère de Dinadan dans le *Tristan* en prose', *Mélanges de linguistique romane et de philologie médiévale offerts à Maurice Delbouille* (Gembloux, 1964), II, 677–86, reprinted in E. Vinaver, *A la recherche d'une poétique médiévale* (Paris, 1970), pp. 163–77; also P. Ménard, *Le rire et le sourire dans le roman courtois en France au Moyen Age (1150–1250)* (Geneva, 1969), pp. 459–61; also E. Baumgartner, *Le Tristan en prose. Essai d'interprétation d'un roman médiéval* (Geneva, 1975), pp. 252–9.

20. P. Waley, 'Juan de Flores y *Tristán de Leonís*', *Hispanófila*, XII (1961), 12.

21. An early 16th-century Castilian manuscript recently acquired by the Biblioteca Nacional (MS 22021) contains among other items a version of a letter from Yseut condemning Tristan's marriage to Yseut of the White Hands, and a reply from Tristan in which he seeks to justify himself. No such reply exists in any other extant version of the story. However, in a paper read at a meeting of the Medieval Spanish Research Seminar at Westfield College, London, in October 1981, Professor H. L. Sharrer suggested that the letters could be rhetorical exercises and not necessarily fragments of a lost Castilian *Tristan* text. Both letters are longer than Yseut's letter in the two extant romances, and their style is even more elaborate than that of her letter in the *Libro*.

22. The Catalan fragment edited by Aramon i Serra (see n. 3, above) is of interest in this respect; the version of Yseut's letter which it contains is very similar to that in the *Cuento*, whereas its accounts of Tristan's parting from his wife and his arrival in Britain with Kaherdin correspond closely to those in the *Libro*.

23. *Coronica nueuamente emendada y añadida del buen cauallero don Tristan de Leonis y del rey don Tristan de Leonis, el joven su hijo* (Seville, 1534). See G. Eisele, 'A Reappraisal of the 1534 Sequel to *Don Tristán de Leonís*', *Tristania*, V (1980), 28–44, and 'A Comparison of Early Printed Tristan Texts in Sixteenth-Century Spain', *Zeitschrift für Romanische Philologie*, XCVII (1981), 370–82.

24. 'A Comparison of Early Printed Tristan Texts', p. 375.

25. J. B. Hall, '*Tablante de Ricamonte* and Other Castilian Versions of Arthurian Romances', *Revue de Littérature Comparée*, XLVIII (1974), 177–89.

26. See J. B. Hall, 'The Ethos of the French Post-Vulgate *Roman du Graal* and the Castilian *Baladro del sabio Merlin* and *Demanda del Sancto Grial*', to appear in *Revue de Littérature Comparée*, LVII (1983).

27. Unlike Lancelot and Tristan, for instance, Amadís does not cuckold his king, Oriana being Lisuarte's daughter and not his wife; the device of the clandestine marriage permits the hero and heroine to have all the thrills and trials of a secret romance without committing any sin. Amadís has right on his side when he finally goes to war against his monarch, for Lisuarte had wished to marry Oriana to the Emperor of Rome whereas she was already legally if secretly married to Amadís and had borne him a son. See J. Ruiz de Conde, *El amor y el matrimonio secreto en los libros de caballerías* (Madrid, 1948). For Arthurian influences upon *Amadís* see E. B. Place, 'Fictional evolution: the old French romances and the primitive *Amadís* reworked by Montalvo', *Publications of the Modern Language Association of America*, LXXI (1956), 521–9.

28. Sharrer, 'Malory and the Spanish and Italian Tristan Texts', p. 38 and n. 7.

29. It should be noted that the kinds of modification which I have indicated are not a purely

Spanish phenomenon. Malory, for instance, who hoped that his work would lead to a rebirth of truly chivalric conduct among knights who read it, modifies the more senseless cruelties of his sources; he also tones down the humour, reducing Dinadan's irony to a comparatively harmless *bonhomie*. See E. Vinaver, *Malory* (Oxford, 1929), pp. 59–69.

The Lion and Yvain
TONY HUNT

* I write on this subject for Professor Diverres in recognition of our common interest in *Yvain* over a number of years and of our increasing agreement on a number of questions, including the romance's relationship to the Welsh *chwedyl*.
1. Hugh of St Victor, *De scripturis et scriptoribus sacris* c. V, *PL* 175, 13B.
2. See, for example, S. Bayrav, *Symbolisme médiéval* (Istanbul, 1957), p. 125; A. Lytton Sells, *Animal Poetry in French and English Literature and the Greek Tradition* (Bloomington, Indiana, 1955), p. 39; Fr. Ohly, 'Vom geistigen Sinn des Wortes im Mittelalter', *ZfdA* 89 (1958), esp. 18–19 and H. Brinkmann, 'Wege der epischen Dichtung im Mittelalter', *Archiv* 200 (1964), esp. 432–5; J. Harris, 'The Lion in Chrétien's *Yvain*', *PMLA* 64 (1949), 1143–63; for Hartmann see the list in Herta Zutt, *König Artus – Iwein – Der Löwe. Die Bedeutung des gesprochenen Wortes in Hartmanns Iwein* (Tübingen, 1979), p. 69, n. 13.
3. See *A. Gellii, Noctes atticae* rec. P. K. Marshall t. 1 (Oxonii, 1968), pp. 206–8 and P. K. Marshall, Janet Martin & Richard H. Rouse, 'Clare College MS 26 and the Circulation of Aulus Gellius 1–7 in Medieval England and France', *Med. Stud.* 42 (1980), 353–94.
4. For a list of earlier studies see Juliette De Caluwé-Dor, 'Yvain's Lion again: a comparative analysis of its personality and function in the Welsh, French and English versions' in *An Arthurian Tapestry: Essays in Memory of Lewis Thorpe*, ed. Kenneth Varty (Glasgow, 1981), p. 237, n. 1. There is surprisingly little overlap between Mme. De Caluwé-Dor's article and the present study.
5. The terms used in the redactions are *serpant* (Chrestien), *wurm* (Hartmann von Aue), *dragoun* (*Ywain and Gawain*), *orm* (*Ivens saga* and *Herr Ivan*), *drakin* (Ulrich Fuetrer), *sarff* (Iarlles y Ffynnawn). On *draco/serpens* and equivalents see Fr. Wild, *Drachen im Beowulf und andere Drachen*, Sitzb. d. öst. Akad. d. Wiss., Bd. 238 (Wien, 1962), pp. 3ff.
6. That Chrestien knew of the tradition seems certain from his description of the lion's behaviour at Pesme Aventure: 'De hardemant et d'ire tranble / et bat la terre de sa coe' (*Yv.* 5532–3). Cf. *Partonopeus de Blois* ed. J. Gildea vol. I (Villanova, 1967), ll. 5803–14: 'De sa cowe bat ses costés: / C'est la costume del lion / Par tot s'a fiere beste non; / De sa coe se seit ferir / Por ire et por coros coillir. / Tant est gentils et debonaire / Qu'il ne seit sens coros mal faire; / Ce fait il as bestes de pes, / Mais les hardis et les engrés / Et les grans tigres et les ors, / Cant il en voit un ou plusors, / Assalt et vaint sens soi ferir, / De lor orguel se vuet marir'.
7. On the symbolism of the lion see M. Zips, 'Zur Löwensymbolik' in *Festschrift für Otto Höfler zum 65. Geburtstag* Bd. II (Wien, 1968), 507–18 (symbol of royal power); G. Heider, *Ueber Thier-Symbolik und das Symbol des Löwen in der christlichen Kunst* (Wien, 1849); W. von Blankenburg, *Heilige und Dämonische Tiere. Die Symbolsprache der deutschen Ornamentik im frühen Mittelalter* (Leipzig, 1943); D. Schmidtke, *Geistliche Tierinterpretation in der deutschsprachigen Literatur des Mittelalters (1100–1500)*, diss. F.U. Berlin, 1968, Teil I, pp. 331–47; F. McCulloch, *Mediaeval Latin and French Bestiaries* (Chapel Hill, N.C., 1960), pp. 137ff.; A. Erler, *Das Strassburger Münster im Rechtsleben des Mittelalters* (Frankfurt a.M., 1954), pp. 18–19; V. Huhn, 'Löwe und Hund als Symbole des Rechts', *Mainfränkisches Jahrbuch für Geschichte und Kunst* 7 (1955), 1–63; F. Oelmann, 'Über alte Bonner Rechtsdenkmäler', *Rheinische Vierteljahrsblätter* 15/16 (1950–51), 171–8.
8. See Peter Haidu's indispensable study *Lion-Queue-Coupée: l'écart symbolique chez Chrétien de Troyes* (Genève, 1972).
9. For bibliographical details see Tony Hunt, 'The Medieval Adaptations of Chrétien's *Yvain*: A Bibliographical Essay' in *An Arthurian Tapestry . . .* pp. 203–13.
10. In a Dutch version of the Reinfried von Braunschweig story a grateful lion has been assailed by a *lintwurm* which uses its tail to control the lion, so that it is the dragon's tail which the hero is obliged to cut off, see Fl. van Duyse, *Het oude Nederlandsche Lied* (Antwerp, 1903), pt. 1, pp. 56ff.

11. Hartmann says 'her Îwein tete der zwîvel wê / wederm er helfen solde' (3846–7). The redactors rely simply on the tradition of the evil monster or reptile, the slaying of which is indispensable to heroic status. In *La Queste del Saint Graal*, ed. Pauphilet (Paris, 1923), p. 94, Perceval helps the lion which is attacked by the serpent 'por ce que plus est naturelx beste et de plus gentil ordre que li serpenz'.

12. The open eyes of the sleeping lion are mentioned, among classical writers, by Plutarch (*Quaest. conviv.* IV, 5, 2) and everywhere in the bestiaries.

13. Ed. Th. Wright, Rolls Series 34 (London, 1863) II, c. 148, p. 230. In the episode copied from *Yvain* in *Gilles de Chyn* ed. E. B. Place (Evanston/Chicago, 1941) the lion joins its master 'et nuit er jor gist a sez piés' (3795).

14. 'And playing about him like a hunting dog which he had reared himself'. There is a similarity to the account of Nequam, *ed. cit.* pp. 229–30: 'Sed et caudae motu liberatori suo blandiens, et lingua manum lingens, *in modo canis* nunc dominum suum cursu laeto processit, nunc ad eundem vultu hilari et jocundo reversus est'. Note that the Welsh lion is found in a cleft in a rock (*hollt . . . yn y garrec*) and Nequam's soldier finds the lion *in recessu quodam*. In Ovid's *Metamorphoses* III, 28ff., the scene of Cadmus's combat with the serpent is a 'specus . . . efficiens humilem lapidum compagibus arcum' and this may have influenced later writers.

15. The quotations are taken, without modification, from the typescript MA dissertation of Meta M. McRitchie (Swansea, 1929) entitled 'A Study of the hitherto unconsidered Yvain Manuscript. National Library of Wales Add. Ms. 444– D. Yvain. (Williams Ms. 530)', p. 4.

16. By far the commonest attribute of the lion in medieval French and German literature is in fact simply its courage or strength, see G. Wüster, *Die Tiere in der altfranzösischen Literatur* diss. Göttingen, 1916, pp. 51ff. and O. Batereau, *Die Tiere in der mittelhochdeutschen Literatur* diss. Leipzig, 1909, pp. 43f.

17. Chrestien was probably aware of the discussion in Augustine's *De doctrina christiana* lib. III, c. xxv where he takes the lion, the serpent and bread as examples of equivocal (Christ-Devil) symbols. Cf. W. Deonna, '*Salve me de ore leonis*', *Revue belge de philologie et d'histoire* 28 (1950) esp. 186f and *id.* in *Genava* 25 (1947), 63–5. See Haidu's sensible conclusion, *op. cit.*, p. 72.

18. See G. Sansone, 'Il sodalizio d'armi del leone e di Ivano' in *Studi in onore di Italo Siciliano* (Firenze, 1966), pp. 1053–60. The uneven odds represented by Yvain's uncourtly opponents may be held to justify the inclusion of the lion as a 'compagnon d'armes', see Katalin Halász, *Structures narratives chez Chrétien de Troyes* (Debrecen, 1980), pp. 21–4.

19. Hartmann 3954 has *bûch*. This may be for the rhyme. It is the only occurrence of a rhyme in *-ûch* in Hartmann's works and, indeed, the only case of the word *bûch*. Despite the blurring of this detail Hartmann is clearly at pains to stress the exemplary nature of the lion's behaviour at this point, hence the hero's recognition: 'nû gît mir doch des bilde / dirre lewe wilde, / daz er von herzeleide sich / wolde erstechen umbe mich / daz rehtiu triuwe nahen gât' (4001–5).

20. An unusual interpretation is suggested by Haidu, *op. cit.*, pp. 63f, who argues that the lion incorporates the characteristic weakness of the knight who is tempted away from home by war: 'Cette interprétation correspond au cas d'Y vain, qui s'est laissé séduire par les aventures des tournois au point d'oublier l'engagement qu'il avait pris envers Laudine. La soif de violence physique, poussée à l'exclusivité et à la démesure, lui aurait fait oublier la fonction sociale attachée à l'idéal de la prud'hommie justement en train de se former'. According to this interpretation the submission of the lion would be 'le signe d'une amélioration progressive chez Yvain'. Haidu recognizes that the systematic application of this view to the text presents various difficulties.

21. Hartmann rightly calls it *trügevreude* (4413).

22. At *Yv.* 4075 MSS PG have *pitié* (MS V *pité*) for the *piëté* of Foerster's critical text.

23. Hartmann makes no mention of the presence of the lion at the beginning of the adventure, so that its appearance at 4815 is awkward.

24. The comparison is preserved in H 4815–57 and *Herr Ivan* 3258, but is omitted in *YG* and the saga. Cf. W. Pangritz, *Das Tier in der Bibel* (München/Basel, 1963), pp. 153–4 and W. Freytag, *Das Oxymoron bei Wolfram, Gottfried und andern Dichtern des Mittelalters* (München, 1972), p. 78 n. 26. In a Christian-allegorical view of the lion, which I find consistently misleading, A. T. Hatto adduces *Apoc.* 5.5 for its christological symbolism, see '"Der Aventure Meine" in Hartmanns *Iwein*', in *Medieval German Studies presented to Frederick Norman* (London, 1965), esp. pp. 97–8.

25. Contrast Lunete's opponent in *Yv.* 3684f.
26. See the *Charrete* ed. Foerster 2582–3; cf. A. Diverres, 'Yvain's Quest for chivalric perfection', in *An Arthurian Tapestry.* . . , esp. p. 217. In Hartmann Iwein says to the host 'mich sterket vaste dar an / iuwer reht und sîn [= giant's] *hôchvart*' (4962–3). In the Welsh the giant commands the lion to withdraw, thus anticipating the same motif in the rescue of Lunete and in Pesme Aventure (the lion is entirely absent in the corresponding Welsh episode).
27. Cf. Hartmann, who anticipates, 4740–41: 'nû erbarmet diz sêre / den rîter der des lewen pflac'. This appellation is found three times (4741, 4957, 5079) compared with eight occurrences of 'der rîter mittem leun' (5263, 5502, 5510, 5685, 6109, 6257, 7753, 8015).
28. See A. Meng, *Vom Sinn des ritterlichen Abenteuers bei Hartmann von Aue* diss. Zürich, 1967, p. 67.
29. Cf. Boethius, *Philosophiae Consolatio* Lib. IV, 2, 45 (ed. L. Bieler), 'ex quibus omnibus bonorum quidem potentia, malorum vero minime dubitabilis apparet infirmitas . . .'. Cf. also *Yv.* 4409–11.
30. Hartmann 5273–80 emphasizes that the odds are even, since Iwein enjoys the support of *got* and *wârheit*, but there is no reference to the lion.
31. Hartmann 5226–8 anticipates the lion's participation in the battle by observing that it draws nearer to its master as soon as it notices his anger. In the Welsh the lion at first joins in the battle and is only later commanded to withdraw. At no point, however, is it wounded.
32. Hartmann's arrangement, in which the prayers clearly precede the intervention of the lion, facilitates the inference that the lion is the answer to the ladies' prayers, an inference he then proceeds to burlesque (5357–61). In *Herr Ivan* the prayer of the ladies is inserted *after* the lion has intervened and temporarily incapacitated the seneschal (3761ff.), an action for which they thank God.
33. *Ywain and Gawain* 2519–22 exhibits a striking innovation: 'For with me es bath God and right, / and þai sal help me forto fight, / And my lyon sal help me; / þan er we foure ogayns þam thre'. This is not easily reconciled with 2575–6: 'Of my lioun no help I crave; / I ne have none oþer fote knave'. *Herr Ivan* 3587–90 omits all reference to justice and the lion, but, like Hartmann, introduces the concept of truth: 'Iak veet at gudh mik hiaelpa skal, / ther alder raetvisa ok sannind aer, / maedhan iak for sannind stridher haer' (3662–4), 'I know that God will help me, who is righteousness and truth, whilst I fight here for truth'. *Yv.* 4533 is clarified in Hartmann 5397 and *YG* 2622 where it is explained that the combatants were two versus two after the elimination of the seneschal.
34. See A. Adler, 'Sovereignty in Chrétien's *Yvain*', *PMLA* 62 (1947), 299.
35. On the *lex talionis* in France see A.-S. Matthias, 'Yvains Rechtsbrüche' in *Beiträge zum romanischen Mittelalter* ed. K. Baldinger, *Z.f. rom. Phil. Sonderband* (Tübingen, 1977), esp. 159. The explanation in *Yv.* 4572–5 is, of course, based on *Ars amatoria* I, 653–6.
36. Hartmann makes the lion's crucial role absolutely clear, 5385–8: 'vor im gewan vrou Lûnete / vride von des lewen bete. / die bete was niuwan der tôt: / des vreut sî sich, des gie ir nôt'.
37. Cf. the most recent treatment of it by A. Pioletti, 'Lettura dell' episodio del "chastel de pesme-aventure" (*Yvain* vv. 5101–5805)', *Medioevo romanzo* 6 (1979), 227–46. In the parallel episode in the Welsh, that of the Du Traws, the lion is entirely absent.
38. In Hartmann the theme of gratitude is reduced to 3 lines (6753–5), in *YG* to 4 lines (3213–6), whereas *Herr Ivan* 5033–44, 5049–52 elaborates it, introducing it by a source reference ('Thet laeter bokin idher haer høra'). The *saga* omits it altogether.
39. Cf. the comment of Machaut, 'Et c'est tout cler que monsignour Yvon / Par bien servir, non pas par vasselage, / Conquist l'amour dou grant lion sauvage' in *Guillaume de Machaut, Poésies lyriques* ed. V. Chichmaref (Paris, 1909), t. II, p. 491, motet V, ll. 26–8. For the evidence that Machaut read the whole of Chrestien's *Yvain* and not just the lion episode as contained in later works like *Gilles de Chyn*, see E. Hoepffner, 'Crestien de Troyes und Guillaume de Machaut', *Z. f. rom. Phil.* 39 (1917–19), 627–9.
40. Cf. *YG* 3271–85, *saga* XIII, 23 and *Herr Ivan* 5122–48. Hartmann does not reproduce Chrestien's description of the surrender, but reports it in 2 lines (6792–3).
41. In Hartmann there are throughout the episode significant references to God: 'got müeze des gastes pflegen' (6719), 'dô liez er in durch got leben' (6794), 'des sî got iemer gêret' (6798).
42. In the first two adventures in the Welsh the lion participates in the battles from the start and it is responsible for the blow which kills the giant. It does not participate in the Du Traws

239

episode (corresponding to Pesme Aventure). Its role in the *chwedyl* is therefore much simplified.

43. The description of Yvain in *Yv* 3203–4 ('Con li lions antre les dains, / Quant l'angoisse et chace la fains') accords, as we shall see, with what the encyclopaedists tell us. John Bednar, *La Spiritualité et le symbolisme dans les oeuvres de Chrétien de Troyes* (Paris, 1974), p. 122 notes of Yvain 'Le lion, symbole de la Résurrection, est attaché à sa personne d'une façon figurée avant qu'il ne rencontre un vrai lion'. A late thirteenth-century gloss in that well-known schoolbook Walter of Châtillon's *Alexandreis* (I, 36) reads 'In vexillo Alexandri erat depicta ymago leonis ad designandum ferocitatem et audaciam illius' (ed. M. L. Colker [Patavii, 1978], p. 358).
44. Ed. P. Jaffé in *MGH* SS t. XIX (Hannoverae, 1866), p. 125, ll. 24–8.
45. Ed. W. M. Lindsay (Oxonii, 1911) t. 11.
46. PL 177, 57D. On authorship and date see F. J. Carmody, '*De Bestiis et aliis rebus* and the Latin *Physiologus*', *Speculum* 13 (1938), 153–9. Guillaume le Clerc's *Bestiaire divin* reproduces much of *De Bestiis*, including the detail 'Li lion fet moult grant noblece, / quer nul cheitif home ne blece . . .' (ed. Hippeau [1852] repr. 1970, p. 196, ll. 213–4).
47. ed. Th. Wright RS 34 (London, 1863), pp. 227–30.
48. *Claudian*, with an English translation by Maurice Platnauer, vol. II (London/N.Y., 1922), p. 4 (*De consulatu Stilichonis* Lib. II, vv. 20–2). Some 1000 years after its composition the second book was translated into Middle English, at Clare in Suffolk, by an anonymous writer (possibly Osbern Bokenham), see S. Moore, 'Patrons of Letters in Norfolk and Suffolk c. 1450. II.', *PMLA* 28 (1913), 79ff and for the text see E. Flügel in *Anglia* 28 (1905), 255–99, 421–38. It is a *speculum principis* intended for Richard Duke of York who is compared with Stilico the 'gode prince'. Lines from book 2 of the *De consulatu* are quoted by Gerald of Wales in his *De principis instructione*.
49. Ed. M. R. James in *Essays and Studies presented to William Ridgeway* (Cambridge, 1913), pp. 286–98. Unknown to James, a text, with vernacular glosses, is found in MS Lincoln Cathedral Chapter Library 132ff. 78r–80r. In the Dublin MS, Trinity College 270, the poem is found on ff. 193r–194v.
50. See J. G. Préaux, 'Thierry de Saint-Trond, auteur du poème pseudo-ovidien *De Mirabilibus Mundi*', *Latomus* 6 (1947), 353–66.
51. See A. Boutemy, 'Notes additionnelles à la notice de Ch. Fierville sur le manuscrit 115 de Saint Omer', *Revue belge de philologie et d'histoire* 22 (1943), 5–33, esp. 24.
52. Ed. M. Chibnall vol. IV, Books VII and VIII (Oxford, 1973), p. 130.
53. On this theme see G. F. Jones, 'Grim to Your Foes and Kind to Your Friends', *Studia Neophilologica* 34 (1962), 91–103, H. Kallfelz, *Das Standesethos des Adels im 10. und 11. Jahrhundert* (Würzburg, 1960) p. 16, note 69, and L. Spitzer, 'Le lion arbitre moral de l'homme', *Romania* 64 (1938), 525–30.

The Arthurian Allusions in the Black Book of Carmarthen

A. O. H. JARMAN

1. N. Denholm-Young, *Handwriting in England and Wales* (Cardiff, 1954), 42.
2. *Reports on Manuscripts in the Welsh Language*, Vol. I, Part II (London, 1899), 297.
3. Ifor Williams, *Canu Llywarch Hen* (Caerdydd, 1953), xv.
4. For various opinions concerning the date of the Black Book see E. D. Jones in my edition, *Llyfr Du Caerfyrddin* (Caerdydd, 1982), xiii–xvi.
5. Strictly, H. D. Emanuel's opinion, quoted by T. Jones in *The Proceedings of the British Academy*, Vol. LIII (Sir John Rhŷs Memorial Lecture, 1967), 98, referred to the 'Stanzas of the Graves', found on pp. 63–9 of the Black Book. For Denholm-Young's dating see op. cit., 78.
6. *Llyfr Du Caerfyrddin*, xxiv.
7. Ibid., lxviii; *The National Library of Wales Journal*, xvii, 3 (Summer, 1972), 319.
8. *Llyfr Du Caerfyrddin*, lxviii.
9. F. G. Cowley, *The Monastic Order in South Wales, 1066–1349* (Cardiff, 1977), 44.
10. Ibid., 153. For the text see *Zeitschrift für französische Sprache und Literatur*, xiv (1892), 147–51.
11. See R. Geraint Gruffydd in *Ysgrifau Beirniadol IV*, ed. J. E. Caerwyn Williams (Dinbych, 1969), 16.

Notes to pp. 102–109

12. *Llyfr Du Caerfyrddin*, xxix–xxx; J. E. Lloyd, *A History of Wales from the Earliest Times to the Edwardian Conquest* (London, 1948), ii, 634–8, 691–2.
13. Kenneth Hurlstone Jackson, *The International Popular Tale and Early Welsh Tradition* (Cardiff, 1961), 120–2.
14. *Nennius, British History and Welsh Annals*, edited and translated by John Morris (Phillimore, London and Chichester, 1980), 26, 67.
15. For Cynon see R. Bromwich, 'Cynon fab Clydno', chapter VI in *Astudiaethau ar yr Hengerdd/Studies in Old Welsh Poetry*, ed. by R. Bromwich and R. Brinley Jones (Caerdydd, 1978), 150–64.
16. The texts of the four poems will be found in *Llyfr Du Caerfyrddin*, 1–2 and 25–35.
17. For the Myrddin/Merlin legend see A. O. H. Jarman, *The Legend of Merlin* (Cardiff, 1976, – contains bibliography); idem, 'Early Stages in the Development of the Myrddin Legend', chapter XIII in R. Bromwich and R. Brinley Jones (eds.), op. cit., 326–49. The theme of the wild man is treated in a broad context by R. Bernheimer, *Wild Men in the Middle Ages, a Study in Art, Sentiment, and Demonology* (Harvard, 1952), and D. A. Wells, *The Wild Man from the Epic of Gilgamesh to Hartmann von Aue's Iwein* (Belfast, 1974).
18. For these events see J. E. Lloyd, op. cit., ii, 586–7; *Llên Cymru*, iii (1954), 115–18.
19. R. Bromwich in her English version of *Armes Prydein, The Prophecy of Britain*, ed. by Sir Ifor Williams (Dublin, 1972), 46; Basil Clarke, *Life of Merlin* (Cardiff, 1973), 175.
20. For a general discussion of this theme see 'Prophecy, Poetry, and Politics in Medieval and Tudor Wales', chapter III in Glanmor Williams, *Religion, Language, and Nationality in Wales* (Cardiff, 1979), 71–86.
21. For the reference in lines 90–4 of the *Vita Merlini* see B. Clarke, op. cit., 56–7.
22. Clarke, op. cit., 102–3, lines 929–40.
23. For a discussion of the names mentioned see R. Bromwich, *Trioedd Ynys Prydein* (Cardiff, 1978), 266–8.
24. For the 'Dialogue' see my edition, *Ymddiddan Myrddin a Thaliesin* (Caerdydd, 1967).
25. *Llyfr Du Caerfyrddin*, 12; *Trioedd Ynys Prydein*, 97–107.
26. For Owain see *Trioedd Ynys Prydein*, 479–83.
27. Ibid., ciii–cvi.
28. Ibid., 98.
29. Ibid., cxii, 360–1.
30. *Canu Llywarch Hen*, 27–9; *Llyfr Du Caerfyrddin*, 62–5.
31. *Astudiaethau ar yr Hengerdd*, 286–96. For the Black Book text see *Llyfr Du Caerfyrddin*, 48–9. Professor Roberts's text includes some additional stanzas from the Red Book of Hergest (c. 1400).
32. D. P. Kirby in *The Bulletin of the Board of Celtic Studies*, xxvii (1976), 89.
33. *Trioedd Ynys Prydein*, 357. Ifor Williams also suggests a Devon connection, *Canu Aneirin* (Caerdydd, 1938), 314.
34. *The Gododdin, The Oldest Scottish Poem* (Edinburgh, 1969), 128, cf. 150.
35. *Trioedd Ynys Prydein*, 358.
36. For the text see *Llyfr Du Caerfyrddin*, 71–3. It has been edited by Brynley F. Roberts, *Astudiaethau ar yr Hengerdd*, 311–18.
37. *Trioedd Ynys Prydein*, 416. See also Keith Busby, 'The Enigma of Loholt', in *An Arthurian Tapestry*, ed. by Kenneth Varty (Glasgow, 1981), 28–36.
38. For the text see *Llyfr Du Caerfyrddin*, 66–8, where the poem is entitled, from the first line, *Pa Ŵr yw'r Porthor?*, 'What Man is the Gate-keeper?'. Professor Roberts's edition is in *Astudiaethau ar yr Hengerdd*, 296–309. For a translation by R. Bromwich see pp. 45–6 above.
39. *Trioedd Ynys Prydein*, 304.
40. For Mabon and Modron see *Trioedd Ynys Prydein*, 433–6, 458–63; W. J. Gruffydd, 'Mabon vab Modron', *Y Cymmrodor*, xlii (1931), 129–47; idem, *Rhiannon* (Cardiff, 1953), chapter V.
41. *Trioedd Ynys Prydein*, 520–3; *Llên Cymru*, ii (1952), 127–8.
42. *Early Irish History and Mythology* (Dublin, 1946), 52.
43. *The Bulletin of the Board of Celtic Studies*, x (1939), 41.
44. *Tryfrwyd* can be understood either as a place-name or as a common noun meaning 'battle'.
45. For Manawydan see *Rhiannon*, chapter IV; *Trioedd Ynys Prydein*, 441–3.
46. His epithet, *llauynnauc*, has also been interpreted as meaning 'of the striking hand', and

241

Llwch identified with the Irish god Lug. See Foster in R. S. Loomis (ed.), *Arthurian Literature in the Middle Ages, a Collaborative History* (Oxford, 1959), 34.

47. In *An Arthurian Tapestry*, 28, Keith Busby takes the Black Book reference as meaning that Llacheu was 'a battle-companion of Kei'.

48. *Trioedd Ynys Prydein*, 45–9, 484; Lloyd-Jones in *Ériu*, xvi (1952), 123–31; *Astudiaethau ar yr Hengerdd*, 308–9.

49. *Trioedd Ynys Prydein*, 487. For a study of Capalu see E. Freymond, 'Artus Kampf mit dem Katzenungetüm', *Beiträge zur Romanischen Philologie, Festgabe für Gustav Gröber* (Halle, 1899), 311; Gaston Paris in *Romania*, xxix (1900), 121–4.

50. *Ériu*, xvi (1952), 123–31.

51. So J. Morris-Jones in *Y Cymmrodor*, xxviii (1918), 110.

52. *Ériu*, xvi, 123; *aruthr* = 'terrible, terribly'.

53. For a brief discussion of this poem, with references, see my article, 'The Delineation of Arthur in Early Welsh Verse', in *An Arthurian Tapestry*.

54. Marie-Louise Sjoestedt, *Gods and Heroes of the Celts*, translated by Myles Dillon (London, 1949), 66–9.

55. *The Mabinogion*, translated by Gwyn Jones and Thomas Jones (Everyman, 1974), 107; *The Mabinogi and Other Medieval Welsh Tales*, translated, with an introduction, by Patrick K. Ford (University of California, 1977), 132.

56. Edited by Thomas Jones, 'The Black Book of Carmarthen "Stanzas of the Graves"', *Proceedings of the British Academy*, Vol. LIII (Sir John Rhŷs Memorial Lecture, 1967), 97–137.

57. Ibid., 127; for the Welsh text see *Llyfr Du Caerfyrddin*, 41.

58. *Canu Llywarch Hen*, 127.

59. T. Jones, ibid., 121; *Llyfr Du Caerfyrddin*, 37; J. Morris, *Nennius*, 45, 85.

60. E. K. Chambers, *Arthur of Britain* (London, 1966), 17, 250.

61. Ibid., 249, 'sicut Britones solent iurgari cum Francis pro rege Arturo'.

62. Geoffrey of Monmouth, *The History of the Kings of Britain*, translated with an introduction by Lewis Thorpe (Penguin Books, 1966), 261.

63. Clarke, op. cit., 102–3.

64. Chambers, op. cit., 112–25.

65. Dr Ceridwen Lloyd-Morgan in her doctoral dissertation, *A Study of Y Seint Greal in Relation to La Queste del Saint Graal and Perlesvaus* (Oxford, 1978), 100–1, quotes a reference in the French text to the burial of Arthur and Guinevere at Avalon. In the Welsh translation of *Perlesvaus*, made towards the end of the fourteenth century, the reference is omitted and Dr Lloyd-Morgan believes that it is 'possible that the references to the burying of Arthur and Guinevere were unacceptable to the translator, since they suggest that the disappearance of Arthur from the world is final'. The translation was probably commissioned by Hopcyn ap Thomas, a gentleman and man of letters and 'maister of Brut' of Ynys Dawe in Gower, who in 1403 is said to have been consulted by Owain Glyndŵr about his prospects. Cf. J. E. Lloyd, *Owen Glendower* (Oxford, 1931), 68–9.

The Ideal of Queenship in Hartmann's Erec

LEWIS JILLINGS

This essay derives from a paper given at Gregynog at a DAAD Colloquium on Hartmann von Aue in September 1974.

1. For a review of research on Enite see O. Ehrismann, 'Enite. Handlungsbegründungen in Hartmanns von Aue *Erec*', *ZfdPh*, 98 (1979), 321–44. Quotations and references to *Erec* are taken from the 3rd edition by A. Leitzmann (Halle 1939); to Chrétien's *Erec et Enide* from the edition by M. Roques (Paris 1963).

2. W. Kellermann, 'Die Bearbeitung des "Erec-und-Enide"-Romans Chrestiens von Troyes durch Hartmann von Aue', in *Hartmann von Aue*, ed. H. Kuhn and C. Cormeau (WdF 359) (Darmstadt 1973), pp. 511–31 (originally *Mélanges Jean Frappier*, 1970). R. Pérennec, 'Adaptation et société: l'adaptation par Hartmann d'Aue du roman de Chrétien de Troyes: Erec et Iwein', *Etudes Germaniques*, 28 (1973), 289–303. M. Huby, 'Hat Hartmann von Aue in *Erec* das Eheproblem neu gedeutet?', *Recherches Germaniques*, 6 (1976), 3–17.

3. P. W. Tax, 'Studien zum Symbolischen in Hartmanns *Erec*. Erecs ritterliche Erhöhung', in *Hartmann von Aue* (as n. 2), pp. 287–310 (originally 1963). H. Bayer, '"bî den liuten ist sô guot"'. Die *meine des Erec* Hartmanns von Aue', *Euphorion*, 73 (1979), 272–85. H. B. Willson, '"Ordo Amoris" and the Character of Hartmann's *Erec*', in *An Arthurian Tapestry. Essays in Memory of Lewis Thorpe*, ed. K. Varty (Glasgow 1981), pp. 129–38.
4. Contrast Chrétien 84–6 and 653f. In the French text Erec maintains his equanimity (225–32).
5. R. Fisher, 'Erecs Schuld und Enitens Unschuld bei Hartmann', *Euphorion*, 69 (1975), 160–74.
6. Contrast Chrétien's experienced Enide, 475 and 2413–22, and especially Gottfried's tutored Isolde.
7. In this passage the narrator emphasizes Enite's share in the kingdom; see also 519–24. 2916 'doch geviel im vrouwe Enite baz' diverges specifically from Chrétien 2304 'ne set li quiex d'ax plus li pleise.'
8. Comparison of 2825 'sus verdiente Êrec sîn loben' with 2985 'den lop hete er erworben' suggests ambiguous praise on the part of the narrator; see also 2965. A similar conclusion is drawn by D. H. Green, 'Hartmanns Ironic Praise of *Erec*', *MLR*, 70 (1975), 795–802.
9. It is the function of the subordinate clauses in 2826–51 to emphasize that the whole passage represents Enite's (flawed) perceptions, even in the narrator's commentary (2845ff).
10. Erec seriously courts 'ungewarheit' (2716); subsequently the term, in its positive form, becomes Enite's dominant objective for Erec (3260, 4259, 6749).
11. In the second battle against Guivreiz, Erec specifically seeks to avoid seeming a 'zage' (6882, 6905, 6907).
12. See n. 8.
13. Despite Enite's confused rationalization of her conduct in a moment of despair (5943–56) there is no suggestion in Hartmann's work that she is wrong to inform Erec of his disgrace.
14. See n. 10. R. Schnell, 'Literarische Beziehungen zwischen Hartmanns *Erec* und Wolframs *Parzival*', *Beiträge* (W), 95 (1973), 301–32, pp. 316–18, also detects Enite's increasing ability to act decisively out of 'triuwe'.
15. F. Tobin, 'Hartmann's *Erec*: The Perils of Young Love', *Seminar*, 14 (1978), 1–14, esp. p. 9, rightly assesses the varying degrees of 'truth' in Enite's lament and self-accusations. T. Cramer, 'Soziale Motivation in der Schuld-Sühne-Problematik von Hartmann's *Erec*', *Euphorion*, 66 (1972), 97–112, esp. p. 99, observes that the direct assertions of Hartmann's characters about their guilt or innocence are often contradictory.
16. A. E. Schönbach, *Über Hartmann von Aue. Drei Bücher Untersuchungen* (Graz 1894), p. 211f. U. Ruberg, 'Bildkoordinationen im *Erec* Hartmanns von Aue', in *Hartmann von Aue* (as n. 2), pp. 532–60, esp. p. 554 (originally 1970). B. Thum, 'Politische Probleme der Stauferzeit im Werk Hartmanns von Aue: Landesherrschaft im *Iwein* und *Erec*', in *Stauferzeit. Geschichte, Literatur, Kunst*, ed. R. Krohn et al. (Stuttgart 1979), pp. 47–70, esp. p. 53, notes that the lime-tree is a symbol for legal jurisdiction.
17. A. Hrubý, 'Die Problemstellung in Chrétiens und Hartmanns *Erec*', in *Hartmann von Aue* (as n. 2), pp. 342–72 (originally 1964); and E.-M. Carne, *Die Frauengestalten bei Hartmann von Aue. Ihre Bedeutung im Aufbau und Gehalt der Epen* (Marburger Beiträge zur Germanistik 31) (Marburg 1970), develop the notion of complementary qualities of man and woman.
18. 802, 1317ff, 1456ff, 3010, 3280, 4425, 5755ff. K. Smits, 'Enite als christliche Ehefrau', in *Interpretation und Edition deutscher Texte des Mittelalters. Festschrift für John Asher zum 60. Geburtstag*, ed. K. Smits et al. (Berlin 1981), pp. 13–25, esp. pp. 19ff, has recently presented a number of conclusions similar to the present paper, which however seeks to stress more strongly the woman's capacity for active participation (see for example Enite's initiative against the wicked count, 3838ff).
19. In the modern German translation to his synoptic edition (Frankfurt 1972), p. 183, T. Cramer overlooks the word 'dicke' in 4161 and 4163 which gives the narrator's comment general significance.
20. Erec's compassion for the widows, 'diu ellende schar' (9798), recalls both the suffering of Enite 'in dem ellende' (3030, 5796, 10107) and the compassion of Guivreiz for Erec himself (6860, 6873).
21. 1262, 4629[50], 4877, 4945, 4981, 5091, 5264. For the queen's active role in Chrétien see P.

Noble, 'The Character of Guinevere in the Arthurian Romances of Chrétien de Troyes', *MLR*, 67 (1972), 524–35.
22. R. N. Combridge, 'Ladies, Queens and Decorum', *Reading Medieval Studies*, 1 (1975), 71–83, esp. pp. 74–6.
23. Tobin (as n. 15), p. 6.
24. See for example recent work by J. L. Nelson, 'Queens as Jezebels: the careers of Brunhild and Balthild in Merovingian history', in *Medieval Women*, ed. D. Baker (Oxford 1978), pp. 31–77; and P. Stafford, 'The King's Wife in Wessex 800–1066', *Past and Present*, 91 (1981), 3–27.
25. T. Vogelsang, *Die Frau als Herrscherin im hohen Mittelalter. Studien zur 'consors regni' Formel* (Göttingen 1954), pp. 45f. W. Kowalski, *Die deutschen Königinnen und Kaiserinnen* (Weimar 1913) was not available to me.
26. A. Georgi, *Das lateinische und deutsche Preisgedicht des Mittelalters* (PSuQ 48) (Berlin 1969), pp. 74–81.
27. K. Bosl, 'Der Aufbruch von Mensch und Gesellschaft. Eine epochale Struktur in der europäischen Geschichte', in *Stauferzeit* (as n. 16), pp. 11–27. Also Bosl, *Europa im Aufbruch. Herrschaft – Gesellschaft – Kultur vom 10. bis zum 14. Jahrhundert* (Munich 1980), pp. 200ff, 257ff; these titles are representative of numerous studies by Bosl on social change in the middle ages.
28. B. Thum, *Aufbruch und Verweigerung. Literatur und Geschichte am Oberrhein im Hohen Mittelalter. Aspekte eines geschichtlichen Kulturraums* (Karlsruhe 1980), pp. 291ff, 151 and passim.
29. Pérennec (as n. 2), pp. 295f, lists references to Erec as 'künec' and Enite as 'künegîn'. In Chrétien's romance Enite is not referred to as 'reine'.
30. 4535–69, 4580–5. Guivreiz as king aids the distressed Erec in order to preserve territorial peace (6833–61).
31. Thum (as n. 28), p. 348. Bosl, *Europa im Aufbruch* (as n. 27), p. 301f.
32. H. Bayer, *Gralsburg und Minnegrotte. Die religiös-ethische Heilslehre Wolframs von Eschenbach und Gottfrieds von Straßburg* (PSuQ 93) (Berlin 1978), pp. 151f. Thum (as n. 28), pp. 293ff.
33. H. E. Wiegand, *Studien zur Minne und Ehe in Wolframs Parzival and Hartmanns Artusepik* (Berlin 1972), pp. 53–128. Bayer (as n. 3), pp. 274f.
34. H. Zeimentz, *Ehe nach der Lehre der Frühscholastik* (Düsseldorf 1973), pp. 92–4. G. Duby, *Medieval Marriage: Two Models from twelfth-century France* (Baltimore 1978). Thum (as n. 28), p. 327. For ecclesiastical considerations in the dissolution of the marriage of Frederick Barbarossa and his queen Adela von Vohburg, see P. Munz, *Frederick Barbarossa. A Study in Medieval Politics* (Ithaca and London 1969), pp. 66ff.
35. Smits (as n. 18), p. 24.
36. So, for instance, the fervent renunciation of the peasant girl in *Der arme Heinrich* which redeems her feudal lord. See also Thum (as n. 28), p. 349.
37. V. Mertens, *Gregorius Eremita. Eine Lebensform des Adels bei Hartmann von Aue in ihrer Problematik und ihrer Wandlung in der Rezeption* (MTU 67) (Munich 1978), pp. 73ff.
38. See also Mertens, *Laudine. Soziale Problematik im 'Iwein' Hartmanns von Aue* (Beihefte zur ZfdPh 3) (Berlin 1978), pp. 36f.
39. Thum (as n. 16), pp. 52ff. Mertens (as n. 38), pp. 60ff.
40. J. Bumke, *Mäzene im Mittelalter. Die Gönner und Auftraggeber der höfischen Literatur in Deutschland 1150–1300* (Munich 1979), pp. 172f, 385f.
41. Mertens (as n. 37), pp. 32–7 and 154–62.
42. Thum (as n. 16), pp. 67–70. Bayer (as n. 32), p. 201. Bayer, *Hartmann von Aue. Die theologischen und historischen Grundlagen seiner Dichtung sowie sein Verhältnis zu Günther von Pairis* (Beihefte zum MLatJb 15) (Kastellaun 1978), pp. 91ff.
43. Bayer (as n. 3), p. 283.
44. Bayer (as n. 3), pp. 284f.
45. Thum (as n. 28), pp. 297 and 310.
46. *Die Reinhardsbrunner Briefsammlung* (MGH Epistolae selectae V), quoted by Mertens (as n. 38), p. 68.
47. Quoted by Mertens (as n. 37), p. 75.
48. G. Kaiser, *Textauslegung und gesellschaftliche Selbstdeutung. Aspekte einer sozialgeschichtlichen Interpretation von Hartmanns Artusepen* (Frankfurt 1973).

49. Such a conclusion accords with Thum's interpretation of the theme of the ruler's duty in *Iwein*; see Thum (as n. 16), pp. 60f.
50. The couple are referred to as 'arm' (3770, 3886 and passim), a reference which recalls the medieval formal distinction between *pauper* and *potens*. See Bosl, 'Der Aufbruch' (as n. 27), p. 20.

Rhyme, Reason and Repetition in Erec et Enide
J. C. LAIDLAW

1. See for example Eugène Vinaver, *The Rise of Romance* (Oxford, 1971), pp. 33–7; Tony Hunt, 'Tradition and Originality in the Prologues of Chrestien de Troyes', *Forum for Modern Language Studies*, 8 (1972), pp. 320–44; L. T. Topsfield, *Chrétien de Troyes: a Study of the Arthurian Romances* (Cambridge, 1981), pp. 23–6.
2. Textual and line references are to *Les Romans de Chrétien de Troyes*, Volume I, *Erec et Enide*, edited by Mario Roques, Classiques Français du Moyen Age (Paris, 1955). That edition has been compared with *Christian von Troyes Sämtliche Werke*, Volume III, *Erec und Enide*, edited by Wendelin Foerster (Halle, 1890); some of the differences between the two texts are discussed below.
3. Rhythm is used here in its older sense which associates the term more with rhyme than with beat or stress; see OED, 8, p. 636.
4. F. M. Warren, 'Some Features of Style in Early French Narrative Poetry (1150–70)', *Modern Philology*, 3 (1905–06), pp. 179–209, 513–39; 4 (1906–07), pp. 655–75; see particularly part IV 'The *tirade lyrique* or couplets in monorhyme' (pp. 655–62).
5. R. C. Johnston, 'Sound-Related Couplets in Old French', *Forum for Modern Language Studies*, 12 (1976), pp. 194–205.
6. See for example *Benedeit: The Anglo-Norman Voyage of St Brendan*, edited by Ian Short and Brian Merrilees (Manchester, 1979), lines 359–70 and 467–78 and *Le Roman de Thèbes*, edited by Guy Raynaud de Lage, Classiques Français du Moyen Age, 2 vols (Paris, 1968–9), lines 521–40 and 1573–96.
7. Ornate rhyme is used here as a term covering all rhymes other than simple or sufficient rhyme; it thus embraces rich, leonine and equivocal rhyme.
8. See note 1.
9. Jean Frappier, 'La Brisure du couplet dans *Erec et Enide*', *Romania*, 86 (1965), pp. 1–21 (p. 3). See also Warren, pp. 662–75.
10. *La Chanson de Roland*, edited by F. Whitehead, Blackwell's French Texts, (Oxford, 1962); *laisses* 83–6 and 128–30, read together, illustrate the technique particularly well.
11. *Benedeit: St Brendan*, pp. 8–10 and lines 51–6 and 134–48.
12. Warren, pp. 655–62.
13. See note 4.
14. Chrétien was not the only poet in the second half of the twelfth century to experiment with rhyme; see *Jordan Fantosme's Chronicle*, edited by R. C. Johnston (Oxford, 1981), pp. xxiii–xliii.
15. Examples occur with similar frequency in Chrétien's other romances. Their presence in *Guillaume d'Angleterre* may provide evidence to show that that romance also is by him. I am grateful to Dr Renée Curtis for suggesting that line of enquiry, and I plan to treat the subject elsewhere.

    For a statistical analysis of types of rhyme in *Erec et Enide*, *Cligés*, *Yvain* and *Lancelot* see D. J. Shirt, 'How much of the Lion can we put before the Cart', *French Studies*, 31 (1977), pp. 1–17 (pp. 7–11).
16. Tony Hunt, 'Chrestien de Troyes: the Textual Problem', *French Studies*, 33 (1979), pp. 257–71.
17. See also Glyn S. Burgess, 'The Theme of Beauty in Chrétien's *Philomena* and *Erec et Enide*', in *An Arthurian Tapestry: Essays in Memory of Lewis Thorpe*, edited by Kenneth Varty (Glasgow, 1981), pp. 114–28.
18. In Roques, lines 109–10 have a rich rhyme (*afere, fere*); in Foerster, the rhyme is equivocal (*afeire, a feire*).

245

19. Frappier, p. 14; the lay-out of the quotation has been altered.
20. The audience hears Ydier's name for the first time in line 1042, when he is forced to reveal it. They likewise are not told the name of Enide until line 1979.
21. Foerster's text is slightly different: line 920 (= 916) echoes line 246 but not line 332. For similar examples of repetition see lines 2475 and 3093, Vinaver, pp. 43 and 81–5, and Topsfield, pp. 22, 40 and 46.
22. Line 907 had been foreshadowed by lines 571 and 576, both of which are spoken by Enide's father, and is echoed by lines 1413, 1421 and 1464.
23. Those rhyme-words are used again in combination in lines 2471–2 and 5199–200, at important points in the narrative.
24. In Foerster, lines 2076–7, which correspond to Roques, lines 2022–3, the reference is to Yseuz and Brangiens.
25. The references in lines 5289–98 and 5837–43 to Eneas, Dido and Lavine doubtless have a similar function.
26. *Costume* is used in lines 38, 44, 287, 290, 1761, 1765 and 1798 to refer to the hunt for the white stag, and in line 579 to describe the contest for the sparrow-hawk. The word occurs on only one other occasion, in line 2822, as part of the phrase *costume et us*.

    The examples of *desresnier* (and *desresne*) are first associated with the hunt for the stag (lines 55, 293 and 296), and then with the contest for the sparrow-hawk (lines 575, 598, 640, 757 and 831). Thereafter the word does not occur again until line 6077 where it is used by Maboagrain to describe how Erec has accepted and won the challenge of the *Joie de la Cort*; the repetition is not accidental. See also Burgess, p. 117.
27. Between line 5445, when Erec enters the town, and line 5776, when King Evrain leaves Erec, *joie* is repeated fifteen times.
28. Examples of *mort* and *morir* occur in lines 5475–6, 5488, 5565, 5583, 5658 and 5756, and of *ocis* in line 5661. *Dolereuse* is found in line 5562, *dolant* in lines 5464, 5563, 5776 and 5827, *duel* in lines 5658, 5779, 5781 and 5800. For examples of *enor* and *enorer*, see lines 5575, 5617, 5768, 5770 and 5771.
29. Lines 2492, 2503 and 2517; the effect of the remark is emphasized by the use of *parole* (lines 2476, 2483, 2507, 2519 and 2529). For more distant echoes see lines 2993 (and 2994), 3102 and 4599.
30. Between lines 2439, where Erec's companions first begin to voice their sorrow at his conduct, and line 2763, when Erec and Enide set off 'en avanture', *duel* is used eleven times and *plorer* and associated forms fifteen times.
31. Lines 1241, 1253, 1295 and 1301.
32. Lines 2015, 2017, 2038 and 2067.
33. Lines 2282, 2299, 2313, 2316, 2383, 2396 and 2398.
34. For an account of the different views which have been taken of the authenticity of the *Joie de la Cort*, see Z. P. Zaddy, *Chrétien Studies: Problems of Form and Meaning in 'Erec', 'Yvain', Cligés' and the 'Charrete'* (Glasgow, 1973), pp. 39–54. On joy in *Erec et Enide* see Topsfield, pp. 4–5, 19, 48–55.
35. An earlier version of this article formed part of the Colloquium held in honour of Professor Diverres at Gregynog from 13 to 15 March 1981. It was a pleasure to bring Professor Diverres greetings and good wishes from the University of Aberdeen which he served with distinction for so many years.

    I gratefully acknowledge the assistance which I received in the preparation of this article from the Oxford Text Archive and the Oxford Concordance Program. I am also greatly indebted to the Aberdeen University Computing Centre and in particular to Mr J. S. Lemon and Miss A. L. Meredith for their patient help.

La Mort le Roi Artu: *an Interpretation*

FAITH LYONS

1. J. Frappier, ed. *La Mort le Roi Artu: roman du XIIIᵉ siècle* (Geneva and Lille, 1954).
2. J. Frappier, *Etude sur la Mort le roi Artu, dernière partie du Lancelot en prose*, 2nd edn. (Geneva and Paris, 1961).
3. 'Le Motif du "don contraignant" dans la littérature du Moyen Age' in *Travaux de linguistique*

et de littérature publiés par le Centre de Philologie et de Littérature Romanes, VII. 2, *Etudes Littéraires*, Strasbourg, 1969, 7–46.

4. 'Le Motif du "don contraignant"', 7–8.
5. *Etude*, 230.
6. Chrétien de Troyes, *Yvain or le Chevalier au Lion*, ed. W. Foerster (Halle, 1887), ll. 735–43.
7. Morgan recalls how at Camelot Lancelot always carried off the prize (*Mort Artu*, 53, 24–8).
8. E. Vinaver, *The Rise of Romance*, (Oxford, 1971), 96–7. See review by R. Guiette, *Revue Belge de Philologie et d'Histoire* (1972).
9. *Etude*, 350, n. 1.
10. *Etude*, 231.
11. *Etude*, 231 n. 5.
12. *Etude*, 233.
13. *Etude*, 221 and 233.
14. *Etude*, 348, n. 5.
15. Yolande de Pontfarcy 'Source et Structure de l'épisode de l'empoisonnement dans *La Mort Artu*', *Romania*, 99 (1978), 246–55.
16. Yolande de Pontfarcy, 253–4.
17. Vinaver, 96–7.
18. *Etude*, 316 and 327.
19. *Etude*, 437–8, additional note to 340–1.
20. *Etude*, 186 and 355.
21. *Etude*, 225 and 327.
22. *Etude*, 110 and 277.
23. *Etude*, 235.
24. *Etude*, 317.
25. In his chapter 'Sur la Mort le Roi Artu', *Etudes de Textes Français*, I, Moyen Age, (Paris, 1964), 177, Roland Derche writes as follows: 'On peut juger fastidieux ces récits de batailles de même que ceux des tournois et des combats singuliers. Pour s'y intéresser il faut évidemment posséder une connaissance précise de l'armement et de la tactique au Moyen Age, ce qui n'est guère à la portée que des spécialistes'.
26. J. Frappier, 'La bataille de Salesbieres', *Mélanges Rita Lejeune*, II (Brussels, 1969), 1019.
27. *Etude*, 239.
28. *Etude*, 295.
29. *Etude*, 263.
30. ed. A. J. Holden, I, 1970, SATF, pp. 161–6, ll. 1–142.
31. E. Vinaver writes of Morgan authoritatively in *Rise of Romance*, 90.
32. J. Frappier, 'Le personnage de Galehaut dans le *Lancelot en prose*' *Romance Philology*, XVII (1964), 540.
33. *Etude*, 246.
34. *Rise of Romance*, 83.

The River Humber in French Arthurian Romances
CEDRIC E. PICKFORD

1. Faral, Edmond: *La Légende arthurienne, études et documents*, 3 vols., Paris (Champion), 1929, Vol. III, *Documents (Bibliothèque de l'École des Hautes Études, 255, 256 et 257)*.
2. Arnold, Ivor D. O. (ed): *Le Roman de Brut de Wace*, 2 vols., Paris (Droz), 1938–40 (*Société des Anciens Textes Français*).
3. Loth, Joseph: ed. and trans. *Les Mabinogion du Livre Rouge de Hergest avec les variantes du Livre Blanc de Rhydderch*, 2ème éd., Paris (E. de Boccard), 2 vols., 1913.
4. Plummer, Charles: ed. *Venerabilis Baedae Historiam Ecclesiasticam Gentis Anglorum*, Oxford, 1896.
5. Bell, Alexander: ed. *An Anglo-Norman Brut (Royal 13 A XXI)*, Oxford (Blackwell), 1969 (*Anglo-Norman Text Society, 21–22*).
6. Bullock-Davies, Constance: 'Chrétien de Troyes and England', *Arthurian Literature*, I (1981), pp. 1–61 (D. S. Brewer Ltd.).

7. West, G. D.: *An Index of Proper Names in French Arthurian Verse Romances* (1150–1300), Toronto, 1969 (*University of Toronto Romance Series, 15*) and West, G. D., *An Index of Proper Names in French Arthurian Prose Romances*, Toronto, 1978 (*University of Toronto, Romance Series, 35*); Roach, William J. (ed.) *Continuations of the Old French Perceval of Chrétien de Troyes*, Vol. IV, *the Second Continuation*, Philadelphia (The American Philosophical Society), 1971.

8. Micha, Alexandre: éd. *Lancelot, Roman en prose du XIIIᵉ siècle*, Paris-Geneva (Droz), Vol. I (1978), Vol. II (1978), Vol. III (1979), Vol. IV (1979), Vol. V. (1980), Vol. VI (1980), Vol. VII (1980) (*Textes Littéraires Français, 247, 249, 262, 278, 283, 286, 288*); Kennedy, Elspeth, ed. *Lancelot do Lac*, 2 vols., Oxford (Clarendon Press), 1981.

9. Carman, J. Neale: *A Study of the Pseudo-Map Cycle of Arthurian Romance*, Lawrence, U.S.A. (University of Kansas Press), 1973.

10. Stenton, Lady: 'Communications', in *Mediaeval England*, ed. A. L. Poole, Oxford, (Clarendon Press), 2 vols., 1958, Vol. I, p. 200.

11. Brault, Gerard D.: *Early Blazon*, Oxford (Clarendon Press), 1972, pp. 120–6.

12. Loseth, Eilert: *Le Roman en prose de Tristan, le Roman de Palamède et la Compilation de Rusticien de Pise, analyse critique d'après les manuscrits de Paris*, Paris (E. Bouillon), 1890 (*Bibliothèque de l'École des Hautes Etudes, 82*).

13. *Tristan*, 1489, facsimile reprint, London (Scolar Press), 1976.

14. Malory, Sir Thomas: *Works*, ed. E. Vinaver, Oxford (Clarendon Press), 3 vols., 2nd edition, 1967, Vol. II, p. 700, line 23 (Caxton, Book X, ch. 59).

15. Lathuillère, Roger: *Guiron le Courtois, Étude de la tradition manuscrite et analyse critique*, Geneva (Droz), 1966 (*Publications Romanes et Françaises, 86*); *Gyron le Courtois*, Paris, circa 1501, facsimile reprint, London (Scolar Press), 1977.

16. *Merlin, roman en prose du XIIe siècle* publié par Gaston Paris et Jacob Ulrich, Paris (Didot), 2 vols., 1884 (*Société des Anciens Textes Français*).

17. *Le Roman de Perceforest, Première Partie*, ed. Jane H. M. Taylor, Paris-Geneva (Droz), 1979 (*Textes Littéraires Français, 279*).

18. *La Mort le Roi Artu*, éd. Jean Frappier, Paris, Geneva (Droz), 1954 (*Textes Littéraires Français, 30*).

19. Pickford, Cedric E: 'The Three Crowns of King Arthur', *Yorkshire Archaeological Journal*, XXXVIII (1952–5), pp. 373–82; Loomis, Roger Sherman: 'Edward I, Arthurian Enthusiast', *Speculum*, XXVIII (1953), pp. 114–27.

*Le Lai d'*Yonec *est-il une allégorie chrétienne?*

JACQUES RIBARD

1. Au fil des ans, en effet, nous nous sommes intéressé successivement au *Laostic* ('Le lai du *Laostic*: structure et signification', dans *Le Moyen Age*, 76, 1970, pp. 263–74), au *Chèvrefeuille* ('Essai sur la structure du lai du *Chèvrefeuille*', dans *Mélanges Pierre Le Gentil*, Paris, SEDES, 1973, pp. 721–24), à *Lanval* ('Le lai de *Lanval*: essai d'interprétation polysémique', dans *Mélanges Jeanne Wathelet-Willem, Marche Romane*, 1978, pp. 529–44), aux *Deux Amants* ('Le lai des *Deux Amants*: essai d'interprétation thématique', dans *Mélanges Pierre Jonin*, *Senefiance* n°7, Paris, Champion, 1979, pp. 579–91) et, dernièrement, à *Eliduc* ('Le lai d'*Eliduc*: étude thématique', dans *Mélanges Charles Foulon*, Rennes, 1980, pp. 295–99).

2. Nous pensons en particulier à notre ouvrage *Chrétien de Troyes, le Chevalier de la Charrette, essai d'interprétation symbolique* (Paris, Nizet, 1972). Une autre étude, de même inspiration mais consacrée au Gauvain du *Conte du Graal*, doit paraître incessamment sous le titre 'Un personnage paradoxal: le Gauvain du *Conte du Graal*' dans *Lancelot, Yvain, Gauvain* (éd. Nizet).

3. Les références du présent article renvoient à l'édition des *Lais de Marie de France* par Jean Rychner (Paris, Champion, 1968).

4. *Les lais de Marie de France* (o.c.), Prologue, v. 15–16.

5. E. Hoepffner, dans son ouvrage classique, *Les lais de Marie de France* (Paris, Nizet), va jusqu'à écrire: 'Le lai d'*Yonec* est exactement, abstraction faite du dénouement, le conte que racontera cinq siècles plus tard, en 1785, la comtesse d'Aulnoy, et que connaît tout enfant de France sous le nom de *l'Oiseau Bleu*.' (pp. 72–73). En fait, à y regarder de plus près, les similitudes se

limitent à l'emprisonnement de l'héroïne dans une tour et aux blessures que se fait l'oiseau-prince en se posant sur un cyprès traîtreusement garni de couteaux et de rasoirs. Tout le reste du conte – et c'est considérable – est complètement différent et n'a vraiment aucun rapport avec le récit de Marie de France.

6. L'équivalence symbolique que nous posons ici entre la femme et l'âme humaine, comme nous l'avions déjà fait dans notre essai sur *le Chevalier de la Charette* (cf. ci-dessus, note 2), ne doit pas surprendre. Il semble que cela corresponde à une tradition dont on trouve au siècle suivant quelques témoignages significatifs. C'est le cas, *mutatis mutandis*, dans *la Queste del saint Graal*: nous pensons à l'épisode du *roi Amant* et des deux *dames* symbolisant l'Eglise et la Synagogue, qui, en définitive, représentent, l'une comme l'autre, l'homme dans sa relation à Dieu (*La Queste del saint Graal*, éd. A. Pauphilet, Paris, Champion, 1965, pp. 184–85). C'est le cas aussi et plus nettement encore dans l'ouvrage dont nous devons la référence à notre collègue britannique, le Professeur Maldwyn Mills. Il s'agit d'un passage de l'*Ancrene Riwle* (*The French Text of the Ancrene Riwle*, Early English Text Society 240, 1958, Trinity College Cambridge, NS.R.14.7, ed. W. H. Trethewey, pp. 141–43) dont nous extrayons ces phrases: 'Un rei fu ke ama une dame de lonteine terre. Ceo fu li du ciel ke tant ama nostre alme. . . . Ore entendez isci la similitude. Cist devant dit rei fu Jesu Crist li fiz du rei de glorie, ke tut en cele manere doune a nostre alme.'

7. Voir, entre autres, *Epître aux Romains*, VII, 7–13, et *1ère Epître aux Corinthiens*, XV, 56.

8. Voir notamment dans la *Queste del saint Graal* (o.c.) pages 167, ligne 31, à 168, ligne 14, et page 184, lignes 15 à 30, dont voici la conclusion: 'Ceste bonté, que Diex fist au monde, a moi et a vos et as autres pecheors, vos vint il mostrer en semblance d'oisel, por ce que vos ne doutissiez pas a morir por lui, ne plus qu'il fist por vos.'

9. 'Ta femme Elisabeth t'enfantera un fils, et tu lui donneras le nom de Jean.' (*Luc*, I, 13); 'Voici que tu concevras et enfanteras un fils, et tu lui donneras le nom de Jésus.' (Ibid., I, 31).

10. On pourrait s'interroger aussi sur le nombre de ces vaisseaux: 'plus . . . de treis cenz', précise Marie (v.370). Faut-il y voir une application de la symbolique des nombres, où l'on retrouverait le chiffre sacré de la Trinité – le même qui s'exprime dans les trois chambres successives que traverse la dame – multiplié par cent pour manifester l'universalité du salut?

11. C'est en même temps peut-être 'le glaive de l'Esprit, c'est à dire la Parole de Dieu' dont parle l'apôtre Paul (*Epître aux Ephésiens*, VI, 17) – cette parole de Dieu dont il dit dans l'*Epître aux Hébreux* (IV, 12): 'Vivante, en effet, est la parole de Dieu, efficace et plus incisive qu'aucun glaive à deux tranchants . . .'

12. *Epître aux Ephésiens*, IV, 22–24.

13. Rapprocher *Epître aux Hébreux*, X, 1–10: '. . . la Loi est absolument impuissante, avec ces sacrifices, toujours les mêmes, que l'on offre perpétuellement d'année en année, à rendre parfaits ceux qui s'approchent de Dieu . . . Il [le Christ] abroge le premier régime pour fonder le second. Et c'est en vertu de cette volonté que nous sommes sanctifiés par l'oblation du corps de Jésus Christ, une fois pour toutes.'

14. Nous avons récemment proposé une interprétation similaire de l'épisode du Morrois dans le *Tristan* de Béroul ('Le *Tristan* de Béroul, un monde de l'illusion?', dans *Bulletin bibliographique de la Société Internationale Arthurienne*, Paris, 1979, pp. 229–44).

15. Voir à ce propos Edgar Sienaert, *Les lais de Marie de France, du conte merveilleux à la nouvelle psychologique*, Paris, Champion, 1978, pp. 123–25.

16. Jean Chevalier et Alain Gheerbrant, *Dictionnaire des symboles*, article 'violet', Paris, Seghers, t. IV, p. 397.

17. Rapprocher ce passage de l'*Epître aux Hébreux* (IX, 15–18): 'Voilà pourquoi il [le Christ] est médiateur d'une nouvelle alliance, afin que, sa mort ayant eu lieu pour racheter les transgressions de la première alliance, ceux qui sont appelés reçoivent l'héritage éternel promis. Car là où il y a testament, il est nécessaire que la mort du testateur soit constatée. . . . De là vient que même la première alliance n'a pas été inaugurée sans effusion de sang.' On y relèvera avec intérêt la notion d''héritage' qui nous renvoie au début de notre lai.

Dans ce même chapitre IX, aux versets 1 et suivants, il est fait référence au 'saint des saints', à son autel orné d'or et où se trouve le 'rameau d'Aaron', et l'apôtre y montre le Christ entrant 'une fois pour toutes dans le sanctuaire . . . avec son propre sang' – autant d'éléments qui rappellent étrangement certains passages de notre lai (la 'feste seint Aaron', le lit-autel où agonise l'oiseau-chevalier, etc. . . .).

18. *St Jean*, XIV, 26; XVI, 8.
19. 'Les romans de Chrétien de Troyes sont-ils allégoriques?', dans *Cahiers de l'Association Internationale des Etudes Françaises*, n°28, 1976, p. 17.
20. U. T. Holmes, 'Old French *Yonec*', dans *Modern Philology*, t. 29, 1931–32, pp. 225–29.
21. Pensons au sort qu'au siècle suivant fera à cette notion de 'règne de l'Esprit', se substituant en quelque sorte au règne du Fils, le franciscain Gérard de Borgo, prétendant reprendre à son compte les théories de Joachim de Flore. Sur ce sujet on pourra se reporter au tome II, pp. 287–88 de l'édition du *Roman de la Rose* par Félix Lecoy (Paris, Champion, 1966).

The Welsh Romance of the Lady of the Fountain (Owein)

BRYNLEY F. ROBERTS

1. Saunders Lewis, *Braslun o Hanes Llenyddiaeth Gymraeg*, Caerdydd, 1932, 44.
2. For an account see J. Loth, *Revue celtique*, xiii, (1892) 475–503, J. D. Bruce, *The Evolution of Arthurian Romance*, Baltimore, 1928, ii, 59–74.
3. In Geraint Bowen (ed.), *Y Traddodiad Rhyddiaith yn yr Oesau Canol*, Llandysul, 1974, 153–74.
4. 'The Art of *Iarlles y Ffynnawn* and the European *Volksmärchen*', *Studia Celtica*, viii/ix, (1973–4), 107–20.
5. I have used R. L. Thomson's edition, *Owein*, Dublin, 1968.
6. *Ysgrifau Llenyddol*, Llundain, 1951, 165.
7. art. cit., 118.
8. Another parallel to an episode in *Peredur* is the description of the youths shooting arrows.
9. On these features see Bruce, op. cit., i, 46, 701; R. M. Jones, in *Llên Cymru*, iv, (1957), 204; Rachel Bromwich, art. cit., 157; T. Gwynn Jones in *Aberystwyth Studies*, iv, (1926), 80; Thomas Parry, trans. Idris Bell, *A History of Welsh Literature*, Oxford, 1955, 87–8.
10. See R. L. Thomson, op. cit., xxvi–vii.
11. Cf. R. Bromwich, art. cit., 165.
12. Cf. W. T. H. Jackson, 'The Nature of Romance', *Approaches to medieval Romance*, *Yale French Studies*, li, (1974), 12–25.
13. Cf. Robert W. Hanning 'The Social Significance of Twelfth-Century Chivalric Romance', *Medievalia et Humanistica*, n.s., iii, (1972), 3–29: 'Accordingly, the most sophisticated form of romance is that in which the hero's arrival at self-awareness, and not some external catastrophe or willed quest undertaken simply for profit or honor, initiates the phase of adventures, culminating in a "return" which, even if it completes a spatial circle, in fact marks the new attainment of a fulfilled, perfected self', p. 11.
14. A. H. Diverres, 'Chivalry and *fin' amor* in *Le Chevalier au Lion*', in Rothwell, et al., *Studies in Medieval Literature and Languages in memory of Frederick Whitehead*, Manchester, 1974, 100.
15. op. cit., xli.
16. ibid., xxviii.
17. 'Literary translation and its social conditioning in the Middle Ages: Four Spanish Romance texts of the thirteenth century', *Approaches to Medieval Romance, Yale French Studies*, li, (1974), 206.
18. Though the author of the Welsh *Seint Greal*, which is translated from *La Queste del Saint Greal* and *Perlesvaus*, has linked his story with native tradition by rendering some personal names by equivalent Welsh forms, e.g. Perceval – Peredur, Loholt – Llacheu, his version is, nevertheless, undeniably recognizable as a translation.
19. *Romance Philology*, xxx, (1977), 431.
20. See further, Brynley F. Roberts, 'Tales and Romances' in A. O. H. Jarman and Gwilym R. Hughes, *A Guide to Welsh Literature*, Swansea, 1976, i, 203–43.

Traditional Material in Artus de Bretaigne

S. V. SPILSBURY

1. There is no modern edition of the romance. Bibliographical details may be found in B. Woledge, *Bibliographie des romans et nouvelles en prose française antérieurs à 1500*, Geneva, 1954

and *Supplément*, Geneva, 1975, n° 116. Quotations in this article are, unless otherwise stated, from Ms A, Paris, Bibliothèque nationale f. fr. 761. The title of the romance is hereinafter abbreviated as *Artus*.

2. See S. V. Spilsbury, 'On the date and authorship of *Artus de Bretaigne*', *Romania*, 94 (1973), pp. 505–22.

3. 'One of the most extraordinary instances of the survival of genuine Celtic tradition in unexpected places is found in the romance of *Arthur of Little Britain* . . .' R. S. Loomis, *Celtic Myth and Arthurian Romance*, New York, 1927, p. 172.

4. For information on proper names in medieval French fiction the following reference works have been used: L.-F. Flutre, *Table des noms propres dans les romans du moyen âge*, Poitiers, 1962, abbreviated as Flutre; E. Langlois, *Table des noms propres dans les chansons de geste*, Paris, 1904; G. D. West, *French Arthurian Verse Romances: An Index of Proper Names*, Toronto, 1969, abbreviated as West, *Verse Index*; and G. D. West, *French Arthurian Prose Romances: An Index of Proper Names*, Toronto, 1978, abbreviated as West, *Prose Index*.

5. West, *Prose Index*, makes this identification, adding 'though not necessarily thought of as such but as a kingdom in Bretaigne', i.e. Britain or England.

6. Two manuscripts of the romance, BN f.fr. 19163 and BN f.fr. 12549, contain a continuation by another unknown author who silently transports Sorelois back to the Island of Britain.

7. Ms G, British Museum Add. 10295, reads 'Phesalle', perhaps Pharsalus in Thessaly.

8. West, *Prose Index*, under *Clamadeu*.

9. R. S. Loomis, op. cit., pp. 302–5.

10. Gertrude Schoepperle, *Tristan and Isolt*, revised edition, New York, 1960, vol. I, p. 206.

11. If the *Artus* author was familiar with the *Tristan* version, it is strange that he did not recognize it as being more suitable for his purpose: an unwilling ancillary like Brangien would have been less of an embarrassment than Jehanete whom, true to the tradition, the author presents as a heroine throughout the whole of the first section of the romance. The mutual love which exists between Jehanete and Artus does not prevent the latter from abandoning Jehanete and setting off to seek Florence, the unknown princess whom he sees in a dream and whom he is destined to marry. And Jehanete, at the end of the story, must make do with Gouvernaus.

12. In Greece, for example: see Richard and Eva Blum, *The Dangerous Hour: The Lore of Crisis and Mystery in Rural Greece*, London, 1970, p. 100; and in Brittany: see L. A. Paton, *Studies in the Fairy Mytology of Arthurian Romance*, 2nd edition enlarged, New York, 1960, p. 193 n. 1.

13. See L. Gautier, *Les Epopées françaises*, Paris, 1878–82, vol. IV, p. 111.

14. See L. A. Paton, op. cit., p. 76.

15. See L. A. Paton, op. cit., p. 194n.

16. *Brun de la Montaigne*, ed. P. Meyer, Paris (SATF), 1875, ll. 24–5.

17. See A. H. Krappe, 'Arthur and Charlemagne', *Englische Studien*, 68 (1934), p. 353.

18. E. Faral, *Les Sources latines des contes et romans courtois au moyen âge*, Paris, 1913, pp. 309–10.

19. See particularly W. O. Sypherd, *Studies in Chaucer's Hous of Fame* (Chaucer Society, 2nd series, 29), London, 1907, pp. 144–50; and S. Cigada, 'Il tema arturiano del "Château Tournant", Chaucer e Christine de Pisan', *Studi medievali*, serie terza, 2 (1961), pp. 576–606.

20. *Fled Bricrend*, ed. G. Henderson, London (Irish Texts Society), 1899, p. 103; *Le Voyage de Charlemagne*, ed. P. Aebischer, Geneva, 1965, p. 53; *Two Old French Gauvain Romances*, ed. R. C. Johnston and D. D. R. Owen, Edinburgh, 1972, p. 72.

21. *Le Voyage de Charlemagne*, ed. cit., p. 53.

22. This episode lends some support to Miss Weston's theory regarding a passage from the *Elucidation*: '. . . Is it not possible that there may be a real foundation of historical fact at the root of this wildly picturesque tale? May it not be simply a poetical version of the disappearance from the land of Britain of the open performance of an ancient Nature ritual? . . . That it records the outrage offered by some, probably local, chieftain to a priestess of the cult . . . and the subsequent cessation of the public celebration of the rites, a cessation which in the folk-belief would certainly be held sufficient to account for any subsequent drought that might affect the land?' J. L. Weston, *From Ritual to Romance*, revised edition, New York, 1957, p. 173. The *Artus* episode does combine the three features of the interruption of the worship, the cessation of religious rites and the Waste Land.

23. There seem to be no parallels for this. The combination of the subterranean fire, darkness

which suddenly covers the land and the flight of the people reminds one of the Younger Pliny's account of the eruption of Vesuvius and its consequences.

24. A point discussed by M. Schlauch, 'The *Rémundar Saga Keisarasonar* as an analogue of *Arthur of Little Britain*', *Scandinavian Studies and Notes*, 10 (1929), pp. 189–202. It is, however, pure coincidence that in Lord Berners' translation Artus is referred to as 'He who will give light'. This was an attempt to render 'Or est venus qui auera' (the expression found also in Chrétien's *Chevalier de la Charrette*). Lord Berners perhaps read 'alumera'.
25. *Berinus*, ed. R. Bossuat, Paris (SATF), 1931, vol. I, p. 111.
26. *Fled Bricrend*, ed. cit., p. 103.
27. See R. S. Loomis, op. cit., p. 46.
28. R. S. Loomis, 'The Spoils of Annwn: an early Arthurian poem', *Publications of the Modern Language Society of America*, 56 (1941), p. 892.
29. In Egypt the tombs of kings were sometimes placed so that they were seen on the horizon at the point where the sun went down; this presumably facilitated entrance to the Otherworld. Similarly Samhain, the beginning of winter, was the time when 'any barriers between man and the supernatural were lowered', N. Chadwick, *The Celts*, Harmondsworth, 1970, p. 181.
30. *Le Roman de Balain*, ed. M. D. Legge, Manchester, 1942, p. 100.
31. *Le Roman de Tristan*, ed. R. L. Curtis, Munich, 1963, p. 305.
32. J. L. Weston, op. cit., p. 108.
33. J. L. Weston, op. cit., p. 122.
34. M. Schlauch, art. cit., pp. 193–4.
35. *The Mabinogion*, trans. G. Jones and T. Jones, revised edition, London (Everyman), 1974, p. 96.
36. T. Parry, *A History of Welsh Literature*, trans. H. I. Bell, Oxford, 1962 p. 76. An Indian influence on *Culhwch and Olwen* has also been proposed: see A. H. Krappe, art. cit., p. 357.
37. See *The Mabinogion*, ed. cit., p. 57.
38. See *The Mabinogion*, ed. cit., p. 46.
39. See *The Mabinogion*, ed. cit., p. 67.
40. Ms A f. 52r°.
41. L. H. Loomis in *Modern Philology*, 25 (1928), pp. 331–49.
42. See T. G. E. Powell, *The Celts*, new edition, London, 1980, p. 146; and N. Chadwick, op. cit., p. 180.
43. See T. G. E. Powell, op. cit., p. 144; and N. Chadwick, op. cit., p. 181.
44. See W. O. Sypherd, op. cit., pp. 145–6.
45. See S. Thompson, *Motif-Index of Folk-Literature*, revised and enlarged, Copenhagen, 1956, n° F. 782.6.
46. See *Auctores antiquissimi*, ed. T. Mommsen, Berlin (Monumenta Germaniae Historica, 13), 1898, p. 218, for Nennius's reference to the mountain which turned three times during the year.
47. See *L'Estoire del Saint Graal*, ed. H. O. Sommer, Washington, 1909, pp. 114–9, for the island that turned with the firmament.
48. M. Schlauch, 'The palace of Hugon de Constantinople', *Speculum*, 7 (1932), p. 513.
49. There are some incidents in *Artus* which attract attention because there are no known analogues: the subterranean fire in the Tour Ténébreuse is one; the statue bearing the likeness of both Florence and Proserpine which will place the chaplet of marigolds ('chappel de soussie') only on the head of 'the best knight in the world', ignoring all others who kneel before her. Perhaps one is too reluctant to credit medieval romancers with inventions of their own.
50. When Artus joins Florence, besieged by the Emperor of India in the castle of Blanche Tour, a plot is hatched to defeat the enemy: overnight all the gates are opened wide and Artus's army creeps in and hides. In the morning the Saracens, thinking that the inmates of the castle have fled, enter unsuspectingly. At once the drawbridges are raised, and the trapped Saracens are packed so close together that they have no room to defend themselves and are cut to pieces [Ms A ff. 130–131]. This was what happened to Robert of Artois and his force when, in 1250, ignoring normal military strategy, he led his men into the city of Mansurah in order to capture it. Though Joinville's account of this was probably too late to have been used by the *Artus* author, the incident was no doubt already well-known in France.

On Birds and Beasts, 'Death' and 'Resurrection', Renewal and Reunion in Chrétien's Romances

KENNETH VARTY

1. In James Carlill's translation, *The Epic of the Beast*, London, Routledge, n.d., p. 223.
2. *Reading Medieval Studies*, VII (1981), p. 83.
3. *Medieval Latin and French Bestiaries*, Chapel Hill, University of North Carolina Press, 1960, p. 159.
4. M. R. James, *A Peterborough Psalter and Bestiary* . . . , Oxford, Roxburghe Club, 1921, p. 127.
5. See B. Rowland, *Animals with Human Faces*, London, Allen and Unwin, 1974, pp. 103–4 etc.
6. See his 1981 Strathclyde University Ph.D. thesis entitled *The Image of the stag in literary and iconographical traditions of the Middle Ages*.

Notes on Rhythm in Chrétien's Yvain

B. WOLEDGE

1. *Etude sur Yvain ou le Chevalier au Lion de Chrétien de Troyes*, Paris, 1969, pp. 245–72; 'La brisure du couplet dans *Erec et Enide*', Romania, 86 (1965), 1–21.
2. CFMA, 1960. I have not felt bound to follow Roques' punctuation.
3. Foerster's first edition forms volume II of the *Sämtliche erhaltene Werke*, Halle, 1887 (reprint Amsterdam 1965). This was followed by several smaller editions, the latest dating from 1912. Foerster modified his text and punctuation in successive editions; in his last edition, his rule of putting a comma before every subordinate clause conceals what I imagine to be the rhythm of Old French. The 1887 edition is known as the *Grosse Ausgabe*.
4. The rhymes in Chrétien's romances show strict adherence to nominative *Artus* and oblique *Artu*, though some scribes used *Artus* for the oblique case.
5. I have given other examples of this construction in *La Syntaxe des substantifs chez Chrétien de Troyes*, (Pubns. romanes et françaises, *149*, 1979) § 22. On the differences between *dames, dameiseles* and *puceles*, see Foulet's *Glossary of the First Continuation* (W. Roach, *The Continuations of the Old French Perceval*, vol. III, pt. 2), pp. 244–5.
6. By this time, Foerster had adopted the practice of always putting a comma before a subordinate clause.
7. Frappier, *Etude sur Yvain* (see n. 1 above), p. 18. Frappier does not name the critics referred to as 'on', and I have not been able to identify them.
8. *Grosse Ausgabe*, p. 274 (note correcting the information given on p. 1).
9. Roques lists all Guiot's punctuation marks on pp. 208–10 of his edition.
10. Page 279, note to l. 212.
11. For instance A. Tobler, *Vom französischen Versbau* . . . , 3rd edition, Leipzig, 1894, pp. 60–6 and G. Lote, *Histoire du vers français*, vol. III, Paris, 1955, pp. 79–85.
12. Volume I, Upsala, 1907, pp. 89–202.
13. I quote from Salverda de Grave's edition, 2 vols., CFMA, 1925–9.
14. For example G. Lote, op. cit. p. 83 and Foulet in his edition of *Galeran de Bretagne*, CFMA, 1925, pp. xxix–xxx.
15. Roques claims (CFMA p. xxvi) that non-elision occurs in the Guiot ms. twice, with *dame* 2159 and *sire* 2316. But in l. 2159 the ms. reads *et la dameisele ot mandez*; in l. 2316, Guiot has missed out *en* before *envoie*, so that the line should read *Et mes sire Yvains en envoie*.
16. *Grosse Ausgabe*, p. 279, note to l. 212.
17. A passage from Chrétien's *Conte du Graal* (ll. 5955–83 of Hilka's edition) was very well analysed by Roques in the preface which he contributed to Foulet's translation of the romance, Paris 1947, 2nd ed. 1970. This preface is also in Roques' *Etudes de littérature française*, (Pubns. romanes et françaises, *28*, 1959) pp. 29–42; the discussion of rhythm is on pp. 39–41. Some features of versification in *Erec* are sensitively discussed in Prof. J. C. Laidlaw's contribution to the present volume.